Phillip Williams is a research fellow for the Spanish Commission for Military History. He has previously taught at the universities of Stirling, Bangor and Winchester and holds a DPhil from New College, Oxford.

'Future historians will need to take account of Phillip Williams' well-argued and thought-provoking book, and all students of early modern history will enjoy this engrossing read.'
Bulletin for Spanish and Portuguese Historical Studies

EMPIRE *and* HOLY WAR *in the* MEDITERRANEAN

THE GALLEY AND MARITIME CONFLICT BETWEEN THE HABSBURGS AND OTTOMANS

PHILLIP WILLIAMS

I.B. TAURIS
LONDON · NEW YORK · OXFORD · NEW DELHI · SYDNEY

I.B. TAURIS
Bloomsbury Publishing Plc
50 Bedford Square, London, WC1B 3DP, UK
1385 Broadway, New York, NY 10018, USA

BLOOMSBURY, I.B. TAURIS and the I.B. Tauris logo are trademarks of
Bloomsbury Publishing Plc

First published in Great Britain 2014
Reprinted 2020 (twice)

Cover design: Graham Robert Ward

A catalogue record for this book is available from the British Library.

A catalog record for this book is available from the Library of Congress.

ISBN: PB: 978-1-4411-6532-9
ePDF: 978-0-8577-2575-2
eBook: 978-0-8577-3598-0

Series: Library of New Testament Studies, 2345678X, volume 286

Typeset by Data Standards Ltd, Frome, Somerset, BA11 2RY
Printed and bound in Great Britain

To find out more about our authors and books visit www.bloomsbury.com
and sign up for our newsletters.

For my parents, Margaret and Patrick

Table of Contents

List of Illustrations

6. The Serene Sebastiano Veniero, '*capitano general da mar*' or
commander in-chief of the Venetian fleet in 1571, with
Lepanto in the background. Engraving (dated c.1610).
Courtesy of the Trustees of the British Museum (Museum
number: 1868,0822.8552).   225

Preface

This book examines campaigns fought between the Ottoman Empire and the Spanish Monarchy in the Mediterranean in the sixteenth and early seventeenth centuries. The Ottoman Empire acted as the standard-bearer for Islam, while the Habsburg Spanish Monarchy stood as the defender of Catholic Christendom. The fighting took place in North Africa and on the coasts of Greece and Italy. Menorca suffered serious raids in 1535 and 1558. A salient characteristic of the conflict was the prominence of 'corsairs' or privateers: these were state-sponsored pirates who sailed from Malta, Leghorn, Algiers, Tunis, Djerba and Tripoli to rob the shipping and trade of the other side. They were licensed to take slaves and to sell them on the markets that fed the demand for oarsmen, workers and domestic servants.

The intention of this study is to analyse both the great military campaigns and the phenomenon of piracy with an understanding of the characteristics of the ship deployed in the Mediterranean, the galley. This is undertaken in the belief that the great qualities and strengths of the oared warships have been almost entirely overlooked and that the movement of resources over the seas was vital to both empires. The Italian territories (the kingdoms of Naples and Sicily and the Duchy of Milan) were essential to the military, political and financial systems of the *monarquía* of Spain; the Arab lands played an equally important role in the economic and naval organisation of the sultans of Constantinople.

One of the keys to understanding both empires, therefore, is to interpret the ways by which the Habsburg kings of Spain and the Ottoman sultans justified their rule over peoples in 'foreign' lands whose contribution to their respective empires was essential to their very existence. Scholars of the Ottomans refer to this process as that of 'legitimisation'. There is general agreement that the sultans presented themselves as heirs to the rulers of early Islam – the Caliphs, who (in various guises) governed a unified Islamic empire ('the caliphate') from the time of the Prophet Mohammed (*d*.632) until 1258. This book presents a parallel argument for the Spanish Habsburgs: in order to rule over the fiefs in central Europe and Italy, Charles V (1516/19–56) and his heirs pledged themselves to the Holy Roman Empire of Germany (for Milan, the Franche-Comté and the Low Countries) and to the Holy and Apostolic See of Rome (the Papacy) for the Kingdom of Naples. These fiefs were conferred during ceremonies of investiture in which the Habsburgs promised to rule according to certain conditions and limitations and with a number of 'obligations'. The Apostolic See also claimed 'suzerainty' or 'overlordship' over a wide number of other territories in Europe (amongst them Sicily), North Africa, the Mediterranean and the New Worlds.

The Italian territories occupied a unique role as both the cause of wars and the means of fighting them. In the 1530s, 1540s and 1550s the vast majority of Ottoman campaigns at sea were designed to assist the kings of France, Francis I (1515–47) and Henry II (1547–59), to seize or recover the fiefs in Italy (Naples, Sicily and Milan) to which they had extremely strong dynastic claims.

Empire and Holy War in the Mediterranean therefore examines two basic themes, the character and qualities of the Mediterranean war galley and the concessions and compromises which the Ottomans and Habsburgs of Spain made in order to legitimise or justify their rule in 'foreign' territories. Both lines of argument might be summed up in the idea that any major military campaign or force in the early modern Mediterranean was profoundly international in nature and origin, as only by drawing resources from the numerous microecologies of 'the corrupting sea' could sixteenth-century armies and navies be sustained.

Consequently, 'empires' or 'hegemonic states' were dependent upon the peoples and resources of the 'periphery' and so were drawn into the process of legitimisation mentioned above, with the peculiar outcome that those agents of proto-national modernity – the Spanish Habsburgs and Ottoman Turks – came to commit themselves to the international medieval programme of the Apostolic See of Rome and the template of the Abbasid caliphate respectively.

The book begins with a brief narrative of events in Italy and the major battles and campaigns. It then moves on to assess the Battle of Lepanto (1571) and the approach to it: the argument is that the engagement was characterised by extremely serious deficiencies in both fleets. The focus then moves onto the galley, its characteristics and requirements. It is argued that there was an enormous difference between strong galleys and weak ones, and the chapters then proceed to analyse how the fleets were configured, what results these configurations had upon the fighting and how a timetable of war shaped campaigns.

This understanding leads to a description of the basic stance or strategies of the Ottoman Empire and the *monarquía* of Spain. In turn, this carries the argument forward to an analysis of different contemporary ideas about how holy war should be prosecuted, about what purpose violence served and how to respond to the raids launched by enemy corsairs. Attention focuses on the Order of the Knights of St John of Jerusalem at Malta and the peculiar set of circumstances – specifically, its devotion to the 'service of God' and its status as a fief-holder – which allowed it to launch attacks on the *Dar al-Islam*, the 'realm of Islam' or the 'domains of felicity'. These were the seas and territories which the sultan, as the Caliph and defender of Islam, was bound to protect.

As we shall see, at crucial moments both Charles V and his successor as King of Spain, Philip II (1556–98), expressed profound reservations about the 'Order of Malta', which they viewed as an institution dominated by Frenchmen. These insights hint at much broader arguments about the nature of political power in Christendom. The Habsburgs of Spain were driven by the 'service of God' in their campaigns in the Low Countries, England, Ireland and the New Worlds.

A comparison of the fighting in the Mediterranean and the Atlantic is made and the origins of the war between Philip II and Elizabeth I of England (1558–1603) are examined.

One of the conclusions is that the new historical agents that emerged in the sixteenth century tended to reinvigorate forms of action and organisation that had been prevalent in the Middle Ages and which have generally been dismissed as relics or anachronisms in the era of the 'renaissance state' and 'sea power'. The 'early modern period' (the sixteenth and seventeenth centuries) was shaped by the political legacy of the 'feudalism' of the Middle Ages. Not only was the *monarquía* of the Habsburgs of Spain a 'composite monarchy' (made up of separate states united only in the person of the ruler), but it was also one in which sovereignty was itself divided and divisible, being conferred by one prince (the overlord or suzerain) upon another (the 'feudatory' or *feudatorio*) with certain conditions, limits and 'obligations'. Within the Ottoman Empire, the quest to locate the dynasty in the traditions of Islam was manifested not only in the application of holy law within its borders and the rhetoric, costume and ceremony of universal monarchy that characterised the Vienna campaign of 1532, but also in the foreign policy which drove its expeditions into the Indian Ocean and compelled it to attack Malta in 1565 and to reclaim Tunis in 1574.

Historians need to be careful when claiming contemporary relevance for their work, but two arguments can tentatively be advanced. The first is that as Europe moves inexorably towards a system in which sovereignty is itself pooled or shared, the model of the national monarchy and nation-state can be seen as a historical anomaly belonging to the period between the French Revolution and the Fall of the Berlin Wall. Historians working on other forms of military activity and political organisation have advanced this argument in slightly different terms; here, emphasis is placed upon the nuances of sovereignty that were conveyed in the ceremony of investiture and credit is given to the idea that small territorial states could accept much larger entities as their 'feudatories'.

With regard to the Ottoman Empire, the question of the contemporary relevance is a more sensitive one in that today's militants hold as their final aim the re-establishment of a state based on their model or interpretation of the caliphate. As has often been noted, the Ottoman sultans repeatedly insisted that they sought peace, direct confrontation between the *Dar al-Islam* and the *Dar al-Harb* was relatively rare and cross-confessional alliances were very common. More pointedly, it should be said that the sixteenth-century group that most obviously appeals to today's radicals – the *ghazi* raiders or 'corsairs' of North Africa – were anomalous within Islamic tradition for two reasons: first, the operations of the *'levend'* captains denied one of the most fundamental tenets of the Prophet's teaching, namely that there should be no compulsion in religion; second, that the Islamic corsairs, while drawing on the eternal rhetoric of *ghazi* raiders, commonly robbed, intimidated, enslaved and even murdered the subjects – both Christian and Muslim – of the sultan, the coastal peasants of Greece and Anatolia bearing the brunt of their attacks.

I would like to thank my former colleagues at Stirling, Winchester, Bangor and Portsmouth for their humour and friendship, especially Richard Oram, Siriol Davies, Michael Hicks, Gary Robinson, Wil Griffith, Paul Cavill, Tracy Pritchard Williams, Raimund Karl, Mark Hagger, Alexander Sedlmaier, Marcus Collins, Gillian Mitchell, Peter Clarke, Joe Canning, Rosemary Jane and Christine Woollin. David Parrott was a generous and valued supervisor at New College. Rex Smith and Gigliola Pagano di Divitiis provided me with invaluable advice, as did the late R.B. Wernham, Cesare Mozzarelli and A.W. Lovett. The late Robert Oresko suggested ideas to me which, regrettably, we never came to discuss in depth: I hope that he would have agreed with some of the arguments set out in this book. I must thank Rob Stradling and Robin Briggs for their professionalism, expertise and encouragement. The friendship and encouragement of Davide Maffi, Mario Rizzo, Aurelio Espinosa, Alicia Esteban Estríngana, Sean Perrone, Bernardo García, Christopher Storrs, Claudio Marsilio, Luke S. Wright, Peter Millard, Óscar Recio Morales, Igor Pérez Tostado, Alberto Marcos and Javier Vela has been a great help to me. None of the above, it should be stressed, are responsible for any errors of fact and judgement contained in the following pages.

I am very grateful to Jo Godfrey and Alex Higson for their help and advice in preparing this manuscript. I am very honoured to be working for the Comisión Española de Historia Militar, and am very grateful to Hugo O'Donnell y Duque de Estrada, Teniente General del Ejército de Tierra Alfonso de la Rosa Morena and Coronel Herminio Fernández García for their encouragement and support.

I must thank Audrey Kirkman, James McAuliffe and Sarah Davies. Many people will be grateful – and surprised – finally to see this book in print, among them Kevin Carrigan, Richard Taylor, Paul Woolley, Guy Wilkinson, Andrew Butterworth and Luca Volta – and Sharon, Jo, Suzanne, Helen, Jacquie, *et al*. I am very much in their debt for their friendship over the years. Great thanks are due to Nicholas, Kerrie, Caitlin and Darren Sears – not to forget Holly. At the Archivo General I would like to give thanks to José Luis Rodríguez, Isabel Aguirre, Macu Delgado, Dori García, Luis Mato, Carmen Larriba, Macario Sahagún, Carmen Fernández, Maria Pilar Goyanes, Maïte Hernández, Blanca Tena, Ángel Moreno, Agustín Carreras, Eduardo Marchena and Javier Ortega. I must also thank the *guardas viejas*, Mario Gutiérrez, Juan José Cimas, Juan Carlos Prieto, Juan José Carranza, Valentín Garda, Iván Gómez, José Luis Muñoz, Alfredo Román and Julián Rubio.

Special thanks are due to Professor Enrique García Hernán, of the Consejo Superior de Investigaciones Científicas, Madrid, and to, Ana and Clara – not to forget my number one pupil, Paula. Miriam Hernández is a great friend of mine, as are Carola Herrera, Germán de Castro and Milciades Paredes. In Simancas I have always been very grateful for the friendship of Germana, Juan Carlos Sahagún and María de los Ángeles, while I can hardly put into words my thanks to Carola (and Jordi, Daniel and Rosa) 'Sargento' Paco (and Maribel), Cachorro, Maïte (and Miguel), Rober and Chon, *mi abuela española*. Finally special thanks are due to Michael, Preeti and Isabella and to Russell, John, Katharine and Eva Rose – not to forget Perry, Paddy, Jack, Murphy and Bertie. My greatest debt is to my parents, Margaret and Patrick Williams, to whom this book is dedicated.

Abbreviations

AGS	Archivo General de Simancas
CCE	*Consulta* of the Council of State
CCG	*Consulta* of the Council of War
CCI	*Consulta* of the Council of Italy
CJD	*Consulta* of the *junta de dos*
CSPV	Calendar of State Papers Venice
Est.	Secretaría de Estado
fol.	Folio number
GA	Guerra Antigua
leg.	legajo
Sec. Prov.	Secretarias Provinciales
sf	without folio number

Introduction: The Mediterranean World in the Age of Captain Francisco de Holanda

Captain Francisco de Holanda served King Philip II of Spain (1556–1598) for more than 25 years, and during his lengthy career he was captured and enslaved three times by enemies of the Catholic faith. He entered royal service in the Kingdom of Sicily as a contractor with a warship or galleon which he hired to the Crown. Following the direct orders of Don John of Austria, the King's half-brother and commander of the forces of the Christian Holy League of 1571–73, he was present with his ship at the Battle of Lepanto (7 October 1571), the great Christian naval victory over the Ottoman Turks. The following years were to be more difficult. During a trip to transport a cargo of wine to the fortress of La Goleta, a small bastion constructed on the isthmus of Tunis, his ship was captured by an Ottoman captain or *reis*. His vessel was confiscated and Holanda himself was carried off to Constantinople, where he was to remain as a captive for six months before escaping aboard a Venetian merchantman. He then returned to royal service with another galleon, the *Juliana*. His next great adventure would take place outside the Mediterranean, as his warship formed part of a squadron of six vessels carrying Don Diego Pimentel and the companies of regular soldiers of the army or *tercio* of Sicily as part of the Invincible Armada sent against Elizabeth I of England (1558–1603) in the summer of 1588.

1

Again, fate was unkind to Holanda: the *Juliana* was lost on the coast of Ireland, and with it disappeared the last vestiges of his property and wealth. Worse, he once again found himself a captive in foreign lands, where he would remain for a full year. After his eventual ransom he sailed to Portugal and embarked in Lisbon aboard a merchant ship carrying sugar to Venice, the 'Republic of St Mark' or 'Most Serene Republic'. But near Sicily this ship was overtaken and seized by seven galiots 'of Moors' and 'the third time [he was] lost, captured and carried away' to captivity in Algiers, where he would spend the next three years. Holanda was obviously as resourceful as he was unfortunate and eventually he managed to ransom himself with 800 *escudos* in gold and, intriguingly, a piece of green embroidered cloth, '*una pieca de paño verde*'. Throwing himself at the feet of the new King, Philip III (1598–1621), he stated that he had to support a wife and children and that all of his inheritance had been lost in royal service. His petition brought a modest reward – a salaried position in the galleys of Sicily worth six *escudos* per month.[1]

Captain Holanda's life tells us something about not only the hopes and concerns of those Christian captains and soldiers who fought against the Ottoman Turks, but also about the practices and customs of war.

The empire over which the Spanish branch of the House of Habsburg presided has been variously referred to as 'Spain', the 'Spanish Empire', 'the Spanish Monarchy' or 'the Catholic Monarchy'; the last term offers an indication of its basic stance as defender of Catholic Christendom, that is to say the part of Europe that adhered to the teachings and doctrine of the Roman Catholic Church. The Ottoman Turks played a similar role as champions and protectors of Sunni Islam. The half-century after 1530 witnessed a series of major campaigns in the Mediterranean, in which both sides regularly mobilised for war. The standard interpretation of events holds that after 1575 or 1580 Philip II abandoned the Mediterranean in order to direct his forces against Protestant powers such as the Dutch Republic and Elizabeth I. The subsequent wars were fought primarily in the Atlantic, English Channel and North Sea by galleons like the *Juliana*, that is to say high-sided ships that depended upon sail for their propulsion. Holanda's misadventures can therefore be taken as indicative of what Fernand Braudel, the greatest and most influential historian of the twentieth century, called the 'shift to the Atlantic', the abandonment of the Mediterranean by the Habsburg government based in Madrid and the redirection of its resources to wars against the emerging maritime powers of northern Europe.[2]

For many years it was argued that this change of direction and intent was inherently unfavourable to Spain. The basis for this argument was a somewhat curious one: this was that despite the enormous extent of its maritime possessions in the Mediterranean, Atlantic and Pacific Oceans, the Catholic Monarchy was not a 'maritime power'. Recently, however, this interpretation has been seriously challenged by José Luis Casado Soto, who has examined the ships sent as part of the 'Invincible Armada'.[3] An insight into the arguments of this 'revisionist' school was given by Pimentel (Holanda's commanding officer), who fell into the hands of the Dutch in 1588 and provided the following explanation when interrogated:

> The reason why the king undertook this war against England was that he could not tolerate the fact that Francis Drake, with two or three rotten ships, should come to infest the harbours of Spain whenever it pleased him, and to capture its best towns in order to plunder them.[4]

If the traditional understanding of the technology and events of 1588 has been called into question, then the history of the Mediterranean in the period 1560–1620 continues to be dominated by long-established interpretations focusing on decline and abandonment. Campaigns in the inland sea in the sixteenth century have been portrayed as the end of a tradition, the product of a form of warfare which was in the course of losing its essential *raison d'être:* the eighteenth-century Enlightenment thinker Voltaire famously observed that the Christian victory at Lepanto in 1571 led nowhere. His dismissive assessment has plagued historians. Braudel, I.A.A. Thompson, Andrew C. Hess and Colin Imber have examined his judgement; none have been able to deny that it contains more than a kernel of truth.[5] The enormously influential arguments advanced by Captain Alfred Thayer Mahan about the decisive role of sea power in history served to downplay further the rationale and value of Mediterranean warfare.[6] Indeed the American historian John Francis Guilmartin Jr., writing in the early 1970s, argued that galley warfare was on course to an evolutionary dead end precisely because of the inapplicability of the 'Mahanian model' to it: the oared warship could not 'command the sea' by remaining away from the shore for long periods, and so this form of warfare was condemned to obsolescence by the introduction and spread of gunpowder technology and the modern fortresses of the 'Italian design', the *trace italienne*. Slow, heavily armed armadas of the sort seen in the Mediterranean in the 1560s and 1570s, Professor Guilmartin postulated, were unable to transport the sort of expeditionary force necessary to besiege and overcome the artillery-bearing fortresses which came to be built at strategic harbour positions.[7] The systematic employment of this new military technology signalled the end of galley-based warfare in the inland sea. The advent of major campaigns in the Atlantic in the 1580s seemed to confirm what was already perfectly obvious from the inconclusive expeditions of the previous decades: this was that Christendom and Islam had fought each other to a stalemate in the Mediterranean and that neither the Habsburgs nor the Ottomans could continue to devote the necessary resources and attention to this theatre of arms. Priorities lay elsewhere, in part because the war galley – that is to say the long, narrow oared vessel employed in the inland sea – had been shown to be a much less effective vehicle than the galleon. The impetus in world history lay, as Carlo Cipolla argued in a concise and brilliant study, with guns and sails, not with oars and swords.[8] It should perhaps be added that these lines of thinking dovetailed with the idea that the impetus to contest the Atlantic was itself partly the consequence of the establishment of powerful centralised states based upon the resources of a proto-nation – the Spanish, the French, the English, the Portuguese, the Swedish and (in certain respects) the Dutch.[9]

Holanda's first period of captivity was brought about by the need to carry wine to the outpost of La Goleta: this detail can be tied to many reservations expressed by commanders about this frontier outpost or *presidio*, which did not have access to supplies of fresh water within its walls and had only a small water tank in its courtyard.[10] La Goleta was supplied and re-supplied in two ways: first, by sending ships or squadrons from Sicily; second, by maintaining a relationship with the local Muslim ruler, the Hafsid 'King of Tunis'. It was difficult for planners to have much faith in either supply line.[11] The 'King of Tunis' was, averred the Duke of Medinaceli, viceroy of the Kingdom of Sicily in the early 1560s, a man so driven by his enmity towards the Christians that it blinded him to the danger from the Ottoman Turks, who would surely take his throne from him. Medinaceli lamented the 'obstinacy' of 'such a bad man' who had perhaps reached the point of no return.[12] It was reported in February 1562 that other than a galleon sent from Malta the garrison at La Goleta had not had sight of a Christian ship for six months and was in the greatest need, '*con grandísima necesidad*'. The same dispatch stated, without equivocation, that the 'King of Tunis' was the 'principal mover' of Ottoman plans to send the fleet against the Christian fortress.[13]

One of the problems in understanding sixteenth-century holy war lies in determining the value placed upon this small, vulnerable and isolated position. When Charles V sailed to capture Tunis and La Goleta in 1535 his expedition faced major problems on account of the extreme shortage of water in the area; the fighting for control of two or three wells or water tanks seems to have been particularly ferocious, one contemporary interpretation being that the success or failure of the entire mission had depended upon gaining control of these positions.[14] The chronicler Francisco López de Gómara stated that only the emperor wanted to press ahead with the expedition to the city after the capture of La Goleta. The desolate dry countryside surrounding Tunis offered little to its prospective conquerors: 'There is no river, nor spring, nor more than one well of fresh water, and so everyone drinks from cisterns'.[15] In 1536 an earthquake destroyed part of the walls of La Goleta; the garrison responded by destroying the Roman acqueduct in order to make use of its stones.[16] In June 1565, when it was feared that an enemy fleet might assault La Goleta, Philip II and his then high-admiral or *capitán general del mar Mediterráneo*, Don García de Toledo, addressed the problem of

Fig. 1 The Conquest of Tunis by Charles V, 1535. Showing the fortress of La Goleta and the shallow lagoon as the Emperor's fleet prepares to set sail back to Christendom. Etching on paper after tapestries by Jan Cornelisz Vermeyen (dated 1546–50).

how to defend this isolated outpost. Although they disagreed on how this might be achieved, both men based their deliberations on the fact that there were only two wells near La Goleta, both of them at a distance of 'a good two miles', 'los cuales son a dos buenas millas de La Goleta'.[17] The final loss of La Goleta in 1574 was, almost directly, the result of its isolation: the interruption of the supply lines over the winter of 1573 and 1574 left it fatally vulnerable.[18]

As a strategic position, therefore, La Goleta was profoundly limited: not only was it highly susceptible to attack, but it also commanded an arid terrain and only offered access to the lagoon of Tunis, not to a deep-water anchorage. Holanda's fragmentary autobiography highlights other significant, if often overlooked, themes. In the first place, it would seemingly lead to the conclusion that Sicily was a kingdom of great importance to Philip II, 'His Catholic Majesty'. Modern scholarship has demonstrated that the island kingdom did indeed make a major contribution to Habsburg war efforts in the Mediterranean and Atlantic.[19] In another important respect Holanda's life illustrated the extent to which holy war was also a business transaction; this was true in several senses. First, captives – or nearly all captives – could be ransomed. Second, his story demonstrates how contractors sold their services to the Crown; as Professor I.A.A. Thompson has shown in a major study, the Habsburg government of Spain employed businessmen whose conditions of service were set down in precise, legalistic documents. The King was constrained by contractual terms which specified how, where and when his warships were to serve him. He could, of course, operate his galleys or galleons outside of these parameters, but in doing so he assumed responsibility for stiff penalty payments for damage and losses.[20]

The contractor – the *condottiere* or *asentista* – was of use because he could exploit market conditions in order to achieve the most efficient return on the King's investment. On a similar note Dr David Parrott has recently argued that during the second half of the 'Thirty Years War' (1618–48) the military businessmen (*munitionnaires*) serving Louis XIII of France (1610–43) and the crown of Sweden supplied land forces which, if comparatively small in scale, were highly mobile and well resourced.[21] In a sense, the events of the years from 1635 to 1648 led rulers to adopt principles which had been evident to Andrea Doria and Charles V a century previously: in most circumstances it was better to have five good galleys than 50 bad ones; war could be successfully prosecuted with small, agile and mobile forces, even if this decision inevitably imposed certain restrictions or limitations on the capabilities, both offensive and defensive, of the forces.

There were, however, some drawbacks or difficulties inherent in the use of 'enterprisers'. In the first place, the fragmentation of administrative and military authority entailed the reduction of the power of the state itself. 'Each contractor, each province, lord or city was,' concludes Professor Thompson, 'in its own way a separate administrative and jurisdictional unit.' In Spain this led to a process of 're-feudalisation', in which the great Iberian landholders like the Duke of Medina Sidonia extended and deepened their control over the machinery of government in the provinces. Louis XIV reached similar conclusions, in part because he was haunted by the repeated collapses of royal power in the hundred years before 1660 which he blamed on the privatisation of sovereignty, whose most obvious manifestation was the military contractor. The 'Sun King' was therefore determined to maintain central control of his armies, a decision which may not have enhanced their overall effectiveness.[22]

This was not the only drawback to the privatisation of warfare. For reasons which were clearly demonstrated by Holanda's financial losses, the priority of the *asentistas* lay in the preservation of their forces, which they were determined not to expose to unnecessary risks. The great strength or advantage of the contractor system – the capacity and wherewithal to maintain and run a squadron or army – was also its principal restraint or shortcoming, in that as *hommes d'affaires* they necessarily sought to safeguard their galleys or regiments, rather than engage the enemy in risky set-piece battles.[23]

The *asiento* represented, in Thompson's words, 'not merely an abrogation of government, [but also] an abrogation of sovereignty' itself. In other words, the very authority and prestige of the King was fragmented, as key functions of the state (the provision of military forces; the use of violence; the rights to import and export goods or to buy domestically at a set price) were entrusted to private individuals or groups. Yet similar arrangements involving the alienation or part-alienation of the authority of the state played a prominent role in the political, economic and military history of early modern Europe. The tendency towards the division of sovereign authority came from both the respect for tradition and the need to innovate. In the first place, scholars are becoming increasingly alert to the significance of princely figures such as Charles de Nevers (to Italian historians, Carlo I Gonzaga-Nevers) who were at once independent sovereign rulers and subjects of other royal houses. Nevers's position was an ambiguous one: as a 'foreign prince' (*prince étranger*) he was the ruler of a sovereign territory within the crown of France. He was able to exploit his royal bloodline and status in order to commit his king, Louis XIII, to a conflict which diverged from the overall strategic interest of the French monarchy, in this case the Mantuan succession crisis of 1628–31, a dispute whose origins lay in the conferral or 'investiture' of the imperial fief of Mantua.[24]

Disputes over sovereign rights remained a major source of tensions: this was true even when the territory in question was governed by the infidel Turk. Thus a major source of antagonism among the rulers of northern Italy in the seventeenth century lay in the energetic campaign by the dukes of Savoy to gain recognition of their claim to the royal crown of Cyprus. This drive served to poison Turin's relations with the Republic of St Mark and the Grand Duchy of Tuscany, both of whom maintained rival pretensions to the island and its royal closed crown.[25]

The fact that, as Vittorio Amedeo I, Duke of Savoy, put it in 1632, the island of Cyprus was 'violently occupied by the enemy of Christians' did little, if anything, to reduce the level of antagonism between Turin, Venice and Florence (the island, formerly a Venetian possession, had been conquered by the Ottoman Turks in 1570–71; the nominal intention of the Christians at Lepanto was to recover it). Controversies of this sort were fed by the widespread determination, noted by the late Robert Oresko, to avoid the stigma of innovation and never to allow any dynastic claim, however implausible, to lapse.[26] In this respect, the Ottomans were little different from their Christian contemporaries. The sultans were determined to uphold their claims to 'suzerainty' or 'overlordship'; this undertaking or policy was critically important because a number of borderland territories in central Europe were governed under a form of investiture, with authority conferred by the Sublime Porte (central government) on its vassal rulers. In the early sixteenth century the Ottomans extended claims of 'superiority' over the Republic of Venice, Mamluk Egypt and, after 1526 and in a variety of forms, Hungary.[27]

The authority of the state, therefore, was fragmented by a number of factors: the need to employ military businessmen; the recourse to ancient familial rights based upon ambiguous and, in nearly all circumstances, bitterly contested interpretations of the historical record; the institution or custom of investiture, by which one prince governed a territory on behalf of another. But it was also true that the 'new' forces or developments of this period served to fragment further the forms of sovereignty. The early modern state routinely allocated its sovereign rights to independent or semi-independent bodies in order to establish and run commercial *entrepôts* abroad. The first wave of 'globalisation' was achieved by governments that hived off huge chunks of their authority. The great commercial companies that dominated European trade with the rest of the world functioned according to a model of delegated sovereignty. The Dutch East India Company (often referred to by its initials as the 'VOC'), established in the early seventeenth century, operated as 'virtually a state within a state', 'a semi-sovereign capitalist state where trade and protection were integrated'. The other, less successful, Dutch trading companies (noticeably the Dutch West India Company, 1621) operated under a similar charter, as did their English counterparts and rivals (the Muscovy Company, the Levant Company, the East India Company, the Guinea Company, the Eastland Company).[28] The English colonies in North America were established under a similar framework.[29] Until 1729 South Carolina was a private company, run with the intention of generating commerce and profit.[30]

Royal sovereignty was also commonly delegated to private bodies or individuals in one other way: privateering – that is to say, officially sanctioned piracy – was an extremely prominent feature of nearly all forms of war at sea in the sixteenth, seventeenth and, indeed, eighteenth centuries.[31] Raiding the enemy provided an incentive to governmental service, served as a school for the education of skilled seafarers and, in theory at least, helped to fill the royal coffers by depleting the trade, wealth and seafaring community of the enemy. Thus the Islamic corsairs who captured Holanda and carried him off to Constantinople and Algiers were engaged in a low-level war of attrition, in which the nominal intention was gradually to wear away the resources and trade of the Christians.

The figures of the contractor and privateer loomed large in the Habsburg-Ottoman conflict. The study of the history of holy war in the sixteenth and seventeenth centuries is also, therefore, an examination of commercial negotiation and business acumen; there was virtually no commander or captain who was unaware of how he might benefit financially or in some other way from the crusade against the infidel, misbeliever or heretic.[32] But for the Habsburgs of Spain the relationship between economic organisation and war was best understood in geographical terms: in its most basic form, the demands of war bound Spain to its territories in Italy. As we shall see, the fighting system of the Habsburgs in the Mediterranean depended upon exploiting those areas of 'abundance' or wealth; the 'regular' or professional forces of the Catholic Monarchy were maintained in these productive regions, with the fundamental strategy of the crown of Spain being that the squadrons or regiments would be moved to defend the territories which were unable to sustain professional military resources at the necessary level. Territories like Naples and Sicily made a decisive contribution to the military efforts of the Catholic Monarchy.[33]

Scientific convention holds that it is impossible to prove a negative thesis, but the history of the early modern period would seem to offer recurring and unequivocal evidence of the difficulty of maintaining professional, regular military forces in 'privileged areas' such as Barcelona, Malaga, the Balearics, Cartagena, Valencia, Gibraltar, Murcia and even, in certain respects, in Cadiz.[34] The faltering attempts to establish flotillas in Catalonia and Valencia under Philip III provide particularly clear-cut demonstrations of the difficulty of maintaining military forces in many parts of Mediterranean Spain.[35] The Kingdom of Aragon had an inward-looking psychology in large part because of its economic isolation, 'the vital concern of the majority of its inhabitants being subsistence farming'.[36] Its military contribution was minimal. In 1630 the capital, Zaragoza, provided 200 men to serve in Lombardy; in 1635 the city (probably) sent 300 men for the war against France (the sources leave room for doubt that this contingent was ever raised).[37] In Valencia during the reign of Charles V – that is, during a period of unprecedented confrontation with the Muslim world, during which there were recurring concerns about the presence of the Moriscos, or 'half-Moors', within Spain – the kingdom provided for the reform of the castle of Benidorm, the improvement of the walls at Peñíscola and Villajoyosa, the construction of a chain of coastal towers and the arming and maintenance of a militia corps and coastal guard. Extremely modest though this contribution was, it still far outstripped that of Catalonia, where the political class proved to be very reluctant to assist in the construction of the fort at Rosas, considered a principal tool for the defence of the principality.[38] An older interpretation holds that until 1625 the Council of War struggled to organise effective militia companies in Spain; only in Galicia did the government succeed in establishing a viable militia.[39] This interpretation has been slightly modified by recent studies. In the kingdom of Granada, for example, the summer defensive mobilisation involved professional troops and so provided a level of surveillance and protection that was at least the equal of comparable coastal guards elsewhere in early modern Europe.[40]

Fortresses were notoriously difficult to maintain. Even in vital strategic fiefs like Finale Ligure it proved very difficult to feed and supply a permanent garrison; here, as elsewhere, 'the precarious ecological and socio-economic equilibrium' of the conclave, the 'poverty and natural misery' of its terrain, meant that the small additional burden of supporting a few hundred troops might serve to bring about dearth and considerable hardship for the civilian inhabitants.[41] Contemporaries made similar observations about the relationship between war and economic resources in Catalonia, Andalusia, Sardinia, Majorca, Menorca and Ibiza.[42]

Such considerations only served to underline the value of those regions where professional troops, well-equipped fortresses and flotillas of oared warships could be stationed and maintained. Throughout the period 1560–1620 the number of galleys maintained in Italy (not including Venice) outnumbered those in Spain by a factor of three- or four-to-one. In 1604 the disparity was something like ten-to-one.[43] The Kingdom of Naples was always been loyal and generous to its Habsburg Kings. In part, this generosity was fed by the obvious need to defend its own coastlines.[44] Yet it also readily extended its help to cover costs in Milan.[45] It has been calculated that Naples paid for one-fifth of the entire cost of the Holy League operations of 1571.[46] In the five years from 1631 Naples sent 48,000 soldiers, 5,500 horse and 3,500,000 ducats to Milan. 'From 1631 to 1643 alone, in fact, the kingdom sent about 11 million ducats to Milan – and that sum takes into account only money, not men, arms and supplies.'[47]

The demands of war therefore drove the Habsburgs of Spain to exploit the resources of their three Italian territories, the imperial fief of Milan and the 'Kingdom of the Two Sicilies', or Naples and Sicily. After 1528 another imperial fief, the Republic of Genoa, assumed a vital role in the naval and financial systems of the monarchy. One historian described the reign of Charles V as that of 'the Genoese Empire'; another proposed the model of a 'Hispano-Genoese Italy'.[48] Giuseppe Galasso observed that the Spanish did not have an empire in Europe, but rather an imperial system. Mario Rizzo and Arturo Pacini have referred to the Habsburg imperial system in Europe as being based on a 'sort of amphibious strategy', in which Genoa and Milan played a pivotal role.[49]

In an iconoclastic study, Professor Henry Kamen has argued that the fighting resources of the Monarchy were not exclusively – or even predominantly – Spanish in nature. The great victories of the sixteenth century were achieved by forces in which no more than a small part of the armies of Charles V or Philip II were 'Spanish' in origin. As Óscar Recio Morales has shown, the demands of war in the seventeenth century drove the Monarchy to depend increasingly upon regiments drawn from Flanders, Italy, Ireland, Germany, Switzerland and other European states – the *'tercios de naciones'*.[50] While these studies have added balance and nuance to an older narrative, it remains clear that the *infantería española* were taken to be the 'nerve' of the armies and garrisons of the Crown, that is to say, the most loyal, ferocious and disciplined of the forces available to Charles V and his successors. The problem was that these groups were always relatively small in number.[51]

Like the *monarquía* of the Habsburgs of Spain, the Ottoman sultans depended upon the collaboration of its 'conquered' peoples: theirs was a 'negotiated empire'. 'An astonishing array,' concludes a recent work of synthesis, 'of elites and ethnic and religious communities saw the advantage of their ties to the centre of the empire in Istanbul.'[52] The imperial government - sometimes referred to as the 'Sublime Porte', in reference to the gate through which ambassadors had to pass in order to enter the palace or seraglio - marshalled resources that were brought from across the Black Sea and Mediterranean (sometimes referred to as 'the White Sea').[53] Constantinople was the central point of its military, naval and economic systems, the place 'most apt to command the world' as one English traveller put it.[54] Sultan Mehmed II 'the Conqueror' (1450–81) had recognised as much immediately after his capture of the city in 1453. 'The Empire of the world,' he was reported as saying, 'must be one, one faith and one kingdom. To make this unity there is no place in the world more worthy than Constantinople.'[55] These words hinted at how the Ottoman dynasty – the House of Osmân *ghazi* – sought to locate itself within an older Muslim tradition.

This book will argue that the inland sea was not abandoned by the two major territorial states, the 'Catholic Monarchy' of the Habsburgs and the Ottoman Empire, both of which were essentially Mediterranean powers. It will argue that Christendom and Islam deployed two profoundly different systems of warfare. The galley has been dismissed as a generic form, while in fact its most noticeable characteristic was its diversity. Whereas Braudel wrote of a unified Mediterranean civilisation, and Professor Guilmartin described the 'Mediterranean system of warfare at sea', the differences between the Ottoman and Christian armadas were enormous and reflected in nearly every aspect of maritime planning. The disparity in the number and calibre of warships determined how, where and when the fighting took place. If the model of the modern artillery-bearing bastion held immense attraction for early modern governments, then the reality of their deployment or use was rather different and, in nearly all respects, limited. The strategic value of fortresses was severely restricted by a range of geographical, economical and logistical considerations – so many, in fact, that this study, dedicated to the galley, can do little more than skim the surface of the deficiencies and limitations of the *fortaleza*.[56] Furthermore, the early modern state was simply unable to defend the full extent of its coastlines or to deny the enemy access to rivers and streams. Sources of water could nearly always be secured on 'enemy' shorelines, while very few fortresses commanded the resources necessary (a deep-water anchorage; a prosperous and populous hinterland; a thriving weapons industry; supplies of fresh water in proportion to the needs of its garrison or population) to make them capable, as Rhodes had been in 1522, of resisting a determined attack for a comparatively long period (the Hospitaller forts held out for just under six months). The general trend in the length of sixteenth-century sieges was downwards, becoming noticeably shorter in the course of the 1500s although the following century would see much more successful defences of major bastions at Crete-Candia after 1645. In short, galleys were not so inefficient, nor coastal defences so effective, as to strangle the life from the Mediterranean systems of warfare at sea.

War operated on a timetable, in which the ambitions of the protagonists could be measured not only by the dimensions of their fleets but also by the date of departure. Ottoman offensive actions in the central and western regions of the *mare nostrum* depended upon catching the spring breezes.[57] Somewhere near the heart of the Habsburg assessment of the practicalities of war in the Mediterranean lay the dual idea that one fleet depended upon sail and the other upon its ability to row. In October 1551 Juan de Vega, the Viceroy of Sicily (1546 to 1557), recognised that the enemy fleet was skilled in the use of the sail but unskilled with the oar on account of its being driven by new *chusma* (the term, slightly derogatory in connotation, that was commonly used for rowers). His comment was made in the context of the sudden and surprising withdrawal of the enemy after its conquest of Tripoli. This was, he averred, evidence of the intelligence of its commanders.[58] This assessment was, without doubt, a simplification, although hardly a grotesque one.

The conflict in the Mediterranean operated on a far higher level and intensity than did other forms of war at sea: even in relatively quiet summers – for instance 1615 – around 170 oared battleships were mobilised by the Ottoman Empire and the Catholic Monarchy for war, while Venice, the neutral power, maintained just under 30 or so sail.[59] Judged by the criteria of administrative provision, the mobilisation of men and the implementation of technology, the inland sea was never abandoned: indeed, the opposite was the case. Measured against the campaigns in the inland sea, the outstanding feature of the conflict between the 'English' and 'Spanish' in the Channel and 'the Indies' was the absence of what, in Guilmartin's terms, might be called 'an Atlantic system of oceanic warfare', that is to say an established defensive network of harbour fortresses guarded by well-equipped professional troops and supplied and re-supplied regularly by galleys or lighter oared warships.[60] Elizabethan 'seadogs' like Sir Francis Drake (1540–96) and commanders like the Earl of Essex (1565–1601) certainly achieved a number of brilliant successes, but the entire rationale of their expeditions was predicated upon the deficiencies of the seaside defences that they attacked in the Indies or at Cadiz. The final defeat of Drake's last expedition was achieved by 80 or 90 Spanish troops at a hastily constructed fort called La Capirilla, a makeshift position on the road between Nombre de Dios and Panama.[61] In 1595 the regular garrison of Oran-Mers El Kebir ran to 1,156 men.[62] When Pimentel, Francisco de Holanda's commanding officer in 1588, informed his Dutch interrogators that Drake had sailed in a few ruined ships to infest the best towns of Spain he was instinctively comparing war in the Atlantic and Indies with the standards of maritime conflict in the Mediterranean: this comparison was a very suggestive one.[63] In November 1586 Philip II spelled out this understanding of maritime warfare in a letter to Pope Sixtus V Peretti (1585–90): he played down the English naval threat, and stressed that it would be possible, with warships, convoys and forts, 'to gain command of the seas' so that 'I would be safe and sure of not being open to attack'. The King insisted that only his desire 'to serve Our Lord' had led him to make plans for the invasion of England.[64]

The intention of this study is to understand the great campaigns in the Mediterranean 'from below' – to begin with the basic tactical features of the galley, and to demonstrate how a series of relatively simple procedures, systems and conventions determined the approach to warfare. The aim is therefore to provide a detailed investigation of the oared warship – almost, in fact, a biography of the galley, making use of the invaluable recent research by Luca Lo Basso and others.[65] The justification for this methodology and approach is twofold: first, that Charles V, Philip II and Philip III adopted precisely this approach; they formulated their strategy in the great campaigns in the Mediterranean with an understanding of the well-maintained warship, the 'galera en buen orden'. When it came to the crunch in 1534 (Koron), 1554

(Mahdia), 1560 (Djerba), 1565 (Malta) and 1574 (Tunis), the decision made by Charles V and Philip II was always to preserve the galley fleet rather than to risk it in operations designed to save isolated fortresses. True, Don John saw things very differently in defending Tunis and La Goleta in 1574; but at the very moment when the fighting was taking place the King had already resolved to destroy the first of these fortresses.[66]

These decisions were, in large part, also determined by the characteristics of the Ottoman armada. The qualities, traits and demands of the oared warship directly determined the proportions, characteristics and deployments of fleets during major campaigns. This book therefore focuses upon the galley in order that the salient features of the major campaigns seen in the Mediterranean in the century after 1530 will become evident. A brief narrative account of events may, however, be helpful to the reader.

I

The Domains of War

The Ottoman sultans presided over a vast collection of states whose borders stretched from the plain of Hungary to the Indian Ocean. The Habsburgs of Spain ruled over a comparable collection of territories: these included the crown of Castile (which in turn was made up of the separate kingdoms of Castile, Leon, Galicia, Navarre, the principality of Asturias, the other states of central and western Spain and the territories in America and the Pacific) and the crown of Aragon (Catalonia, Aragon, Valencia, the Balearics and the kingdoms of Sardinia, Naples and Sicily). From 1554 Philip II of Spain ruled as Duke of Milan; this vital strategic fief was conferred upon him through the ceremony of investiture by his father, Charles V, in his capacity as Holy Roman Emperor (he ruled as emperor from his election in 1519 to his abdication of the title in 1558).[1] In 1580–83, Philip II annexed the crown of Portugal, which had fallen vacant. The acquisition of the Portuguese empire brought extensive possessions in the southern Atlantic, Africa and the Far East into the Catholic Monarchy. In addition to their Mediterranean territories, the Spanish Habsburgs possessed a collection of 17 fiefs in the Low Countries.

Events may be profitably divided into three periods: from 1494 to 1530; from 1530 until 1560; and from 1560 until 1620. In the first period, the Ottomans were able to achieve major advances, in large part because the Christian states were engaged in a series of bitter and exhausting wars for the control of territories in Italy and the Low Countries.[2] While the Christian powers were involved in this bloody

19

fratricidal war, the Ottoman Turks made monumental territorial advances. In 1516/17 Sultan Selim I 'the Grim' (1512–20) conquered the Mamluk Empire, making him ruler not only of Egypt and Syria but also over the Two Holy Cities of Islam, Mecca and Medina. The acquisition of these territories decisively advanced his claim to leadership of the Muslim community. Taking further advantage of the princely rivalries in Christendom, the Ottomans proceeded to seize and occupy Belgrade (1521) and Rhodes (1522), before moving to dismember and claim most of Hungary (1526) after routing Christian forces at the Battle of Mohács.

Things were very different after 1530, in part because from this point until 1560 the Ottomans practically became a participant in the Christian civil wars, becoming allies of the Kings of France and therefore enemies of the Habsburgs of Spain. The principal cause of these wars, like those of the previous 40 years, largely lay in the rivalry between the crowns of France and Spain for the control of fiefs in Italy, although after 1530 the fighting focused on efforts to win the Duchy of Milan rather than the Kingdom of Naples. After 1560 the conflict assumed the characteristics of a more direct confrontation between Christian and Muslim: this saw the forces of Philip II confront the Ottomans at Djerba (1559–60), Malta (1565), La Goleta and Tunis (in 1573 and 1574), and during the engagements of the Holy League of the early 1570s.

Crucial to an understanding of all of these wars was the nature of political sovereignty: temporal authority in Italy was highly fragmented. Throughout the peninsula sovereignty was invested by one prince upon another: many territories in the northern half were unequivocally imperial fiefs like Milan, Mantua and Florence. Great controversy surrounded the status of fiefs like Ferrara, Urbino, Parma and Piacenza, Reggio and Modena. Popes such as Alexander VI Borgia (1493–1503), Julius II Della Rovere (1503–13), Leo X de'Medici (1513–21) and Clement VII de'Medici (1523–34) insisted on exercising the Holy See's claim to the temporal overlordship or 'suzerainty' over states such as the Duchy of Urbino.[3]

At the centre of these conflicts that raged from 1494 to 1559 ('the Italian Wars') lay the status of the Kingdom of Naples. The Church exercised an uncontested claim to 'the Kingdom', '*il Regno*', as its fief; it also asserted its overlordship over Sicily, arguing that these two territories ('The Kingdom of the Two Sicilies') were rightfully one state that had been ruled by its dependent kings since their conquest in the early Middle Ages.[4] In 1494 Charles VIII of France invaded the peninsula in order to exercise his dynastic claim to the Kingdom as the heir of the deceased houses of Provence and Anjou. His invasion ultimately failed because of the opposition of the Pope, Alexander VI, who refused to confer the investiture to 'His Most Christian Majesty' and consequently Charles VIII was unable to arrange his coronation in Naples. Subsequently Alexander VI promulgated a 'Holy League' to expel the French from the peninsula.[5] In 1496 Charles VIII withdrew, in part because of the diplomatic success of Alexander VI's call to arms.[6] In 1500 (the 'Treaty of Granada' or 'Treaty of Chambord') Charles VIII's successor, Louis XII, agreed with Ferdinand II of Aragon (1479–1516) and his wife Isabella I of Castile (1474–1504) to remove the existing King of Naples, Federigo (a relative of Ferdinand), and divide *il Regno* between them; they did, however, specify that they would respect the temporal authority of the Holy See, its claim to overlordship. The terms of this treaty were successfully executed, although the division of the kingdom in this manner proved highly unsatisfactory to both parties and quickly resulted in the outbreak of a second war, this time between Louis XII and Ferdinand. For Ferdinand and Isabella, known as 'the Catholic Monarchs', the preliminary step to securing 'the Kingdom' was to drive the French army from it; their *Gran Capitán*, Gonzalo Fernández de Córdoba, achieved this in a brilliant campaign launched in April 1503 and which culminated in the Battle of Garagliano (December 1503) and the conquest of Gaeta in January 1504. But success on the field of battle was only half of the equation. Upon the death of Alexander VI (18 August 1503) Ferdinand and Isabella recognised that the success of 'the war of Naples' depended upon the election of a friendly candidate to the Chair of St Peter.[7] And so it proved. In 1507 Ferdinand sent a delegation to proffer his oath of vassalage for Naples to Pope Julius II, who declined to accept it. His Holiness did not confer the investiture until July 1510, when it better suited him to recognise the King of Aragon as his fief-holder or 'feudatory'. One later writer argued that the conferral was made in recognition of Ferdinand II and Isabella I having conquered Granada, Oran and the Indies.[8] More immediately, the Bulls conferring the investiture were handed over when 300 troops arrived from Naples to serve in campaigns against Alfonso I d'Este, Duke of Ferrara (1505– 34), and Louis XII of France. Another Holy League (with Florence, Ferdinand II of Aragon, Venice and England) was formally convened to this purpose in 1511.[9]

Ferdinand II of Aragon had won Naples, but the Kingdom had also been conferred upon him. The role of the Church in bestowing these territories was certainly appreciated by Luis Cabrera de Córdoba, the contemporary biographer of Philip II. He recorded that Julius II gave the Bull of investiture to 'Don Fernando el Católico' and the Bull 'of deprivation of the Kings of France because they did not abide by the conditions of the fief nor by the oath of fidelity to the Church'.[10] The importance of the Holy See's claim to 'the Kingdom' was again to come to the fore during the pontificate of Clement VII de'Medici (1523–34). One of the key terms of the Treaty of Cognac (22 May 1526) between the Pope and Francis I, king of France, was the restitution of 'il Regno' to the Church; Francis I was 'prepared to bide his time with regard to Naples'.[11] Clement VII's excommunication of Charles V and declaration that Naples, as a lapsed fief, had reverted to the Holy See led to the 'War of the League of Cognac'. In 1527 Rome was sacked by an army under Charles de Bourbon, a disaffected French grandee who had pledged himself to the service of the emperor, but in the months after this outrage matters quickly deteriorated for the Habsburgs. In the spring and early summer of 1528 the position of Charles V appeared desperate; his forces were confined to a few forts within the city of Naples, and following a decisive naval action (28 April 1528) by galleys owned by the Genoese condottiere and admiral Andrea Doria, the supply lines from Sicily were cut; the French army, assisted by the barons of Angevin descent whose estates lay on the eastern regions of il Regno, advanced unopposed on the capital. On 4 July 1528 Habsburg fortunes improved dramatically when Doria, moved by concerns over French ambitions in his native Genoa, switched his allegiance to the Habsburgs. The

Ligurian Republic would play a pivotal role in the system of the *monarquía*.[12]

Charles V was henceforth able to call upon Doria's warships to ferry resources – above all foodstuffs – to his troops in Naples.[13] Denied access to the seas, the French army withered away. Naples had been secured, but Charles V needed Clement VII to confirm the investiture of the Kingdom and to crown him as Holy Roman Emperor. In order to underline his devotion to the Church, Charles made a public avowal of his desire to serve the Holy See. The terms of the investiture of *il Regno* bound the King of Naples to the Apostolic See of Rome 'for the propagation of the Christian religion': in the ceremony of investiture he swore an oath of fidelity, homage and liege obligation, promising to send 300 soldiers to serve in the wars of the Pope; in more general terms he vowed to obey, revere and serve the Holy See 'in the spirit of filial devotion'; he committed himself to fight against all infidels ('saracens') and pledged that he would never tolerate heretics, schismatics or usurpers of Church property as subjects but instead would persecute them with great alacrity, *sed illos efficaciter persequentur*.[14]

This pledge stood at the centre of a settlement that brought a degree of stability to the Italian peninsula with an accord (the 'Treaty of Barcelona', 29 June 1529) between emperor and pope. In his capacity as Holy Roman Emperor, Charles V conferred the duchy of Florence upon the Pope's nephew Alessandro de'Medici (the city had first to be conquered, at great cost, by an imperial army). Charles V also resolved the status of a number of other contested fiefs, including Reggio, Modena, Ferrara, Ravenna, Cervia and Milan.[15] Clement VII, for his part, was persuaded finally to confirm the investiture of Francesco Maria Della Rovere as Duke of Urbino (12 December 1529).[16] In March 1530 Malta, Gozo and the city of Tripoli were conferred by Charles V upon the Order of the Knights of the Hospital of St John of Jerusalem, the 'Hospitallers' or 'Knights of Malta'. This chivalric order of 'warrior monks', whose members swore allegiance to the Pope, had been evicted from Rhodes by Süleyman I (1520–66) in 1522.[17] Clement VII saw fit to confirm the investiture.[18] In Bologna on 22 and 24 February 1530 the Pope crowned Charles V as Holy Roman Emperor, King of the Romans and King of Lombardy.

'The coronation of Charles V is usually referred to as a triumph for the emperor; it was also a triumph for Clement VII.'[19] Great attention has been paid to the two imperial coronations of February 1530; perhaps some consideration might also be given to the ceremony of 5 November 1529, in which Charles paid reverence to the Pope by kissing his foot, hand and head before presenting him with 1,000 gold crowns.[20] The settlement between the Medici Pope and Habsburg Emperor of 1529–30 therefore made important progress towards the resolution of the wars that had raged across the peninsula since 1494. The Republic of St Mark was one of the losers. In 1529 Venice surrendered the cities of Ravenna and Cervia and six Adriatic towns (Monopoli, Polignana, Mola, Trani, Brindisi and Otranto) which Ferrante II of Naples (as king) and Pope Alexander VI (as feudal overlord) had conferred upon her in the 1490s.[21] These towns, which commanded the productive regions of Apulia, Venice 'had craved for half a millennium'.[22] The Republic was compensated with a range of concessions or privileges granted in the Kingdom of Naples.[23]

Later settlements in Italy were based upon the political institution of investiture and referred back to the pacification achieved by Clement VII and Charles V. Thus in 1557 Philip II conferred the fief of Siena upon Cosimo I de'Medici, Duke of Florence (1537–74). The grant was made with very specific conditions or 'obligations' (the King bestowed Siena 'in feudum nobile, ligium et honorificum'), which in turn harked back to the investiture of Florence by Charles V upon Alessandro de'Medici (ruled 1530–37). The *presidios* of Tuscany – the strategic harbour bases of Piombino, Orbetello and Porto Ercole that helped to ensure passage for the galleys along the western Italian seaboard – were exempted from the investiture of 1557 (previously they had formed part of the duchy of Siena). The fief of Portolongone, on the island of Elba, was purchased by Philip III in 1605.[24] In this instance, as in others, the Habsburgs remained profoundly conscious of the terms of conferral. The Catholic Monarchy paid attention to the writ of 'His Caesarean Majesty', the emperor and temporal overlord of many territories in northern Italy, as can be seen in the withdrawal, after a heated exchange, of Spanish troops from the strategic enclave of Finale Ligure in 1573.

This territory, on the western coastline of the Republic of Genoa, was finally secured by the crown of Spain in 1602, although it was not until 1617 that the investiture was confirmed.[25]

In northern Italy the larger independent or semi-independent states (Parma, Florence, Ferrara, Savoy-Piedmont, Urbino, Genoa, Mantua) existed in a state of ferocious rivalry, constantly invoking their immemorial and inalienable rights and forever trying to play 'Spanish' interests against 'French' ones (or vice versa). Indeed, a lower strata of urban and feudal power-holders ('communities, factions, fief-holders, ecclesiastical and lay estate-holders, magnates and personalities of various levels') succeeding in making their voices heard on a vast range of political, administrative and military issues.[26] Above all the Church continued to exercise its claims of suzerainty in the peninsula. The Holy See duly reclaimed the duchies of Ferrara (in 1598) and Urbino (in 1631) as lapsed fiefs, citing the terms by which they had been conferred or 'invested' upon the respective houses of d'Este and Della Rovere.[27] Such moments were viewed with extreme trepidation by the Habsburgs, for whom the 'quiet of Italy' – the 'tranquilidad de Italia' or the 'quietud de Italia' – stood as one of their outstanding strategic goals.[28] To this end they sought to limit the 'humours' that the dynastic ambitions of the Farnese or Medici could unleash: this was no easy task, as the predatory instincts of the rulers in Florence or Turin were supremely well tuned to any signs of vulnerability in enclaves like Piombino or Monaco; moreover, behind these expansionist or acquisitive tendencies Habsburg statesmen invariably suspected the agency of His Most Christian Majesty, whose presence in Italy would constitute a major threat.[29]

Julius II made a famous assessment of the political history of 'il Regno': that Naples had always been given as a fief, sometimes to one nation, sometimes to another. In 1494–96 Charles VIII's campaign had been undermined by the refusal of Alexander VI to recognise him as king of Naples, just as in May and June 1528 the Habsburg or imperialist position was on the brink of being fatally isolated by Clement VII's maneouvres. As historians such as Carlos Hernández, Maria Antonietta Visceglia and Angelantonio Spagnoletti have shown, in Naples Ferdinand and his successors (technically, the kingdom was invested upon the kings of Aragon) governed a nobility and aristocracy whose loyalty was far from assured or unconditional. Even within the Aragonese faction there were important tensions (Andrea Doria, for instance, acted as one of the focal points of opposition during the viceroyalty of Don Pedro de Toledo in the 1530s, 1540s and 1550s); there was always, until at least the 1550s, a tension between ruler and ruled.[30] Paradoxically the demands made by the Spanish kings of '*il Regno*' over the coming centuries served to entrench the influence and authority of the indigenous barons and princes. The nobility and aristocracy in Naples exploited the financial needs of the Spanish government to their own ends, 'thereby strengthening its control over the provinces and acquiring a large share of the assets (titles, lands, new taxes) that the monarchy was forced to sell'.[31] The Neapolitan model of evolution towards 'the modern state' was remarkable for generating enormous military and financial resources by means which appear paradoxical or contradictory: first, the state presided over a constant distribution and redistribution of estates, titles and revenues, many of them 'feudal' in character; second, the government conceded enormous tranches of political, economic and legal authority to the Church, the final aim being the control of the Conclave of Cardinals and, with it, the election of the next pope.[32]

Historians of domestic political arrangements in Spain now tend to view the concept of 'absolutism' with considerable scepticism, the emphasis being on the accommodation between the crown and municipalities and noble and aristocratic groups, rather than on their political eradication.[33] In Italy the difficulty for governments lay in isolating their territories from those around them; this was especially true in Naples. Again, the status of the kingdom as a fief of the Apostolic See imposed a sense of internationalism. In a public ceremony the ambassadors of His Catholic Majesty 'gave obedience' to the Pope on behalf of their sovereign; the procession from the villa of Julius III to St Peter's saw the nobles of Naples march 'each one between two Roman barons', in order to underline the traditional brotherhood of these groups.[34] As Professor Spagnoletti has shown, the Spanish Monarchy bound the great Italian families to them by conceding them fiefs in the *mezzogiorno*, thus strengthening the dynastic ties that transcended political boundaries.[35]

The governments of the Spanish Habsburgs were supremely sensitive to the 'humours' of Rome. In an excellent revisionist study Professor Michael Levin has shown how nervous Charles V and Philip II's ambassadors in Venice and Rome became at the mention of any prospect of innovation in Italy. Above all else, the mechanics for papal election caused the Habsburgs and their diplomats frequent headaches. In the late 1520s and early 1530s the imperial faction in the College of Cardinals was relatively small. A diplomat warned that if 'by some disgrace' a Frenchman or an ally of the League of Cognac were to be elected as the next pope 'we' would be in deep trouble, '*ternianmos harto trabajo*'.[36] In 1537 the Habsburg government in Naples was faced not only with a joint Franco-Ottoman offensive against Piedmont and Naples (Brindisi was a point of particular concern), but also with a serious shortage of infantry. The emperor ordered 6,000 Swiss troops to be sent to guard the less important fortresses in the southern regions of the Kingdom. His plan was to employ his German infantry battalions in Piedmont and Lombardy. This scheme was met with profound scepticism from the viceroy, Don Pedro de Toledo, who reminded Charles V that the Swiss were and always had been enemies of the imperial crown and friends of the King of France. The presence of such large numbers of Swiss infantry would, he warned, serve to inspire the enemies within the kingdom – the faction of France, '*la parte de Francia*' – to remove their masks and reveal themselves.[37] In 1551 the deterioration of the relationship between Don Pedro de Toledo, Viceroy of Naples, and the leading noble, Ferrante Sanseverino, prince of Salerno, led to the latter's rebellion and exile. Continuing a long tradition of family intrigue, Salerno immediately went to serve Henry II of France and sought to mobilise his extensive influence within the kingdom.[38] He developed a conspiracy in Gaeta. Luckily the plot was betrayed by another exile, Cesare Mormile, who divulged information on it in return for a pardon and the restitution of his lands.[39] In 1552 the Ottoman fleet, with Salerno aboard it, arrived near Messina. The Kapudan Pasha, assisted by Turgut *reis* ('Dragut *reis*' to his Christian contemporaries), interviewed a junior official from Sicily on the whereabouts of the 'prince of Bisignano', a client or 'creature' of Salerno. They flatly refused to believe that Bisignano was loyal to Charles V and obedient to the viceroy.[40] In July Juan de Vega, Viceroy of Sicily, stated that the enemy had been unable to do any damage on its coastlines (in Messina they were in good spirits and, he noted, 'the women are as calm as if the Turkish fleet was in Constantinople'); he was concerned that in Naples, 'where the French have many understandings', things might be very different.[41] In August 1552 Süleyman's armada did indeed land and try to seize Gaeta. The janissaries were disembarked and a siege attempted.[42] 'Once again,' writes Braudel, 'we may note how obsessed French policy was with Naples.'[43]

If the Franco-Ottoman alliance was one thread in the history of the Mediterranean, then the ongoing rivalry over control of the mechanics of apostolic election was another. The conclave of 1549–50 was one of the most bitterly contested papal elections of the century, as 'French' and 'Spanish' factions strove to secure the elevation of their rival candidates.[44] The election of Julius III brought relief, but only temporarily. The ongoing dispute over the conferral of the duchies of Parma and Piacenza threatened, in Cardinal Granvelle's words, to 'be the worst break there has ever been between pope and emperor'. At its heart this was a war over the conferral of two fiefs, which Charles V, as Holy Roman Emperor, and Julius III, as Pope, claimed to be part of their respective overlordships. In a remarkably complex series of events, a war (1551–52) occurred that pitted emperor and pope against Ottavio Farnese, Duke of Parma and Piacenza (1547–86), supported by Henry II.[45] Once again the terms of investiture stood at the centre of Italian conflict, with the rivalries between the Habsburgs and the Valois of France serving to lend authority to the rival pretensions of empire and Church. A similar pattern of events played out in the war of Siena (mentioned above), a duchy-fief that was eventually invested in 1557 by the crown of Spain upon the Medici of Florence, and in the controversy over the terms of sovereignty in Ferrara in the later 1560s, although this did not result in armed conflict.[46] The tensions were the result, in

Professor Daniela Frigo's words, of the 'institutional fragility of a [form of] state whose legitimacy still rested on dynastic and feudal criteria of seigniorial origin'.[47] Symbolism was extremely significant: 'beneath the controversies over formulas, rituals and titles there simmered a much more profound inter-dynastic conflict that involved the conception of sovereignty itself'.[48] The practicalities of Italian politics meant that diplomats – even saintly ones like St Francis Borja – had to take into account the feudal claims which the Holy See, sometimes in competition with the Holy Roman Empire, advanced to the polities of the northern half of the peninsula.[49]

In 1556 Pope Paul IV Carafa seized upon the Peace of Augsburg, the religious settlement arrived at by Charles V in the Empire which recognised the right of rulers to establish Protestant churches in their territories, to declare that the Habsburgs had forfeited their right to Naples by their disobedience. Paul IV called upon Henry II of France to 'liberate Italy'. The Duke of Guise, at the head of the French army, marched over the Alps and down through the peninsula.[50] It was widely believed at the time that Paul IV's plans went beyond the manipulation of the French to remove the Spanish from Naples. After his death, Carlo Carafa, Paul IV's nephew, was brought to trial for a number of crimes committed under the pontificate of his uncle, the most serious of which was that he had sought to bring the Turks into Italy to evict His Catholic Majesty.[51] Whether or not there was any truth to these allegations, it is clear that Henry II of France had been 'particularly attracted by the prospects of having an invasion legalised by the pope' – a statement that takes on greater meaning when the successful exercise of apostolic jurisdiction in Naples in 1494–96 and 1528 is taken into account.[52]

Whatever Paul IV's true intention in 1556 – whether it really was to liberate Italy or, as Braudel rather cynically but persuasively suggested, to secure the conferral of the fief of the Duchy of Siena for the House of Carafa – he was compelled by military defeat to confirm the investiture of Naples on Philip II.[53] Famously, the Duke of Alba knelt before his erstwhile enemy and kissed the foot of the Pope on 27 September 1557.[54] The Iron Duke, in other words, performed the ceremony of reverence, the expression of feudal duty to the heir of St Peter.

Changes in the 'humours' of Italy were said to cause tremors across the continent. 'Things in Italy change often,' wrote an experienced cardinal in the mid-sixteenth century, 'especially with new popes, changes in the College of Cardinals, and in the entire court, which is often renewed with the new principate; these innovations give rise to the mutations and universal alterations of Italy and of all Christendom.'[55] Charles V tried to ensure that the imperial succession – the title of 'Holy Roman Emperor', with the prerogatives as suzerain – should pass to his son, the future Philip II; this initiative having failed, he attempted to secure the title of Imperial Vicariate in Italy for his successor, as this honour came with jurisdiction over the imperial fiefs of the north of the peninsula.[56] In his *Testaments* Charles V warned Philip II that tensions would be caused by three matters: papal suzerainty over Naples; Rome's claim to the monarchy of Sicily – in other words, to Sicily as a domain of St Peter's by right of it having been conquered by its Norman vassals; and the Church's attempt to impose the Bull *In Coena Domini*.[57]

At the death of Pius IV (1565) Don Luis de Requesens, a prominent Spanish statesman, stated that the election of the wrong candidate would entail catastrophic consequences: the 'accession of an insolent Pope or a bad Christian would level to the ground what is left of Christendom'.[58] A little later he was more specific: the election of a Pope 'who is the enemy of Your Majesty is a much greater threat than either the Turk or the King of France', as conflict against these rulers offered the chance to gain territories, something which was not the case when fighting against the Pope. 'And such a war must end with Your Majesty asking for forgiveness and kissing the foot of the pontiff, as God cannot permit that the kings of Spain fail in the obedience that is owed to this Holy See.'[59] As Pius V lay waiting to be buried Cardinal Pacheco, one of Philip II's representatives in the College of Cardinals, wrote of the need to ensure the election of a malleable, pro-Habsburg candidate, 'as upon the good mind of the Pope hangs the peace of the kingdoms of Your Majesty in Italy'.[60] The passage of time did not alleviate 'Spanish' fears about the emergence of a 'bad pope'. The election of Alexander de'Medici ('the Cardinal of Florence') as Pope Leo XI in April 1605 caused consternation among Philip III's statesmen: it was believed that the new pontiff was pro-Florentine and pro-French, '*un deudo de los reyes de Francia y del Gran Duque*'. The Viceroy of Naples, the Count of Benavente, immediately recognised the danger posed by the 'rivals of Your Majesty [who] would not fail to take advantage of the situation' and requested that 10,000 to 12,000 Spaniards and a couple of million *escudos* be sent to Italy.[61]

These moments of tension notwithstanding, the settlement of 1529–30 brought about significant changes in Italian and, indeed, European history. Certainly, after this juncture war adopted a very different structure and pattern. From this point on, Charles V was able to oversee the defence of the frontiers of Christendom in the Mediterranean and Hungary with far greater confidence than had previously been the case. He repeatedly stated that his fundamental motivation in doing so lay in his devotion to 'the cause of God'; he might also have added that he was able to do so because of the effective system which was established using the regiments, or *tercios*, and high-grade galleys. Andrea Doria played a crucial role; he was promoted to the new position of high-admiral or 'Captain General of the Mediterranean Sea', *capitán general del mar Mediterráneo*. The Genoese businessman-admiral was granted an estate in the Kingdom of Naples which conferred upon him the title of 'Prince of Melfi'. In September 1532 he led 30 or so Christian galleys into the Levant; a number of towns in Greece were put to the torch and a garrison installed in Koron. Patras and Castilnuovo di Cattaro were taken, burnt and abandoned.[62] The justification for this campaign was that it served to divert the Sultan's forces away from Vienna. Whether Süleyman ever genuinely intended to attack the city is another matter. It has been persuasively argued that his 1532 campaign was a response to Charles V's coronations at Bologna two years previously. The Sultan's theatricality – his flamboyant ceremonial entrances into Nish and Belgrade, his four-tier parade helmet – was the real purpose of the mission, which was a skilfully choreographed procession and display of imperial grandeur, rather than a campaign of conquest. The campaign of 1532 was undertaken, according to a contemporary Italian source, to advertise the Sultan's status as '*imperator del mondo*'. Having said this, the sultanic programme explicitly referred to the question of sovereignty

Fig. 2 'Barbarossa, King of Algiers and arch-pirate'. This representation of a ferocious but somehow vulnerable or wary figure captures the assessment often made of the corsair-admiral by his direct Christian adversaries. Engraving on paper by Jérôme David (dated 1610–47).

in Italy (the northern part of the peninsula was to be given to the King of France; the southern half was to be ruled by investiture).[63]

Whatever his intention in Hungary in 1532, Süleyman's response to Doria's action in Greece was to instigate a new naval structure; at the end of the 1533 campaign he recruited the most talented, fearsome and ruthless of the North African corsairs, Hayreddin Barbarossa (sometimes 'Barbaros Hayreddin Pasha', henceforth 'Barbarossa') to serve as the first high admiral or 'Kapudan Pasha' and governor of the province of the Aegean islands (*Cezayir-i Bahr-i Sefid*). This title made him 'responsible for the protection of the seas and the islands (*cezayir*)'. At this juncture he was already recognised by the Ottomans as governor general of 'Barbary' or Algiers.[64] The Habsburg garrison was withdrawn from Koron in the spring of 1534, the troops embarking on Doria's galleys on the inauspicious date of 1 April. In the following year Charles V in person led an expedition to Tunis, where Barbarossa had established himself. The small fort at La Goleta fell after a month's fighting; as we have seen, the emperor then pressed ahead, against the advice of his councillors, with the conquest of the town of Tunis. His crusade was greatly assisted by a rebellion of the Christian slaves held in the city, an event which seems to have convinced the corsair-admiral of the impossibility of defending its walls.[65]

The other great innovation after 1530 was that the Turk practically became a participant in the Christian civil wars, as Süleyman sought to intervene in the fighting in Italy in order to favour the cause of his new 'ally', the king of France, Francis I and Henry II. To this end the Sultan sent fleets against Habsburg territories in 1534, 1537, 1543–44, 1551 (seizure of Tripoli), 1552, 1553 (successful operations in Corsica led by Turgut with 60 galleys), 1554, 1555, 1556 (the campaign against Oran, which was spearheaded by corsairs from North Africa) and 1558 (the raid on Ciudadella de Menorca).[66] These expeditions repeatedly foundered on the well-protected coastlines of Italy, which the emperor and his ministers were actively fortifying. Thus the enormous armada launched in the summer of 1537 failed to make significant headway in Naples; almost as an afterthought, in September Barbarossa sanctioned a raid on Corfu, a Venetian territory. By this juncture the Ottoman fleet was in a very poor state, and in purely military terms the landing resulted in little more than superficial skirmishing. Yet this contretemps was enough to convince the Most Serene Republic that an alliance with the other Christian princes was necessary and in 1538 a Holy League was duly convened by Pope Paul III Farnese (1534–49). An engagement, or partial engagement, took place between the two fleets off Preveza in late September. The Ottoman armada was again in some disarray by early autumn and headed back towards Constantinople; it was caught in a storm and dashed against the Greek coast. Taking advantage of the unguarded seas of the Adriatic, Doria seized the small and isolated fort at Castilnuovo di Cattaro (Herçeg Novi) in October. An enormous Ottoman force was mobilised to reclaim the position in the following year. Doria's decision to seize and retain the outpost proved enough to convince the Venetian patricians that nothing good could be achieved by the Holy League and in effect the Republic of St Mark withdrew from the confederation at the end of 1538; it remained neutral throughout 1539 and was forced to conclude a humiliating peace treaty with the Sublime Porte in 1540.

The experience of the 1530s therefore demonstrated how quickly Christian unity would break down under the pressure of war, in no small part because of the economic difficulties faced by the Most Serene Republic in feeding itself in times of conflict and the consequent dependence upon exports from Naples.[67] In military terms, the first decade of the fighting also served to underline the limits of the Christian position, in that Koron and Castilnuovo di Cattaro had proved impossible to hold, while the town of Tunis was returned to a vassal-king, the Hafsid ruler Muely Hassan, who swore an oath of homage to the emperor in 1535.[68] Only La Goleta – the position which would lead to the capture of Holanda's galleon – was retained by the Catholic Monarchy. In many respects the campaigns of the 1540s and 1550s conformed to the pattern set down in the 1530s. In 1541 Charles V himself led a campaign against Algiers in the later stages of the campaigning season; the expedition was overcome by a fierce storm in October. A large part of the fleet was lost, the galleys alone able to resist the winds and therefore to avoid being dashed on the jagged shoreline.[69] The fracas convinced Francis I to re-open hostilities in northern Italy and the Low Countries in the following year; again, he was assisted by Süleyman, who dispatched Barbarossa with an enormous armada to the coastline of Italy in 1543; in an infamous incident, it wintered in Toulon and ravaged the Ligurian and Tyrrhenian coastlines until September of the following year.[70] This was the last major campaign of Barbarossa, who died in Constantinople in July 1546.

In 1544 Charles V was able to bring Francis I to the negotiating table and made extensive concessions in order to secure, as he put it, 'the common good of Christendom'; specifically, his intention was to bring about a General Council in order to reform the Catholic Church of abuses and to moderate its theology in the light of the challenge posed by the Protestants.[71] In order to convince Francis I to agree to this, he was willing to surrender either the Low Countries or Milan, a concession which would have surrendered many of the gains of the previous 20 years.

In the following year Charles V succeeded in agreeing an informal truce with Süleyman (it was formalised in 1547); it held until 1550, when the town of Mahdia ('Africa' in documents of the time) was seized and garrisoned by Doria.[72] This incident led to a resumption of major hostilities at sea, with an Ottoman fleet taking Tripoli (14 August 1551), which had been held by the Hospitaller knights since its investiture in the settlement of 1530. The fortress was surrendered, in extremely controversial circumstances, after a short siege. Henry II's ambassador to Constantinople negotiated the terms with knights who belonged to the two *langues* or languages (strictly speaking, 'tongues') of France.[73] At this point the Order of the Hospital appeared to be an institution on the point of rupture on account of the accusations levelled by the Spanish knights at their French colleagues.[74] Having lost Rhodes in 1522, the Hospitallers seemed unwilling or unable to defend Malta almost three decades later. A knight, Frey Juan Bautista, arrived in Sicily with a papal decree or *Breve* allowing it to transfer its headquarters from the island to another of the territories of 'His Catholic Caesarian Majesty', Charles V. The viceroy, Juan de Vega, was extremely reluctant to allow this transfer. In the first place there was no immediate danger, the enemy fleet having headed back to the Levant; afforded respite from the enemy advance, Malta, a rocky outcrop without soil, might be fortified to a very high level. In no way would it be advisable to leave a garrison consisting predominantly or wholly of French knights without experienced leaders.

Should the Ottoman fleet arrive at the island and face such a garrison then these *chevaliers* might very well negotiate the terms of their surrender, as had happened at Tripoli, where the commander had forgotten his honour and the vow he had made to defend the fort in order to save his person and property. It was, Vega argued, foolish to throw away Malta in this manner and, given that the purpose of the Order – and the justification for its numerous estates scattered across Christendom – was to make war on the infidel ('*su profesión es guerrear a los infieles*'), it seemed wiser to require the knights to remain in the city, the 'castle' (which was *fortísimo*) and the *Burgo* or fort near the Grand Harbour, all of which might be easily strengthened.[75] In November the viceroy again expressed profound scepticism about the Order of the Knights of the Hospital of St John of Jerusalem: if the Hospitallers were now more unified in purpose, then nobody could have any confidence in their government 'especially if they were to see themselves in some trouble'.[76] But the emperor himself clearly felt even more strongly than his viceroy. As Beatriz Alonso notes, in October 1552 Charles V expressed extreme mistrust of the Knights of Malta: he ordered that in no circumstances was Mahdia to be given to the Hospitallers, for their possession of it would lead to the 'total destruction of the kingdoms of Sicily and Naples and of the other regions of Italy and of the frontiers that we have in Africa'.[77]

In 1552 Doria had a lucky escape when a much larger enemy fleet launched itself upon his 40 galleys in waters to the south of Rome, between the island of Ponza and Terracina; seven Christian galleys were taken after a chase that lasted a day and a half. As mentioned above, the Ottoman armada then made a brief and, in truth, half-hearted effort to besiege the coastal town of Gaeta. In 1553 Süleyman's fleet was deployed to assist operations in Corsica, where Henry's II's forces were sponsoring a rebellion under Pedro Corso. The island was conquered, although it was retaken by the Republic of Genoa in the following two campaigns. In 1555 the commanders of the Ottoman fleet showed little inclination to bolster the efforts of the King of France; they stood off the assaults on positions in Corsica (Calvi and Bastia). In 1558 the Ottoman fleet again provided minimal genuine assistance to Henry II's forces, although on this occasion the large fleet was successful in raiding the small town of Cuidadella on Menorca before heading back to the Levant.[78] Again, it must be stressed that this operation was a Franco-Ottoman enterprise: the Sultan's commanders at the siege of Ciudadella reportedly invited the people to become subjects of His Christian Majesty, an invitation which they refused.[79]

Nearly all operations from 1530 until 1560 were, therefore, a manifestation of the war between the Franco-Ottoman alliance and the Habsburgs, rather than a direct Christian-Muslim conflict. In 1552 Süleyman ordered his admiral, when on the coasts of Naples, to operate at all times with the French galleys, exercising extreme caution when the two armadas were not united.[80] Prince Philip believed that Henry II's ambassador in Rome had provided refreshment for the enemy fleet when it arrived at the Roman coastline or 'beach'; the 'enterprise of Naples', he averred, was the intention of the Ottoman high command, an objective which they hoped to achieve with the help of the King of France, the Prince of Salerno and the other outlaws. (It had been impossible, he explained, to send Spanish infantry to Italy 'as the seas are full of corsairs'.)[81] Even as late as May 1566 Toledo took the possibility of a Franco-Ottoman assault upon Corsica seriously, citing the preparation of galleys in Marseille as evidence for such a plot.[82]

After 1560 the Kingdom of France collapsed into the anarchy of the Wars of Religion, and the fighting in the Mediterranean from this point adopted the characteristics of a more straightforward confrontation between Christians and Muslims, with the Habsburgs of Spain and their allies or 'confederates' being pitted against the Ottomans. In the summer of 1559 Philip II gave orders for an attempt to reclaim Tripoli , which he hoped might be snatched by a late-season campaign.[83] The expedition ended in a major defeat at the island of Djerba (11 May 1560), when an Ottoman armada routed the Christian fleet and captured a large number of galleys and galiots.[84] The Kapudan Pasha then successfully besieged the garrison guarding the small and isolated castle on the island.

In 1556 and 1563 the Islamic corsairs of Algiers (armed by Genoese and French ships) attacked the North African *presidio* or outpost of Oran, which guarded the sea lanes to the east of the Straits of Gibraltar;

both expeditions were eventually rebuffed; in the latter case the Ottoman commander, the corsair Hasan Pasha, abandoned the siege when it appeared possible that the Christian fleet, which had been slowly brought over from Italy, might be about to arrive (Philip II's galleys duly appeared on 8 June, the siege having lasted over two months).[85] In an operation designed to obviate all possible risks, in September 1564 Philip II's fleet captured the small fortress or 'mole' known as the Peñón de Vélez de la Gomera. In 1565, after five years of relative inactivity at sea, Süleyman dispatched a fleet of 200 or so galleys to Malta. The expedition was to prove unsuccessful; after a siege lasting nearly a third of a year, the Turks withdrew. The renowned Sultan died in the following year during a campaign in Hungary.

On Christmas Day 1568 a rebellion broke out among the 'New Christians' or 'Moriscos' of Granada in southern Spain, the Moorish communities who retained a strong attachment to the Muslim faith. It was in response to the efforts of the government to eradicate not only their confessional beliefs – the majority of Moriscos had continued to observe the Islamic religion, rather than the Christian faith to which they had been nominally converted in the early sixteenth century – but also their cultural and ethnic identity. The fighting in southern Spain, known as the 'War of Granada' or the 'War of the Alpujarras', took place in bouts of extreme ferocity and lasted until the spring of 1570. In this year Sultan Selim II (1566–74) dispatched a vast expeditionary force to embark upon the conquest of the Kingdom of Cyprus, a Venetian territory. The attack upon Nicosia led to the convocation of a Holy League (1571–73), whose principal sponsor and architect was Pope St Pius V (1566–72). In 1570 the Christian relief force, or the vanguard of it, sailed as far as the straits between Scarpanto (Kárpathos) and Rhodes (18 September) and reached Kastellórizon (Meyísti) three days later, only to disband when it heard of the fall of Nicosia (the city had fallen on 9 September). On their return to Italy, the Venetian representatives and the overall commander, Marc'Antonio Colonna, an Italian prince with estates in both the Papal States and 'il Regno', made serious allegations against Gian Andrea Doria (1540–1606), Andrea Doria's heir and successor as Prince of Melfi and Philip II's commander during this summer. The basic theme of these

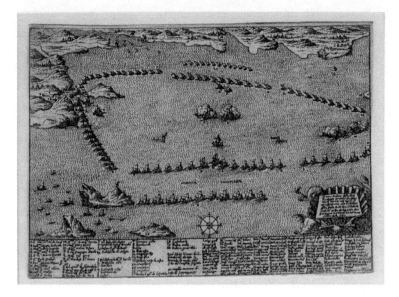

Fig. 3 Lepanto. This print by Martin Rota (dated 1571) shows 'the Naval Battle' as it came to be represented and remembered in Europe – as a decisive Christian victory over a highly disciplined and well-prepared Ottoman armada.

complaints was that Doria's only intention had been to preserve his galleys.[86]

With the help of Francisco de Holanda's galleon, the fleet of the Holy League, commanded by the King's half-brother, Don John of Austria, engaged the Ottoman armada at the entrance to the Gulf of Lepanto at the very end of the campaigning season of 1571. The result was a spectacular victory for the Christians. In 1572 Don John was unable to follow up his initial success, as the Ottoman fleet, once again ably commanded by a corsair recruited in North Africa, Uluç Ali Pasha, avoided the ineffective Venetian armada in high summer before withdrawing to Navarino (Pylos Bay) and Modon (Methoni) in September and October. Its forces then skilfully rebuffed a landing party led by Alessandro Farnese, the heir to the Duchy of Parma-Piacenza and one of Don John's deputies. As in 1570, the complaints made by Venetian statesmen against 'the Spanish' were acerbic; unsurprisingly the Republic of St Mark made peace with the Sublime Porte in the spring of the following year. A complicating factor in 1572 lay in the machinations of international diplomacy, as Elizabeth I of England was rumoured to be planning to assist Charles IX of France (1560–74) in an attack upon Philip II's territories in Milan or the Low Countries; the Queen of England certainly complicated things for His Catholic Majesty by expelling the 'Sea-Beggars', a group of pirates whose arrival in the Low Countries re-ignited the rebellion against Philip II. The complexity of events in 1572 cannot be underestimated, as the King of Spain was also clearly considering a move against Algiers.[87] In 1573 Don John of Austria led a campaign that seized the town of Tunis in the last moments of the 'fine season'; once again this initial success proved impossible to follow up, as the Habsburg commanders were unable to defend the twin forts at La Goleta and Tunis, where Don John had begun building a new bastion, against an Ottoman force of vast proportions in 1574. The principal difficulty for the Ottomans in this year lay in sailing the gargantuan fleet from Constantinople to the city on the North African coast; having made a late departure, it was constantly delayed by bad weather, being forced to take water in Calabria and at Augusta and Licata in Sicily.[88] The two forts in North Africa were quickly won, the hastily constructed bastion at Tunis holding out for just under three weeks.[89]

The forms and character of the fighting after this point will be set out in some detail in this study; suffice it to say that it has always been argued that the Mediterranean was abandoned after the second loss of Tunis in 1574 or 1580, the year in which Philip II claimed the crown of Portugal and its extensive overseas possessions as his inheritance.[90] Certainly from 1572 the Catholic Monarchy was involved in a series of interrelated wars against Protestant states in northern Europe; foremost among these conflicts was 'the Revolt of the Netherlands', the attempt to suppress a Calvinist revolt in the Low Countries. This conflict merged into the war fought against Elizabeth I and intervention in 1590 and 1592 on behalf of the Catholic League in the French Wars of Religion. The fighting with England lasted until 1604 and the Revolt of the Netherlands was temporarily halted in 1609 by a truce of 12 years. The pact was signed on 4 April 1609; on this very day the Council of State met to recommend to Philip III that the New Christians or Moriscos of Spain should be expelled: the congruence of the two decisions has led historians to wonder if they are somehow related, one widely accepted interpretation being that, as Voltaire put it, the King had been unable to defeat the Dutch and so took revenge on the Moorish minority at home.[91]

Voltaire's condemnation of Philip III must, however, be placed in context. In their classic study, Antonio Domínguez Ortiz and Bernard Vincent pointed out that in recommending the expulsion the primary concern of the Council of State was the security of Spain in light of the threat from the Muslim world. The religious beliefs and practices of the minority communities were in fact the secondary reason for their removal. Curiously, the threat of French involvement over the Pyrenees was not mentioned. The justification for the expulsion, notes one recent study, was the threat of the imminent loss of Spain itself (in this case the author is, unfortunately, unable to say where the threat came from).[92] Moreover, few people seem to have feared that *reputación* was in particularly short supply for the King of Spain in 1609. Far from being ashamed of the decision to expel the Moriscos, Philip III believed that this achievement would stand as the crowning glory of his reign.[93] Indeed, in December 1610 the King's ambassador in Genoa wrote to congratulate him on the expulsion of the New Christians, the assassination of the King of France and the capture of the Moroccan port of Larache (Al Araich): these three 'miraculous' events surely demonstrated that 'Our Lord is with Your Majesty'. The year had, he added, finished better than had seemed likely and there was every chance of further successes.[94]

When the agreement with Amsterdam ('the Twelve Years Truce') elapsed in 1621, the fighting against the Dutch Republic was resumed. It was finally brought to an end in 1648 as a part of the general treaty (the 'Peace of Westphalia'), which concluded the European conflagration known as the 'Thirty Years War'. Philip II and Philip III repeatedly stated that they were driven to protect Christendom and purify it from the 'stain of heresy'; their one overriding intention, they claimed, was to perform the service of God.[95] If decisive changes in the direction and tempo of fighting were brought about by events in 1530 or 1560, then the military system of the Habsburgs of Spain was characterised by important continuities: the territories in Italy which had been the cause of so much of the fighting against Charles VIII, Louis XII, Francis I and Henry II of France certainly served the Catholic Monarchy extremely well in the long succession of wars fought against its many enemies after 1560.

II

The Habsburgs, the Ottomans and the 'Naval Battle'

Warfare in the Mediterranean Sea in the sixteenth and seventeenth centuries was fought between two sides who had either too few good galleys or too many bad ones. This painfully simple dichotomy dominated nearly all campaigns. Christendom and Islam, the Habsburgs of Spain and the Ottoman Turks, engaged in a war of unequal measures and obscure objectives. A degree of futility hung over the fighting; a sense of charade clung to most major enterprises; an element of self-contradiction was never entirely absent from the correspondence of the Christian 'captains general' (*capitán general* or *capitanes generales*) and the officials who laboured under them. Yet if the fighting promised meagre rewards and fleeting advantages it was still perhaps true that the naval war fought in the *mare Mediterraneum* was the longest, the most continuous and the greatest conflict of its age. The fighting refused to ebb away; it persisted long after any realistic chance of victory had vanished – if indeed any such opportunity had ever really existed.

The principal feature of this curiously dissonant form of warfare was the reliance upon the oared warship as a means of conducting campaigns; indeed, in many respects the galley provided not only the basic characteristic of the fighting but also the major objective of it. At least this formulation holds true for the Habsburgs of Spain, whose main operational goal appeared to be to maintain and, if possible, improve their fleet from year to year. Having said this it should immediately be added that the task of identifying their basic aims or ambitions in the Mediterranean is a profoundly difficult one. In trying to pin down the strategic interests of the Habsburg kings Philip II (1556–98) and Philip III (1598–1621) the historian is faced with the most glaring of contradictions, in that while their principal military concern was to improve their fleet and to keep it away from danger they nevertheless swore that they would sacrifice their kingdoms in their entirety in order to serve the common good of Christendom.

A profound and irreconcilable contradiction therefore loomed between what the Habsburgs professed as their ambition to the Pope and other Catholic rulers, and the tactical and operational objectives that governed the running of their fleet.[1] The Habsburgs protested that they needed to keep their galleys safe from harm for two reasons: first, because high-grade galleys were practically impossible to replace; second, because the royal squadrons served to maintain communications between Spain and Italy and therefore made possible the overall programme to which the dynasty was pledged, which was not only to defend Christendom's borders against the Ottoman threat but also to purge Europe of the 'stain' of heresy. If, as they repeatedly averred, their final or overall dynastic purpose was the very cause of God, then this grand aim had to be prosecuted with worldly prudence. The imperative that shaped the royal instructions in years of major campaigns such as 1565, 1572 and 1596 was that the fleet was the single tool that preserved the integrity of Catholic Christendom: this same rationale provided the justification for deployments in those years of less significance, in which the armada was employed on patient patrols that were designed to improve its strength.

Habsburg strategy was therefore driven by two competing ideas: on the one hand stood notions of chivalry, honour and carrying the attack forward into the domains of the infidel; on the other there loomed the priority to preserve the royal armada at all costs. Needless to say, the tension between these two imperatives was a serious one: it was no coincidence that to his contemporaries Philip II was both 'the Prudent

King' (*el rey prudente*) and 'His Holy Royal Catholic Majesty' (*Su Sacra Real Católica Majestad*). This contradiction has sometimes been understood as a legacy of Charles V's imperial programme: unlike his father, Philip II would never be elected emperor, but the dream of a Habsburg universal monarchy remained alive. The problem with this line of argument lies in the extreme attention to detail exhibited by the king. Approaching holy war with a legalistic view of his duties and responsibilities, he had a very clear understanding of the value of his royal armada and of the obligations of his 'confederates', 'friends' and 'vassals' in Italy. In January 1561 the King was certainly able to contain his concerns over a prospective attack upon Malta. His basic assumptions were made clear in response to pleas from the Grand Master, Jean Parisot de la Valette, who forwarded reports that a large Ottoman force might be about to besiege the island. In response Philip II allowed the Order to take double its usual export of wheat from Sicily, specifying that this was to be an extraordinary concession made for this year only. In the same letter he instructed the viceroy 'to do something to help and favour the Grand Master and the Religion so that they should escape from any difficulty in which they might find themselves', referring to the island as being as important to him as one of his own territories. To the Grand Master he was more precise and even less forthcoming: he expressed his conviction that la Valette, guided by his own valour and prudence, would make such preparations as to convince the Sultan to abandon any idea he might have of attacking the island; should the Turk proceed to invest the forts, the King stated that he had no doubt that the Hospitallers would be able to conduct a successful defence.[2] In April the King sent an extraordinary ambassador to Genoa, Savoy, Florence and Piombino to ask for the use of their galleys, explaining to them the importance of defending La Goleta 'for the navigation of all Christians and to serve as a break on the infidels of Barbary'. His representative was then instructed to visit Rome, 'and to kiss the foot of His Holiness on my behalf'. He was to present Pius IV with a letter which set out the 'love, respect and observance which in all things we have for him'.[3] At this point the King also sought to convince the Grand Master that 'the service of God' and 'the Service of Our Lord' was to send the Hospitaller galleys to Messina by the middle of May so that they could help to protect 'our states' and those of 'our confederates and friends'. He stressed that the deployment of the flotilla on the seas with the Catholic Armada represented a much better use of it than to have the warships in the Grand Harbour of Malta, where they could do no good.[4]

These missives and instructions reveal a series of crucial assumptions about the role of the oared fleet, the resources available to the crown, the strategic value of fortresses and the quality of the Hospitaller squadron; they perhaps hint at how the interests, instincts and nature of the Order were perceived in Madrid. They also indicate that Philip II held that the 'service of God' in the Mediterranean had to be a very restricted or cautious policy, a defensive strategy based upon equipping and maintaining good galleys and deploying them with craft and discretion. In 1565 the King was even more rigorous and circumspect in his orders. 'We hope,' he wrote to the high-admiral, Toledo, in March, 'in God that with your prudence, diligence and good preparation, some actions can be undertaken that, whatever the circumstances, the enemies will not be able to do anything of substance.'[5] In May and June he was no more specific or forthcoming: 'I am confident in God and in your good diligence and experience that you will do what is most convenient.'[6] Unsurprisingly, Toledo found it difficult to determine exactly what his instructions were and repeatedly asked the King for clarification of the 'law by which I am to abide'.[7] In his final instructions of 27 July for the expedition to relieve Malta, the King ordered his Captain General of the Mediterranean Sea that under no circumstances whatsoever was he to fight the enemy at sea. The conservation of the fleet was more important than the relief mission, since if the island were lost, 'which God will not want', there would be other means of recovering it, *'en caso que Malta se perdiese, lo que Dios no querrà, habría otros medios para tornarla à recuperar'*. If the Christian armada was defeated or destroyed, in contrast, there would be no means of rearming in many years. In an oblique reference he added that in the wake of a major defeat those enmities that were then in abeyance would be reanimated. A disaster on land, 'which Our Lord will not permit', would be of 'much less inconvenience than putting the fleet in any danger'.[8] A similar set of priorities dominated the other great campaigns in the inland sea. In instructions issued to Don John of Austria on 17 May 1572 Philip II stressed the need to defend the Netherlands from Anglo-French attack; the galleys were needed in order to ferry the armies to Finale Ligure, whence they would march to Brussels. Later he came to modify these instructions, but the underlying rationale remained. In instructions of 4 July he allowed Don John to pass into the Levant with a part of the fleet, although his reservations about holy war were marked: he referred to the defence of the Low Countries or Milan, 'which is of so much more weight and importance than anything that can be undertaken in the Levant', before going on to reiterate his desire to serve as a confederate of the Holy League, 'an act of such Holiness and such service to Our Lord, of such damage to the enemy of Christendom and [one that will] give satisfaction and contentment to His Holiness, whom I desire to please and satisfy above all else ...'.[9] The obvious contradiction within his letter – the statement of the comparative futility of a campaign in the eastern Mediterranean and the simultaneous insistence that it was the very service of God – cuts to the heart of the question of the problem of holy war in the sixteenth century; indeed, in many respects it offers insights into the 'mentality' (or worldview) and religiosity of the period.

Many historians have argued that the reason for the King's involvement in Mediterranean holy war lay in the taxes conceded by the Church; these monies, 'the Three Graces' (or *cruzada*, *subsidio* and *escusado*) represented an important source of income for the King.[10] The difficulty with this argument is threefold: first, the taxes may not have actually brought in as much money as they were nominally supposed to do, at least in the first instances. Second, the significance of the Three Graces as a negotiating tool was surely undermined by the lack of alternative strategies available to Rome in June 1565 or August 1570: if Pius IV or Pius V was going to break with the King of Spain, then the possibilities of rescuing the knights at Malta or the Venetian garrisons in Cyprus in 1570 were slight, if not negligible. The third reason for doubting that the Three Graces could have been the central motivation of the King lies in the 'service of God', the war against all heretics and infidels. Philip II's case was that his galley fleet was crucial not only to campaigns in the Mediterranean, but also to his military efforts in central and northern Europe and in Spain and its Atlantic seaboard; the King's efforts in these domains were dedicated to the 'service of God'. Popes tended to link the Three Graces to the investiture of Naples and the Constantinian prerogatives and messianic destiny of the Papacy ('the Vicar of Christ'); the Holy See was the sole source of authority on relations with the infidel Turk and the inspiration for the princes of Christendom to unite under the banner of the cross.[11] The problem with this line of argument was that it was impossible to deny that Philip II was true to his word – that the *monarquía* was engaged in a war against all heretics and infidels in line with the terms of the investiture of *il Regno*. Even Pope Pius V, who was driven by a profound spirituality that led him to a messianic vision of Christendom, accepted the case advanced by the Habsburg King and his diplomats. In his first audiences with the ambassador Juan de Zúñiga in January 1568 Pius V expressed his love for Philip II ('This Holy See has no other defender'), and admitted how much the affairs of France pained him. Zúñiga responded by lamenting that His Christian Majesty had not taken advantage of the offer of help recently made to him by Alba. 'His Catholic Majesty,' observed the Pope in another audience shortly afterwards, 'is the sole defender of all of Christendom.' At this point, Zúñiga sought to tie the King's many campaigns 'in service of religion' against heretics and Turks to the exhaustion of the royal patrimony and the need for the concession of the *cruzada*.[12]

During the reign of Charles V the church revenues were always justified by the wars against both heretics and infidels: as Professor Sean Perrone notes in his masterly study, the dedication of these monies to the galleys and war in the *mare nostrum* was nothing more than nominal. The Three Graces were spent on all of the emperor's wars, not only those in the *mare nostrum*.[13] This continued to be the case. The *escusado*, first conceded in 1567, was granted in order to allow the King to travel to the Low Countries in the wake of Alba's repressive measures.[14] In November 1569 Zúñiga penned a paper on how to win the *cruzada*: in order to do so, the King would have to intervene in Ireland and England.[15] In September 1571, His Holiness granted the

King a dispensation to dedicate 'whatever portion of the *escusado* that his Majesty should consider necessary for the enterprise of England, without incurring the penalty of excommunication or censure set out in the Bull'.[16]

For the moment it is not necessary to ask why, in the days before Lepanto, His Holiness was already convinced that His Catholic Majesty was planning to invade Ireland and England. The point is that the consideration of the problem of the 'service of God' moves inevitably from the unifying role of the oared squadrons to the monies provided by the Church and the military campaigns of the crown of Spain, that is to say the unrelenting series of wars against heretics (within Christendom) and infidels (on its many, long borders). These themes were inextricably linked in the thinking of statesmen. Thus in July 1563 Medinaceli expressed the hope that the success of the fleet in repelling the Ottoman assault on the *presidio* of Oran would 'give heat' to the King's interests at the Council of Trent. Christendom, he pointedly insisted, had one true defender 'on this planet'.[17] Others began from this same premise but reached radically different conclusions. In the late 1570s and early 1580s Philip II negotiated a series of secret, temporary suspensions of arms with the sultan, Murad III (1574–95). In response Pope Gregory XIII mobilised the Holy See's rights in protest against these accords. Making use of the papacy's claims as feudal overlord of Naples, its control over the granting of Three Graces and the rather vague theological arguments outlined above, Pope Gregory XIII effectively sought to curtail the sovereign authority of the *monarquía*, in this case through impeding its conduct of foreign policy. Understandably, this intervention led to a 'great storm' (Cardinal Granvelle's words), a 'veritable crisis' – and a triumph for papal diplomacy. In 1582 the King had to cede to Rome the right to veto any future treaties or accord with Constantinople, a concession which effectively ended the possibility of any lasting peace.[18]

The galley stood, therefore, as the objective of strategy and as the source of controversy. Part of the reason for the centrality of the oared warship lay in the limited strategic value of fortresses and harbour positions: there were very few seaside towns or ports which offered the prospect of decisive advantage to either side, and if any such fort or location existed then it was certain that it had to be constantly supplied and re-supplied from the sea.[19] Given the geographical and environmental conditions in the Mediterranean, by far the best means of achieving this logistical operation was by the employment of the oared warship; to be precise, the best means of provisioning important forts lay in the use of the high-grade oared warship, 'the reinforced galley' ('la galera reforzada') or 'galley in good order' ('la galera en buen orden'). The oared warship was, by virtue of its capacity to make progress against headwinds, to row through summer calms and to race away from predators, essential to the maintenance of any fortress. As the King's letters of 1561 suggested, a flotilla offered governments the ability to deploy their fighting forces in the most effective manner. It could also protect seaborne trade and could offer employment to hotheads, thus giving vent to those violent tendencies – what contemporaries often referred to as the 'humours' or 'bad humours' – that might otherwise have disturbed the peace of the commonwealth. 'It is an excellent plan,' wrote the philosopher Giovanni Botero at the end of the sixteenth century, 'to keep a fleet of galleys, so that those who are of a restless disposition can find an outlet for their youth and courage in fighting the true enemies.'[20]

The relationship between the galleys and their home provinces was a complex and multifaceted one. On one level the squadrons were taken to be a reflection of the economic, geographic and, in certain respects, political and legal systems of the territories in which they were maintained. Thus the poverty and sterility of Catalonia loomed over the attempts to found a flotilla in the principality under Philip III; in contrast, one of the difficulties in recruiting oarsmen in Sicily was precisely the productivity of the region, its dedication to agriculture and the consequent reluctance of its peoples to serve as *chusma*.[21] Sicily's position on the frontier of the Islamic world presented both a challenge and a considerable advantage to its flotilla; the long and difficult coastline of Spain, where there were so few harbours or points offering safe anchorage, greatly restricted the activities of the galleys based in Gibraltar and Sanlúcar de Barrameda. The all-powerful barons and princes of the Kingdom of Naples, with their numerous privileges or liberties, cast a shadow over the squadron of *'il Regno'*.

If the oared squadrons were to some degree shaped by the laws, customs and geography of the territories and seas in which they were based, then the fundamental feature in determining their quality or 'order' was the logic of piracy or *el corso*. The strength, or weakness, of a group of galleys was shaped by the Darwinian logic of hunter and hunted, of capture and captive. The calibre of any group of warships – specifically, this was true of the flotillas of the Catholic Monarchy – was a direct result of their exposure to the opportunities and dangers that lay in the regular pursuit of enemy privateers. The most trusted commander of the Habsburgs of Spain, the Genoese-Neapolitan Gian Andrea Doria, Prince of Melfi, was remarkably consistent in his assessment of the best means of employment for the royal galleys, which was to run them in defence of their own seas and in the areas where Islamic corsairs were known to operate. This choice was designed to improve the running order of the ships by adding slaves to their crews and by exercising the existing oarsmen or *chusma*, while avoiding the many dangers that lay in campaigns in foreign seas. Doria's views on this matter dovetailed perfectly with those of Philip II himself.

The Habsburgs formulated their policy according to the dictates of prudence; in practical terms this meant that they accepted that their fleet would always be numerically inferior to that of the Ottomans; indeed, it was considerably smaller than even the (nominal) size of the armada of the Republic of Venice in years such as 1538 and 1571. The trade-off was in seamanship: the reinforced galleys of Charles V, Philip II and Philip III were clearly and decisively superior to those of the Ottomans and the Most Serene Republic of St Mark.

What this meant in the simplest terms was that Charles V, Philip II and Philip III were convinced that it was better to have 50 or 60 good galleys rather than 100, 150 or even 200 bad ones. Whether they chose this strategy or had it imposed upon them is a difficult question: certainly, they were very much aware of the (relative) scarcity of oarsmen and troops; they also recognised the cost of hangers, hulls, sails, oars, provisions, guns and all the other things necessary for war at sea; they were constantly reminded by their high command that there were relatively few safe harbours in the western half of the *mare Mediterraneum* and that the demands made of their squadrons were particularly onerous; somewhere within their overall outlook lay the assumption that the Mediterranean was a domain of relative 'sterility' or poverty and that military resources must be correspondingly small and limited, if mobile and expert or 'exercised'.[22] Certainly the Habsburg preference for high-grade seamanship was extremely closely tied to the overall function of the galleys, which was to serve as the bridge between Italy and Spain. In this capacity the squadrons had to make long voyages in testing conditions. While one of the recurring complaints made by admirals was that the fleet should be used only in summer, it was the very centrality of the royal armada as the link between Barcelona, Cartagena, Seville, Messina, Genoa and Naples that forced the monarchy to call upon it: in February 1596 Philip II addressed a letter, apologetic in tone, to Doria. It followed the loss of a number of galleys in a storm. 'The shipwreck,' wrote the King, 'has been great, although of those ships that were separated two have re-appeared.' The real point of this communication was to explain why he had failed to heed the advice sent to him by the admiral on so many occasions over so many years. 'But I well remember the times that you have warned me of the need to avoid winter sailing, and I desire to do this and would do so were it not for the unavoidable events that prevent me from doing so, and in fact compel me towards the opposite course of action.'[23]

The characteristics of the Christian squadrons were taken to be a reflection of a variety of factors: regional customs; geographical features; the employment of the flotilla in cleansing the seas and thus securing captive oarsmen. Financial investment was also significant, as some states, most notably the Hospitaller Order in Malta, the Grand Duchy of Tuscany and (in the 1580s) the Papacy, were able to invest heavily in their flotillas and so secured and maintained ships that were considerably more seaworthy than those of Philip II and Philip III. The seven Hospitaller galleys were 'marvellously armed', in the words of Medinaceli in the summer of 1562.[24] The recent work of Michel Fontenay and Luca Lo Basso helps to explain why this was so: these warships were manned almost entirely by slaves and convicts, groups which tended to make excellent oarsmen.[25] The squadrons based in Genoa, Leghorn and Nice paid for part of their upkeep by travelling to Messina to collect the annual shipments of silks in late summer. The degree of variation within Italy was, therefore, considerable. Yet Christian contemporaries clearly believed that the respective fleets of cross and crescent were also reflections of the civilisations that they represented; in this regard, the armadas served as an embodiment of the rival principles of Christendom and Islam. It is true that their thinking in this matter was sometimes confused or unclear and, moreover, at many points it was infused by a certain form of chauvinism. Part of the value of this dismissive, jingoistic strain of thought lies in what it tells us about the temper of the Christian crusaders who espoused it; its principal significance, however, lays in the misgivings that the Habsburgs and figures such as Toledo and Doria expressed about such dismissive views of the enemy.

The Christian view of the *armada del Turco* consisted of two distinct but overlapping strands of thought. The first dealt purely with galleys: while the Ottomans equipped vast fleets which were propelled forward by huge numbers of weak or novice oarsmen, Christians had a fleet depending upon forced labour, in which slaves, criminal oarsmen and professional rowers were proportionately much more significant. The Ottomans consequently had a large but weak fleet equipped by novices; the Christians had a smaller but expert armada propelled forward by experienced oarsmen, 'a forced fleet' (*'una armada forzada'*), as it was sometimes referred to.[26]

It is much easier to pinpoint how the two fleets differed so dramatically than to explain why this was so. The dry correspondence of admirals and officials rested on a number of assumptions: that the Christian states were more willing to condemn their own believers to serve *en galera*; that they were much less willing to accept the convert; that they were much more successful in recruiting and retaining oarsmen on a professional basis as paid rowers. It was said that the peasants recruited to row on the Sultan's fleet hated 'the galley as much as death', and refused to re-enlist: 'And this is why the Turks always have new oarsmen who, being unused to the sea, are of almost no service and then the majority of them die.'[27] Islamic holy law stipulated that no member of the brotherhood of believers or *Ummah* could be forced to row on the oar banks unless he had been convicted of a serious crime. Many adult Christian captives in Algiers or Tunis clearly converted to Islam in order to avoid the horrors of being forced to serve as a manacled *esclavo*.[28] It is noticeable that 'there was no legislation determining what offences were punishable by condemnation to the galleys', and that many criminal oarsmen gained release after a period of no more than six months.[29] Islamic holy law and the peculiarities of the Ottoman system of jurisprudence may have made it particularly difficult to condemn oarsmen and to retain them on the galleys. Given conditions on the warships, it seems highly likely that anyone convicted of a crime who was able to pay an indemnity would have chosen to do so; given the fact that their income in part depended upon the collection of 'blood money' and similar penalties and fines, it seems probable that many regional officials would have been happy to see cases settled in this way.[30]

One of the recurring difficulties in interpreting the warfare of the sixteenth and early seventeenth centuries lies in the stubborn prevalence of the two models: why, in other words, did the Ottoman Empire fail to make the reforms that would have improved the calibre or *orden* of its armada? The pattern certainly had a long history.[31] At points individual Kapudan Pashas did focus their resources into a core of expert galleys. Towards the end of July 1537 Barbarossa selected 80 galleys in good order to seek out the evasive Christian armada captained by Andrea Doria.[32] In 1543 Süleyman instructed Barbarossa to preserve the fleet at all cost, an order that conveys an understanding of both the cost of the fleet and the sense that it would be improved gradually over a number of summers.[33] Throughout the 1550s the fleet was very active in consecutive years, and may have been relatively well maintained. In 1572, perhaps the most decisive year, Uluç Ali came to use a band of highly reinforced ships. In the final operations in September and early October he may have been sailing with no more than 32 galleys.[34] Yet these instances remained the exception to the rule; in other campaigns emphasis fell on the need to provide the spectacle of an enormous fleet, rather than an effective one. The intention was – or at least appeared to be – to arm more galleys than the combined fleets of the Christian powers. Prestige, rather than prudence, appeared to be the governing principle of the *armada del Turco*.

Warfare in the inland sea was fought by two armadas of very different sizes and calibres; as a result, it operated according to a certain timetable of opportunity, as for most of the campaigning season the Ottoman fleet was so large that the Christian admirals simply could not contemplate facing it. The unfolding of events therefore followed a certain formula or pattern. Major campaigns were shaped by the calendar of the winds, knowledge of which played a major role in the formulation of strategy – to be more precise, it provided yet another reason why the fighting was trapped in a sort of strategic stasis, with success tantalisingly beyond the reach of both sides. But beyond these narrowly naval parameters, many western writers and statesmen believed that the political and military systems of the Ottomans and the Habsburgs were almost exact opposites. Islam was remarkable for its unified political leadership; Christendom, in complete contrast, was characterised by its extreme divisions. There were, reflected Pope Pius IV in the autumn of 1565, 100 princes in Christendom and should they unite in crusade then they would certainly defeat the Turk, who was but one.[35] Ottoman commanders before major battles were reported to have encouraged their men by dismissing the enemy as being divided by fierce hatreds ('which we know is their ancient custom'); the Christians were always, they suggested, likely to turn and flee, 'as they did at Djerba [in May 1560], each captain trying to save his own ship'.[36] This was a conventional assessment: Toledo, in fact, voiced similar concerns just before Lepanto.[37] In central and western Europe warriors were invested with fiefs when they swore homage to serve their suzerain lord on the field of battle: it has often been held that the sixteenth century witnessed the abandonment of this principle as a political system, but it could be argued that in fact the *Cinquecento* saw a startling reinvention of it.

In setting out their claim to universal sovereignty, the Ottomans located themselves within an old tradition of Islam. In an inscription dating from 1538 on the citadel of Bender, Süleyman the Magnificent gave expression to the nature of his authority:

> I am God's slave and sultan of this world. By the grace of God I am head of Mohammed's community. God's might and Mohammed's miracles are my companions. I am Süleyman, in whose name the *hutbe* is read in Mecca and Medina. In Baghdad I am the shah, in Byzantine realms the Caesar, and in Egypt the sultan; who sends fleets to the seas of Europe, the Maghreb, and India. I am the sultan who took the crown and throne of Hungary and granted them to a humble slave. The *voivoda* Petru raised his head in revolt, but my horse's hoofs ground him into the dust, and I conquered the land of Moldavia.[38]

Islam was a community in which it was the universal obligation of all believers to defend the values of peace, serenity and brotherhood and, moreover, to do so at the behest of the Caliph, 'the Deputy of God' or 'successor to the Prophet of God'. In claiming to be the Caliph or leader of the brotherhood of Muslims, the Ottoman sultans positioned themselves and their dynasty as the custodian of the political and legal traditions that had been passed down by Allah to Mohammed and had been established by the Four Rightly Guided Caliphs after the death of the Prophet in 632 (Christian calendar).[39] Crucial elements of this legacy were the defence of the Holy Cities (Mecca and Medina) and the pilgrimage route to them.[40] The Sultans frequently employed the title 'Servant of the Two Holy Places', *Khādim al-Haramayn*.[41] As leader of the Muslim brotherhood, the Caliph was obliged to uphold Islamic legal traditions. Süleyman was given two epithets: he was 'the Magnificent' to his Christian contemporaries and 'the Lawgiver' to his Muslim subjects and chroniclers. In broader terms the Caliph was charged with the protection of the *Dar al-Islam*, the 'Domains of Islam', from which no territory could be alienated or lost. In his instructions to Barbarossa Süleyman referred to 'my protected lands', a phrase which indicated the nature of his sovereignty.[42] The Ottoman Turks also employed the term *Padishaw-i Islam*, 'Emperor of Islam'.[43] As such, the sultan was the guardian or protector of all Muslims.

Recently historians have come to appreciate the importance of the institution or ideal of the caliphate in shaping Ottoman grand strategy. In an excellent revisionist study, Giancarlo Casale has shown that the Ottoman Empire was highly successful in penetrating the Indian Ocean under Selim II (1512–20) and Süleyman. Its motivation was to assert its claim to the caliphate, a consideration which had enormous political and economic importance to the sultanate and led it to organise the defence of the pilgrimage routes, to try to put an end to Portuguese depredations at sea and to pay for the Sultan's name to be read out during Friday prayers in mosques across the subcontinent.[44]

Did the Christians understand this legacy? Did they comprehend the implications or consequences of these Islamic precepts for the fighting? Often the correspondence is ambiguous. In 1553 Juan de Vega put forth the idea that the Catholic Armada should venture to inflict 'some notable damage' as 'his [the Sultan's] authority is the principal means by which he maintains his estates'.[45] Other statesmen spoke of the Turk's power being dependent on fear and tyranny and that it was important or necessary to embarrass the Grand Signor, to show him to be a paper tiger.[46] A more balanced and educated assessment was sometimes filtered through the intelligence reports. In March 1565 reports from Constantinople detailed the appeals made by the Hafsid 'King of Tunis' via the Chief Mufti, the most senior religious scholar (the *sheykhulislam* or *mufti el-enam*). The call was made to Süleyman as 'the first emperor of the world' ('*che essendo il gran signore il primo imperator del mondo*'), before referring to his duty to protect Muslims and to liberate 'Barbary' from the Christian garrisons in La Goleta and Oran. While Corsica was another option for attack, Malta remained the most likely target, as the Turk received complaints every day about the Hospitallers.[47] The terms were Christian in connotation, but the logic or rationale was Islamic in origin.

The clearest evidence of an understanding in western circles of the Ottoman claim to sovereignty in the Muslim world can be found in an official description of the imperial Ottoman standard captured from Ali Pasha's flagship at Lepanto. The flag of the sultan was, the scholar Luis del Mármol explained, that of the Caliphs, 'Popes of the Muslim Arab

Empire', 'la bandera de los Halifes Pontífices del imperio arabé mahometano'. The standard included no heraldry or coats of arms; instead it consisted entirely of 'the letters of their faith'; it was emblazoned with the names of the first leaders of Islam (the Four Rightly Guided Caliphs), passages from the Qur'an and the name Allah, which was inscribed 28,900 times. 'And this flag is created in imitation of the first flag that Mohammed raised against the Christians ... and this flag proclaims the Grand Signor as Lord and Caliph in spiritual matters, as well as being supreme over all Islamic princes, as he claims to be'. When 'the Turk' sent this emblem, accompanied by certain tokens or objects (a scimitar and copies of the Qur'an) it served as a demand that the recipient acknowledge him as the leader of the Muslim community. In the recent past, Mármol explained, these symbols had been sent to the 'Sharif of Morocco' and 'the King of Persia', 'el Rey de Persia', both of whom had refused to recognise Ottoman claims to supremacy. The paper then touched upon the division between Sunni and Shi'a branches of Islam, before adding that since the conquest of Constantinople no sultanic standard had ever been lost.[48]

Scholars disagree as to whether the Ottoman state was based upon the need for continual conquest. One interpretation is that 'Süleyman was unable to go beyond the (imperial) political framework of medieval Islam' and headed a regime built upon a fusion of the conquest ethos derived from the Nomadic Turkic origins of the dynasty and Islamic universalism. In this line of argument, 'a totalitarian system of requirements and compulsions underlay the expansive ideologies'; the janissaries carried the state forward, driven by the need to conquer for conquest's sake.[49] The alternative explanation is that the Ottoman elite was engaged in trade and that the Ottoman state consciously developed its navy; it was a merchant state that inherited 'Euro-Asian commercial patterns and cannot [therefore] be assessed as a separate and isolationist block set apart by Islamic philosophy or slave state military ethos'.[50]

However the basic character of the Ottoman state is viewed, it is clear that the Empire boasted a military and administrative elite, the kapikulus, whose martial qualities have recently been compared favourably with those of their Christian adversaries. The janissaries served as salaried troops and the *sepahis* operated as a fief-holding cavalry regiment; both groups were formidably disciplined and effective on the field of battle.[51] Modern scholars would, therefore, query the assertion, made with great insistence in May 1565 by Jean Parisot de la Valette, Grand Master of the Order of Knights of the Hospital of St John of Jerusalem at Malta, that the enemy troops were 'mostly a rabble and wholly inexperienced soldiery' and unprepared for the trials of warfare.[52] The Grand Master's dismissive assessment of the Ottoman expeditionary force was not made without some documentary basis, but it was in part motivated by the predicament in which he found himself at this juncture; it was also, undoubtedly, an expression of that sense of social exclusivity upon which the Hospitaller Order depended.

The use of the terms 'Islam' and 'Christendom', the *Dar al-Islam* and the *Dar al-Harb*, is both tempting and dangerous, useful and misleading: on the one hand, the Ottomans emphatically identified themselves with the legacy of the caliphate and associated titles such as the 'Defender of the Holy Places', the *Padishaw-i Islam* and the 'Shadow of God on Earth'; on the other hand, the claim to be the Caliph depended upon important innovations (their Turkic origins were frequently taken to disqualify them from this role) and the empire clearly sanctioned activities which, in strict terms, failed to conform to Islamic precepts.[53] The *devishirme*, or levy of boys from Christian communities within the Empire, was 'of dubious propriety in Muslim law'; the activities of the corsairs were even more questionable, in that there could be little doubt that the privateers of Algiers and Tunis operated by the forceful conversion of captive Christian youngsters and so broke one of the pivotal injunctions of the Prophet, that there should be no compulsion in religion.[54]

The use of the term 'Christendom' was no less ambiguous or, at times, controversial. In the first place Philip II and Philip III certainly distinguished between those actions that were undertaken in defence of Christendom and 'in the service of God' and those that were done 'for my particular service'. Even when they claimed to be performing the 'cause of God', their assertions were viewed with considerable scepticism by their Christian confederates; certainly during the Holy Leagues of 1538–40 and 1571–73 there were many in Venice or Rome who saw Habsburg claims to be serving and protecting Christendom as little more than self-serving rhetoric. For their part Philip II, Doria and Toledo believed that their 'confederates' in Venice, Rome or Malta were drastically underestimating the forces of the Turk while simultaneously overplaying the qualities and potential of their own forces.

If these disputes served to underline that the ancient custom of the Christians was indeed to fall into bitter acrimony and division, then in certain respects the Habsburgs and Ottomans were very similar. As Professor Faroqhi has pointed out, both the sultans and their Christian rivals strove to associate their respective dynasties with glorious wars undertaken in defence of the faith.[55] At this point a crucial caveat must be added: that, in both Muslim and Christian eyes, the claim of the Ottoman sultans to be the Caliph did not necessarily commit them to an expansionist policy based on the concept of the lesser *jihad*. On the contrary the pacific or conciliatory nature of Ottoman aims was evident from the very beginning of the confrontation between the Habsburg and Ottoman empires. In 1533 Süleyman protested his desire to secure peace and to bestow it 'for eternity' upon those Christian princes who kept their word; yet simultaneously he and his envoys insisted that Hungary must be surrendered in its entirety; that he could not return Algiers to the King of Spain even if he wanted to do so; and that the fortress at Koron must be evacuated by Charles V's forces.[56] He placed particular emphasis upon the cessation of the privateering expeditions which had been launched by the garrison from the Greek town. A number of lightly armed vessels or *fustas* had been active throughout the Archipelago: Habsburg diplomats warned that these expeditions carried the danger of setting the whole world on fire in a greater war than had ever before been seen.[57] While such claims were obviously exaggerated, Charles V subsequently informed his diplomats that the abandonment of the fort had been inevitable; 'if there had been no other cause for it, it was owing to the fact that many men and even princes said it would be a useless irritation of the Turk'.[58] The emperor subsequently displayed little interest in seizing territory in Greece or the Levant: during the Holy League of 1538 he was willing to allow any territory conquered in the Levant other than Constantinople to be conferred upon Venice.[59]

From the 1530s western diplomats were therefore conscious of the duties of 'el Turco', and that these responsibilities precluded the possibility of alienating territories from his domains. Yet if these negotiations underlined the extent to which peace would have to be conferred on terms dictated by the Turk, they did at least suggest that some sort of peace or understanding was attainable. 'If anyone,' Süleyman wrote to the Archduke Ferdinand (Charles V's brother and successor as Holy Roman Emperor), 'seeks peace of us with honesty and good faith, it is proper that we should not refuse him. We ourselves seek peace from everyone with honesty and good faith.'[60] Orations made by diplomatic representatives of the Sultan to the Republic of Venice opened by referring to his status as the 'Emperor of the Muslims', 'Imperator di Messuramani', before going on to state that he would always seek and treasure peace and value those friends who maintained it with him.[61] Good faith and integrity were qualities which the Habsburgs could recognise. In his Testament of January 1548 Charles V stressed to his son the absolute importance of being a man of his word. This was especially important when dealing with the Ottomans, 'as without faith and word there is neither perfection nor credit a second time'. By breaking his word his son could only present the King of France with a chance to cause trouble in Germany and Italy and 'to disturb the service of God'.[62] It is worth noting that the emperor apparently assumed Sultan Süleyman to be inherently more trustworthy than was His Most Christian Majesty; it is also noticeable that he seems to have believed that the Ottoman Empire was not inherently expansionist in nature and that the 'service of God' did not, in 1548 at least, commit the Catholic Monarchy to campaigns of conquest in the Mediterranean. The precise opposite, or something akin to it, was the case: lasting peace could be secured between two men of honour, princes who valued their word.

'It is perhaps worth underlying,' writes Braudel, 'the pragmatism and lack of preconceived notions in Spanish policy on at least four occasions (1558–59, 1563–64; 1567; 1575–81) and no doubt at other times unknown to us: a policy very different from that traditionally allotted to her by history.'[63] This pragmatism originated in the understanding of 'el Turco', the idea that the Sultan's priority might lie in securing peace and administering justice within his domains, rather than in acquiring new ones. This view was often insisted upon by the Ottoman sultans themselves, as in 1551, before the expedition to Tripoli. Here Süleyman and his ministers repeatedly asserted that they wanted peace with Charles V, whose seizure of Mahdia had contravened the accord of 1547.[64] A Hospitaller knight presented the following description of Sultan Murad III to Don John of Austria in 1575:

> [The Sultan] spends a lot of time in the study of his Laws ... This Lord seems a moderate and stable man, more given to reasoning than to feelings, and he proceeds to acquire more renown with the observance of justice and the laws, and through the good governing of his States, than by arms; therefore, unless I am mistaken, this Lord will not go to war unless he is either provoked by other princes, or induced by authority, counsel, and insistence of those who are very near to His Majesty.[65]

This passage can be read as a specific portrayal of the Sultan's individual characteristics; equally, it can be seen as a reflection of the duties of the 'Emperor of the Muslims' with regard to the Domains of Peace. But another crucial consideration underpinning all assessments was that of practicality: was it really possible for the Turk to undertake the invasion of Italy? As we shall see, a recurring thread in the western assessment of the enemy was the idea that the Ottomans were provoked or 'irritated' into war by the actions of the Christian corsairs; this line of interpretation dovetailed with a more pragmatic assessment which held that the conquest of a territory in Italy was simply beyond the Ottoman fleet, and that actions in years such as 1534 or 1558 were really motivated by a desire to assist the pernicious ambitions of His Most Christian Majesty of France in the peninsula. The documentation was therefore permeated by the perception that neither side could win this war: in the first place the vast dimensions of the Ottoman armada restricted the offensive opportunities open to the Spanish Habsburgs and their confederates; on the other hand, it was believed that if the Turk might be inspired or lured into attacking Christendom, his forces would always be restricted by the tactical superiority of the 'Catholic Armada', the redoubtable coastal fortifications of Italy and the protocol of prudence that guided the forces of His Catholic Majesty. Writing to the viceroy of Sicily in 1553 the future Philip II expressed his astonishment that the Turk, now engaged in a war with 'the Sophi' (the Safavid Persian), should have sent his fleet on an expedition to assist the French positions in the western Mediterranean (the support for Pedro Corso's rebellion in Corsica).[66] Writing from England in January 1555, the Prince hoped that reports of Süleyman's reverses in the war against the Persian might prove to be accurate: 'the more that things deteriorate for the Turk, the more he will have to leave us in peace, and the less comfort will His Most Christian Majesty take from the sultan's fleet.'[67] Philip II would be more specific in detail – and much more cautious in tone – in the strict instructions he issued to his admirals over the coming decades; it is also true that the fighting after 1560 adopted a very different rhythm and character. But this unguarded or offhand comment is valuable because it conveyed the sense that Mediterranean holy war offered meagre rewards to both of the major protagonists, each of whom fought on terms set down by others.

The contradictions or tensions inherent in the Mediterranean policy of the Habsburgs of Spain were therefore profound. While evoking the grand legacy of European kingship, a warrior tradition of the defence of the faith that was traced back to Charlemagne and Constantine, Charles V, Philip II and Philip III were intensely conscious of the value of wretched men toiling at the oar in the most degrading of conditions. If lost, the 'forced galleys' would require many years to replace. It was axiomatic that it was difficult, if not impossible, to establish functioning galleys without a core of experienced oarsmen and a major defeat at sea would mean that there would be very few veteran rowers to train or carry the new recruits during their lengthy period of adaptation. In this sense the principal adversary of the *monarquía* was taken to be the sea itself, whose exactions and sudden dangers stood as a perpetual threat to the 'bridge' between Spain and Italy. Their first priority being the need to move resources and men over the seas, the plans of the Habsburgs of Spain began with an assessment of galleys and their rowing crews. While nominally committed to regain the Holy Lands denoted by their title of 'King of Jerusalem', they were very much aware of the dangers in sailing the southern coast of Sicily or the Gulf of Lepanto. Standing at the apex of a culture in which religious war was extolled as a sort of abandonment of personal autonomy to common destiny and providential design, the Habsburg Kings of Spain remained determined to control the fate of their fleet, issuing instructions that prescribed, point by point, what their commanders could, and could not, do or attempt to do. While committed to the *'guerre sainte'* in the Mediterranean, they nonetheless recognised that their royal armada was considerably smaller, if tactically superior, to the enemy; that there were very few harbour positions which offered anything like decisive leverage to either side; that the proposals and outlooks of their Christian allies were invariably ambiguous or ambivalent, being at best a hopelessly optimistic assessment of what might be achieved in the arid environment of the Mediterranean summer. Finally, the outlook of Charles V, Philip II and Philip III encompassed the idea that the conquest of Italy might well be beyond the capabilities of the enemy fleet and that the Ottoman Turk might have been provoked into war by the actions of the Christian corsairs or lured into it by the hollow promises of His Most Christian Majesty. But then, in the final instance, there was the problem of Spain, where large communities of Muslims or pseudo-Muslims lived in Valencia, Aragon and, until 1570, Granada. The Habsburgs of Spain, who had pledged themselves to defend the cause of Catholic Christendom, were perhaps uniquely well placed to understand how Ottoman pretensions to leadership of the Muslim community might drive the sultans to try to rescue the 'New Christians' of *Al-Andalus*. Yet the problem of the Moriscos led back, inexorably, to Italy: it served to underline the perception that in military terms the *monarquía* of Spain could not operate effectively without its Italian fiefs. Charles V, Philip II and Philip III may have presided over an empire of unprecedented global reach, but their military capability in southern Europe depended upon small but mobile squadrons of galleys and experienced troops who might be just a few thousand in number and who were garrisoned at a distance of hundreds of miles across the seas. The kings could never overlook or forget the value of their subalpine fiefs, or what they had committed themselves to do in order to secure them.

The problem in trying to identify Habsburg interests, outlook and strategy in the Mediterranean is, therefore, an acute one in that rhetoric and reality were so diametrically opposed. The essential tensions within Habsburg policy can be best demonstrated by an examination of the event that has sometimes been regarded as the greatest confrontation between the forces of Christendom and Islam, the Battle of Lepanto (7 October 1571). The engagement saw the destruction of the vast majority of the Ottoman fleet of 240 or so sail; only 30 galiots or light galleys escaped, and these were commanded by Uluç Ali, an Algerian corsair who, as we have seen, was appointed Kapudan Pasha or high-admiral in 1572.

The Christian triumph was heralded as a singular historical success, a turning-point in history and an affirmation of Catholic faith.[68] Those who had been present at it simply referred to it as 'The Naval Battle', *la batalla naval*. Later generations came to regard it as a pivotal moment. 'The battle of Lepanto,' concluded Sir Francis Bacon in the early seventeenth century, 'arrested the greatness of the Turk.'[69] When informed of the event Pius V expressed his gratitude to God and declared that He had not given such a victory to Christendom for a thousand years.[70] Shortly after Lepanto a son and heir, Fernando (1571–78), was born to the King of Spain. In a celebrated painting, *The Offering of Philip II* (Museo del Prado, Madrid, 1573–75), Titian commemorated and linked the two events by portraying the King raising his heir to a providential – indeed celestial – light while a Turk, having lost his turban, sits chained on the floor.

Lepanto takes its place within an extraordinary period of European history, one which would shape events across the face of the world. It has been argued that from the late 1560s Philip II's grand strategy became dominated by a 'messianic imperialism'. From this juncture he apparently issued orders for campaigns that were based upon the conviction that the Almighty would intervene to assist Spanish forces. Tactical considerations were overridden, it has been argued, by the need to perform 'the service of God', the propagation of the Catholic faith through wars against heretics and infidels. In November 1569 the King instructed his Governor of the Low Countries, the Duke of Alba, to undertake an operation against England without the forces necessary for such an intervention.[71] Professor Geoffrey Parker has recently argued that '*la batalla naval*' confirmed the messianic tendencies of Philip II, who henceforth embarked on campaigns in the certain knowledge that he was God's agent on earth, carrying forward His Providential Design.[72] Certainly the King recognised that the crusade against the Ottoman infidel was the very cause of God. On the other hand, he repeatedly argued that any enterprise undertaken against the Turk should be limited in scope and ambition and designed specifically to obviate all possible risks to his own forces.

Long before the engagement of 7 October, the Prudent King had expressed his reservations about any significant success being achieved that year. In mid-February 1571 he stated that it was already too late in the calendar to think about gathering the forces necessary for a large-scale incursion into Ottoman territories, '*una empresa general en tierras de enemigos*': the preparations for an undertaking of this kind simply could not be made in time and, besides, he added that the Republic of Venice sought to engineer such a campaign in order to improve her hand in the ongoing negotiations with the Sultan. Only a localised campaign, one which might perhaps serve to divert the focus of the Ottoman attack from Cyprus, could be undertaken. Nothing more could be attempted: 'this argument is,' Philip II concluded, 'so certain and so simple that it cannot be denied or even cast into doubt.'[73]

The most serious problem for the Habsburg King lay in his relationship with his Christian 'confederates'. If their long-term strategic position caused concern, then their short-term tactical decisions provoked alarm. The key to Philip II's entire strategy in the Mediterranean lay in the idea that the value of military forces did not depend upon the number of galleys or troops but rather in their effectiveness and substance: '*las fuerzas no consisten en el número de galeras sino en el efecto y substancia*'. His confederates did not begin from this premise. Their grandiose plans hatched to arm 250 galleys were an expression of vanity, an emphasis upon the 'number and name' of forces rather than their efficacy.[74] The King's firm assumption was that the fleet of the Republic of Venice, while of a spectacular size, would be severely deficient in nearly all regards. One of his first priorities in negotiations

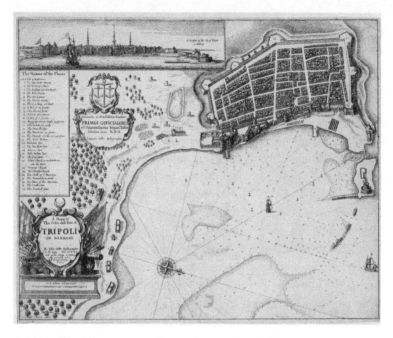

Fig. 4 'A map of the citie and port of Tripoli in Barbary'. Print (book-illustration by Wenceslaus Hollar, published by John Seller, 1675). Note that even in this rather optimistic view of the fortifications of Tripoli the harbour appeared to offer relatively little protected anchorage.

with Rome and Venice was to stipulate that his squadrons should not be required to make the journey to Cyprus unaccompanied and that under no circumstances should they be required to winter there. His armada could help the Republic with campaigns in the 'Morea' (Greece) and venture as far to the east as the Negropont: they could do no more than this.[75] Another point of contention lay in the appointment of the overall commander; this was significant not only because the King sought to engineer the appointment of his half-brother, Don John of Austria, but also because of the inevitable imbalance that would exist within the fleet: the Catholic Monarchy's galleys and captains would be more experienced, while those of the Republic of St Mark would be more numerous. Mistrust and jealousy would be endemic.[76]

In the eyes of the King and his senior ministers the crucial problem in waging war in collaboration with Venice and the Holy See was the refusal of his allies to accept the grim realities of war. As Philip II's contemporary biographer Luis Cabrera de Córdoba put it, the Venetian captains wanted to be authors of great acts but they would not submit to naval discipline.[77] The essential critique advanced by Philip II and Doria was that their confederates believed they could summon enormous fleets into being with immediate effect. To place hopes in 'new' or unexercised forces was, at best, wishful thinking; in effect, it entailed some degree of self-deception. The travails of the Venetian fleet throughout 1570 and 1571 emphatically confirmed the basic assumptions and outlook of the King and his doughty Genoese admiral. The Doge and Senate were informed by their own officials in the early summer of 1571 of the dire state of the fleet: typhus was so rife aboard the Republic's galleys that priests and chaplains absconded or fled, leaving the afflicted to die without the sacraments of confession and communion.[78] Don John of Austria was shocked when he visited the galleys of the Venetians in Messina at the very end of August, finding them 'in such poor shape in terms of men of war, oarsmen and seamen that it has given me very great cause for concern. They have artillery and arms, but without the men to fire them these will not be of much use.' Another worry – a serious one, given past events – was that there was little or no discipline or 'obedience' among their officers and captains. 'The more I learn about this, the greater my concern, as it will surely affect everything that I have to do.' Yet what caused him the deepest anxiety was that the world would look at the number of ships under his command and judge that he ought to undertake an aggressive campaign in the Levant, 'counting the galleys by their number rather than by their quality'. In his own hand he stressed his intention 'to console' his allies but lamented that their galleys were without soldiers, mariners or discipline and that their oarsmen were desperately unhealthy, 'ruines remeros'.[79]

So on 30 August 1571 – just 38 days before la batalla naval – Don John's overriding concern was that expectations far outstripped reality and that he, as overall commander, was charged with somehow both addressing these deficiencies and dealing with the emotional reaction of his allies.[80] The King, who had clearly anticipated this problem, had provided a partial solution to his half-brother: this came in Don John's right, as *capitán general* of the Holy League on both land and sea, to station professional Spanish and German infantry aboard the squadrons of Rome and the Republic of St Mark and to command their captains – on pain of death – to engage in battle.[81] These prerogatives, which *el rey prudente* had obtained in long and tortuous negotiations over the previous year and a half, meant that Don John would be able to engage the enemy in a reasonably coherent formation and with a fair chance of success. Still, the navigation from Messina towards the coast of Greece proved a trial of nerve and endurance. Eight of the Republic's galleys went down in Otranto harbour and a number of others caught fire due to bad seamanship.[82] At the end of September the King again expressed his concern about the ragged state of the Venetian warships at Candia, Crete, 'upon which the decision depends'.[83]

If the Venetian squadrons were in a ragged state, the one saving grace for the Holy League was that the Ottoman fleet was in an even worse condition. From the outset enormous difficulties had been reported by the western agents. In March a spy in Constantinople informed the Christian governments that Piyale Pasha, who boasted a distinguished record of success as a naval commander, had striven to avoid being pressed into service aboard the fleet in 1571. The captains (referred to as the '*reis*' or '*azabs*' in Turkish) and sailors 'have come out of this very unsatisfied'.[84] Reports dated 30 May 1571 stated that the Sultan would send out a total of 200 ships 'although very badly armed'.[85] Dispatches from mid-June held that Famagusta remained very strong, and that Mustafa Pasha's army was suffering greatly from illness, '*padecía mucho de enfermedad*'. The condition of Ali Pasha's fleet was no better, riddled with plague as it was.[86]

Another dispatch described the enemy in the most dire of terms: aside from two select squadrons – those of the Guard of the Archipelago and Algiers – the fleet was in bad order; every ship had a notable lack of oarsmen, '*per ogni galera mancha zurma assai*'; the men that were aboard the fleet were of the lowest calibre, '*gente villísima*' – in this instance, as in many others, the Christian assessment of the martial qualities of their adversaries was inextricably linked to a consideration of their social origin or status. The report went on to state that there were few fighting men and that a sizeable number of the troops were unarmed – many, in fact, did not even carry a scimitar. The artillery, moreover, had been badly cast and was consequently inadequate. The fleet's progress, marked by attempts to burn or attack villages and towns on the Venetian islands, was haphazard and faltering. At Corfu it had been resolutely rebuffed.[87] The bulk of the enemy force was, another dispatch stated, 'in the most bad order for both fighting men and rowers', '*malissimo ad ordine di gente cosa da combattere come da remo*'. Mortality rates were high. 'This year they have set upon the worst imaginable means of arming, on account of the lack of men. When they left Constantinople, they found it necessary to sail along their own coasts and along their own country, seizing the very subjects of the sultan and putting them to the oar.' Yet, despite these inherent difficulties, these dispatches affirmed that the Sultan had ordered his commanders to engage the Christian fleet should it offer battle or venture into his seas.[88] By the end of August it was known that the Ottoman armada was on the point of exhaustion and that new troops would have to be raised to man its galleys.[89]

From July onwards there was widespread confidence in Venice and Rome that the Christian armada would be 'very superior' to the enemy fleet, which had been decimated by disease and consequently 'has such a shortage of men'. His Holiness promised the young captain general that victory certainly awaited him, '*que cierto spera la vitoria*'.[90]

A very similar picture of Ali Pasha's fleet emerges from the Turkish sources. The Ottoman documents refer to these months as the 'time of confusion and disorder'. In August or September the Ottoman *timariot* cavalry (the *sepahis*) had been granted their request to leave the fleet and return to their homes; Uluç Ali, the corsair captain who was to win renown as high-admiral in the following campaign, warned against an engagement with the enemy. 'In his view the ships were worn out owing to the six-month campaign that they had been involved in.'[91] 'Many of the Janissaries in Famagusta,' reads a Christian report from mid-July, 'want to abandon the campaign, as they have been away from their homes for two years.' The '*generale*' was doing all that he could to retain them.[92] Christian *avisos* spoke of the ineffective raids launched by the Ottoman fleet in September and August; the Turkish accounts added the detail that during these amphibian skirmishes the troops simply abandoned the armada and headed for home.[93] Intelligence gathered after the battle from captives confirmed this picture. The interrogation of the tutor of the sons of Ali Pasha revealed two valuable details: first, that 60 or so ships had been allowed to carry the sick to Koron and Modon; second, that pressgangs had emptied the town of Lepanto and its adjacent countryside of all its inhabitants, 'and there only remained behind the women to lock the doors'.[94]

A cogent argument could therefore be made from both the Turkish archives and the Simancas records that by the first week of October 1571 the Sultan's armada had already been defeated; indeed, Philip II certainly believed this to be the case. Royal orders issued to his 'commissaries' or negotiators in Rome dated 13 October 1571 began from the premise that the Ottoman armada had lost a great number of men in the summer operations and consequently that in the coming year, '*el año que viene*', it would be much smaller in size. Yet it would still be necessary, he reaffirmed, to destroy what was left of it before proceeding to attempt a general expedition, '*una empresa general*'. To fail to do so was 'to throw away everything' as the enemy fleet, reduced in scale though it might be, would nevertheless be able to recapture any position in Greece or the Levant with ease, '*con facilidad*'. He also warned that a raiding expedition along the enemy coastlines would serve very little purpose and, pointedly, once again urged his confederates to equip their squadrons in good order, selecting experienced soldiers and oarsmen. As with his letter of the previous February, he insisted that his argument was backed up by the inevitable and unquestionable force of logic and empirical observation: it was therefore undeniable, 'as easily can be understood by anyone who looks into the matter', '*como facilmente queriendo mirar en ello se deja entender*'.[95]

It could be argued that the outstanding feature of *la batalla naval* was that both fleets were marked by such profound inadequacies. In August Toledo sent a valuable piece of advice to Don John: if an engagement took place in the coast of the enemy, then he should allow the Kapudan

Pasha to station his galleys near the shoreline. This tactical concession would simply allow the enemy to disintegrate: 'a great number of the soldiers and oarsmen' on the *armada del Turco* would avail themselves of this opportunity to flee to land. 'And if the battle should take place in our seas, you should do the opposite.' His meaning was that inexperienced Christians, no less than novice Muslims, would abandon the fray.[96] His prediction was unerringly accurate. One account speaks how, after the triumph in the centre, the Christian galleys moved to the right flank. 'There was', reads one of the accounts of Lepanto written just hours afterwards, 'a great group of enemy ships which had not fought', *'un gran golpe de galeras en aquella parte de los enemigos que no habían peleado'*, and 'some ships belonging to the League which were not as far forward as was necessary'.[97] 'We made so many of their ships flee to the land,' recorded Francisco de Murillo in his triumphal account, 'that it is an embarrassment to say it.'[98] In the aftermath of Lepanto one of the priorities for the Ottoman government was to identify those captains who, in the heart of the battle, had hoisted sail and fled towards the coast.[99] Prior to the engagement Don John, who paid great attention to Toledo's advice, had clearly feared that he might be shamed by his own men: he had ordered that the smaller ships, the *fregatas*, *fustas* and brigantines, should be stationed far from the main body of the fleet, 'so that no man should have hope of saving himself but by fighting, so that they should either die or achieve victory'.[100] The corsair Uluç Ali had provided identical advice to his superiors; it was not heeded. The Turkish chronicler Peçevi (1574–1650) recorded that 'the oarsmen and warriors on the Ottoman ships evacuated their ships and fled ...'[101]

If the correspondence of Don John of Austria, Philip II and Toledo and the other commanders in the months leading up to 7 October 1571 was imbued by a profound sense of caution and even cynicism, then the immediate aftermath of the fighting saw the beginning of a process in which *'la batalla naval'* came to be celebrated as a decisive confrontation between two energetic and healthy fleets.[102] The historical background that informed the assessments made by Philip II and his councillors will be studied in detail: an understanding of the galley, its strengths and failings, will explain why they were moved by such ambivalence or pessimism about the longer cycle of events. The very details of Lepanto – specifically, the manoeuvres on the Ottoman southern flank and the engagement, more pursuit than skirmish, in which the flagships of Doria and the Marquis of Santa Cruz gave chase to the Algerian galiots led by Uluç Ali – underscored the challenge facing the Holy League in *el año que viene*.

Lepanto has always been understood in heroic terms, and as such has been interpreted in a number of ways: as a manifestation of the age-old conflict between western European civilisation and eastern Islamic powers; as a confrontation of forces representing two empires driven by blind religious bigotry; as the death-pangs of a system of warfare based upon the oared warship; as the concluding chapter of the history of the Mediterranean before its abandonment and replacement by the Atlantic as the principal motor or theatre of historical change; as the zenith of Spanish power before it entered into a process of precipitous decline; as the last of the Crusades or the first rehearsal of gunpowder weaponry in a battle at sea.[103] What is, perhaps, certain is that for neither Philip II nor his senior statesmen and advisors did Lepanto assume the features of epic confrontation and ecstatic triumph. The documents that passed over the King's modest desk clearly held that the overwhelming majority of the Venetian and Ottoman warships were diseased hulks that sailed at the mercy of the elements at the end of the 'fine season'; this was the outcome, more or less inevitable, of their respective naval systems. The judgement of the overall strategic panorama was equally rigid: Venice was waging a bad war in order to secure a good peace; there was little prospect of the Holy League achieving any meaningful objective.[104] As we shall see, the tactical details and requirements set out by the King in his letter of 13 October 1571 – the need to capture the galiots of Uluç Ali and so eviscerate Ottoman naval expertise for once and for all – can be closely tied to the basic strategic stance of the Catholic Monarchy: that the most profitable employment of the fleet was to deploy it in defensive patrols in the western Mediterranean, where it could strengthen itself by capturing the Islamic privateers of North Africa.

Voltaire was, then, guilty of a certain form of historical plagiarism: the essential point is that on 13 October, six days after *la batalla naval* and before he even knew that it had taken place, Philip II of Spain already feared that it would lead nowhere. His reasons for doing so were profoundly historical in nature; they were rooted in an understanding of recent campaigns and a familiarity with 'the laws of the sect of Mohammed', that is to say a grasp of the basic precepts of Islamic civilisation. The King's basic outlook was mathematical and mechanical rather than chivalric and heroic; with certain limitations, it might be said to have been both deeply pessimistic and thoroughly deterministic. He and his senior advisors might perhaps have been more comfortable with the statement that their thinking began with empirical observation and broadened into an appreciation of systems and structures, a logical and dispassionate assessment of history, both ancient and modern, that led to certain conclusions based upon rational projection, *como facilmente queriendo mirar en ello se deja entender*. However the event is addressed, the greatest and most evocative feature of *la batalla naval* was the question, recently addressed with great élan by David García Hernán and Enrique García Hernán, of what to do in the days after it.[105]

To the King, the event at Lepanto on 7 October 1571 had to be understood in reference to his vast responsibilities as guardian and protector of Catholic Christendom; in itself it did little to alleviate them. In many regards *la batalla naval* was simply another pitfall avoided. And over the previous 18 months the burden and scope of his obligations had dramatically widened.

III

Chusma

'If there is a hell in this world,' ran a sixteenth-century saying, 'it is in the galleys where rest is unknown.'[1] In 1579 the painter El Greco came to represent Hell in his *Dream of Philip II* (Museo del Prado, Madrid); this canvas depicted an allegory of the Holy League that had fought the Battle of Lepanto: he had the wretched toiling in linear banks which looked very much like the benches of an oared warship. The galley represented an incongruity: it placed wretchedness and splendour in immediate proximity; it was at once the most horrific affront to the senses and the superbly decorated representation of its prince. Visitors to the squadrons were taken aback by the assault upon both their senses and their sense of decency. John Evelyn visited Marseille in 1644 and sailed aboard a richly gilded warship. The discomfort of the oarsmen astonished him: 'Their rising forwards, and falling back at their Oare, is a miserable spectacle, and the noyse of their chaines with the roaring of the beaten Waters has something of strange and fearfull in it to one unaccustomed. They are ruled, and chastised, ... without the least humanity: Yet for all this they are Cherefull, and full of vile knavery.' Another description comes from a Frenchman who was himself condemned to the galleys:

> Picture to yourself six men chained to a bench naked as they were born, one foot on the stretcher, the other lifted and placed against the bench in front of him, supporting in their hands a vastly heavy oar ... Sometimes

the galley slaves row ten, twelve, even twenty hours at a stretch, without the slightest rest or break. On these occasions the officer will go round and put pieces of bread soaked in wine into the mouths of the wretched rowers, to prevent them from fainting. Then the captain will call upon the officers to redouble their blows, and if one of the slaves falls exhausted over his oar (which is not uncommon) he is flogged until he appears to be dead and is thrown overboard without ceremony.[2]

Historians tend to view contemporary descriptions of this sort with a touch of scepticism, aware that they were sometimes exaggerated in order to lend colour to a narrative. Yet it is difficult to imagine that conditions *en galera* could have been much better than these passages suggested.

The humanist culture of the *Cinquecento* could hardly ignore the pivotal role of skill and experience in war at sea. Conclusions to this effect were ingrained into the very fabric of history. In a famous passage, Thucydides (born 460–454 BC; died after 399 BC), the 'Father of History', has the Spartan king Archidamus admit to his countrymen that they were inferior to the Athenians at sea, and that it would take some time for them to train and acquire maritime skills. On the other side Pericles galvanised the Athenians by reminding them how difficult it had been to acquire their naval skills. 'Seamanship is an art like any other; it is not something which can be picked up in one's spare time, indeed, it leaves no leisure for anything else.'[3] The Athenians were a seafaring people with extensive overseas possessions and numerous naval offices. 'The majority are able to pull an oar when first they set foot aboard a warship, having had the preliminary training man and boy up to that moment.'[4]

The historians of antiquity – Thucydides, the Greek Polybius (*c*.201–*c*.120 BC) and even Caesar himself – therefore stressed the value of maritime skills and elevated oarsmen to a privileged position.[5] The formula had a particular relevance to sixteenth-century naval warfare, as races of men who could row were certainly very important to the greatness of the states in the Mediterranean. Throughout the late Middle Ages there had often been a scarcity of skilled seafarers in the

Mediterranean; Venice had experienced considerable difficulty in finding rowers. Consequently, the *Signoria* made full use of criminal oarsmen, establishing a form of 'debt slavery for many of the poorer members of the crew'.[6] For the Habsburgs and their Genoese admirals the consideration of manpower was always the crucial one. When Andrea Doria took ten Ottoman supply ships (*esquirazos*) and two galleys in July 1537 he had the Muslim slaves transferred to his warships and then burnt all of the hulls but for one galiot. His priority was to avoid the disarming of the galleys, '*por no desarmar las galeras de gente*'. He simply could not afford to weaken the crews of his ships by manning these vessels.[7]

Braudel suggested that sixteenth-century society treated oarsmen, and even slaves, with a degree of compassion.[8] Certainly, governments of this period sought to ensure that the rowing crews were cared for humanely. In his exhaustive instructions of 1568 to Don John of Austria, Philip II himself issued orders that the *chusma* were to be treated well.[9] 'The galley without *chusma*,' ran a popular Venetian refrain, 'would be like a body without life.'[10]

Gian Andrea Doria held it to be a fact of almost sacred importance that oarsmen were much more valuable and more difficult to replace than soldiers. An army, he observed, could be recruited at relatively short notice; in contrast the galley fleet had to be groomed and maintained over a period of years.[11] The argument set forth in the following pages will be based upon the outlook and interpretation of Doria. The Genoese admiral's argument was a very simple one, which extolled the skills, experience, fortitude and resilience of the oarsman as the key feature of any successful and sustainable fleet. The only way for the oarsman to gain the necessary qualities was through exposure to the many dangers inherent in his profession. In practice this meant an initial period of debilitating illness from which very many would not recover. The oared warship was, by its very nature, a Darwinian creature. Those squadrons that thrived did so at the direct expense of weaker competitors; those oarsmen who survived did so as many of their colleagues died and were thrown to their watery grave. To serve '*en galera*' was to face a daunting challenge of endurance and survival. The skills, robustness and value of the rower increased in proportion to his service on the oar banks.

Oarsmen varied greatly in their levels of ability, stamina, strength, health and resistance to disease: the best galleys were, logically, those that had the largest proportion of well-trained, experienced *remeros*. Since Professor Guilmartin was undoubtedly correct in arguing that the galley was defined by its propulsive system – Doria would certainly have agreed that the oars were the 'feet of a ship' – it follows that a reassessment of the 'training' and qualities of the oarsmen used by the powers of the Mediterranean will bring about a more complete understanding of the respective merits and characteristics of the various flotillas of the sea and, with it, a view of the benefits and limitations of the system as a whole.

The argument set out in the following pages will therefore be based upon the writings of Doria, whose basic premise was that the output of a trained oarsman, inured to the biological trials of the prison warship, was greatly superior to that of a new recruit. The Prince of Melfi systematically applied this thesis to all considerations of strategy and tactical deployment. It is true that he never addressed the mechanical and mathematical issues set out by Guilmartin and scholars such as W.L. Rodgers and André Zysberg. Doria and his contemporaries had little to say about the physical process of rowing, the achievement of propulsive power output in relation to the angle at which the oar entered the water, the mass-weight distribution and drag of a hull, acceleration and sustainable levels of output. This omission was not simply due to oversight or to an infatuation with the writings of Thucydides and Polybius; rather it was because their outlook was focused upon the differentiation between rowing crews, between strong and weak galleys. Their assessment of warships took into account both the level of medical resilience and the skill or athletic coordination necessary for the exercise of the oar stroke: good crews were not only physically stronger and biologically tougher, but also much more efficient in their use of the oar. A crucial element of sixteenth-century thinking was the sense of drawing strength from collective endeavour: the basic criteria employed by Don García de

Toledo in 1565, for instance, held that there was a direct correlation between the size of the rowing crew and its final or absolute value and performance. It was better to have more men aboard each ship, although this preference was based on the premise that a high overall proportion of oarsmen would be trained and experienced and that the novices would be well cared-for during their summer exertions. To this end he laid up about 30 galleys, a third of the total available to him, in order to concentrate their crews in the other warships. He also responded enthusiastically to proposals for recruiting almost 3,000 *buenas voyas*.[12] The mathematics behind such calculations remain obscure; as we shall see, the best explanation for the overwhelming preference for bigger crews is that they increased the efficiency of the oar stroke, whose rhythm was the crucial element in accelerating the ship and maintaining its speed through the water.

In 1590 the Genoese contractor Leonardo Spínola, sailing in command of two galleys belonging to Gian Andrea Doria, captured the flagship or *capitana* of Bizerta on the coast of the Papal States. Doria subsequently described the vessel as 'the best and the best armed' he had ever seen. It was a galiot carrying 130 Turks, among them 100 janissaries, who had 'put up the very greatest resistance' ('*grandísima resistencia*'). Two hundred and twenty Christians were liberated from its banks. The *reis* or captain, Amisa, was 'a man of very great understanding and valour' who had escaped 'on many occasions' from the Christian *capitanas*. Only the previous summer he had evaded four Florentine and three Genoese galleys which had surrounded his ship. Doria suggested that the key to the speed under oars of the galiot was that, as a rule, it was lighter than a galley but carried an equal or larger number of oarsmen. As was often the case, this galiot did not carry artillery; the absence of heavy weaponry helps to explain why its crew sustained disproportionately heavy casualties in the skirmish. Doria's account was written to reflect glory upon the galleys that had finally put paid to the career of this feared corsair – his own. The viceroy of the Kingdom of Naples, the Count of Miranda, rather churlishly informed Philip II of the decisive detail in the skirmish: that the Christian slaves downed their oars at the decisive moment of the chase. The Turks, seeing that their situation was hopeless, turned their fury upon the oarsmen, killing ten and badly injuring 30.[13]

Doria's account may therefore have been selective, and Miranda's was certainly peevish, but both men would have concurred that the reason for the excellent performance of the galiot lay in its oarsmen. The oared fighting ship was, essentially, an amalgamation of muscle and experience, athleticism and health: its *chusma* had to be seasoned, toughened-up, carefully prepared by being exposed to the great hardships and risks of life at sea over many years. As was the case for all forms of naval warfare in the early modern period, disease carried away a far larger portion of the crews than did enemy fire.[14] In January 1565 an official expressed surprise that only 234 oarsmen had died on the galleys in the previous five months: such clemency was clearly a sign of God's good will, although he added that he and the other officers were doing all they could to allow the crews to rest and recuperate.[15] In a perceptive study Professor Thompson suggested that up to 50 per cent of *forzados* or criminals condemned to the galleys of Spain died in the course of their time on the ships; Tenenti arrived at the figure of 60 per cent mortality for Venetian criminals, although with good medical provision this figure could be much lower, with just one in ten perishing.[16] Zysberg's study of the lives of 60,000 French oarsmen in the period 1680–1748 concluded that one in two died in the course of their sentence.[17] Oarsmen with no previous exposure to life at sea were guaranteed to suffer. We can follow the history of 838 forced oarsmen serving in the squadron of Naples in the early seventeenth century. Just over 1 in 8 *forzati* (128 of a total of 838) died in the period from October 1601 to March 1602, and around a third (260 of 838) were totally inactive after these six months. By this point 260 men had been freed at the completion of their sentences.[18] The 107 slaves purchased for the galleys of Spain in 1603 fared little better. Four years later 52 were still at the oar; 55 had died or 'gone'.[19] Of course not all of those *forzados* who disappeared from the musters died; a proportion of them must have escaped or been allowed to escape. Corruption and negligence, in other words, were known to be major problems. It was common for the government to issue decrees that the officials charged with the supervision and care of *forzados* and slaves were to be financially liable for their escape.[20]

The mortality rate of 50 per cent therefore emerges from several detailed studies and registers of oarsmen. To put this figure in context, Stalin's Gulag archipelago killed 14.6 per cent of those who entered it between 1934 and 1947. This figure was inflated by the jump in death rates in the years 1941 to 1944, when the mortality rate spiked as a result of shortages of food and medical supplies caused by the war.[21]

The documents tell us relatively little about medical provision.[22] Admirals believed that badly prepared or poorly preserved food and drink would lead to illness among the crews. One of the duties given to Santa Cruz in 1571 was to oversee the proper preparation and storage of biscuit, wine and other provisions.[23] It was axiomatic that crews should be well fed and well rested in winter in order to compensate for the deprivations of summer. Meat had to be provided in December and January because biscuit would form the staple diet in June and July.[24] Commanders sometimes made mention of a hospital ship, but this arrangement appears to have been an informal one in which the desperately sick were left, with minimal medical supervision, to recover or perish.[25] On the other hand, sixteenth-century medical provision, rudimentary as it was, may have been superior to those forms found in later periods. The galleys of Louis XIV of France were constructed with cramped rooms below deck which served as hospitals. To venture into them was to crawl into grim compartments without light or fresh air. One priest who had regularly to visit the sick and provide the last rites spoke of moving into a chamber existing in 'the shadows of death', '*les ombres de la morte*'.[26]

One of the practical constraints upon the exercise of sea power in the early modern Mediterranean was that novice oarsmen were certain to fall ill and to be of little service in their first two years of activity. During this period the sick were quarantined in the hospital ships or left ashore; those who remained *en galera* were carried along largely by the efforts of others. Those who survived acquired the skills in the use of the oar and built up their strength and immunity to disease. One of the perennial obstacles to the health and effectiveness of a galley was therefore the employment of new *chusma*. A squadron propelled by recently recruited rowers was by definition a weak squadron: 'Your Majesty will never have good galleys while the *chusma* is new,' Doria warned Philip II.[27] In July 1570 the captain general of the papal squadron, Marc'Antonio Colonna, had to admit that he had encountered great difficulty in arming 'these galleys' (*'ho havuto difficoltà grande ad armar queste galere'*).[28] Doria reported in May 1573 that 'a great number' of the new oarsmen recently recruited in Genoa had already died; 500 more were sick. There would be barely enough for six vessels, never mind the nominal number of ten new warships that he had offered to fit out.[29] Fleets diminished in proportion to the amount of *gente nueva* on them. In 1564 four galleys, three of them belonging to the duke of Florence, had to be sent to Gibraltar as their crews had fallen ill. There was no other option, and the hope was that, given time to recuperate, they would later be able to serve.[30] Three or four galleys full of ill oarsmen were sent back from the 1604 Catholic Armada; most of the sick were novices and Benavente cautiously referred to the fact that 15 of the galleys of Naples were rowed by new recruits.[31] It was inherently dangerous to mix veteran and new *chusma*, especially if the latter were ill. Some galley commanders flatly refused to do so, fearing that disease would spread from the recruits to the veterans.[32]

One of the tensions within the Habsburg fleet was the need to make use of all the oarsmen; the recruits had to be trained – there was, after all, no other way of producing good *chusma*. In practice the mixing of the blood of the galleys was almost impossible to avoid.[33] At some points the commanders claimed that their diligence had allowed them to recruit and employ new oarsmen without incurring a devastating outbreak of mortality. Santa Cruz was proud to have armed 20 ships from 14 in 1570; these were, he claimed, among the best in the Christian fleet. He had achieved this by recruiting *buenas voyas* who, he added, could be hired in Spain and Naples in great number. These novices had served very well, in large part because of his efforts to ensure their health. This experiment having proved successful, he proposed to the King that he could fit out many new galleys by mixing new and experienced oarsmen.[34] A similar proposal was later rejected by Doria, who was very reluctant to remove one rower from each bank in order to arm another 20 or so ships.[35] The trade-off, in other words, was a bad one. In December 1572 the Genoese admiral pointedly observed that galleys armed entirely with new *chusma* simply could not match the efforts of 'forced galleys' and so, he added, being unable to endure the workload they usually came to fall apart, '*que por no poder durar el trabajo se suelen deshacer*'.[36]

Santa Cruz's plans in 1570 made it evident that his assessment tended to be more aggressive or assertive than Doria's. It was, however, based upon the supposition that the performance of rowing crews consisting of equal proportions of veteran and novice oarsmen would still be markedly superior to those of Venice and the Ottomans, the majority of whose ships were '*armadas de gente nueva*'. The King approved the proposal to remove a number of oarsmen from the more highly equipped warships in order to equip new ones (thus 38 ships were to be fitted out from the squadron of Naples). He did so on the grounds that the enemy would not be armed 'with more than for three-by-three' and, indeed, recent reports stated that many of Ottoman ships would be equipped below this level.[37]

By definition a new galley could not be armed without experienced oarsmen: aside from the question of health, its crew would lack physical strength as well as the technique that was of enormous importance to the maintenance of the oar stroke and the ship's balance. The importance of a core of veteran rowers was central to all stages in the life of a galley. Without a starting group of experienced oarsmen, it was difficult to properly fit out a new galley – '*sin algún principio de chusma vieja mal se puede ordenar una galera nueva*'. Any new vessel would have to be manned in part by experienced oarsmen taken from established galleys.[38] By extension a good warship was one that had been seasoned over the previous summers and rested in winter, one in which novices were introduced sparingly – for their own benefit and that of the other oarsmen. Such a vessel had to be introduced slowly and carefully; a long process of improvement – of exercise, recuperation and further recruitment – was necessary to establish it as a fully functioning warship. There were, therefore, inherent limitations that the health, fitness and technique of crews placed on the ability of governments or private individuals to create new squadrons or to expand existing ones.

Balancing old and new rowers was therefore a difficult but necessary task. The royal government sometimes issued instructions to the captains general to share out the *chusma* 'in a way that the galleys go armed in an equal manner and can all serve with the same diligence'. Stragglers – galleys lagging behind the rest of the squadron – were an inconvenience.[39] It was an ongoing concern for Philip II throughout his life; much as he acknowledged that the *Real* or royal flagship needed additional oarsmen, he continued to insist that the galleys of Spain could not be prejudiced as they 'have so much sea to run and guard', '*lo mucho que han de correr y guardar*'.[40]

A new squadron would require time, money and careful husbandry before it could function properly. 'The Pope puts such efforts into arming his galleys that soon he will have ten of them running,' Doria observed in the spring of 1588, 'but for all his efforts it will be several years before they are good and of service.'[41] As things turned out, Sixtus V was surprisingly successful in establishing his new squadron, in part because he threw money at the project, in part because Doria himself provided a contingent of experienced oarsmen.[42] Was it worth fitting out ships manned entirely by novices? In August 1566 Toledo weighed up the option of arming around 10 of the recently completed hulls with *buenas voyas*. He chose not to do so for two reasons; the first was that the cost would serve 'to irritate' the Kingdoms of Naples and Sicily. The second reason was more surprising: 'this was because, being new galleys, they could not serve me, or could do so only to fight with the enemy, and to do so they would not be enough.'[43]

At first glance Toledo's rationale in 1566 was slightly confusing: his meaning was clearly that a direct engagement with the enemy would somehow require less skilled ships than would be needed in other operations. His thinking began from the premise that the enemy would enjoy an advantage of numbers; it then moved to the precept that the reliability, endurance and performance of his crews would be much more valuable to him than the simple arithmetic of how many ships could take to the seas. Indeed, earlier that year he had noted that, given the considerable difference in size between the Ottoman fleet and the Catholic Armada, the fitting out of ten, 12, 15 or even 20 new ships would hardly serve to address the imbalance of numbers; on efforts to run additional vessels he had reflected that 'being new galleys we cannot bring them with the security that is offered by those that are already armed'. It would be better to use the recently raised oarsmen to reinforce the existing galleys, although the orders for the construction of 40 new hulls in Barcelona offered, perhaps, the possibility of a more assertive policy in the future.[44]

The need to replace those rowers who died or were released forced the commanders of the oared squadrons into a relentless recruitment drive. It would have been ideal for the replacement oarsmen to be experienced but, since such men were impossible to find in sufficient numbers, it became inevitable that unskilled recruits were put to the oar. 'Your Majesty's armada having such a large amount of new *chusma* is one of the causes that it does not have galleys of service, as before an oarsman is useful it is necessary for him to spend at least two years on the galley banks, since in the first year he is of absolutely no use and in the second of little.' Writing in 1601 Doria went on to lament that there were very few slaves belonging to the armada; servile labour used to be the core – '*el nervio*' – of the fleet. This shortage was a result of the galleys being forced to sail in winter and being inactive in summer 'and as a result they are weak and have not been able to take galiots which they have seen and chased'.[45] As this analysis suggests, the conscripted oarsman (*buena voya*) and convict (*forzado*) were of limited value in relation to the slave. Oarsmen only really began to be of genuine service after 24 months, and yet by this point a majority of convicts had served their sentences. Indeed at points the Genoese admiral suggested that a minimum sentence of three years would be necessary for the proper manning of galleys with *forzados*.[46]

Good oarsmen were jealously guarded. When the contract for two galleys of Stefano de Mari ended in 1566, Toledo ensured that his crews were divided up among the rest of the squadron, 'for they are also armed with *forzados* and *esclavos*, who can be shared out among the other ships to put them in better order'.[47] Immediately after the death of another contractor, Juan de Mendoza, the officials compiled an inventory of his slaves, making sure that they were claimed as royal patrimony.[48] Royal officials specified that oarsmen should be returned to His Majesty when the *asiento* was completed.[49] Competitive contracts for oarsmen led to rivalry between states. The death of the crusading Pope Sixtus V signalled a reduction in the size of the papal squadron from ten galleys to half that number. Doria was quick to point out the inconvenience of the redundant vessels – some of the best in the Mediterranean – being sold to a rival prince, especially as there was some rumbling of a maritime 'league' of the Papacy, Genoa and the Grand Duke (in fairness, there were nearly always rumours of a league or alliance of one sort or another) and it would be inconvenient to increase the squadrons of the 'potentates of Italy'. Specifically, he stated that he would not want the new pope to continue with the squadron that his predecessor had established. Instead, these crews should be purchased and incorporated into the squadrons of Sicily and Naples, which then suffered from an acute shortage of *chusma*.[50]

No commander liked to release experienced oarsmen; few could do so without expressing regret. It was a wrench to let go men who had just started 'to be of service'. Commanders – even Doria – had to be reminded by the King of the need to unshackle *forzados* who had served their time.[51] In 1574 investigations unearthed a group of French 'prisoners of war' who should have been released 15 years previously.[52] The following year Don John proposed that old or crippled *forzados* should be able to commute their sentence by purchasing a slave for the fleet.[53] This idea perhaps sheds light on a wide problem. Not many historians have accused the early modern judicial system in Spain and Italy of being unnecessarily lenient on criminals, but this was precisely the allegation levelled at it by Doria, who called for stiffer sentences (minimum three years) to be imposed. Many criminals were sent down 'not for two years, but for one, or even for a few months'. Instead of condemning the able-bodied, the courts sent down 'disabled men' who, it has to be assumed, would be of no use and were therefore immediately released. No explanation was given for this reluctance to condemn criminals to the galleys.[54] On the one hand, it may have been that an understanding of the brutish conditions aboard the warships made judges unwilling to send men down; on the other hand, economic factors could not be overlooked. Santa Cruz was given to complain that the 'barons' of Naples did not send *forzados* to the central court of the *Vicaria* in Naples, which would normally forward them on to the galleys. The nobles, having extensive legal prerogatives within their estates, commuted the penalties.[55]

Conditions for oarsmen on both sea and land were always difficult and frequently dangerous. Yet those individuals who survived the initial shock to their system could enjoy careers of remarkable longevity at the oar. Tata de Natolia served aboard the galleys for 40 years, initially as an oarsmen but later as a gunner aboard the galley *San Martín*. He was employed during the campaign against Felipe Strozzi in Portugal (1582) and then aboard the Invincible Armada (1588). The details of his petition suggest that he had remained a Muslim throughout his life.[56] Ahmed of Larache, a Moorish giant in his mid-twenties, became the object of competition among the admirals in 1610. One captain had even offered to swap two slaves for him. The documents do not record what crime Angelo Bruno was guilty of, but it must have been a very serious one; having served as a *forzado* in the flagship of Spain for more than 35 years, he was into his sixties before the King granted him his freedom.[57] Miguel Dezea, the son of an Old Christian father and a Morisco mother, spent 37 years on the galleys of Spain.[58] Strong Christian oarsmen were valued by the corsairs of Algiers, who bought and sold the most skilled and experienced slaves.[59]

Don Quixote, then, was misinformed by the guard who told him that a sentence of ten years *en galera* was a 'civil death'.[60] It was not necessarily so simple. We find numerous and reciprocal complaints among the top rank of Christian commanders that their rivals had kept the best *chusma* and men for themselves.[61] In May 1565 Philip II was forced to adjudicate in a dispute over the ownership of 40 Turks who had been rounded up after their ship went down off Sardinia.[62] The following year he was still asking for details to be sent to him before he could reach a decision; in the meantime a similar dispute had broken out over the allocation of Moors captured in the confines of Porto Ercole, Piombino and Orbetello.[63] It is, perhaps, easy to see why the King might want to eschew responsibility for adjudicating these arguments. Jealousy often got the better of the admirals, as Santa Cruz's words from 1570 demonstrate:

> I have worked long and hard to arm these galleys, and so that they can be sustained and go on to increase it would be best if Your Majesty allocated to them all of the *forzados* of this Kingdom [of Naples]. In Milan they do not provide the 200 that they are supposed to allocate to the galleys of Gian Andrea Doria, and he always comes here to claim half of these, and he takes the best ones.[64]

Similar laments were heard in many years. In October 1610 the Count of Elda claimed that, although his two galleys were well equipped with oarsmen, he hoped to take some from the galleys of Spain, which were 'overflowing with rowers'.[65] In 1631 new rules were introduced to prevent rowers being moved or traded from one galley to another, a measure which had been introduced many times previously but whose failure was pretty much assured.[66]

If oarsmen acquired medical resilience through exposure to disease, they became stronger and more skilled through exercise. This improvement had to be accomplished during the period from May to September. Being in port in summer did the men of the galleys no good for two reasons: first, they did not improve as oarsmen and, second, conditions there were reckoned to be at least as bad as those at sea. The various port authorities across the Mediterranean instigated a primitive system of quarantine, but it is clear that this provided little or no protection to large squadrons, let alone fleets. Reports of oarsmen lost to disease during bouts of summer inactivity can be found in any year.[67] The 'bad airs' were notoriously damaging to large contingents of men, many or most of whom were physically restrained. Galley captains took note of the health of a coastline, seeking to avoid those ports that had an unhealthy reputation or were known to be infested. Corsica, for instance, was characterised by its 'bad airs' in winter.[68] If summer activity was vital to the health of a galley fleet, then avoiding sailing in the period from October to April was equally important. Winter navigation was ruinous, in part because it ate away at the fabric of the vessels, wrecking their hulls, oars and rigging, but primarily because it killed the *chusma*. Of course, the new *chusma* were most badly affected: as Andrea Sauli put it, there was the gravest danger (*'gravissimo pericolo'*) in making galleys manned by new oarsmen navigate in winter on account of the levels of illness and death to which they were subjected.[69] Yet even those sea-hardened oarsmen who had spent many years on the oar – and therefore built up a formidable degree of immunity to disease – were likely to perish if forced to row regularly in the winter months.[70] Winter navigation destroyed both the ships and their men, meaning that they would not be able to serve in summer.[71] Bad weather was less of a threat than the cold, which the second marquis of Santa Cruz took to be the real danger to his crews.[72] When the galleys from Naples, Genoa and Sicily were still in Spain in November 1597 they presented a wretched image; if the oarsmen were not given clothing, predicted an official, then few of them would arrive back in Italy.[73] A similar picture emerged from the Ottoman fleets.[74]

When identifying the characteristics of the best-equipped Christian squadrons – those of Rome, Florence and Malta – Doria observed that these flotillas enjoyed a range of advantages over the King's armada: not only were they heavily financed (with double the salary of the royal ships) and garrisoned with expert troops, but they were excused winter navigation.[75] Simply being forced to winter away from base could be catastrophic for the *chusma*: this was one of the greatest lessons that could be learnt from the Tripoli and Djerba expedition undertaken in the autumn, winter and spring of 1559–60.[76] The Hospitaller galleys suffered terrible losses on a long voyage to Marseille in the early months of 1562. On their arrival in Sicily the ships elicited suspicion that they carried the plague. It turned out, however, that the symptoms of illness were the result of the long navigation, the large number of passengers and having spent the winter in a bad way, *'malpasar del invierno'*.[77] It was later said, with some exaggeration, that the flotilla only made it back to Malta because of the fortuitous capture of a small brigantine with 30 Turks which fell into their midst. An added problem during this expedition was that the high winds made it impossible to raise the awnings above the rowers, an inconvenience which served to exacerbate the 'excessively' cold weather.[78] The galleys of the Genoese contractors suffered extremely high levels of mortality in the winter of 1610–11 when employed on the coast of Spain in the expulsion of the Moriscos. To make matters worse, the usual consignment of *forzados* from Milan had not arrived, meaning that the galleys had been considerably weakened over the course of the previous 24 months.[79]

The rowing crews had to be able to recuperate in the cold months: in 1566 the Grand Master of the Hospitallers asked to use the Monarchy's galleys to assist with the construction of the new city (later Valletta). Toledo resolutely rejected the proposal. 'If this request were granted, it would lead to the total destruction of the galleys, as the *chusma* is so tired after last summer, and they need the winter to recover and to be able to resist the work that will surely come next summer.'[80] Spending the winter in their home ports, Benavente observed in November 1608, was key to the conservation and expansion of the oared flotillas.[81] But the viceroy then directly contradicted himself, as he was sometimes prone to do. Over the coming months he employed oarsmen from eight of the galleys of the Kingdom of Naples to build a new fortification at Orbetello, which he subsequently named after himself. He did, at least, offer the mitigation that the air in those regions 'is so healthy and [because of] it the *chusma* improves its health and is better able to sail'.[82]

IV

Those Esteemed Dreadful Monsters

The history of the galley has always been written from the perspective of technological progression and historical progress. The oared warship has routinely been condemned as a failure, an anachronism in the age of Atlantic 'seapower'. Yet the Elizabethan 'seadogs' certainly retained a deep respect for the oared flotillas. Sir Walter Raleigh referred to the galleys of the squadron of Spain as 'those esteemed dreadful monsters'.[1]

These monsters had in part won their esteem in the Atlantic. The Kingdom of Portugal was annexed by essentially Italian forces – that is, by Habsburg forces based in Italy – under the command of the Marquis of Santa Cruz in 1580. The same forces claimed the Azores in 1582–83. These campaigns demonstrated that an armada partially composed of galleys was capable of decisively defeating Franco-Portuguese fleets consisting of well-armed galleons.[2] Philip II's appreciation of Mediterranean technology may also help to explain why in 1585 he chose to send galleys to the Indies, 'something never before heard of or seen'. Cabrera de Córdoba recorded that Pedro Vique was entrusted to oversee the transfer of an oared squadron and the construction of modern fortifications; the network that he established succeeded in keeping the *corsarios* from the seas for ten years.[3] This successful transplantation may serve to justify and explain the assertion made in 1600 by the *Adelantado Mayor de Castilla*, the Count of Santa Gadea, who reflected that the problem for the galleys of Spain over the previous decades was that ships had been sent to 'Brittany, Flanders, Portugal and even to the Indies'.[4] In the simplest terms, one theatre of action had decisively exerted its influence over another in the later sixteenth century: Mediterranean forces had quickly and easily taken control of the Atlantic world.

Sixteenth-century captains would have been slightly perplexed by the idea of the galley. Oared warships were rarely referred to or described as a generic form: they were said to be strong or weak, sickly or healthy, new or old, reinforced or in bad order. A vessel might assume very different characteristics and qualities depending upon how its captain wanted to fit it out. Any squadron contained at least two different designs of ship: the larger *capitana* and *patrona*, sometimes referred to as 'lantern vessels' (in other words, the ones carrying the torches by which the squadron navigated in the dark), were different in function from the rest of the squadron. They were considerably longer, with a deeper keel and more sail, having two masts (fore- and mid-ship), and they required considerably larger rowing crews than did 'regular' hulls of 24 to 26 banks. A *capitana* might have 30 banks or more; its greater length allowed it to achieve a smoother transfer of the water along its hull and so slightly improved its level of stability. The galiot was the lighter design of oared warship; typically it was a ship of between 18 to 22 banks, although smaller variants were far from uncommon. Below the galiot there was the brigantine (usually said to have 12 to 18 banks; commonly the crew of a *corso* brigantine numbered between 37 and 85 men), which in turn morphed into smaller species of vessels, the *fregata*, *felucca fusta*, which were nearer to being a boat than a ship.

Essentially, statesmen saw that each and every regular sized galley of between 25 and 26 banks could be fitted out in three different ways. In 1594 Miranda set down the two basic configurations of the galley: for normal ferrying operations around 164 or so oarsmen would suffice; when the fleet went on *en orden de guerra*, in the order of war, or to clean the seas of corsairs, it was important for them to be able to catch other ships but also to withdraw or retire, should it be necessary. In either case, the quality of the sailors and oarsmen was decisive, 'as it is so difficult to find any men of whatever quality, and so much more to recruit men who are experienced and skilled'.[5] When the galleys were reinforced, each ship could carry up to 250 *remeros*. These figures were very close to the configurations of crews and ships in the 1560s.[6] If little changed in this regard, it is clear that this period did witness a marked growth in the size of the prestige galleys, the flagship (*capitana*) and vice-flag (*patrona*), and the Royal Galley, the *Real*.[7]

There were, then, three basic models for the arming of a regular-sized warship of 24 banks – with 164, 200, or 240 oarsmen. It would be remiss to fail to point out that Philip II, Philip III and their captains general believed a fourth configuration of the warship to exist, although they hardly ever considered it as a serious choice for their deployments. This option involved the galleys being deployed as floating platforms which supported large numbers of fighting men. In this guise as many hulls as possible were sent to sea. Consequently, each vessel was, or would be, equipped with fewer oarsmen, although emergency attempts were nearly always made to recruit auxiliary *chusma*, experienced or not.

Only on one occasion did Gian Andrea Doria seriously countenance this fourth option. This was in memorandum ahead of the 1595 campaigning season, in which he predicted that the Ottomans would be able to send out an armada of some 125 sail, all counted. While this was a relatively impressive number of vessels, the great majority of them would sail in very poor order. The *capitán general del mar Mediterráneo* therefore proposed that the large but technically weak Ottoman armada carrying an impressive number of janissaries and fighting men should be opposed by a Christian armada of comparable characteristics, 'for it does not matter if the legs are weak, as what counts is the strength of the arms'. The Christians could depend upon the decisive tactical advantage of having superior infantry. In these circumstances the Christian armada should, he reasoned, emerge victorious from a large-scale engagement, but even in defeat it would be able to inflict such heavy damage on the enemy fleet that it would not be able to undertake any significant campaign that summer.[8]

These observations help to explain Toledo's curious decision in August 1566 not to arm the ten or so new galleys available to him: given the scale of the Ottoman fleet, ten or 15 new ships would hardly serve to bring about parity with the enemy; furthermore, battle was considered an option of the last resort for the Catholic Monarchy precisely because in a general confrontation the element of seamanship was largely removed from the equation. For these reasons, Doria's paper of 1595 very much constituted an anomaly. Indeed the desultory assumption or rationale implicit in it – that in the mid-1590s the royal armada was now so feeble that it might be compelled to engage the enemy on his terms – might very plausibly be interpreted as an effort to inspire or rebuke the King to return his fleet to its former state. As such, it might be taken as a warning that proposals and judgements should not be isolated from the political and administrative context in which they were made.

When faced with undertaking difficult or risky missions, Doria and Toledo operated according to the maxim of 'the fewer the better': the best option was to have a smaller fleet with larger and more 'exercised' crews. From at least the 1550s the priority was to run galleys 'in very good order'.[9] Not everyone understood the logic behind these decisions. In November 1561, at perhaps the most perilous moment for the Christians, Medinaceli was astonished when the galley commanders chose to sail with 'so few ships, but they must have a better idea of what they are doing that I do'.[10] Charged with escorting the two sons of Carlo Emanuele I, Duke of Savoy (1580–1630), to Spain in the winter of 1602–03, Doria thought it best to reduce the 16 galleys of the Genoese contractors to eight rather than ten: 'as it is no little thing when from two galleys you reinforce one well; for it appears to me that it is better that eight excellent galleys sail rather than ten which would not be so good'.[11] It was accepted by the Ottoman Turks that operations outside the campaigning season required reinforced craft.[12] Some of the Venetian *capitani generali* understood the military significance and utility of the reinforced galley in exactly the same way as did the other Christian commanders, although like the Ottomans their capacity to reinforce their ships appears to have been restricted by their comparative shortage of oarsmen secured on a long-term basis.[13]

Doria, Toledo, Philip II and Philip III, and figures as eminent and experienced as the first and second marquises of Santa Cruz, all held a view that appears directly counter-intuitive on first impressions: they believed that bigger, heavier ships with more oarsmen were much more effective and seaworthy than were the lighter vessels. To put this in the simplest terms, they believed that a 30-bank galley armed with five or six rowers per bank (a crew of 300 or more men) was more seaworthy than a 25-bank vessel with five oarsmen per bank (a total of 250 men). By extension they believed that a 25-bank ship with 250 oarsmen offered superior levels of performance than a 25-bank ship with 160 rowers. (A bank was taken to refer to the oars on both sides of the ship, so a 25-bank ship had 50 oars. It was usual to have more men on the banks towards the stern of the ship.)[14] In 1607 the Council of War clearly believed that the current generation of warships offered superior stability under both oar and sail precisely because they were built with broader and deeper hulls. In addition, these ships could store more sail.[15]

The assessments penned by Toledo and Doria necessarily lead back to the arguments about the restricted potential of the human rower advanced by Rodgers, Guilmartin, Zysberg and Professor John H. Pryor.[16] According to calculations made by Rodgers, an oarsman could provide 140 watts of output for ten hours, 170 watts for four hours and 200 watts for one hour; the very highest level of exertion (300 watts, enough for 26 strokes per minute) could be sustained for only a very short burst of just 20 or so minutes.[17] This was, Guilmartin argued, a relatively short amount of time and power in relation to the demands of the new form of fighting that emerged in the course of the sixteenth century as a result of the implementation of new technology.

At this juncture four separate strands of argument can be set out about the oarsman, his capacity and limits.

The first of these is that of improvement and differentiation. An emphasis upon human frailty fails to take into account the self-evident observation that some oarsmen were much healthier, fitter and stronger than others. It fails, in other words, to consider the improvement in the performance of the oarsman over the first two to three years of his employment on the banks. As the burden of an experienced oarsman (the weight of his person, provisions and equipment) was not significantly different to that of a novice, the improvement in his performance over the first 24 to 36 months of his service brought about a considerable increase in overall output. By extension, the efficiency of a crew increased in proportion to the number of well-trained oarsmen: a galley with 200 trained oarsmen would be more powerful and seaworthy than one with 160 oarsmen of the same calibre; the additional 40 oarsmen, all of them providing more power in relation to the increase in weight and drag, improved the level of power in relation to the amount of additional draw or friction in the water.

The second strand of argument is that the basic outlook or assumption of the captains general was comparative: when Doria or Toledo referred to the royal fleet being *en buen orden*, they were really saying that it could be in much, much worse condition. For all their emphasis upon the capacity of the human rower to adapt to conditions *en galera*, sixteenth-century captains were certainly conscious of the fact that even the best oarsmen could not be driven too hard for too long or exposed to too many hardships. In other words, their principal point of reference in assessing the calibre of the royal armada was with the performance of new or unexercised crews, groups that might provide very little power, and sometimes none at all. Of the 200 galleys equipped by Süleyman's officials in 1537, 80 were said to be in good order, 'and [the] rest are almost disarmed'.[18] In 1551 the majority of the galleys of the Ottoman fleet were unable to exert any force at the oar whatsoever.[19] 'Some say that the majority of the Turk's galleys are in bad order,' read a report from April 1565, 'on account of the little skill of the *chusma*.'[20] It was reported from Constantinople in January 1569 that a captain was fitting out a 23-bank galiot and recruiting a crew of *buenas voyas* before sailing to Algiers 'and everything will be badly armed. He will leave here in early February, and will be in Modon until 10 March.'[21] This was too good an opportunity for the Christian admirals to pass up. In 1570 the Venetian commanders Girolamo Zane and Sforza Pallavicini were dismayed to find that of 80 galleys at Corfu only 30 could leave port: 'the rest, for the shortage of oarsmen, could not move from where they were'; here they were stuck for a month (23 June to 23 July) 'amidst the dead and dying'.[22] In September of that year Doria provided Marc'Antonio Colonna with a written testimony to the effect that many of the galleys of the Republic of St Mark 'were not in the state to be able to make the voyage to Cyprus without help'.[23] The 30 galleys that departed from the Golden Horn on the last day of June 1595 were 'in such bad order that no effect can be expected of them'.[24]

The third point to be made about the performance of galleys was that in nearly all circumstances the lowest level of exertion – the calculation made by Rodgers of an output of 140 watts – was precisely what was required. Navigation was a grinding slog; even chases of galiots unfolded through hours of tedious rowing before the sails were unfurled and the pursuit would suddenly become a sprint for life and liberty. Good galleys could trudge against adverse conditions for days. The squadron carrying the emperor fought spring headwinds 'which have never faltered' all the way from Spain to Nice in 1538.[25] In April 1566 the rains prevented Santa Cruz from sailing from Spain to Italy; having arrived in Barcelona, his squadron had to row into easterly winds for two-thirds of the voyage back to Genoa in May 'and so the *chusma* is very fatigued, because a large part of it is new'.[26] In July of the following year a band of the King's galleys battled exhausting headwinds just off the Cape of St Vincent; the winds just off Cadiz, it was noted, were so strong that it was often impossible to *proejar* – to row into them.[27]

The most detailed account of the ability of the galleys to row can be found in the various memoranda discussing the relief of Malta in 1565: Toledo envisaged that the oared fleet, travelling unencumbered, could make the 40 or so miles overnight and surprise the enemy at dawn (the plan was to travel from over the horizon, beyond the sightlines of the island). Yet he thought it very unlikely that this distance, or even 25 miles, could be covered while towing provision ships.[28] Rowing was understood primarily as a means of traction rather than as an expression of velocity; considerations of speed had relatively little use or application, although captains commonly thought about how far they could travel overnight. On the other hand, the galley could set its sails to tack against the wind: both Zysberg and Professor Olesa Muñido have shown how the triangular form of the lateen sail allowed it to catch a part of the wind.[29] These craft were also able to sail at an angle of 90 degrees to the wind direction; thus the Ottoman fleet, when first spied by a reconnaissance craft in 1566, was using north-westerly winds to navigate towards the south-west.[30]

It is true that when it came to discussing the flagships, the consideration of military utility shaded into the personal vanity of the *capitán general*. There can be no doubt that sixteenth-century aristocrats liked having galleys which were bigger than those of their colleagues and peers. Early in his tenure of command Toledo resolved to build a large *capitana*, 'as it is not possible to avoid confronting the armada of the Turk one day' and the flagship was the vessel 'that gives the whole fleet spirit and hope of victory, as everything depends on the good or bad of the *capitana*'. This was a curious statement for a man who so assiduously avoided contact with the enemy; it can be judged a rare expression of pride. In any case his plan was torpedoed when the Viceroy of Naples refused to accede to his demands and pointed out that the *capitán general del mar Mediterráneo* did not have permission to lay down a new hull.[31]

Toledo did, in fact, succeed in building a new flagship, although she had a rather sad career. Throughout the great confrontations of the 1560s and 1570s half of the hulls of the squadron of Sicily were left in the docks in Messina; there was simply not enough *chusma* to crew them. Before Lepanto the King wrote to Don John to mention these ships, which could only be used in exceptional circumstances. He specifically referred to the royal flagship that Toledo had ordered and which had never been used; the viceroy wanted to have it broken up and used for parts, and the King reminded his half-brother that, whatever his decision in this regard, he was to make sure that the materials were put to good use.[32]

Nobody denied that the flagship or *capitana* and vice-flagship or *patrona* played a role of disproportionate significance within a squadron: they headed the pursuit of enemy ships and so captured the slaves who would improve the performance of the squadron. These vessels were allocated the largest proportion of the best oarsmen, and logically their level of performance was considerably higher than that of the other vessels in their squadron. Therefore in many routine journeys it did not matter too much if, say, eight of the ten galleys within a squadron were comparatively weak, as the performance of the leading ships was vital to the apprehension of enemy corsair craft.

The fourth major consideration in understanding Doria's assessment of the war galley lay in the improvement in rowing technique over time. Steven Redgrave, five-time Olympic champion, points out in his recent guide to the sport that it is essential in rowing that the oars enter, move through and leave the water at the same time in order to avoid incurring any additional drag; a rower whose stroke is out of time with those of his colleagues serves only to slow the hull.[33] 'Like any complex movement performed well, the rowing stroke *does* look simple, even monotonous, but in fact the components of the stroke are difficult and require very considerable amounts of training.'[34] Rowing is, therefore, a profession requiring very specific skill sets. The momentum of the ship through the water in fact poses considerable dangers to those who take the oar. The achievement of a coordinated, balanced and rhythmic stroke was a decisive characteristic of good Mediterranean warships. French experts writing in the time of Louis XIV emphasised the need to have each bank functioning with equal power and precision, '*bien égaliser la chiourme*'. This precept required the officials to devote a great attention to the allocation of men to each bank, none of which could support more than one new rower.[35] The way that crews invested their athletic energies held enormous importance. Since antiquity, the captains of oared warships had found that inexperienced crews had a propensity to cause instability to the ship; the rips and currents of the Straits of Messina, for instance, could throw a novice crew into a panic.[36] Strong currents running from the sea of Marmara towards the Aegean, often accompanied by northerly winds, presented a hazard in the approaches to these straits.[37] Aside from his physical weakness, the novice oarsman is hindered by a tendency towards causing instability; a boat is easily destabilised by 'technical failings' or 'roughness' – these can, for the sake of simplicity, be termed the tendency to wobble the hull by losing rhythm or balance, by moving too far or too little or too late or too soon. It is essential for the novice to learn how to propel the oar through its cycle without unbalancing his vessel. For this reason many rowing clubs have boats with flat, broad bottoms on which novices can learn the basic skills. ('A flat-bottomed boat,' notes Redgrave, 'is a stable, but slow boat.')[38] Elite oarsmen have the necessary technical qualities to transfer their physical power into and through the oar stroke without causing instability to their craft; as the novice becomes more adept and improves one skill, he finds that he is much more able to eliminate whatever other technical failings are afflicting his rowing.[39] Similarly modern coaches are convinced that smaller rowing boats are more sensitive to failings in technique or adverse conditions; a larger crew is more able to 'dampen out' the errors, roughness or inconsistencies in its members' stroke.[40]

These considerations are important because they dovetail very closely with the arguments and assumptions found in the correspondence of sixteenth- and seventeenth-century officers: if today's eight-man racing boats are quicker and overall more efficient than two-man craft, then it seems inherently logical that in the *Cinquecento* crews of 250 oarsmen were quicker and more efficient than those of 160 *remeros*. Still, within this formulation the key criteria remained the qualities of the oarsmen; the technical failings of 250 unskilled oarsmen would have rendered a ship unstable and ineffective; logically, a crew consisting of 180 skilled oarsmen would have been able to assimilate 60 or 70 less experienced rowers, to 'dampen out' their failings as rowers.

Experienced oarsmen were, therefore, not only more powerful but also more efficient than novice crewmembers. Galleys equipped with *chusma vieja* or *chusma forzada* not only exerted much more physical power, but also employed it much more effectively than did those warships that were propelled by unskilled rowers, regardless of their propensity to fall sick. The consideration of technique and rhythm helps to explain how some crews were capable of maintaining a regular pace for hours on end, although doubtless in doing so they did not row anywhere near their full capacity. It also explains how contemporaries could spot *galeras en buen orden* so readily, or why *galeras en mal orden* were summarily dismissed as such. The order of its stroke told a witness all that he needed to know about an oared warship. It conveyed immediately, and without the possibility of deceit or deception, the quality of the blood running through its veins.[41]

The drawbacks or limitations in the use of the galley that formed an important part of the studies of Zysberg, Rodgers, Pryor and Guilmartin cannot be overlooked or dismissed; the larger designs created greater drag and were more difficult to start moving; they were also less manoeuvrable than the narrower, shorter galiots. On the other hand, sixteenth-century captains seem to have believed that these difficulties were marginal in relation to the advantages that were brought about by equipping their bigger ships with larger crews.

The reaction to Toledo's proposal to lay down a new flagship in 1566 demonstrates the degree to which the Habsburg system was imbued with an inherent rivalry in which criticism, constructive or otherwise, was quite freely vented. Yet in all of the correspondence no voice was ever raised against the fundamental rationale advanced by the Genoese businessman-prince. Indeed, the complaints voiced about the Habsburgs and their servants in 1565, 1570, 1572 or 1605 tended to underline precisely how effective their fleet was: the protests of la Valette in August 1565 or Giacomo Foscarini in October 1572 were based upon the premise that the royal armada of Philip II could and should have done much better, that its officers could and should have been much more ambitious.[42] The rationale underlying both complaints was that of good *chusma* and the discipline, regularity and strength of the oar stroke. In this respect they were no different from the explanations proffered by Toledo and Doria or the instructions issued by the King.

The swiftest galleys in the western Mediterranean were the bulky Christian *capitanas* and the sleek galiots of Algiers and Tunis.[43] In 1538 Charles V oversaw the pursuit of a French squadron near Marseille. The imperial flagship chased down and overcame its prey; two other French warships headed to sea and were hunted down by the pursuing pack; only Francis I's royal flagship, rowing into the wind, managed to reach the relative safety of La Ciotat.[44] Turgut *reis* was captured on 1 June 1540; the corsair made the mistake of springing out to attack a Genoese squadron under Juanetín Doria, thinking that it consisted of only six ships. He took advantage of favourable winds in order to launch his attack from a cape on the western seaboard of Corsica, near Bastia, and only realised his error when it was too late to do anything but fight. The outcome of the skirmish was determined when the prow of his ship sustained heavy damage from a cannon shot and began to sink; the other captains of his squadron, incidentally, seem to have given little thought to fighting the Christian squadron and turned to run, '*sus galeras echaron cada una por su cabo*'.[45]

In many respects, the accounts of pursuits left out most of the details; certainly they say little or nothing about seamanship, leewardliness, the capacity of oarsmen to maintain a rhythm or speed, tacking into the wind or the actual details of the fighting when it occurred. Yet the documents frequently report chases of 60 or 70 miles and, moreover, stated that these distances were traversed in a matter of hours.[46] Clearly the dice were loaded in favour of the *capitanas*: the best oarsmen, the fiercest soldiers, the most accurate gunners and most skilled mariners served under the direct command of the captain general. The flagship boasted the largest masts, and doubtless the best sail. By the same standard it is clear that not all of the other galleys in the squadron would carry cannon as a matter of routine.[47] The length of a 30-bank ship afforded it considerable additional streamlining and buoyancy over a 22-bank vessel; its transfer of water from prow to stern was smoother. The drawback for the flagships would lie in a comparative slowness in changing direction, as the vessels with shorter hulls would have been more immediately responsive when turning.

The performance of galleys in pursuits can be set out and studied in relation to one particularly well-documented pursuit. On 8 June 1606, during a period of poor weather, the Neapolitan squadron under the second Marquis of Santa Cruz chased three galiots for around nine hours, making up 13 miles on them. With two hours of daylight left to him, Santa Cruz succeeded in positioning one galiot downwind, while two galiots remained upwind (or ahead) of the Christian pack. Up until this point, the pursuit had taken place under oars; unfortunately, a fresh wind coming from the Gulf of Taranto created a heavy sea. Santa Cruz calculated that he would not have enough time to overtake these two advanced vessels before darkness fell. The prospect of nightfall therefore forced his declaration: unfurling his sails he swept down upon the disadvantaged galiot. Faced with the superior sailing qualities of the flagship, the galiot had little chance of evading the hunting pack. With 120 minutes of daylight at his disposal, Santa Cruz had allowed himself ample time, and duly claimed his prize.[48]

A few inferences, all fairly self-evident, can be drawn from Santa Cruz's account: first, that he – or, rather more specifically, his oarsmen – had rowed almost directly into the wind during the first stages of the hunt; second, that the galiots also headed directly into the wind; third, that this phase of the chase accounted for by far the most significant part of it, perhaps something like seven hours out of a total of nine or so. Clearly the figures of 60 or 70 miles quoted by captains included not only the distance rowed under oars, but also the pursuit under sail, which would have constituted the greater part of the pursuit.

The narratives of pursuits reveal a pattern.[49] Having been sighted, the captains of the galiots nearly always headed directly into the wind. Their hope was that they would simply sprint away from the larger ships under oars and so avoid a pursuit under sail. The unfurling of the canvas was more than half the battle: as soon as the winds became the key factor in the hunt the clear advantage lay with the larger, more stable flagships. The narrower the hull of the vessel, and the shallower its keel, the greater the imbalance brought about by the use of sail would have been; in this respect the slender hull and shallow keel of the galiots would have put them at a considerable disadvantage in relation to the flagships.[50] The galiot was further disadvantaged in that the logic of rowing into the wind meant that when the sails were unfurled both hunter and hunted would turn and head back in the general direction from which they had come, and therefore towards the main body of the pursuing squadron. This observation may help to explain why the Barbary galiot was often surrounded by Christian galleys at the death; as we have seen, Amisa *reis* had distinguished himself by being able to extradite himself and his ship from this unfortunate position on a number of occasions.

Given the superior sailing performance of the large Christian *capitanas*, it was generally true that they exercised a greater advantage in rougher seas: many successful pursuits consequently took place in more turbulent conditions. Of the 20 galiots and brigantines captured during Don John of Austria's tenure as Captain General of the Mediterranean Sea, 11 were arrested in May, September and November, and only 9 in June, July and August.[51] A pursuit in the 'calm seas', '*las calmerías*', of July and August was not guaranteed to end in success; even long pursuits of 70 miles could end in failure.[52] Chases in winter, between November and February, offered the galleys important advantages over galiots and smaller craft – although the bonus of an occasional prize did not prevent Doria from complaining about being ordered to sail in bad weather late in the season.[53] Of course, hunting in winter was a dangerous game, yet it was a risk that many captains were willing to take. At the very end of 1601 a group of Philip III's galleys was blown back into Barcelona; when news arrived of a band of galiots on the coast, it set off again in the direction of Valencia.[54]

Bad weather, therefore, was not necessarily a bad thing. Apart from the navigational advantages set out above, the Christian admirals sometimes found that corsairs were sheltering from the winds on coves and bays.[55] One of the few successes achieved by the Catalan squadron in its short and unhappy history came in November 1612, when it chased down and overpowered a *saetia*.[56] On the other hand, it was relatively easy for the galleys to inspect merchantmen in the *calmerías* of the Mediterranean summer; yet in July and August there was always a reasonable chance that, appearances being deceptive, a freighter might turn out to have been hijacked by the enemy and manned with a skeleton crew.[57]

A few more deductions can be made. It was obviously true that the amount of daylight was a key consideration in the corsair's hopes for escape; when night fell he would often be able to extinguish his lantern and glide away into the dark seas. If a pursuit in April or October may have offered the Christian galleys marginally more favourable conditions, then they also offered less daylight and therefore less time. Commercial and passenger vessels making a voyage in waters where a more powerful enemy squadron was believed to be lurking might shorten the time they spent on the sea, venturing from harbour only after midday; they would also send light frigates ahead to scan the waters for signs of trouble.[58] On the same note large fleets sent out swift vessels to act as their eyes and, more ambitiously, to capture enemy reconnaissance craft.[59] This tactic was often used as part of a plan to hide the fleet, moving it undetected, with sails withdrawn in day and sometimes in night as well, and navigating at considerable distance from the shore. It seems to have been surprisingly difficult to spot other vessels at sea; this was true in both darkness and bright sunlight. In 1566 a reconnaissance patrol sent into the Levant from Sicily arrived near Cephalonia. The captain, Don Juan Zanoguera, spied what he took to be two enemy ships limping along 'in bad order'. Having little doubt that his craft would be more than a match for these vessels, he lay in wait for them in a cove or bay. He was surprised and very disappointed to find, as the sun moved and his view cleared, that before him was the entire Ottoman fleet.[60]

Zanoguera managed to avoid capture, using his skill and capitalising on the deficiencies of the enemy armada (by his account, there was only one galley capable of maintaining a pursuit of his ship.) Concerns about visibility served to underline the importance of guarding the shoreline. López de Gómara writes that the emperor fortified the most important places on the seaside of Naples and Sicily, 'knowing that the galleys are like rays of sunshine, and although they are seen and heard, you do not know where they are going to attack until they fall upon it'.[61] Large mobilisations were simply much more easily followed. 'Although the saying goes that the sea is a forest,' noted Toledo in one of his more reflective moments, 'by this it is meant that a few galleys are very difficult to track.' A large fleet was very different, as it 'has to take water and at every stage leaves a footprint of where it is going'.[62]

The fact that one or two vessels among a group of galleys were so much quicker and stronger than the others could present a major handicap. A very rare Turkish narrative account of a skirmish in 1560 tells us that Uluç Ali's flagship was far ahead of the rest of its squadron: 'The ships that should have accompanied him were not alongside him, so he was alone.' After the initial burst of fighting 'Uluç Ali turned his galley, which resembled a sea dragon, around' and headed back towards the rest of his flotilla.[63] After a pursuit of 70 miles Doria had to abandon the chase of the eight galiots sailing under Arnauti Memi *reis* on 16 October 1590, in part due to adverse winds off the Catalan coast, in part because the other nine vessels of his squadron had fallen so far behind his excellent *capitana* and *patrona*.[64] The hunter was in danger of becoming dramatically outnumbered by those he was chasing. In this instance, as in many others, the *reis* chose to lead his galiots straight out to sea, hoping that bad weather might force the captain of the hunting pack to ask himself if it was worth risking his precious flagships in a pursuit taking place 20, 30 or 40 miles from shore. In July 1607 Santa Cruz was faced with precisely this conundrum. Having discovered a corsair squadron at a distance of five miles in the gulf of Bonifaccio – that is, in the passage of sea between Corsica and Sardinia – his squadron made up four miles on its prey in two hours. But then the wind and sea got up to such an extent that the marquis decided to turn back to the shelter of the island.[65]

Heavy weather might pose a problem in other ways. Doria was unable to locate Turgut *reis* in the difficult weather experienced in the later stages of the 1550 season, '*non lo havendo potuto ritrovar per li tempi contrari*'.[66] In 1589 the papal squadron had secured what should have been a winning position in pursuit of two large galiots after their discovery in the Cala di Forno, on the Tuscan coastline. This chase had begun in rough weather, and as the sea became more violent the relative advantage of the larger galleys became more marked. With the winds in its large fore- and mid-sails, the Christian flagship was very well placed. 'But,' Oratio Lercano reported, 'being full of hope that the galiots could not in any way escape from my hands, the mast of one of our galleys broke and we had to break off the chase and go to the rescue of the stricken ship.'[67]

If the difficulties in the chase are taken into account – that is spotting; stalking into the wind under oars; and finally hounding down the prey under sail – it would seem fair to conclude that the sixteenth-century captain general was justified in being proud of any successful pursuit. The advantages lay with the corsairs. Like gunslingers of the Wild West, the Christian *capitanes generales* had to find an edge, to engage an enemy squadron on the most favourable terms, perhaps after it had become tired from battling against winds and elements. The Cape of Denia was an excellent point from which to spring an ambush, especially if the corsairs had laboured into headwinds across the Gulf of Valencia.[68] The Cape of Bonifaccio was another excellent position. And when a captain had no luck here, he could always sail around the other islands, which were sure to offer him glimpses of the enemy.[69] But there were dangers here too; as Turgut had found to his cost in 1540, there was always the prospect that a bigger predator might be waiting around the next blind-spot on the coastline.[70]

These patterns of action had been found in the *mare nostrum* since the time of Carthage and Rome, when Mylae, Tendari, Lipari and 'the Cape of Italy' had been launching positions from which to surprise the enemy. 'If you want to catch these corsairs,' Don Luis de Requesens advised the emperor in the early 1520s, 'then the galleys should lie in wait in the Channel of Piombino, where they would surely come across many Turkish ships.'[71] The coast could serve as a trap for entire fleets. The curve of the coastline at San Felice Circeo, near Terracina, afforded an excellent position from which to spring an attack; in 1552 a hundred or so Ottoman galleys lay in wait there for the imperial squadron under Andrea Doria. The pursuit was begun at night and continued for almost 20 hours, resulting in the capture of seven galleys. Lorenzo Capelloni, Andrea Doria's first biographer, blamed his 'old age', the obvious and slightly embarrassing deduction being that the Prince was asleep when his fleet sailed into the trap; the author also mentioned as contributing factors that the lieutenant had chosen to sail too close to the island of Ponza; that the currents of the sea, *corriente del mare*, had favoured the Muslims; that the day and night guards had been negligent; and that the enemy took a great deal of encouragement and impetus from its sudden appearance and descent.[72]

V

The Sea-Wolves

Warfare depended upon the wretched. Convicts, slaves and poor men whose only way of making a living was hard physical labour – these were the essential component of the great fleets of brilliant princes. If, as Braudel says, the Mediterranean spoke with many voices, then Philip II and his galley captains listened most attentively to those speakers who gave grim, wearying details about experience and strength, hardiness and survival.[1] Philip II referred to the '*gente de buena volla y marineros*' as 'the principal, and most necessary and difficult [to find]' of the components of his fleet.[2] It was more difficult – much more difficult – to find oarsmen than it was to secure new hulls and rigging; hulls without *chusma* were of no use.[3] In 1535 Paul III ordered the Roman courts to condemn as many men to the galleys as was possible.[4] Braudel points out that the most serious problem in reconstructing the Neapolitan squadron after the losses at Djerba in 1560 lay in finding oarsmen.[5] In December of that year Doria stated that his priority was to return his *capitana* to good order: in fact, his flagship had been captured by the Ottoman fleet in the rout off Djerba (11 May), and so the Prince must have been referring to his need for oarsmen – the right sort of oarsmen – to be employed aboard a new warship.[6] In Sicily the government saw things in the same light. In the summer of 1562 the viceroy, Medinaceli, was happy to sell the Grand Master of Malta a hull – although he drove a hard bargain, insisting that the Hospitallers pay in slaves rather than in specie (he believed that la Valette's two private galleys had taken many slaves that summer). He was confident that the King would back his policy as 'without slaves it is impossible to arm your galleys', 'sin esclavos es imposible armar sus galeras'.[7] When the transaction was completed, the Grand Master handed over no more than 50 slaves claiming, somewhat implausibly, that the Order could not afford to be more generous as its last patrol had come up very short, 'por no haber traído presa esta última vez'.[8] In this case his decision to buy a new hull was a slightly curious one.

In 1565 there were six new hulls in Barcelona. But it was never really likely that there would be enough oarsmen to arm them or even that it would be a good idea to do so, as to dilute the existing *chusma* would tire it, forcing the better, older ships to tow the weaker, newer ones.[9] Toledo, incidentally, tried in 1565 to requisition slaves in Sicily – he hoped that as many as 1,200 might be enlisted – only to be thwarted when the cities of Palermo and Messina invoked their extensive and ancient liberties. (He also initially hoped to recruit 2,000 *buenas voyas* in Naples.[10]) In the following year the King instructed his ministers to be as diligent as possible in recruiting volunteer oarsmen.[11] It was a routine instruction, almost a platitude. At this juncture Toledo hoped to recruit 2,000 *buenas voyas* in Sicily.[12] Braudel, I.A.A. Thompson and Francesco Caracciolo have pointed out that in the early 1570s the government threw anyone and everyone – travellers, criminals and vagabonds – to the galleys. But were these measures productive? The balance of evidence suggests that they were not.[13] In June 1570 Santa Cruz wrote of the shortage of slaves, who were 'very few' in number, *muy pocos*. He was trying to arrange for a credit of 12,000 ducats with a view to buying some *esclavos* in Spain.[14] In Venice and Naples at this time oarsmen – any and all oarsmen – were gratefully put to the oar.[15] In December 1571 Don John hoped to arm the six new hulls that would be available for the next campaign. But this already appeared unrealistic. The captain general of the squadron of Sicily, Don Juan de Cardona, thought that at best two of these ships could be equipped 'for the shortage that there is of *forzados*, of whom many have died, and with the disorder that there was in unchaining oarsmen on the day of the Battle, on account of which many have fled and some were freed'.[16]

Shortly after the Venetian abandonment of the Holy League in April 1573, Don John advanced a proposal to arm 300 or 350 galleys; the King responded that, much as securing the new hulls, rigging, arsenals and weaponry would present enormous obstacles to the implementation of this proposal, the greatest difficulty would lie in finding *chusma* and *marineros*.[17] He clearly expected his half-brother's proposal to be impossible to implement – as, of course, it was. A couple of months later, in July, and after much discussion, complaint and procrastination, Doria finally launched the five new galleys whose preparation he had been overseeing for some time; yet no sooner were the hulls in the water than their crews became incapacitated by illness, 'and if something is not done to remedy this they will shortly be useless'.[18] In 1587 it was understood that the greatest difficulty in arming the two recently completed galleasses would be in finding oarsmen.[19] These enormous vessels were to sail with the Invincible Armada in 1588; in the end they took much of the best *chusma* with them.

Maintaining an oared warship was a labour worthy of Sisyphus: the greatest adversaries of the *galera en buen orden* were time itself, the seas and the elements, each of which took their toll on the battleship and its rowers. The common assumption of all commanders was that the ability of their crews to resist the demands and trials of service at sea was determined by their collective history, the sum total of how they had been trained and employed over the previous years. And here lay the different character of the squadrons across the seas. As the excellent work of Luca Lo Basso has shown, the various flotillas had different manning patterns. For all the complaints about the shortage of oarsmen in Naples, the *forzados* always constituted the largest group on the galleys of '*il Regno*', usually accounting for around 60 per cent of the crews.[20] The corsair galleys or galiots of Valetta, Algiers, Tunis and Leghorn were propelled by oarsmen who were almost exclusively slaves; the slaves aboard Ottoman galleys included amongst their number a high percentage of Poles and Hungarians.[21] Aboard the Ottoman squadrons in the Levant, the contracted, voluntary oarsmen – western sources sometimes used the term 'militias' but recent Ottoman scholars have employed the Turkish term, *kürekçi azap* – were predominant. One recurring feature of the reports from the East was that there were comparatively few Christian slaves in Constantinople. There were no more than 2,000 of them in 1599, and of these less than half were ever put to the oar.[22] Many of the slaves were skilled craftsmen employed in the construction and maintenance of the ship hulls; they were not required to row. Venice freed her Muslim slaves as a condition of the peace treaties signed with the Sultan in 1540 and 1573. Only those who had been convicted of piracy or serious crime were retained.[23] The Venetian fleet therefore did not employ Muslims as slaves until the outbreak of war over Crete in 1645, although it did make use of convict oarsmen, whose loyalties could be just as uncertain and their attempts to escape as dangerous.[24]

The relationship between the King and his galleys, the way that the *galera reforzada* corresponded to the essential outlook of the Catholic Monarchy, will become clear in the course of the following pages. Suffice to say that the oared warship *en buen orden*, upon which the Catholic Monarchy based its military strategy in the Mediterranean, was itself a template for the expedient investment of athletic energy. The examination of the qualities of the high-grade galley leads directly to another of the inherent restrictions to the Christian system of warfare at sea – the difficulty in finding the right sort of slave. The capture of civilians or of men with no previous exposure to the rigours of life at sea was of very limited value, as they would have little or none of the necessary resilience, strength and skills. In 1619, as part of his reasoning for a defensive campaign over an aggressive one, Don Pedro de Toledo, fifth Marquis of Villafranca, stated that of 500 slaves captured during raids upon coastal villages and towns, fewer than 20 would be suitable for service at the oar.[25] The other major difficulty in raiding coastal communities was that when the adult male population of these settlements was present expeditions of this sort entailed a high degree of risk. Even small villages could put up fierce resistance.[26]

Whereas the crews of merchant ships provided, in theory, a rich source of servile labour, in practice their capture was of limited value. This was for three reasons: first, because of the plethora of diplomatic complaints that inevitably accompanied any action; second, because the majority of seafarers aboard Ottoman, French and Venetian shipping tended to be Christians, Greek Christians or Levantine Jews – groups who could not be enslaved; third, because conditions aboard oared warships were much, much worse than those on merchantmen. Commercial seafarers did not row as a matter of course, and so would have to go through the process of acclimatisation and training.[27]

In practice the slave markets proved to be a very unreliable and rather expensive source of oarsmen. Santa Cruz's plans to buy slaves in Spain in 1570 appear not to have been successful. In 1604 the price quoted in Genoa was 80 *escudos* per slave. This made it a relatively costly option, the normal price being 55 to 60 *escudos*.[28] Clearly, it was not going to be easy or cheap to buy 1,000 slaves: 80,000 *escudos* would have been enough money to run around four galleys in Genoa or around six or seven in Naples. Yet the conditions of the slave market in 1604 were generally favourable, as supply was fed by the war in Hungary. The reverses suffered by Austrian armies and the subsequent winding-down of hostilities in central southern Europe meant that the number of Muslim slaves available to purchase in northern Italy was reduced.[29]

All of the considerations and criteria about the slave, his athleticism and price can be found in a detailed proposal put forward by a Hospitaller knight, Roberto Dati, in 1606. He offered to purchase a contingent from Leghorn and Malta: the slaves should be young (between 18 and 30 years old) and 'tall of body, healthy, robust and brave'. Perhaps 500 might be purchased in this way, he suggested. If the government sought to buy slaves directly then the best option would be to secure them from the Uskoks, a nation of corsairs based at Sejn in the Adriatic, 'as the majority of the hundreds of Turks sold there are from the seaside areas, they are better oarsmen than slaves captured from inland areas'.[30]

The market was therefore a relatively unreliable and expensive source of servile power. Precisely because of these inherent restrictions in obtaining slaves through the market or raids on villages, defensive patrols *en corso* occupied a position of extreme importance in the proper running of the oared warships – as the Duke of Feria put it in 1603, these were 'the principal means for their conservation and augmentation'.[31] A crew

of corsairs was likely to have built up the requisite collective resistance
to disease and the elements. Moreover, the expense and risk involved in
defensive patrols was relatively low, the King was obliged to protect 'his
vassals' and the exercise of the galleys was held to be inherently
beneficial for the existing oarsmen.[32]

The health of the Christian war galleys of the sixteenth and
seventeenth centuries was, therefore, determined by their capacity to
hunt the hunters, to catch the galiots and brigantines fitted out in North
Africa. For all the political and cultural importance attached to the role
of the galleys as defenders of the seas of Christendom – the incessant
outpouring of rhetoric about resisting the fury, arrogance and insolence
of the infidels – the western galley squadrons depended upon their
direct adversaries, the Islamic corsairs of Algiers, Tripoli, Djerba and
Tunis, without whom they would have been unable to operate as
effectively as they did. The perspective of the captains general was,
therefore, governed by the paradox that the capture of their direct
opponents was essential to the proper running of their warships. In this
paradigm, Christian civilians occupied the anomalous position of
enticing the enemy into a trap, tempting him to reveal himself.
Merchant ships, and even coastal communities, served essentially as
bait. The coastline of Sicily was the most frequented by the Muslim
corsairs. Yet this exposure was, paradoxically, a benefit to the kingdom's
galleys, 'for there is greater facility to capture slaves and they have sailed
less in winter'.[33] A proposal made in 1612 functioned on this same
premise – that a vulnerable island like Mallorca ought to be able to
exploit its position on the frontier with the Muslim world in order
to maintain a strong squadron of oared warships. It asked Philip III to
consider establishing a group of galleys on the island, underlining the
value 'of having in this port galleys occupied solely in running as corsairs
and eradicating the pirates', 'galeras ocupándolas solamente en corsear y
extirpar los piratas'.[34]

This proposal went on to outline a series of other advantages and
benefits, the details of which might certainly have been queried.
However, the rationale or perspective underlying it was clear and widely
accepted: that an effective royal squadron of galleys protected its

peoples, coastlines and seas but, as it did so, it improved itself. One of
the central features of the Christian system of warfare at sea was
therefore that defensive patrols were fundamental to the health, and
indeed the improvement, of a galley. A squadron dedicated solely to
catching the right sort of oarsmen – that is, Muslims with previous
exposure to the grim existence of life *en galera* – should, over the course
of a number of years and with proper support and investment, establish
itself *en muy buen orden*.

  Throughout the period under study the galleys of Philip II and Philip
III were placed into bands of reinforced galleys in order to sally in
pursuit of the Islamic corsairs of North Africa. The Christian
commanders were intensely conscious of the large number of enemy
ships; danger and opportunity sat side by side, in that until at least the
1590s there was always the possibility that a large Algerian flotilla was
lying in wait around the next bend in the coastline or just over the
horizon. In the 1520s statesmen such as Don Hugo de Moncada urged
'Caesar' (Charles V) to send his galleys in good order after the corsairs,
who went about in *fustas*, light ships.[35] In 1522 a band of Venetian
trading galleys were arrested in Southampton. As the *capitano*, Vincenzo
Priuli, contemplated the journey home he saw that they would have to
be put in good shape 'as the seas are so full of corsairs', '*che cum tanti
corsair che sono sopra il mare bisognerà esser ben in ordine*'.[36] In 1530 and
1531 Charles V and Andrea Doria established the routine of patrol and
skirmish around the islands.[37] In 1540, 55 Christian galleys set out to
clear the seas of the corsairs, leading to the capture (mentioned above)
of Turgut in waters off Corsica.[38] In 1554 a band of 60 galleys sailed
under Don Sancho de Leyva with the intention of hunting down Turgut
reis, who, having ransomed himself from captivity in Genoa, had
returned to his old ways and was reliably reported to be stationed in
Preveza with his flotilla. The expedition certainly went out with high
hopes ('with our galleys being in such good order that it will allow them
to achieve some good success'), but the usual allegations and
recriminations engulfed the officers on their return 42 days later:
'nothing more was done because everyone looks for his own benefit and
advantage more than for the service of Your Majesty ...'. It travelled no

farther than the cape of Santa Maria – that is, Santa Maria di Leuca, on the tip of the heel of Italy – before heading back to Messina on account of the shortage of provisions.[39] In January 1556, 14 galleys *muy buen en orden* were sent on a patrol of Sardinia, Corsica and Mallorca en route to Catalonia.[40] In 1559 galleys were sent from Genoa to accompany the squadron coming from Spain to Italy; together they were to run along the coasts to clear them of corsairs.[41]

In the wake of the disaster at Djerba, Philip II circulated plans to maintain 100 galleys on a permanent basis. He had a very clear idea about how his fleet should be established. 'Although I see how important this is for the good of my kingdoms and to attack the enemies of the faith, it is necessary first to look at the order and form by which we are to maintain them. They should be very well paid for, as if this is not the case we will not achieve the end that we are aiming for.'[42] The principle underlying the royal armada was that there was no point in having galleys if they were not *en buen orden*. This precept or conclusion was largely determined by the characteristics of the enemy. In March 1562 Doria presented a sober assessment of the balance of power on the seas, in which the Ottoman enemy enjoyed a marked advantage. The Ottomans might attack La Goleta or Malta, and thus make things more difficult for Sicily. Nevertheless, he would be able to gather 80 or so galleys in Messina and he expressed confidence in them ('I do not doubt that there might come a chance to do some great service'). On the other hand, if there was no prospect of an enemy attack then the best deployment of the galleys would be to divide them into two bands and to sweep the home seas for corsairs, as there would be about 60 privateering ships from Algiers, Tripoli and Djerba to pursue: 'For this it would also be necessary that Your Majesty ask for the galleys of your confederates, as it would be a better [to send out] reinforced galleys rather than ones that are not good and spoilt.'[43] The King sent out instructions couched in precisely these terms for the summer expeditions of 1562, 1563 and 1564, the aim being (in Sancho de Leyva's words) 'to destroy the corsairs, who increase in such a way that there will not be a little work in it, and if we delay it then there will be more still'.[44] Everyone – even the Grand Master of Malta – was in agreement about the wisdom of this policy, which was undertaken in the very service of God.[45] This enthusiasm did not, however, prevent the Hospitallers from sending their galleys out into the Levant in September 1562 on the grounds that Doria had been delayed and that they had received intelligence of a rich prize.[46]

In 1566 the Count of Altamira, in command of a band of royal galleys, took eight privateering ships during his passage to Italy, capturing more than 300 Turks and two of the best ships in Algiers. The high-admiral, Toledo, addressed the issue of whether it would be wise to strangle the two *reis* or captains, 'as if this is done it could result in very great damage to the important persons who are captive' in Algiers.[47] In March of the following year the King endorsed Toledo's plans to run the seas with a band of galleys on the way down to La Goleta; it would be a major success, he added, to intercept the ten galiots that were said to be heading from Constantinople to Algiers.[48] In the summer of 1567 Doria was one of the commanders of a band of 50 galleys that swept the western Mediterranean from the Balearics to Gibraltar and captured seven galiots. For the rest of his life he retained an enduring sense of pride in his actions in this year; indeed, in his mind the decade later came to assume the glow of a sort of golden age of galley warfare, one which he could cite and refer back to in order to lament circumstances, conditions and colleagues in the 1580s and 1590s.[49] His later recollection seems to have overlooked, however, that crews of six of the seven enemy craft escaped after running their ships aground in North Africa. At the time the King was sanguine about this missed opportunity ('nothing else could have been done') and pleased to hear about the many Christians who had been freed.[50] It was also a profitable year for the Christians in the Tyrrhenian, as four galiots were captured in the seas off the Papal States.[51] In May 1569 a band of galleys was sent to sweep the Tyrrhenian Sea while Spanish infantry was marched to Genoa from Milan (Doria, incidentally, took advantage of this window of opportunity to recharge his batteries at the baths of Lucca).[52] The Genoese sought to send out similar patrols every year, as they always enjoyed a good chance of success.[53]

A memorial prepared by the government of the Papal States at the time of Lepanto began with the premise that the overall interests of the

Holy See and the Catholic Monarchy must be different to those of the Republic of St Mark, as the difficulties in navigation of the Mediterranean lay entirely in the actions of the corsairs of Barbary.[54] This was music to Habsburg ears, although it should be added that the passage was probably designed to give hope to the King that the pirate 'nests' might be seized during the campaigns organised and led by the Holy League. In the spring of 1571 the King issued instructions to his captains general in Naples and Sicily that they were to lead the usual patrols for corsairs; he added, in a curious aside, that the squadron of Sicily might proceed as far as Genoa.[55] In the dramatic summer of 1572 Doria remained in Messina with a band of 20 or so galleys and 9,000 troops when Don John ventured to Corfu to meet up with the main body of the fleet of the Holy League. For a brief moment the destiny of civilisations seemed to hang in the balance. But amidst the fevered excitement, as cardinals dreamed of the re-conquest of Constantinople and, perhaps, even of Jerusalem itself, there was one man who was not going to let his dreams run away with him. The Prince of Melfi admitted that, given that the conservation of the fleet must always be the principal concern, he could envisage nothing better than to sweep the coast and islands of Italy. The King later penned a letter to Doria in which he averred that Venice and His Holiness must understand that 'what was done was undertaken with the intention of cleansing the seas and chasing corsairs, which is for the common good of all'.[56]

Deviations from this basic plan were seldom successful, in part because they greatly exacerbated jealousies within the Christian high command. Towards the end of the campaigning season in 1575 Don John of Austria advanced the plan to divide the fleet into three squadrons (one was to venture into the Levant under Santa Cruz; one was to head towards North Africa under Don Juan de Cardona; one was to sweep the waters around the islands under Doria). Previously the King had issued more conventional instructions, having stipulated that a squadron was to sail in the waters near Genoa to give heart to the 'old nobles' (the pro-Habsburg faction) within the Republic. At news of Don John's revised proposal acrimony broke out.[57] Objections were raised on the grounds that Santa Cruz was to take all of the veteran soldiers on his galleys and would likely obtain 200,000 ducats from the expedition. Taken aback at this criticism, Don John penned a long and windy justification which concluded with a plea to be give the authority to serve and a warning that one day catastrophe might occur because of the rivalry between separate ministers of the crown.

In 1585 and 1589, once again, the King and his Genoese admiral thought along exactly the old lines: if there was news – or even a rumour – of an enemy fleet then the Catholic Armada was to congregate in Messina; if not, 'it would be best for the galleys to be divided up into squadrons to cleanse the seas, to guard the coasts and to chase the corsairs'.[58] So beneficial was the summer patrol *en corso* that in 1592 Doria was willing to send out the squadron 'without soldiers' in order to exercise his squadrons; in doing so he was taking a calculated risk, judging that the damage done to them by being inactive over the summer outweighed the potential threat to them on the seas.[59] Unfortunately they returned with only one brigantine carrying just 21 Moors.[60] This sort of gamble would not have been taken a generation earlier, when the North African corsairs ruled the waves.[61]

Exercise was therefore at least as important for the galley as financial investment: or, rather, the need for investment was so closely tied into the requirements of summer exercise and winter rest that the three can hardly be separated or isolated from each other. At the end of 1605 Benavente made the prevalence of 'new' oarsmen aboard the Ottoman fleet the central plank in his policy proposal for the coming years: he argued that the Catholic King should leave the Ottoman fleet unmolested. On the basis that no forces could be diverted from the war in Flanders, he argued that the best way to proceed would be to continue to exercise and increase the number of the Monarchy's galleys by deploying them *en corso* in the western Mediterranean, only venturing into the Levant 'from time to time'. The Turk, not being immediately or directly provoked, would allow his navy to stultify and decline. When, at some point in the future, Philip III decided to deploy the full force of his arms in the Mediterranean, he would do so with a healthy and efficient galley fleet and, moreover, a debilitated and unprepared adversary.[62] It was interesting that Benavente arrived in December 1605 at a conclusion which, in practical terms, Doria and Philip II had reached many decades previously.[63]

At first sight, the *galera en buen orden* took from governments much more than it offered them. Its demands were great and its limitations serious: it was prone to deteriorate very quickly; and it certainly had to be used very sparingly. Given these restrictions, the principal objectives of its commander could be said to have been to sustain it at an equivalent level from one year to the next. The high-grade or reinforced galley was, in many respects, a means of deterrence rather than a tool of war: it was valued not simply because of what it did, but because of what it allowed others to do – to conduct trade over the seas or to move men, silver, foods and weapons so that they were employed in the most efficient way on land.

The tension within the Habsburg system – that is the rivalry between the ideals of valour and prudence, between the desire to protect Christendom against its most terrible and dreaded enemy and the imperative to preserve the fleet at all costs – dominated the major campaigns and, indeed, the very way that these campaigns were discussed and remembered. The King alluded to this tension in his instructions of 1560, 1565 and 1572. Yet if the decision to deploy the galleys 'cleaning the coasts' represented the triumph of prudence over reputation, it nevertheless appealed to ideals about hunting and lineage which were persuasive in the European court culture of the day. The exchange of hunting weapons and animals – specifically horses – was an important feature of diplomatic courtesies. The Hospitallers were pledged to send their feudal overlord, the King of Sicily, a hawk each year as tribute.[64] These ceremonial acts and the philosophical or cultural significance attached to hunting were not, however, of any real significance or use to the *capitán general*, whose outlook was dominated by grim practicality.

The corollary between loss and gain in galley warfare accounts for the way in which prestige was so directly attached to material concerns and military success: the loss of men, rowers, equipment and reputation could only result in the strengthening of the enemy and the consequent further debilitation of naval forces and, by extension, economic opportunities and military resources. The first setback, in other words, made it more likely that other, more serious, defeats would follow. Of course, this formula might be applied to nearly all armies and navies in the early modern period. However, it can be claimed that *el corso* transcended the simple considerations of the quest for booty and the elimination or reduction of enemy forces. Within galley warfare there was a perfect symmetry: one year's defeated janissaries and *gente de cabo* were next summer's *chusma*; captured corsairs would directly assist the future apprehension of other Algerian brigantines. Captives became equipment.

The peculiar attraction of *el corso*, and the characteristics of its relationship with and place in the system of Mediterranean galley warfare, lay here. The galley or galiot squadron operated on the assumption that its minimum annual attainment would be to be self-sustaining. As such, galley-based privateering can be seen as a logical extension and evolution of the crusading ethos or *razzia* and *jihad* and a rationale that could be traced back as far as seafaring history itself; it was also a philosophy of deterrence, protection and conservation.

VI

The Royal Armada

In a long letter, addressed to the King, of 5 July 1565, Don García de Toledo described Gian Andrea Doria as a man of vivacity, spirit and intelligence, *'viveza, ánimo y intelligencia'*.[1] Not too many of his contemporaries would have agreed with this judgement, and very few historians have been tempted to do so. The problem in assessing Doria is one of repetition and continuity: his perspectives and concerns altered little from the beginning of his voluminous correspondence, in or around 1560, until his death in 1606. The great events of this period – events over which he presided as the *éminence grise* – had little or no impact upon his advice or outlook. Djerba, Malta, Granada, Cyprus, Lepanto, Navarino, Tunis, Cadiz, Algiers: he approached these events with a single, if not singular, outlook, and their outcome only served to underline how indisputably correct he believed himself always to have been.

The problem in evaluating Doria's assessment of galleys and, beyond this, his understanding of Mediterranean holy war lies in the comparative shallowness of the alternatives. No other commander provided a systematic and thorough assessment to rival that of the Prince of Melfi; those leaders – Don García de Toledo in 1565, Don John in 1571 – who achieved significant successes readily acknowledged their debt to the Genoese admiral-prince. Indeed, in certain significant respects Toledo was even more conservative in outlook than was the Prince of Melfi. Philip II was clearly convinced by Doria and repeatedly approved of his tactical decisions; the King admired his seamanship (his 'art and diligence') and implemented plans based upon his strategic assessment, unchanging as it was.[2] If Philip III was distinctly underwhelmed by the Genoese's leadership of the 1601 campaign to Algiers then the operations conducted after this point (the expulsion of the Moriscos; the stealth missions into the Levant in 1604, 1605, 1614 and 1619; the seizure of Larache in 1610 and Mamora in 1614) were characterised by principles very similar, if not identical, to those of the Genoese *capitán general del mar Mediterráneo*. And in fairness to Doria it should be pointed out that at the dawn of the seventeenth century he had provided over 40 years of continual service. Few figures of this or, indeed, any other age boasted a comparable record of service. Retirement was long overdue.

Doria frequently referred to the long lineage of his complaints. He expressed exasperation that problems which should have been so easily resolved were allowed to fester, year after year, without remedy. Indeed so repetitive and frequent was his grumbling that at times he apologised for it; on at least one occasion even Philip II responded with irony.[3] The tone of his many complaints sometimes suggested that the Prince of Melfi was perhaps conscious of the way that he, as a historical figure, would be defined by them. Some of his letters present glimpses of a life on shore which, if not exactly one of harassment, was at least marked by constant irritation: his debts were mentioned many times and his creditors loom in the shadows. At points he gave free vent to his deepest frustrations, alluding to some sort of conspiracy against his person; these moments hinted at a troubled demeanour beneath the rather prickly and superior façade.[4] Doria was given to portraying himself as a man of duty who was unable to support the basic costs of his household, let alone his galleys, well armed though they had always been.[5] While it is difficult to imagine the Prince of Melfi, Councillor of State, victor of Lepanto and (after 1584) Captain General of the Mediterranean Sea, as a sort of Dickensian figure of the *Cinquecento*, a seafaring spendthrift pursued around Genoa by a gang of debt-collectors, then it is clear that he felt that he deserved better. And perhaps, in truth, he did.

His colleagues and peers can hardly be said to have escaped very similar predicaments, although the Prince of Melfi might have insisted that the problems that he encountered were of a unique historical gravity. The surviving correspondence of Andrea Doria is characterised by complaints almost identical in nature to those that would flow from his desk over the next half-century.[6] Getting grain from the Viceroy of Sicily was one of the great chores of the House of Doria in the 1550s and following decades. It was no easier to extract monies from the King.[7] In his last years Andrea Doria reflected that after 30 years of Habsburg service he did not want to be compelled to abandon the galleys by his debts.[8] His finances were exhausted, as were his ships: 'And in times of need, friends cannot be found', *'et amici nel tempo de bisogni no se ne trovano'*.[9] In December 1557 Andrea Doria stated that the galleys had not enjoyed an hour's rest in the previous four years and that his debts were spiralling exponentially. As was so often the case, this complaint fed into another: there had been high prices in Italy throughout this period because of the 'extreme sterility', *'una carestia estrema in tutti i paesi et luoghi d'Italia'*.[10] In late June 1559, as the galleys prepared for the Tripoli expedition, Andrea Doria once again wrote to the King reiterating his poverty and financial exhaustion, 'with all of my credit lost', and with no means of supporting himself or his galleys.[11] A few weeks later he presented a bleak memorial to the King: it began by stating that his galleys had sailed throughout the previous eight years in both winter and summer, before moving on to list a plethora of problems which had led him to pawn (*empeñar*) his furniture and silver 'so that [I] should never fail in any service of Your Majesty'.[12] In April 1560 he stated that his galleys had not enjoyed one day's rest in the previous 12 months: 'Your Majesty must consider how much it has cost me to support 1,400 men, aside from the *chusma*.'[13]

In his twilight years Gian Andrea Doria portrayed the 1550s and 1560s as a sort of golden age of galley administration, a depiction which can be easily and quickly contradicted by the letters that both he and Andrea Doria wrote in these years.[14] In November 1564 he complained that his galleys were exhausted and would not be of service; the oarsmen were sick and a period of rest was desperately needed. His flotilla had always shouldered the lion's share of the work, while the other royal squadrons enjoyed a much lighter workload. He himself had not been paid and consequently would not have had the money to eat had the Republic of Genoa not sold him some foodstuffs on credit.[15] Professor Thompson found that the government based in Madrid ended up owing vast sums of money to the house of Doria; similarly gargantuan amounts were due to some of the other Genoese *asentistas*.[16]

The parallels between the lives of Andrea Doria and his successor as Prince of Melfi were uncanny: the younger man can hardly have been unaware of them. Their careers elicit a profound sense of repetition. The decision made by Gian Andrea Doria in September 1570 was eerily similar to the one that Andrea Doria had made at the same point of the year in 1537. In 1554 Sancho de Leyva stated without reservation that Prince Doria's galleys were not in good order and he was so old that he lacked the strength necessary for command, '*ya de tanta edad que le faltan las fuerzas*'.[17] Four decades later the Count of Olivares made almost identical complaints of Gian Andrea Doria.[18] Other statesmen of the time came very close to the same conclusion.[19] Even the characters of the two princes of Melfi were cut from the same cloth. William Robertson's fine description of Andrea Doria is only a fraction away from the spirit of the man found in Rafael Vargas-Hidalgo's vast collection of Gian Andrea Doria's correspondence: 'a stranger to the arts of submission or flattery necessary in courts, but conscious, at the same time, of his own merit and importance, he always offered his advice with freedom, and often proffered his complaints and remonstrances with boldness'.[20]

The careers of both Andrea Doria and Gian Andrea Doria were characterised and defined by their very prominence as, on the one hand, leading ministers and representatives of a monarchy dedicated to the defence of Christendom against its greatest enemy and, on the other, as businessmen whose fortunes were based upon the preservation and steady improvement of the fleet of expensive, fragile warships. In their more extreme moments they veered between a sense of utter resignation and a barely concealed conviction of superiority: whether they truly felt what these words expressed, or simply used melodramatic expression as a way of highlighting their oft-repeated grievances, is open to interpretation. It has often been said that both men were caught between the ideals of chivalry and the practicalities of the businessman; within their own correspondence the template of the heroic individual clashed with a profound sense that the impact and role of any one man was drastically curtailed by the tactical and technical demands of running a fleet of galleys. Gian Andrea Doria might perhaps have objected here that any assessment of his role in purely naval terms overlooked the vital importance of the flotillas as the bridge between Spain and Italy: the preservation of the armada, he might have argued, *was* the very service of God. If he followed the course of greatest circumspection it was because there was no other way of uniting Cadiz and Naples, Genoa (strictly speaking, Finale Ligure) and Valetta, Messina and Seville.

Needless to say, at every stage the Prudent King endorsed this *política de prudencia*, curtailing all risks and providing instructions that specified how, where, why and when the galleys could be sailed. Often the royal instructions were the direct consequence of Doria's advice: if the two men thought as one it was because of their adherence to the same set of simple, but rigorous, principles. The war galley, which was driven by the most collective of efforts, also produced a sort of common outlook or mentality, one which was all but immune to change, challenge or innovation. In years when the royal galleys operated with the Venetian squadrons as part of the fleet of the Holy League both Andrea Doria and Gian Andrea Doria served as lightning conductors for anger and accusations which, in truth, might justifiably have been directed against Charles V or Philip II themselves.

While both Andrea Doria and Gian Andrea Doria were peculiarly vulnerable to criticism arising from the contradiction between worldly prudence and heavenly zeal, the other captains general were caught in a very similar paradox. In mid-August 1565 Don García de Toledo envisaged leaving this world in a blaze of glory, fighting the enemy on Malta. There was a chance that 'I might be killed in some misfortune' and 'His Majesty would lose me from his service'. He would remain humble and continue to define himself by his actions: 'And in these times I believe this might be beneficial, as what matters is to secure the present, as in the future there will be someone else to govern, and perhaps to do so better than I.'[21] These were heady sentiments, but any assessment of them must take into account that the King had issued him with detailed and unequivocal instructions to safeguard his person – indeed Toledo later pointed out to colleagues that the King had 'explicitly and specifically' ordered him not to remain on Malta with them.[22] What this explanation did for morale is not known. At other points he employed the messianic rhetoric in order to address very worldly concerns: 'God, Our Lord, knows that if I could remedy this problem with my own blood, I would gladly do so in order to serve Your Majesty'. He was, of course, referring to the impossibility of securing monies from the viceroy of Naples.[23] A generation later, in 1593, Don Pedro de Toledo, captain general of the galleys of Naples, concluded a long complaint about the poor condition of his squadron with a request that he be given absolute authority to run it; if he was not to be granted this concession, he begged for a licence to retire: 'for although it is what I most desire to serve Your Majesty in any occupation whatsoever in which I can venture my life, in this matter, in which honour is involved, it would not be mine to value it more than any other thing'. Typically for a captain general, this grand sentiment immediately preceded a reminder of the need for a period of reform and recuperation in which the royal purse strings would be loosened.[24] Other figures combined grand rhetoric with much more earthly concerns. 'So much do I want to increase this squadron of galleys,' stated Feria, the Viceroy of Sicily in 1604, 'that I would even give the blood of my arms if it were necessary.'[25] The letter went on to emphasise the need to capture slaves; it would be remiss to fail to point out that it was penned at a time when Philip III was attempting to clamp down on the viceroy's sponsorship of a community of corsairs. It seems highly likely, therefore, that whatever his rhetorical somersaults, Feria very much envisaged others spilling their blood to arm the squadron.

In December 1614 Osuna struck a similar note, asking that the King either send him infantry with which to defend Sicily or allow him to retire and 'I will put myself in two galleys and a galleon that I have and will go to face the armada of the Turk in order to die an honourable death ...'[26] Grand rhetorical constructions therefore served as a cloak for more direct, and worldly, concerns. This perspective corroborates arguments advanced by Professor R.A. Stradling. He has pointed out that 'the Spanish system and its policy-decisions were not in any immediate sense dependent on conventional economic criteria, and usually functioned without significant reference to their logic'. The falling-off of silver receipts in the 1640s 'did not in practice, drastically affect the monarchy's ability to wage war'.[27] In many ways this thesis is triumphantly vindicated by the history of the galleys. Complaints about the overall financial plight of the Monarchy – the exhaustion of the kingdoms; the impossibility of wringing another ducat from the depleted treasuries or over-extended lines of credit; the physical and emotional exhaustion of the chief ministers and, indeed, of His Holy Royal Catholic Majesty – can be traced back to the 1530s.[28]

The difficulty in assessing the financial health of the fleet lies in two areas: first, that one complaint seamlessly merged into another – almost always the mention of one problem led to an entire chain of laments, recriminations and proposals for reform; second, the fact that, true to the Stradling paradigm, the plethora of complaints greatly outnumbered the positive assessments or records of payments and, yet the galleys sailed. Sometimes they did so in spite of royal instructions, as in October 1572 Don John of Austria had to admit that he had been forced to ignore orders not to borrow money in order to mobilise the fleet.[29] Money also presented a profound problem for the *capitán general del mar Mediterráneo* during his attempt to organise the defence of Tunis and La Goleta in 1574.[30]

At this juncture the historian has to confront the problem of dishonesty, which could be found on all sides: the kings, presumably, knew that the contracts left a healthy margin of profit for the businessmen and so took the myriad complaints with more than a pinch of salt; the contractors knew that, however often they threatened to leave service, there would always be someone else willing to pick up the reins.

There was, of course, an administrative reality beneath these rhetorical exercises, a history of missed opportunities that suggested that with just a little additional foresight a great deal more might have been achieved. An insight into the many complex issues and factors that affected the health of the fleet can be found in discussions held in 1589. Philip II requested of Doria a list of areas requiring adjustment and received by return post a breathless catalogue of abuses and their remedies. Both ailments and solutions must have been thoroughly familiar to the King. The pressures and demands in the years leading up to this point had, without doubt, taken a very heavy toll upon the royal squadrons. The best oarsmen had been allocated to the galleasses that had gone to Spain and sailed as part of the Invincible Armada in 1588. The galleys of the Genoese *asentistas* had worked for seven winters without rest, and so it was highly unlikely that their over-burdened owners would sign a new contract when the current agreements expired. The essential requirements of the oared fighting ship – regular funds, vigorous oarsmen, winter rest and summer exercise – were not being met. Part of the problem was administrative: the government needed to coordinate the ferrying of men and money more effectively so that squadrons did not have to wait idly for months in Catalonia or Cartagena. When the squadrons sailed they should carry a good number of veteran soldiers trained in the use of the harquebus, 'the skill that is worth most aboard the galley'. To rectify the shortage of slave oarsmen, the second Marquis of Santa Cruz had recently asked for a licence to attack the Kerkennah islands in conjunction with the galleys of the Knights of St John, whose commander had proposed the expedition. This did not seem a good idea to Doria, as there were no corsairs in the Kerkennah islands, and 'it would be better to capture one hundred Moors at sea than 300 on land'. There were other dangers or potential drawbacks in this sort of mission.

> I have never known that Your Majesty's armada should be occupied in taking villages in Barbary, and it does not seem fitting to the authority and decorum [*decoro*] that this expedition should be undertaken by a large number of galleys, and with a few ships it would be something of a risk. Indeed, employing the royal armada on a raid such as this one might inspire the Turks to do the same with their fleet, as they have discussed this sort of action on occasions; and so, at this junction, and with the galleys of Your

Majesty being in the poor state they are in, it would be the greatest inconvenience to undertake this mission.

It was an emphatic reaffirmation of the simple ideas that had guided Doria throughout his career. The best policy, he reiterated, was for the galley squadrons to be employed in defensive patrols to try to capture the corsair ships 'which infest the coastlines of Your Majesty's kingdoms, as, apart from preventing damage to their coastlines, the men captured aboard these ships are of greater use and service as oarsmen on the [royal] galleys'. But if the Ottoman fleet came out to attack Christendom, the galleys of Spain and Italy would not be enough to prevent the infidels from 'doing the greatest damage'.[31]

The background to this letter provides an interesting context. Previously Doria had refused to give Don Pedro de Toledo, fifth Marquis of Villafranca and captain general of the galleys of Naples, a licence to raid the Kerkennah islands. Indeed he went further than this, and set a number of limitations on any *corso* expedition undertaken by Villafranca. In March 1588 the King approved of this decision.[32] By this point the relationship between Doria and Villafranca had collapsed, never to recover. Yet just a few months later the Genoese backtracked. Assessing a proposal for a raid made by Santa Cruz, he advised Philip II that 'the shortage of slaves is so great that we should organise a raid in the lands of Moors'.[33] His endorsement of this sort of campaign was unique and may be attributed to the strong friendship that he had struck up with Santa Cruz during their joint patrol of the southern seas in 1588.

From the 1560s – even, indeed, from the 1530s – the danger for the royal armada lay in the way that the secondary, and more rudimentary, function of the ships – to unite Spain with its fiefs in Italy – was steadily overtaking their primary or chivalric purpose, to serve as the scourge of the infidel enemies of Christendom. This inevitably involved a high degree of wastage, needlessly sacrificing men in the winter and, by extension, passing up summer hunting opportunities.[34] Consequently, the galleys were seldom in the order that was 'desired' or 'necessary'. The mistake made by Andrea Doria after the capture of Tunis in 1535 was to send no more than 14 galleys 'and these in very poor order' in pursuit of

Barbarossa. The corsair escaped and subsequently raided the Balearics before settling in Algiers.[35] The galleys under the Genoese captain general were not impressive in 1550, being short of at least 1,000 men.[36]

There was a routine to these complaints, a sense of inevitability to them. From the 1530s there had been allegations that the galleys of Naples were not only disproportionately costly but also deficient and not as shipshape as those of the other squadrons. Such observations inevitably fed strong rivalries; the fractious relationship that Andrea Doria had with Don Pedro de Toledo, second Marquis of Villafranca and Viceroy of Naples (1532–1553), was very similar in tone to the one that his successor as Prince of Melfi maintained with the fifth Marquis of Villafranca.[37] The Genoese contractors tended to complain that they were at a disadvantage in comparison with the captains general of the squadrons of southern Italy, who received regular payments directly from the chancelleries of Naples and Sicily. Gian Andrea Doria was given to asserting that the Genoese flotilla was by far the most cost-effective.[38] The squadrons of galleys found themselves in competition for oarsmen and, to a lesser degree, for biscuit, wheat, export licences and other resources.[39] The rivalry for men, assets and payments sometimes led to bitter exchanges. Even small advantages could cause resentment.[40] Jealousies were seldom too far beneath the surface; it is tempting to argue that a degree of social tension can be found in these rivalries, in that collaboration aboard the fleet quite often obliged scions of the grandest Spanish houses to serve with – and sometimes under – Genoese contractors of relatively modest lineage. The principal problem with this line of argument is that the figure most convinced by the tenets of the *política de prudencia* was the King himself.

Each and every captain general sought to underline his own achievements, devotion and – if he could legitimately include it in a complaint about biscuit or awnings – his ancient and unbroken lineage, the immemorial services of his predecessors, his willingness to lay down his life in the service of His Catholic Majesty; none overlooked or omitted the numerous shortages and deficiencies that he faced or the manifold advantages enjoyed by his colleagues and rivals in Genoa or Sanlúcar de Barrameda. 'It is impossible to describe or imagine the condition in which I found the fleet,' complained Don García de Toledo, appointed Captain General of the Mediterranean Sea in 1564.[41] In February 1565, he reiterated his exasperation at the demands made of the fleet.[42] Yet the reform of the galleys was, he averred, a fool's errand. He subsequently claimed that when first offered this position he was minded to decline it, even though it was the greatest office bestowed by the king. The officials, selfish and corrupt men, bitterly resented any effort to correct them; they enjoyed a free rein to pilfer from the royal treasury and to employ the galleys for commerce. 'Your Majesty can be certain that the majority of the galleys destroyed at Djerba were lost for this reason. They carried a great load of olive oil and other merchandise, and consequently could not exert force at the oar' when it was needed.[43] So was the defeat at Djerba really caused by capitalism? The assessment of Toledo was clearly influenced by his desire to portray the armada on his arrival as a den of iniquity – and, by direct inference, to underline exactly how exceptional his reparatory efforts had been. The document might, then, be said to tell us as much about Toledo as about the armada, in that the very rationale of much of his correspondence functioned upon the idea that the armada required long-term husbandry and could not be suddenly improved in short periods of time.

The judgement must always rest on a degree of comparison, as the laments made by the two Doria admirals in the 1550s and early 1560s to an extent support Toledo's complaints. Officials voiced similar grievances – for instance about the misappropriation and misuse of slaves – during these years.[44] The same difficulty in judging the veracity of statements of pessimism clouds other areas. In the 1580s and 1590s Doria constantly complained that his authority as Captain General of the Mediterranean Sea had been seriously diminished, that he enjoyed very little authority in comparison with his predecessors. In turn this merged into his serious misgivings about the failure of discipline aboard the other royal squadrons in Italy.[45] Yet this observation is difficult to substantiate. The correspondence of Toledo from the mid-1560s is replete with similar laments about his diminished status, and in turn (as we have seen) these matters seamlessly merged into serious misgivings about the conduct of his esteemed colleague, the Viceroy of Naples.[46] In

June 1570 Don John himself complained that 'nobody could believe that I can serve with relish [*gusto*], not having the place and authority that a son of such a father and the brother of such a brother should have'.[47] Five years later he warned his half-brother that divisions within the command structure brought about serious difficulties for the Catholic Monarchy and might, one day, precipitate a disaster.[48] His words once again demonstrated that the naval system balanced on a tension between limited resources and grand objectives; the forces of the Catholic Monarchy remained separate and the various commanders were as much rivals as colleagues, and yet collectively they were charged with the defence of the borders of Latin Christendom against its most implacable enemy. Doria had served with distinction in this period and can hardly have been unaware of the tensions that had curtailed the authority of Andrea Doria, Toledo and Don John in the 1550s, 1560s and 1570s. Did he really, then, believe in the substance of his complaints in the 1580s and 1590s? Or were his words simply a means of making a point, of trying to claw back prerogatives from the viceroys?

Whether these tensions were positive or negative in effect was, of course, a question which nobody would have thought of addressing; it seems possible that in the final instance the Habsburg government functioned as well as it did precisely because it had a tendency towards compromise: cooperation and constructive criticism were built into it. Of course major campaigns heightened the tensions within the top rank of statesmen and officials. With rare exceptions, the viceroys in Messina or Naples and the Governor of Milan tended to prioritise their own areas of responsibility. They sometimes gave little thought to the overall needs of the Catholic Monarchy and its quixotic campaigns on behalf of Christendom. Their case was, by inference, that the defence of Calabria, Gaeta, Apulia or Piedmont should be the immediate priority, and that the relief of Malta or Famagusta or the seizure of Tunis were secondary considerations. 'Members of the high command tended to focus on their individual duties in relation to the administration of their respective territories, to the detriment of the general interest of the fleet. This was especially the case when they considered that the armada's demands for provisions stood in conflict with their own responsibilities.'[49] Disputes between the captains general of the Catholic Monarchy were features of nearly every major expedition. In 1565 and 1566 Toledo was painfully aware that his actions were being viewed critically in Rome, Naples and Madrid.[50] On 17 June 1570 Doria wrote to the Pope employing the standard rhetorical conventions (kissing his foot, reminding him that 'it has always been the custom of the King to defend Christendom'). He then sent news that the 51 royal galleys would sail to defend the Venetian territories and a promise that 'they will lack for nothing, apart, perhaps, for soldiers' whom the Viceroy of Naples was unwilling to release to him.[51] As Professor Manuel Rivero Rodríguez notes, the loss of Tunis in 1574 was attributed by contemporaries to the enmity existing between Don John and the viceroy of Naples, Cardinal Granvelle.[52] In the sixteenth century few statesmen would allow themselves to be drawn into bitter dispute with the King's half-brother; probably, Granvelle had good cause for his complaints.

Astute ministers knew how to exploit the Catholic Monarchy's overarching duties to their own ends. It is not too much of a simplification to state that Doria took advantage of the arrival of the Ottoman fleet at Malta in 1565 to try to solve his credit problems, which were indeed considerable (continuing a family tradition, he had been forced to sell his silver and pawn his wife's); his political sensitivity was astute, and he certainly won the King's attention.[53] He spent much of 1570 playing a similar game. As Professor Rafael Vargas-Hidalgo has shown, he set about trying to sell his galleys to the Crown in 1571 – in other words, to gain an improvement in his terms of service at precisely the moment when his value to the Monarchy was most evident. His plan was thwarted by the King's astute decision to let it be known that the galleys, once purchased, would be given *por asiento* to Nicolas Grimaldi, one of Doria's principal rivals.[54]

It is clear that even Philip II himself knew how to underline the failings of his fleet in order to stave off calls for aggressive expeditions and to appeal effectively for funds. In July 1568 he expressed his disappointment to the papal ambassador or nuncio, Castagna, that his armada had not been in the sort of shape that would allow it 'to pass into the Levant to make the Turk live in fear' ('*dare una passata per le marine per far paura al Turco*'). However, he promised that shortly it would be in shape to do so.[55] It would be difficult, however, to reconcile this statement with the instructions sent to his officers, although, as we shall see, the King was considering the conquest and destruction of Tripoli (Chapter IX). It would be going far too far to accuse His Majesty of deceit on the basis of this one episode, relatively minor in nature, but perhaps it would be fair to conclude that he made a very sharp distinction between his general ambitions and his immediate priorities.

Galley warfare seldom allowed its participants to think beyond their immediate priorities; to do so was to fall into the trap of hubris. If the King or his ministers made too many grand claims for the royal armada, then in Rome thoughts would inevitably turn to putting the Grand Turk in fear, and an invasion of the Levant represented the precise opposite of the Catholic Monarchy's overriding policy of constructive deterrence. The negative descriptions of the fleet – the plethora of laments, grievances and criticism – cannot therefore be read as a simple record of military deficiency, financial insolvency or administrative chaos. A sort of rugged pessimism was, more or less, what was expected of the viceroy, captain general or contractor, whose correspondence was governed by the principle that they would be foolish to keep their complaints to themselves. This line of analysis – and this line alone – can resolve what is, on the face of it, a perplexing contradiction at the heart of the correspondence, the combination of deep pessimism and bullish confidence that so characterised the outlook of the Habsburg monarchs and their *capitanes generales* in years such as 1538, 1565, 1572, 1596 and 1601.

If admirals complained bitterly about the burdens, restrictions, injustices and shortages that they endured, then they nearly always asserted the superiority of their squadron over those of their direct rivals. 'It appeared to me,' Doria calmly informed His Catholic Majesty on 8 September 1565, 'that no one could serve better than I.'[56] His many complaints about the exhaustion of his squadron sat uncomfortably next to his reminder to the King of 'how well my galleys have always been armed'.[57] 'My intuition,' he reminded the King on 24 August 1572, 'has been proved good, as it always will be.'[58] Other captains general were no less confident or assertive. 'My services are not,' opined de Vega in 1551, 'inferior to those of others of my time.'[59] 'In the end,' wrote Don Sancho de Leyva on 8 September 1565, 'the relief [of Malta] was done in the very way that I proposed to Your Majesty in my letter from Palamós.' Here, clearly, was a man who was not plagued by self-doubt: 'If my advice had been listened to and followed from the very beginning, we would have saved ourselves a month and a half and excused many great costs, and far fewer knights and men would have died at Malta.' His only consolation lay in the thought that it was better that his peers had, eventually, come to their senses and employed his proposal.[60] In August 1570 the Marquis of Santa Cruz declared that his galleys would prove themselves to be the best in the Christian fleet in 1570; this may not have been too far from the truth, as his flagship was certainly a fine racer.[61]

Given the rivalries between the captains general, the not-infrequent complaints about approaching administrative chaos and the common laments about impending financial collapse, it would be easy to portray the life of the royal armada in the bleakest terms. The counterbalance to this pessimism must be that, however much they complained about each other or their conditions of service, the officials seldom failed to express a sense of collective superiority. Don García de Toledo's serious complaints about the organisation of the fleet on his appointment as *capitán general del mar* in 1564 have already been mentioned; yet these qualms did not prevent him from expressing absolute certitude in the capacity of 84 or so royal galleys to defeat an Ottoman fleet of comparable dimensions.[62] As we have seen, the King shared this confidence, placing his faith in God and the prudence and diligence of his admirals.[63] One of the paradoxes of 1565 was that la Valette had much greater confidence in the forces under Toledo than did the Captain General of the Mediterranean Sea himself.[64] Again, there was a very real sense that the Grand Master underestimated the enemy. A similar pattern can be discerned in the early 1570s, when Venetian officials could hardly fail to be impressed by the 'order' of the King's fleet, much as at the same time they were infuriated and puzzled by the extraordinary and, to (nearly) all extents and purposes, inexplicable delays that overcame the royal armada.

This is not to deny that Doria, that emblem of prudence, was beset by contradictions. A man who often accused his detractors of knowing nothing of the sea did so by evoking a vast hinterland of knowledge and experience to which he had unique access. Yet this was the very same figure who incessantly elaborated a few simple principles and ascribed all subsequent failures to the ignorance of them. A similar contradiction could be found in his personal qualities and demeanour. A man who presided over the forced labour of thousands of manacled men in the most wretched of conditions clearly felt little if any embarrassment in requesting a licence to retire to the baths at Lucca to cure his ills.[65] He was not a man to suffer in silence. In an extraordinary letter of May 1565 he stated that, should God give him life and allow him to serve that summer, he would return to his homeland to decide upon the manner of his death; at the end of this year he remarked that having 'served all summer' he was so overcome by illness that he 'could give thought to nothing else other than to making a recovery'. He was 25 years old (or thereabouts) at the time.[66] That he saw no anomaly in this attitude or outlook was doubtless in part a consequence of his personal character; it was also, perhaps, a feature of the polarity found in early modern society, particularly in the dockside community of large ports, where rich and poor, privileged and wretched, existed side-by-side to an extent that was remarkable even in an age of contrasts. Again, Andrea Doria emerges as a man caught in similar constraints and contradictions, if perhaps one slightly more conscious of the hardships endured by his crews.[67]

Philip II himself frequently expressed his concerns about the shortage of funds: these complaints, so often voiced to the nuncio or via his ambassador in Rome, were hardly dissimilar in tone or content to the letters addressed to him by his contractors, governors and ambassadors. Typically, they contrasted his volition (*voluntad*) to serve the cause of God with his limited resources, and complained that his poverty and exhaustion would not allow him to continue, much as his only desire was to spend everything he owned in the cause, indeed to lay down his own life for it.[68] Indeed in a truly remarkable letter of July 1570 the papal ambassador Castagna outlined the many financial burdens of the

Catholic Monarchy and drew particular attention to the threat posed to the Indies convoys by Protestant corsairs that year. He warned that the psychological strains might one day prove too much for Philip II: 'not being of a strong complexion, the travails of the mind might one day cause the king some harm'.[69]

Again, the King was caught in the tensions and troubles that affected his senior commanders. Perhaps the greatest contradiction in the mind of Gian Andrea Doria was, on the one hand, to insist upon the historically decisive role of the fleet and yet, in the same breadth, to argue that the options for its deployment were so few and restricted. His outlook, limited or contradictory though it was, permeated the thinking of nearly all of his peers. Again, the King himself was caught in exactly the same quandary. Much as he voiced the need to win reputation and to demonstrate his *voluntad* to serve the Holy See in its unending campaigns in defence of the faith, his priority in formulating a strategy for holy war in the *mare nostrum* centred around the need to avoid misfortune. The rationale of both men was based upon an understanding of the nature of the oared warship, that is to say an awareness of both the vast potential of a high-grade fleet and the enormous difficulty of equipping, maintaining and improving galleys *en buen orden* from one year to the next.

VII

The Shadow of God on Earth

'However important the administration of land affairs,' wrote Lufti Pasha, a sixteenth-century Ottoman statesman and reformer, 'the affairs of the sea are far more important.'[1] Scholars have been unable to decide whether Lufti Pasha's words were an accepted tenet of Ottoman strategy, or an aberration to it. There can be no doubt that the Sublime Porte invested vast amounts of money in its fleet. Professor Daniel Panzac has calculated that the construction and fitting-out of a fleet of 223 galleys at the end of the sixteenth century would have cost roughly three-quarters of the state's entire income.[2]

Western commanders focused their thoughts on the vast human, financial and administrative demands of maintaining a fleet through just one campaigning season, a perspective which served to underline the limits of the offensive potential of the enemy. In a highly rhetorical piece that was clearly designed for public consumption, Pietro Aretino wrote to Francis I beseeching him to conclude a peace treaty with Charles V so that Christendom could resist Süleyman in 1538. Perhaps little faith should be put in a letter so public in nature and so influenced by the rhetorical conventions and the political circumstances of its day. However, it perhaps struck a chord when it evoked the image of the 'grand monster Süleyman, the power of whom scares us more than it actually hurts us'.[3]

Christendom was highly fortified. In a valuable recent study Professor Luis Ribot concludes that the majority of the works of fortification in

Italy were undertaken in the sixteenth century.[4] Liliane Dufour, Antonino Giuffrida and Valentina Favarò have provided detailed accounts of the fortification of Sicily, where new works were begun at Siracusa in 1532, at Palermo in 1535–36 and at Catania in 1542. If Messina and Palermo were quickly 'brought to perfection' the other medieval coastal fortresses were slowly improved, with gun towers ('*torrioni*') being built alongside the old high, thin walls.[5] In Naples, the phases of the fortification programme can be seen as a response to the great campaigns of 1527–28, 1532–34 and 1537.[6] It was the success of this drive that brought about the frustrations of the 1540s and 1550s, when the patience of both Ottoman admirals and French commanders quickly frayed under the pressure of joint actions.[7]

By the same criteria, the limitations of the Christian position were all too obvious. After 1533 the Ottoman armada was, as Professor Murphey has pointed out, usually far larger than its adversary.[8] In conversation with an imperial diplomat in 1535 Henry VIII of England affirmed that 'even if the Turk had lost two or three hundred thousand men, he would not feel it, he was so rich and powerful'.[9] English diplomats found Francis I in jovial mood when he heard of the Venetian submission to the Sublime Porte in the negotiations of 1540:

> He is not inclined to war, nor to assist the Emperor against the Turk; 'and what resistance can the Emperor make against him (the Turk) if his power come to Tunis lacking the Venetians' and the French king's aid?' Andrew Doria has but 40 galleys. The Turk has rigged this year 200 new galleys, 'and what Barbarossa had before I need not to express'. This Venetian news will not be so pleasant to the Emperor.

Francis I, His Most Christian Majesty, had considerable difficulty in disguising his glee at Ottoman operations against Charles V, 'His Catholic Caesarean Majesty'.[10] At the height of the sixteenth-century crusades Cardinal Granvelle analysed the Ottoman threat as being limited by the capacity of the Constantinople fleet to ferry the practically unlimited number of Turks capable of bearing arms, 'for [the Sultan's] strength lies in numbers'.[11] In 1570 this advantage was made manifest. Once the fleet had ferried Selim II's huge army to Cyprus there was little hope for the Venetian fortresses. 'The reasons for our going to Cyprus,' Doria put it in his long and precise dissection of the tactical possibilities of 16 September 1570, 'are founded on the weakest of hopes.'[12] His assessment was based on a number of criteria, but foremost among them was the sheer scale of Ottoman mobilisations on land and sea, which were capable of sending a massive fleet to face the Christians and maintaining the siege of Nicosia.

If the Turk's superiority was obvious in the number of ships rigged, then commanders on both sides recognised that the small squadrons of western galleys were tactically superior to those of the Sublime Porte. In his manifesto setting out the need for reforms Lufti Pasha wrote that '... many of the past sultans have ruled the land, but few have ruled the seas. In the management of naval expeditions the infidel is superior to us.'[13] Ottoman chroniclers referred to the Christian galleys as being 'as agile as frogs' in sea battles, but believed that Christendom possessed inferior soldiers and was therefore incapable of land warfare.[14] In 1552 the Imperial Council warned the Kapudan Pasha to beware the tricks and ruses of the Christians; this, like other instructions, betrayed a lack of confidence in 'the science of the seas'.[15] This view has been confirmed by a pivotal paper by Professor Imber, who underlines 'the abundance of materials, money and men, which allowed the rapid construction of new fleets' but stresses that the armada of Süleyman tended to be of a lower calibre, and dismissed as such.[16]

For most of the period under study the Christians faced considerable perils in sailing through their own seas. The operational imperative was determined by the threat from the corsairs of Algiers, Tunis, Djerba and Tripoli. An excellent recent paper by Aurelio Espinosa has documented the many maritime problems faced by the government of Charles V in the 1520s and 1530s. The need to run men, biscuit, money and correspondence over to its fortified outposts in North Africa, and to maintain contact with the imperial armies in Italy, proved a recurring headache to the Emperor and his ministers in Spain.[17] In 1552 and 1553 Salah *reis*, based in Algiers, was able to sail at the head of 40 vessels including galleys, galiots and brigantines.[18] There were 32 oared ships in Algiers in 1563; in October 28–30 ships under Turgut sailed up and down the coasts of southern Italy.[19] Indeed the Viceroy of Sicily had taken every precaution when, earlier in that year, he had sent out the squadron on a tour. His thinking was shaped by the dimensions of the enemy, the observation that the fortunes of the island's galleys over the previous years had been 'so contrary' and the presence of the Hospitaller knights, who might not offer the wisest counsel.[20] Throughout the 1560s Doria and Toledo exercised considerable caution before venturing beyond the harbour walls of Genoa or Messina, in part because of their shortage of troops, in part because of the 25 or so high-grade galiots that put out from Algiers alone.[21] There was, as ever, a hint of exaggeration and political opportunism in these letters of caution and complaint, which proceeded to rehearse the usual grievances and demands for money, foodstuffs and infantry; on the other hand, the dimensions of the privateering threat were remarkable by any contemporary standards. In 1565 the North African reis, led by Turgut reis and the governor general (beylerbeyi) of Algiers (Cezayr-i Garb), arrived at Malta with 50 galleys and 22 galiots. Thirty-four of these came from Algiers alone, although many of them were said to be badly prepared.[22] As a demonstration of his faith in his corsairs Süleyman had entrusted them with helping to maintain the patrols around the besieged island.[23]

The dimensions of the Habsburg fleet were determined by the corsair threat in the western basin of the Mediterranean rather than by the dimensions of the fleet from the Levant. In a survey written in the mid-1550s, Andrea Doria had suggested that at least 80 well-armed galleys were necessary to defend Christendom against the enemy on the seas.[24] After 1580 the privateering menace began to decline. Still, the idea that the Barbary corsairs were worthy military adversaries remained an enduring tenet of Habsburg naval planning. In 1590 Doria described what he believed to be the realistic level of the Monarchy's naval presence in the Mediterranean. His thinking was based on the supposition that the royal squadrons should not be vulnerable to attack from numerically superior corsair flotillas, although he allowed for extenuating logistical and geographical considerations. Spain, he began, was close to Algiers and possessed such a long coastline that it was necessary 'on many occasions to divide the galleys of the kingdom into two bands'; he calculated that 26 to 30 galleys should be regularly maintained, depending upon the availability of *chusma*. In Genoa, where the contract galleys served so well at such little cost, there were currently 17 warships in addition to the *Real*. Given the centrality of this squadron, it being so close to all parts, it was important not to reduce this number. Naples should sustain between 22 and 24 galleys, including two galiots. Sicily required 12 to 14 galleys, again including two galiots. This was a comparatively low number, especially in the light of the island being on the 'frontier' of Barbary. But Doria's reckoning was influenced by the kingdom having so many ports and consequently the facility to attack the corsairs without the royal galleys themselves being exposed to serious danger. Also important was the proximity of Malta, whose powerful vessels could be summoned.[25]

The examination of numbers of ships fitted out in North Africa provides a general context for Christian privateering: throughout the period under study, the practice of *el corso* in the waters of North Africa or the Levant by captains from Trapani or Alicante was a gamble against the odds. For the same reason the deployment of the royal armada was largely determined by the proportions of the enemy: the consideration of the simple number of ships mobilised by the enemy after 1534 was both the cause of this *política de prudencia* and also, in a very specific sense, the principal objective of it. The sea-lanes off Sardinia, Ibiza or Valencia offered the royal galleys rich pickings, and given the intensity of the threat, the impossibility of matching the Turk galley-for-galley and the dangers of navigation, the priority had to be to strengthen the oared flotillas, upon which everything depended. The general strategic panorama – that broad sense of Christendom having adopted a defensive position after 1530 – was clearly expressed in the low-level *guerre de course*.

The vast majority of *chusma* aboard the Sultan's fleet were recruited through the annual levy and were know as the *kürekçi azap*. The system was calibrated according to the demands of the expedition which was about to be undertaken. The oarsmen were paid a salary that was collected from the other households within the community. Muslim oarsmen, incidentally, were paid more than non-Muslims.[26] The *kürekçi azap* were conscripted on the basis of one year's service *en galera*. Given the grim experience of the oarsman in his first year of service, it would be logical to argue that, having served for one campaign *en galera*, very few men would choose to repeat the experience.

A common perception among the western planners was that the military power of the Ottoman Empire was predominantly land-based. The greatest military asset of the Turks remained their cavalry, the *sepahis*, who numbered between 150,000 and 200,000 in the sixteenth century.[27] It was impossible to imagine that the Christians could engage this sort of force in open battle on land. Professor Murphey has persuasively argued that the janissaries and *sepahis* enjoyed terms of employment, regimental discipline and *esprit de corps* that were perhaps superior to those of their Spanish and French equivalents.[28] Whether or not the best of the Sultan's troops were willing to serve on the fleet was another matter. Certainly, at crucial junctures Christian hopes focused on the idea that enemy troops were not of a high quality: one of the hopes expressed by Christian statesmen in 1565 was that around 6,000 or 7,000 veteran infantry (German or Spanish troops) would have a good chance of fighting their way through or around the Ottoman besiegers and reaching the Hospitaller forts.[29] As we have seen, a considerable amount of evidence suggests that at Lepanto the great majority of professional troops were absent from Ali Pasha's fleet, having died, been injured, secured their release or absconded. Concerns about the calibre of marines appear to have been fairly consistently held. Reformers in Constantinople clearly worried about the poor level of training of the soldiers who were available to the navy.[30]

Westerner observers believed that the Ottoman Empire entered into a process of decline after 1580, and they identified the corruption of the warrior ethic as one of the principal causes of this reduction in military effectiveness and political stability.[31] Having said this, it should be added that many reports posted back by ambassadors and agents over previous generations presented the Ottoman court as an institution of peculiar volatility and that previous sultans – specifically Bayazid II (1481–1512) – were taken to be peace-loving in character.[32] The very first Kapudan Pasha, Barbarossa himself, was reported to have been at the centre of fierce rivalries and jealousies.[33] In June 1559 the civil war against one of his sons was said to have brought Süleyman to his knees, the Sultan lamenting that in one hour his son had cost him the reputation he had acquired in the previous 40 years.[34] It was also true that the assessments of Ottoman decline after 1580 were based upon a set of criteria which were often inconsistent, curious or blinkered. In 1604 the empire was widely perceived to be on the point of collapse. The Turk still had, by one calculation, 300,000 men under arms in Persia and Hungary.[35] This was, roughly, about ten times the number of veteran troops found in Philip III's renowned Army of Flanders.

The advantage of the Turk was, then, one of numbers.[36] In July 1537 Andrea Doria passed on what he considered to be reliable and specific intelligence on the enemy: 'The whole fleet does not have forced galleys, except for those of Barbarossa, who has shared out the [spare] 800 Christians that he had among his captains in groups of 20 to 30 ...' Apart from the 40 or so ships entrusted to Barbarossa's 'old captains', the fleet made its way with 'bad oars [and] few mariners, and they can sail only with great difficulty'. It was disintegrating as it moved westwards; 30 or so ships had been left in Constantinople and Gallipoli and a further 20 more had fallen behind the main body of the fleet. In short, there was not a lot for the Christians to fear: 'their navigation thus far has been made with great disorder, in part because these galleys can travel very little under oars, in part because of the bad feeling' between the commanders. Confirmation of these details was to arrive when the Christian fleet took three enemy warships in a skirmish. Aboard these three galleys there were only 50 Turks at the oar, 'the rest being Greeks and Christians of *buena volla*'. On the other hand, these vessels were stocked with ample quantities of provisions and weaponry and their Muslim crews certainly fought ferociously.[37]

Barbarossa's fleet in 1534 carried a total of 24,400 men.[38] Professor Imber's study of the Ottoman registers shows that in 1539 the government was able to raise 23,538 oarsmen for a fleet of about 150 ships.[39] The fleet of 1545, had it sailed, would have been an enormous force; it would appear from the records that the supply of hulls, rather than the provision of oarsmen, was the principal consideration of administrators. (The 100 or so galleys were, incidentally, to be financed from the booty or *gazâ malî* from three previous expeditions.)[40] In March 1556 it was reported that the Kapudan Pasha would sail with 100 or even 200 galleys.[41] Philip II remained optimistic about the possibility of saving Oran, trusting in God, the good diligence of Andrea Doria and the certainty that the enemy armada was armed with volunteers and so was *muy mal en orden*. 'And to this end we charge you to make sure that our galleys go in very good order.'[42] The 70 Ottoman warships sent out in August 1559 were in poor shape and aboard them there were no janissaries or other capable military men, *'gente de facción'*. They had been dispatched 'precipitously' in the hope of impeding the progress of the Catholic Armada.[43] The enemy warships were all, Venetian officials affirmed, very badly armed, *'que estaban todas muy mal armadas'*.[44] In January 1562 there were threats of 150 galleys being put in order for an attack upon La Goleta, a project which, incidentally, was said to have been enthusiastically sponsored by Turgut *reis*.[45] Yet the talk of campaigns of conquest was merely one theme – and, on balance, a marginal one. In his last years it was consistently reported that Süleyman did not have 'a greater nor more cruel enemy than his son', who continually plotted to have him assassinated.[46] In March 1563 there were concerns about Ottoman intentions with regard to Cyprus, but then it was widely believed that the Turk, old and unwell, had resolved not to undertake another campaign on land or sea; the Viziers, moreover, would be handsomely bribed by the Venetian ambassador or *bailo*. There were threats of sending out 100 galleys, 'but it is not known that they have recruited the *chusma* nor equipment, and many are of the opinion that if a fleet goes out it will be no more than 50 galleys to protect the archipelago'.[47] The inference was that the Sultan guarded his reputation as an unvanquished champion of Islam. It was 'the common opinion', reported Medinaceli in February 1563, that Süleyman was keen to preserve his reputation and would not send a major fleet against Christendom while there was peace between France and Spain.[48] There were so few slaves in Constantinople in October 1564 that they would not be enough to equip ten galleys. 'And if the Turk should have to arm, he will take advantage of his subjects as he used to do, and they will send out the orders so soon that we will know of their mobilisation well in advance.' The Sultan, old and unwell, would only do this if he were provoked into a fight.[49]

The first batteries of the assault upon Fort St Elmo were ringing in the ears of Jean Parisot de la Valette when he informed Philip II that all of the oarsmen of the enemy fleet were volunteers, '*que sono tutte armate di bona voglia*'.[50] He had a direct motivation for stressing the inexperience of the Ottoman forces at this juncture – his increasingly desperate need for rescue – and there can be no doubt that, like other Grand Masters of the Order of the Hospital of St John of Jerusalem, he found in reports what his institution needed to see in them; yet his dispatch was consistent with many others before and after the event and, moreover, fell in line with Ottoman sources, which leave no doubt that many of the Sultan's galleys were built and manned specifically for this campaign.[51]

In December 1565 Philip II's spies in Constantinople reported that the officials had counted 30,000 casualties. Was it true, as was reported late in the year, that the Viziers played down the damage done to the armada in Malta, 'as it consisted solely in the loss of men, of which they have a great abundance'? Whatever the losses, preparations were afoot for the next year: 100 galley hulls were to be laid down in the Arsenal.[52] As late as April 1566 Doria was concerned about the ability of the Catholic Monarchy to prepare its positions 'if the enemy fleet comes out as powerful and as promptly as they write'.[53] So the Christian victory at Malta had led nowhere: Ottoman ascendancy – Ottoman numerical superiority – quickly reasserted itself.

But if this was the case, then the traditional failings of the *armada del Turco* were also still evident. The 120 or so galleys of the Sultan's fleet were consistently reported to be in bad shape and the Kapudan Pasha, Piyale Pasha, achieved very little in the Adriatic; his one success that summer lay in occupying, without a fight, the Genoese enclave of Chios.[54] In July 1568 the Ottoman fleet was reported to have arrived at the island a few weeks previously, 'in a very bad way on account of contagion'; six ships had already keeled over. Even with the corsairs from North Africa the most that this fleet could hope to do was 'to come into the seas of Your Majesty to rob, as they know that the royal armada is scattered across the seas'.[55] Towards the end of the season the Ottoman fleet was in Rhodes, 'in such bad condition for men and weapons that 30 galleys in good shape would be enough to destroy them all'. The shoreline of Naples, it seemed, was safe, in part because of the 'good order' of the preparations there.[56]

From time to time a report painted a more positive picture of the enemy. This was the case in the early summer of 1570, when 150 galleys were said to be prepared, two-thirds of them armed with veteran *chusma*.[57] But was this *aviso* reliable? A dispatch from Constantinople of January of this year fell more in line with western expectations. If, it read, the Christian princes were to arm 200 galleys and 30 ships they would certainly defeat the enemy fleet, 'as it is in very bad shape for leadership, *gente de facción*, and troops. This is because the Turks pay no attention to anything other than to send out a great number of ships, placing no weight on the need to arm them as is necessary.'[58] As late as June 1570 there were no more than 30 functioning galleys in the capital; the Viziers were reportedly trying to dissuade the Turk from moving against Cyprus. Perhaps Selim II really had, as some dispatches suggested, been astonished by the refusal of the Republic to surrender the island.[59] On its return to the capital, 30 galleys sailed in to great acclaim during the day; the rest – 100 or so sail – returned under the cover of darkness 'so that no one could see in what bad shape they were in'.[60]

In the year of 'the Naval Battle' another renegade, going by the name of Martín de Morales, reported that the enemy fleet was in fine fettle; on the other hand, his account of his own life contained some curious details.[61] Suffice to say that once again Philip II was confident that his galleys, being in good order and guided by the principles of prudence, would have little difficulty in opposing the fury of the infidel over the coming months.[62]

In 1572 Captain Jacobo de Nicolao counted 160 galleys in Constantinople. But 'the men for them, both for the oar and to fight, was new and not good.'[63] Toledo thought there could be little to fear from 'an armada with new *chusma* and a shortage of mariners'; it was put out that the Kapudan Pasha might venture into the Christian seas, an eventuality which, Toledo averred, was 'more to be desired than feared', as the destruction of what was left of the Sultan's navy was the best possible outcome that year. The enemy fleet would have neither the legs to run nor the arms to fight.[64]

These same patterns continued to recur over the coming decades. It was reported late in 1590 that the Ottomans planned to send out an armada of 200 sail and so needed 40,000 oarsmen; the empire did not need to recruit an army 'because the men of war are paid in normal circumstances'. It would be wrong to dismiss this report out of hand, as a large number of troops (around 7,500 *sepahis*) were available to the fleet in the early 1600s. These regiments were stationed in the 'Province of the Archipelago', the domains governed directly by the high-admiral. On the other hand, an armada mustered with new oarsmen but experienced troops would have certain strengths and weaknesses. The calibre of its officials and leaders was also an issue: the 'Turks have few men who know how to command, and those that do are all renegades. At present they can send out 25 galleys with difficulty.'[65]

The early seventeenth century produced many *avisos* along these lines. In late May 1600 Cigala-*zade* Yusuf Sinan Pasha was waiting for men who had been raised in Anatolia, and when they arrived he would set off with as many as 60 galleys, all of them well armed with troops, and head for the coast of Calabria or, perhaps, for Gozo.[66] Vast numbers of new, fresh oarsmen might be called up by the Sultan. In the autumn of 1613 orders were sent to the Khan of the Crimea for 20,000 peasants to be recruited for the oars.[67] The register of oarsmen raised in 1640 shows that 62,946 households produced 6,634 oarsmen, enough to man around 40 galleys. (The system had been slightly improved after 1600.)[68]

The Ottoman fleet was, therefore, larger in size than the Catholic armada but technically weaker; it was, moreover, manned by *gente nueva* with the result that as the campaigning season progressed its crews were ravaged by disease. Its novice oarsmen fell ill with what reports very often referred to as *el peste*, 'the plague', a blanket description for typhus, consumption and the other ailments that afflicted men at their first exposure to the raw elements while being simultaneously denied many basic forms of hygiene. The fleet of His Catholic Majesty, in contrast, was guided by the principle that its oarsmen were 'old' or experienced; of course, this precept was little more than an operating ideal, and complaints proliferated about the shortage of skilled and hardened oarsmen. Conditions were perhaps not substantially better for the manacled or salaried *chusma* of the squadrons of Christendom, but their capacity to endure hardship and squalor had been raised by the simple but brutal and unforgiving process of exposure and survival. While the Catholic Armada was more or less consistent in terms of the number and calibre of ships available to it over the calendar year, the eastern fleet showed marked variation in number from year to year and throughout the campaigning season itself. True, during the lifetimes of Cervantes and Shakespeare there was a decline in the regular or habitual size of the Ottoman fleet in some years, although this reduction in the numbers of warship was nothing like as steep as has sometimes been suggested (from about 85 in 1568 to around 60 in 1602).[69]

In Rome, Naples and Madrid all plans were predicated upon the inexorable decline of the enemy armada over the summer. Shortly after raiding Ciudadela of Menorca in 1558, the oarsmen of the Ottoman fleet were being decimated by disease, forcing the Kapudan Pasha to head home with 15 or so 'empty galleys'. His journey was predicted to be at least a very uncomfortable one, above all in the Adriatic, which was characterised by violent and unforgiving autumnal storms. The 1559 fleet was, as Braudel says, 'rather the worse for wear' and ventured no further than the Albanian coast. By October it was at the point of collapse with as many as 15,000 deaths (again, a clear exaggeration).[70] Piyale Pasha himself recognised in 1560 that 25 galleys belonging to the fleet of the Christians ('the abject miscreants') could attempt some movement in the 'well guarded lands' at the end of the summer, after the 'august armada' had returned to Constantinople.[71]

'What I desire,' wrote Francisco de Eraso from Madrid in early July 1565, 'is that God may have given some illness or shortage of food and water in the enemy camp which will force them to raise the siege.' His prayers seem to have been answered: when the Christian relief force finally landed at Malta, its leaders were ordered not to attack the plague-ridden Ottoman camps in order to avoid contagion. Many captured Turks perished, even those who had suffered no injury or flesh wound.[72]

Another crucial feature of the Ottoman naval system was that it was able to lose vast numbers of men without this having any apparent effect upon its capacity to send out another massive fleet in the following year. In July 1532 Barbarossa lost around 35 galleys and galiots in a series of squalls, the most serious of which overtook a raiding party from Algiers near the island of San Antioco, just off Sardinia.[73] The departure of Barbarossa's fleet from Castro and Ugento in 1537 was attributed to the extreme shortages of water and foods and to the 'great mortality' among its men.[74] López de Gómara recorded that the Turks lost 20,000 men and 60 ships in a storm late in 1538; another 37,000 men were said to have been killed at the siege of Castilnuovo di Cattaro in the following year.[75] Some 15 ships were lost in 1546, while the losses in 1558 and 1565 have already been mentioned.[76] The official Christian accounts of Lepanto speak of the death or capture of 35,000 Turks, while the Ottoman sources gave the more realistic figure of 20,000 dead – this number referred specifically to the casualties at the naval battle, as opposed to the vast lost of manpower sustained at Nicosia and Famagusta in the previous 14 or 15 months.[77] Braudel cites reports that the Ottomans lost 15,000 oarsmen and troops and a total of 50,000 men at Tunis in 1574.[78]

These grim descriptions and statistics – doubtlessly inflated – should not detract from the undeniable observation that the Turk had more galleys and fighting men and, logically, his ministers expressed frustration that their Christian opponents hid behind fortresses and refused to give battle on the seas unless it was on their terms. In his debriefing in August 1571 the renegade Morales reported that the Ottoman high command had been boasting that 'the Christians are chickens [gallinas] who would not dare to appear before us'.[79] The taunt had a ring of truth to it and was repeated in later Turkish accounts of the campaign.[80] On the other hand, Ali Pasha could hardly have been surprised by the cautious deployment of the fleet of the Holy League. In 1572 one of Philip II's officials was critical of the failed Venetian attempt to engage the enemy near Cerigo in early August. A better tactic would have been to keep the Ottoman armada in isolation: 'as if they wait, as they must, then the enemy armada will be consumed [by disease] this year even more than it was last summer'.[81]

One of the most pronounced features of the Ottoman threat was that it was inherently unpredictable. If the western fleet required years of preparation and prudent husbandry, the *armada del Turco* could emerge over one winter of intense activity organised from Constantinople. The efforts in Constantinople to rebuild the fleet and replenish its crews in the aftermath of the campaigns of 1537 and 1538 must have been very considerable, in the latter case perhaps even comparable with the reconstruction after Lepanto.[82] In 1565 and 1570 a fleet emerged with little warning; on both occasions the call to the *kürekçi azap* compensated for a few years of comparative inactivity in the Arsenal of Constantinople.[83] In June and July 1572 Marc'Antonio Colonna could not refrain from expressing his admiration for the 'unimaginable' resurgence of the enemy, and in September – less than a year after Lepanto – Doria was writing with concerns about the vast *armada del Turco* that was promised for *el año que viene*.[84] In 1573 Don John consulted his trusted adviser on the possibility of arming 150 galleys: Toledo replied that even a Christian fleet of these proportions would be purely defensive in nature, it being unable to face the enemy *'en batalla determinada'*.[85]

Of course, such efforts at reconstruction required an intense concentration of discipline, investment and energy over the winter months. A dispatch from December 1569 stated that the workers in the Arsenal clocked in at midnight, 'and so for the great efforts, they send three galleys out each day'. It went on to report that all members of the military orders – *'todos los de la orden militar'* – were being called up to serve.[86] But reports of these bursts of activity reinforced the notion that the Ottoman fleet might present more of a spectacle than a threat; after all, in January 1569 Venice had taken the trouble to inform Philip II's diplomats that the Sublime Porte could arm no more than 130 galleys 'with great difficulty on account of the shortage of seamen', *'con harta dificultad por la falta de gente de mar que tiene'*.[87]

After 1580 the capacity of the Ottomans to build a fleet from scratch was considerably reduced. True to form, Doria repeatedly warned against complacency. He pointed out to Philip III in 1601 that the Turk would be able to assemble a large transport fleet with astonishing speed, as was demonstrated by the reconstruction of the Ottoman armada after 'la batalla naval'.[88] But nearly everyone else believed that the Sultan would need two or even three years to return his armada to the proportions of the 1560s and 1570s. In February 1591 the Ottomans boasted that they would have 200 to 300 galleys ready for the summer of 1592 – a figure which could not be met in two years even with 'extraordinary diligence'.[89] In the wake of the impressively large Ottoman fleet of 1594, the Count of Miranda, Viceroy of Naples, lamented that the efforts this year would make it easier for the Sultan to return next summer with still greater forces.[90] In January 1614 Don Pedro de Toledo, the fifth Marquis of Villafranca, expressed concern and regret that the Turks were now returning their attention to the seas after so many years of neglect. He estimated that this year they would be able to gather 150 galleys – not enough to inflict serious damage on Christendom, 'but next year they would do more, and the third year more still'.[91] In the autumn of that year Osuna, Viceroy of Sicily, presented intelligence reports stating that in *el año que viene* the Ottomans would be able to fit out 82 new galleys to accompany the 75 they had armed that year.[92]

Carl von Clausewitz referred to major battles in the Age of Sail as 'cash transactions'.[93] In galley warfare these monetary transfers affected the powers in very different ways. As we have seen, major setbacks had little or no long-term effect upon the overall Ottoman naval capacity. Sokullu Mehmed Pasha was obviously exaggerating when he claimed in the aftermath of Lepanto that the empire could send out a fleet with sails fashioned of satin and anchors cast of silver, but since 1532 the imperial government had called a new fleet into being in every spring.[94] In the immediate aftermath of *la batalla naval* the Duke of Alba wrote that Venice must understand that Ottoman power could not be destroyed in one expedition, 'as if the forces of the Turk were so limited that one very great defeat might reduce them'.[95] Even Giacomo Foscarini, the Venetian general, came to accept the essential veracity of Alba's argument, much as the logic of this rationale led inexorably to the conclusion that it would be impossible to defeat the Ottoman

Empire without attacking it simultaneously in the Mediterranean and in Hungary.[96]

In complete contrast, Charles V, Philip II and Philip III operated on two premises: first that their high-grade galleys were practically irreplaceable, requiring years of careful husbandry; second, that the squadrons served to link Spain with Italy and so make the Habsburg military system a cohesive reality. Decisive defeat in battle at sea was therefore held to entail near-catastrophic consequences not only for their armada but also for their entire military-administrative system. As Toledo put it in December 1572, the operations in the Levant over the previous three campaigning seasons had been an unprecedented gamble with the fate of Christendom, in which 'all of the estates and kingdoms of His Majesty' had been staked on the outcome of just one battle.[97] Any major 'cash transaction' at sea therefore threatened the Catholic Monarchy with absolute bankruptcy – the breakdown of its entire military-administrative system because of the isolation of the *plazas de armas* in Italy from each other and from Spain.[98]

Sophisticated or highly advanced forms of naval conflict are based to a large degree upon a war of attrition, the long years of mobilisation and frustrated or indecisive actions that are occasionally punctuated by major confrontations. The principal failing of the Ottoman naval system was that the 'quiet' years – those of patient attrition – were almost guaranteed to be marked by devastating raids by the Christian corsairs in the Levant.[99] Three, four or five reinforced galleys, sailing according to the peculiar ethos of the corsair knights, could – and repeatedly did – wreak havoc on the peoples and trade of the eastern Mediterranean.

The most marked and important consequence of the two Mediterranean administrative systems was that naval conflict functioned according to a strategic timetable. The galleys of the Catholic Monarchy were 'older', more 'exercised' and therefore less prone to succumb to illness: the longer that the campaigning season went on, the more the scales tipped in their favour. It can be no coincidence that most of the major Christian offensives – Koron and Patras (from September 1532), Tripoli/Djerba (late 1559/early 1560), Algiers (October 1541 and late August 1601), the *jornada de Navarino* (Don John sailed to Corfu in

September 1572), the expulsion of the Moriscos of Valencia (from mid-September 1609) – and all of the major achievements – the capture of Koron (25 September 1532) and Castilnuovo (27 October 1538), the relief of Malta (the galleys departed from Sicily on 26 August 1565 and landed infantry in the early hours of 8 September), the battle of Lepanto (7 October 1571), the capture of Tunis (Don John's fleet sailed from Marsala two years to the day after *la batalla naval*) – took place towards the end of the campaigning season. History had taught the Christian commanders that their hand became stronger with the waning of the summer. For the same reason, all of the major Ottoman successes were completed before mid-September: this was true of the retaking of Castilnuovo di Cattaro (7 August 1539), the fall of Tripoli (14 August 1551), the twin victories at Djerba (the naval engagement took place on 11 May, and the Christian garrison surrendered on 31 July 1560), Nicosia (9 September 1570) and Famagusta (1 August 1571), and the capitulation of the forts at La Goleta (23 August) and Tunis (13 September 1574). The steady growth of disease aboard the Ottoman galleys ensured that at some point in or around August, the Sultan's fleet and expeditionary force became trapped in a downward spiral of illness, vastly reducing its fighting capability.

One of the benefits of the western model of a professional and regular armada was that it would be highly disciplined; its crews would be able to resist the corrosive effects of the winds, colds, seas and 'bad airs'. In September 1572 the Duke of Urbino placed his faith in the failings of the enemy.[100] Perhaps the only hope for the relief of Tunis and La Goleta in the summer of 1574 was that bad weather would blow the Ottoman fleet into Portofarina (Puerto Farina or Ghar El Melh lake) or Bizerta, allowing a band of reinforced galleys from Sicily to reach the besieged garrisons in the fortress on the edge of the lagoon.[101] On both occasions, these hopes were to be disappointed. By the same criteria, a small Catholic Armada in good order would have to bide its time before exercising its superiority. In 1606 Benavente informed Philip III that the Turkish fleet would run to no more than 60 to 70 galleys 'and these in poor shape'. He suggested that 30 highly reinforced warships might venture into the Archipelago at the beginning of September. 'Should these galleys come into contact with the enemy, I presume that they, being in such good shape, will be safe to do whatever should be best.'[102] The Viceroy's proposal stopped short of actually advocating an engagement with the *armada del Turco*. In this it was perfectly representative of western thinking over the previous decades, which had functioned on the premise that the enemy should be engaged only if it was with an advantage that was both manifest and manifold.

The decline in health of the Ottoman fleet therefore offered the Christians the opportunity to strike. The only other realistic option – the only other realistic option after 1535, it should be said – was a campaign in spring as the Ottoman fleet was gathering. In 1573 one plan formulated before the break-up of the Holy League was to have the fleet in Corfu by mid-April, a plan which very probably meant that the German and Spanish infantry, dispersed across the western half of the sea, would not be present.[103] This sort of expedition was talked about a great deal in the first decade of Philip III's reign, during which the Ottoman Empire was perceived to be in crisis. One of Santa Cruz's proposals for the 1609 season was to send 53 reinforced galleys into the Levant. These would sail under the cover of darkness for the entire journey, moving from one unoccupied island to the next and beyond the sight of the reconnaissance towers. The expedition would then hijack and destroy the Ottoman galleys before the Kapudan Pasha could embark soldiers at Moron, Koron and La Preveza.[104] The problem with this plan was, of course, that, even if successfully executed, it would only achieve what illness and the seas could be relied upon to do – that is, wreak havoc among the weak and unprepared. In 1614, when a major Ottoman offensive was threatened, Santa Cruz put a similar plan into action, his intention being to burn the Sultan's biscuit stores at Vólos. The expedition was, however, delayed: on 23 April the marquis wrote to express disappointment that bad weather had kept him in Messina for almost two weeks; it was now 12 days since his departure from Naples, and in this time Venice would surely have forewarned the Ottoman government of his coming.[105]

The strategic timetable was based therefore on the emergence of Ottoman supremacy in the early stages of the campaigning season and its gradual waning over the course of the summer and autumn. From this starting point three observations should be made. The first of these is that in these circumstances it was practically impossible to foresee circumstances in which the Christians could adopt the offensive position. Indeed, only when Venice was involved in the Holy League could the western powers seriously entertain the possibility of an engagement with the Ottoman fleet, and even then the union of so many different squadrons and 'nations' beneath the banner of the cross promised a difficult navigation.

Outside of years such as 1538 and 1570–72 things were very different, as the simple numbers of ships and men available to the Sublime Porte made any plans for a Christian attack fanciful. This is not to deny that the Christian commanders, even Doria, sometimes discussed the capture of Ottoman fortresses and believed that many positions could be seized. From time to time the old plan to recapture Tripoli or Tunis was dusted off and sent around for discussion. Another option that was periodically considered was that of an attack upon the two *presidios* guarding Constantinople itself, 'by which Your Majesty might deprive the Turk of all his territories in the Mediterranean'. Benavente was confident that the towers could be stormed; the difficulty – and it was not a small difficulty – was perceived to lie in retaining them 'since the Sultan will devote all of his forces to their recapture'.[106]

The second major observation about the general conditions of Mediterranean warfare is that, outside of the Holy League, it was evident that the spring period would be crucial. In years of major actions both sides raced to have their forces out on the seas early: if the Christian fleet was to undertake any sort of pre-emptive operation, or simply gather to shadow the lumbering enemy, then it was imperative that it be ready to sail as and when the enemy mobilised.[107] If the enemy were to arrive on the coast of Naples or Sicily before the Catholic Armada could sally to shadow it 'then all the money spent in preparations will be thrown away with great loss of reputation and without having been able to prevent the damages which are usually caused by delays'.[108] Again, this understanding was widely shared, although inveterate crusaders like Jean Parisot de la Valette tended to express it in the most confident terms. In 1562 he stated unequivocally that the enemy, however large his fleet, would not dare to put men ashore at La Goleta or anywhere else if the Catholic armada gathered in Messina; the congregation of 60 or so galleys would, he continued, put an end to Ottoman arrogance, which only ever manifested itself because the royal armada was spread out across Italy, Spain and the islands.[109] Christians felt uncomfortable if the enemy enjoyed the run of the seas without opposition, even if the military threat posed by, say, a fleet of 80 sail on the highly fortified coastlines of southern Italy was deemed to be relatively limited.[110]

These considerations dovetailed into an awareness of the enormous logistical requirements of any campaign, especially one that was offensive in nature. It was standard procedure that proposals for *empresas* had to be forwarded as autumn gave way to winter in order for everything to be in place by the following spring.[111]

There was, therefore, an inherent contradiction in the western mindset with regard to the timetable of mobilisation: on the one hand, it was deemed essential to have everything in place in April or May; on the other, experience demonstrated that no action could be taken against the fleet from the East until August, September or October. The two commanders of the Holy League of Paul III, Andrea Doria and Ferrante Gonzaga, certainly were delayed in 1538, reaching Corfu as late as 7–8 September.[112] Similar misfortunes and misunderstandings affected the armada in 1565, 1570 and 1571. The observation of delays quickly became an allegation: Charles V and Philip II were able to dispatch squadrons across the seas to re-stock their fortresses and coastlines in April and May; yet the King and his fleet were then unable to come to the defence of Christendom until much later in the summer – until, in fact, its final moments.

These allegations of intentional delay lead directly to the third major feature of warfare imposed by the different systems of East and West: that, given the quantitative and qualitative difference in the respective forces of cross and crescent, it was all but impossible for the western galleys to engage the Muslim fleet in battle. Working from a paper written by Don García de Toledo in 1564, Professor Guilmartin placed considerable importance upon the fact that 'at no point was the possibility of a general fleet engagement even considered'.[113] This was certainly true, but not for the reasons that *Gunpowder and Galleys* proposed – that galley warfare was essentially a form of amphibian warfare waged by two enormous, slow-moving fleets that could not remain at sea for any length of time. Don García's reasoning in 1564 was very different indeed to that of the commanders during the Holy Leagues of Paul III and Pius V, as the presence of the Venetian contingent in 1538 and 1570–72 made up the enormous disparity in numbers between the fleets of Christendom and Islam. In the set of circumstances envisaged by Toledo in 1564 the impossibility of a general fleet engagement was due to the respective tactical qualities of the fleets and strategic intentions of the commanders, namely that the Christians could not face a much larger fleet *en batalla determinada* and were therefore committed to a defensive strategy; conversely, the Ottoman fleet would be unable to catch and engage a smaller but tactically superior armada. In contrast, when the Holy League was convened in 1538 and 1570–72 a general fleet engagement at sea in the lower Adriatic or Ionian Seas was pretty much the only outcome that anyone envisaged or hoped for. This was because of the proximity of two large, immobile fleets consisting of a majority of 'new' or 'unexercised' warships, albeit with significant groups of high-calibre galleys belonging to the Catholic Monarchy, its Italian confederates and the corsairs of North Africa incorporated into them.

The Catholic Monarchy therefore looked to a policy of prudence to defend its territories in the Mediterranean; indeed, this strategy was on the whole successful in protecting the frontiers of its friends and confederates. If there were fault-lines or recurring difficulties – the Franco-Ottoman alliance; the danger of being caught and surrounded by the enormous armadas from the Levant; the violent Hospitaller actions – then these proved manageable. The major threat to the *política de prudencia* lay in Spain itself, where large populations of Muslims, or crypto-Muslims, lived.[114]

In the early 1950s a Catalan historian, Joan Reglà, advanced the argument that the Moriscos or 'New Christians' were widely seen as a fifth column in early modern Spain. Drawing heavily from the earlier work of Pascual Boronat, Reglà showed that the converted communities were believed to be actively assisting the privateering raids of the corsairs of Algiers; indeed the New Christians were said to be willing to fight with the forces of the Ottoman Turk in a prospective invasion of Spain. He went on to suggest that, as the Ottoman threat receded, Morisco communities sought alliances with the powers aligned against Philip II in the Triple Alliance (1595), namely Henry IV of France, Elizabeth I of England and the Dutch Republic.[115]

Reglà published his article in 1953, and Boronat's work had first seen light in 1901. The problem for subsequent historians has been that the argument for the 'great conspiracy' drew upon a wealth of contemporary documentation that left little room for doubt: Charles V, Philip II, Philip III, their senior statesmen and highly educated figures like Juan de Ribera, Archbishop of Valencia, clearly believed that the humble communities of Moriscos in southern and eastern Spain posed an existential threat to the country.[116] Documenting these reports and concerns was relatively easy; explaining their pervasive and persistent nature has proved much more difficult. Many scholars have doubted the veracity of the 'great conspiracy', while being unable to deny that contemporaries of Cervantes and El Greco did indeed believe in it.[117]

The answer to this conundrum lies in five main areas: the balance of naval power on the seas; the deficiencies of the coastal defences in Spain in general and the Balearics and Valencia in particular; the experience of the Marquis of Denia (later the Duke of Lerma and favourite of Philip III) in Valencia in 1596; the circumstances of 1609, with the apparent stabilisation of the Ottoman Empire, the resurgence of its armada and the prospect of the re-establishment of the traditional alliance with the King of France; finally it is important to return to the perception of 'the Turk', that is to say to the resonance of the idea of Islamic nationhood ('the *Ummah*'), and the role of the sultan, as emperor of the Muslims, in protecting all believers.

Perhaps the major point of weakness in the western defensive system was the inability to defend Spain against the Ottoman menace. As we have seen, the Ottoman fleet exercised an advantage of numbers.[118] If 60 or 70 Christian galleys could not expect to engage the enemy, then at least they could shadow it, waiting for an error or opportunity, and ferry reports, men, weapons and provisions to the fortresses wherever possible. In June 1559 Gian Andrea Doria expressed confidence that the King's galleys, sailing with those of Florence and Malta, would be able to follow the larger Ottoman fleet and give it some hard work, 'sara seguitata et travagliata'.[119] Following the disaster at Djerba, the King recognised that the galleys that remained to him in June 1560 were not enough to face the Ottoman fleet in open battle; they would, however, be capable of tracking it, trying to check its ambition and preventing it from disembarking all of its troops.[120] His thoughts and concerns were shared by Gian Andrea Doria, who referred back to the successful guerrilla operations conducted by Andrea Doria in 1537.[121]

The one scenario in which the King envisaged having to run considerable risks on the seas in 1565 – that is to say, sailing as many galleys as possible, all of them loaded to the brim with soldiers, and emptying Naples, Piedmont and Lombardy of Spanish infantry – was if the Ottoman fleet headed to Oran, Mers El Kebir or the Peñón de Vélez de la Gomera. In this case Philip II ordered that 25,000 to 30,000 men were to be brought over to the Iberian coastline, 'as the good and security of everything depends upon this'.[122] His instructions in 1568 were that, should it be necessary, the Catholic Armada was to form 'a good band of reinforced galley' to sail on 'the tail of the enemy and impede him so that he cannot do anything of any moment nor inflict any great damage while he lives in fear of our galleys'.[123]

These concerns would not be allayed by subsequent events. In March 1591 Philip II warned his ministers and officers that the Ottoman fleet would certainly be offered the chance to winter in Toulon. He gave instructions that if the enemy fleet headed to Algiers, then all the galleys of Italy, even though they were 'discomposed', were to come to Spain. 'I well see the difficulties and concern that this will cause you, as well as the dilapidated state of things here ['ruin aparejo de acá'], as well as the forces of the enemy. I feel in this the same as you, but I hope in God that He will help and will order it as is best.'[124] To this same end he appealed in October 1592 to the Pope and the other princes of the peninsula, whose assistance would be vital in *el año que viene*.[125] In 1596 the King again gave instructions that the royal armada was to pursue the enemy while 'stinging at its tail' (*'picándole a la cola'*) if it moved westwards towards Spain or towards the coast of North Africa.[126] Even the brilliantly eccentric Duke of Osuna, successively Viceroy of Sicily and Naples in the decade from 1610, held to the same understanding of the essentially defensive nature of the Christian stance. In proposals advanced at the end of 1614, he suggested that the 60 or so reinforced Christian galleys could harass and sting the outer fringes of the Ottoman fleet.[127]

Military commanders were concerned not only by the disparity in numbers on the sea, but also by the unevenness of defences on land. One of the causes of concern in 1569 – that is, at the moment that the War of Granada was raging – was that the spies in Constantinople reported that the Ottoman Kapudan Pasha had asked for extensive information on the coast of Spain. 'And he has been informed that Cartagena is a most secure port for a very large fleet, and that the fortress could be taken very easily, especially if the rebel Moors were not defeated when the fleet arrived there.'[128] In 1574 Toledo believed that it was absolutely essential to defend Malta, Alghero, Cagliari, La Goleta and Corsica:

> And it would be good to see if the problem of the Moriscos of Granada has been remedied [by their removal to other parts of Spain]. If anything needs to be done, it must be done immediately. The fortifications of Cartagena and Gibraltar have to be finished, as it is to be believed that the Turk will want to come to claim vengeance for the past defeat, and I fear more for the coast of Spain than for the shorelines of Italy, as it is not as well fortified, and because the force of the Moors is greater in that part than here.[129]

Other senior strategists shared these concerns. In 1588 Doria prepared a short paper assessing the possibility of a major Ottoman campaign in the *mares de poniente*. Naples, Sicily and Malta were thought to be impregnable to attack; in Sardinia and Mallorca the enemy would be able to do much damage; however, the greatest danger was to Menorca and Ibiza. Not only were these islands small but they would also be defended by few men and brittle fortifications. Provisions would be in very short supply. Furthermore, it would be impossible to relieve these positions once 'the Turk' had established control of the major harbours. If the Sultan threw 10,000 troops ashore, both Menorca and Ibiza would almost certainly fall after a short siege. Oran and Mers El Kebir were similar in that it would be impossible to get help to these positions once the enemy fleet was upon them and had secured the major anchorage (at Mers El Kebir). While 'some' did not take seriously the threat that the Ottoman fleet might descend upon the Balearics, Doria was of the contrary opinion: in summer the Sultan's fleet could even reach the coast of Spain. In such an expedition, the defences of the Balearics would play a significant role; denied Menorca or Ibiza as fallback positions, the Ottomans would face a 'very great danger' in sailing to and from Spain. Cartagena would be the only port in the region large and secure enough for the sort of fleet he envisaged – one of at least 100 sail. 'But if the Moriscos of Aragon, Valencia and Murcia were to rise up Your Majesty will know better than anybody what the Turks could do.'[130]

Doria went on to state that it was precisely the problem of following the large enemy fleet into the western seas that concerned him, as the band of reinforced galleys would be much smaller than the enemy and unable to cause the Ottoman commanders concern or 'to do some good thing'. The assessments made by Toledo and Doria were revealing in that they underlined the relationship between the different parts of the Catholic Monarchy: the same outlook that envisaged the defence of Italy as a matter of calculation, restraint and the intelligent deployment of resources thought in the most absolute of terms about the prospective loss of Spain.[131]

Boronat's case in part depended upon the events of 1596, when the Marquis of Denia, Viceroy of Valencia, expressed extreme concern about the Moriscos. These concerns are worth examining in detail; the background to them was the devastating Anglo-Dutch attack upon Cadiz. In letters of 13 and 17 July Denia complained that he would be unable to defend the kingdom as he had been ordered to do. He had no faith in the *gente del pueblo*, the civilian militias and home guards given the task of manning the coastal towers. These groups, he complained, were afraid of using gunpowder weapons and refused to confront the corsairs when they landed on the shore. Although the government would be able to muster enough veterans to hold the important coastal fortresses against an attack from the armada of Algiers, it was clear that if a fleet as powerful as the Anglo-Dutch one were to attack then the key positions of Denia, Peñíscola or, as was most probable, the ramshackle castle at Alicante, then the defenders would certainly be overpowered. The viceroy continued that the only way to ensure that the kingdom would be able to protect itself in the event of the arrival of a large enemy fleet would be for it to have an established *tercio*. In the absence of a regular garrison force, Denia was obliged to ask Philip II for a large sum of money, supplies and arms as well as a good band of men, '*un buen golpe de gente*'. The King had given orders that Murcia and the surrounding regions were to provide help to Valencia in the event of attack. However, the viceroy foresaw little prospect of success in these measures: these reinforcements would be both too small and too late, 'and the enemy will have accomplished whatever he intends to do'.

It was not, however, the Dutch and English who most worried Denia: 'The areas which can give us here the greatest difficulty are the *aljamas*, the regions inhabited by the Moriscos, and I have sent out spies and am proceeding with the caution that is necessary. I trust in God that, as this is His cause He will look after everything.' In early August the viceroy was reporting that it was a 'certainty' that the Moriscos of Valencia and Aragon would rise at the arrival of a large fleet from the East, an eventuality which, he added, might occur at any point until the end of September. The one positive aspect of the intelligence reports throughout the summer was that the New Christians would not trust any 'nation' other than the Turks. On 17 July the viceroy reported that the Moriscos were 'very quiet'. Yet if anything could disturb their calm it was precisely the suggestion that they were under suspicion, and so Denia was being careful not to make too obvious his concerns or investigations, while his agents scoured the countryside looking for hidden arms caches.[132]

These concerns, or elements of them, have been examined previously. Braudel and Tulio Donghi both cited a document detailing the deliberations of the Council of Aragon, whose members dismissed the fears voiced by Denia out of hand: '[the Moriscos] possess neither arms, nor supplies, nor fortified positions to gather and wait for the Turkish fleet even if it were for only a few days'. The councillors also pointed out that the majority of the Moriscos lived in the western part of the kingdom around Alicante, that is to say the *sierra* of Bernia, and this region was commanded by a fort with its own water supplies.[133] But Denia's letters to the councils of State and War give a broader picture: the royal government clearly had few arms, supplies and soldiers. Alicante, he reported, was '*necesitadíssima de todo*', in the very greatest need of everything.

It is true that the tone of Denia's correspondence in July and August was far from conventional. He seemed almost determined to read the evidence so as to support his conviction that an enormous conspiracy was afoot. When, for instance, a Moorish captain was captured and admitted that he had been recruited to sail a group of refugees to Algiers, the viceroy thought it possible that his confession was a ruse to hide the real plans for a rising. It was not until mid-August that Denia came to declare the kingdom safe; his reasoning for doing so was profoundly revealing of his outlook. He uncovered another conspiracy hatched by affluent members of the Morisco community to escape to Algiers, 'something that they would not do if they held any hope of the arrival of the armada of the Turk, in which case they would all be planning to rebel'.[134]

There were, therefore, inconsistencies – perhaps even important inconsistencies – in Denia's correspondence and, aside from protests about his physical frailty that were overblown even by the conventions of the day, his conclusion was perhaps overly influenced by reports whose provenance or reliability might have been more thoroughly questioned and investigated. The point must be, however, that from at least the 1560s Philip II seems not to have doubted that the Ottoman fleet might indeed head towards Spain. Moreover, this conviction was shared by both Toledo (in his paper of 1574) and Doria (in his memorandum of 1588). Indeed in certain important respects the concerns voiced by Denia in 1596 echoed the fears expressed in Toledo's paper of 1574:

Italy was safe and fortified, while Spain, where the Moors had their strength, was weak and vulnerable. As with complaints about the state of the galleys, a degree of deliberate exaggeration must be factored into any assessment, although it is worth pointing out that even Philip II recognised in his instructions of 1591 that the problem lay in the failings of the military infrastructure and administrative apparatus in Iberia, '*el ruin aparejo de acá*'. The lineage of this concern could be traced back to the 1530s, to the Admiral of Castile's plea to Charles V not to believe that with 'the waters of Spain he can quench the enemy fire in Hungary'.[135] It was a consistent, recurring concern. Furthermore, it should also be pointed out that the Ottoman threat was a genuine one: in 1594, 100 galleys had run along the shoreline of Calabria, burning Reggio di Calabria; two years later a force of comparable dimensions sailed from Constantinople.[136]

After 1596, many senior figures in government and the church continued to voice their beliefs in the threat. The Count of Benavente, Denia's successor as Viceroy of Valencia, was concerned in August 1598 by news of the departure of the armada from Constantinople. This kingdom, he fretted, was not short of those who would be happy if the fleet arrived on its shorelines.[137] Archbishop Ribera, who served as Viceroy of Valencia from 1602 to 1604, claimed in 1601 that although he was nearly 70 years old, he was certain that if the King did not undertake the expulsion of the New Christians, then he would live to see the day in which Spain was lost.[138] In 1602 Philip III had agreed that the expulsion was the best option, 'if it can be done in good conscience'.[139] In 1608 the Count of Chinchón made the case to the Council of State for removing the New Christians, warning Philip III that it might be another 20 years or more before as clear an opportunity presented itself.[140] By the summer of that year reports were beginning to suggest that the window of opportunity was closing. Having dealt a decisive blow against the long-running Celali rebellion in June 1608, the Grand Vizier, Kuyucu Murad Pasha, was proving himself 'to be one of the most effective commanders in Ottoman history'. In August Benavente expressed concerns about the intentions of the enemy fleet.[141] The highest ranks of Philip III's statesmen were beginning to express the conviction that the Sultan might shortly 'send all of his forces against Christendom'.[142]

The decisive report was filed in Constantinople on 24 January and was transmitted via Venice with other information detailing the retreat of the rebels of Asia Minor ('Anatolia') to the mountains. It detailed the preparation of 130 galleys in the Ottoman capital, and stated that the Grand Vizier was to accompany the Kapudan Pasha aboard the fleet. Orders had been sent out for biscuit and gunpowder. The report reached Venice in late February and Valladolid on 4 April.[143] On that day the Council of State met to discuss the report, and the decision to expel the Moriscos was taken.

It is true that similar reports had been filed in previous winters; it was perhaps also the case that, given the drastic nature of the decision to expel the minority, Philip III placed rather too much weight on the threat to Spain, and not nearly enough on the likelihood of the Ottomans being able to mobilise at such short notice.[144] On the other hand, the Ottoman-Morisco conspiracy had very often been understood within the context of the Sublime Porte's alliance with the crown of France; this had certainly been the case for Philip II in 1591, and in 1596 the governor of Oran voiced concerns about the prospect of the Ottoman armada wintering in Toulon and Marseille before embarking upon an attack in the 'mares de poniente' in the following year.[145] By 1609 the likelihood of war with His Most Christian Majesty, Henry IV, was looming. The cause lay in the claims of a French prince, Charles de Nevers – Carlo I Gonzaga-Nevers to Italian historians – to the duchy of Kleve and the perceived challenge to Habsburg interests in Italy posed by Carlo Emanuele, Duke of Savoy.[146]

In defence of the decision made on 4 April 1609 it might also be said that the nature of the Ottoman fleet held within it the prospect of a sudden re-emergence and that an impressive armada del Turco did indeed venture out that summer. In June the Council of State was discussing intelligence reports detailing the movement of 90, 120 or 130 enemy warships, and some dispatches mentioned as many as 200 sail with 20,000 janissaries. (The emergence of a fleet of this size was improbable, as Juan de Idiáquez, *Comendador Mayor de León*, recognised).[147] In Mallorca and Malta the threat was taken seriously; Lerma personally annotated the reports from the Balearics before passing them on to Philip III.[148]

In truth the fateful decision had been taken long before this point: in June and July 1596 the Marquis of Denia, who is much better known to history as the Duke of Lerma and favourite of Philip III, had made up his mind about the new Christians of Valencia and Aragon. And so from September 1609 the expulsion was executed 'in silence' and 'at the entrance of winter'.[149]

VIII

Dear Prudence

Fernand Braudel famously wrote that Philip II never conceived of the Mediterranean as a unified whole and that no trace of strategy could be discerned in the vast collection of letters, instructions and memoranda fired off to his servants.[1] Figures such as Don García de Toledo and Gian Andrea Doria provided a structured and precise approach to the deployment of the squadrons, one which was almost mathematical or geometric in tone and nature. The truth of the matter is surely, though, that the timetable and structure of warfare was imposed upon the Christians by sheer force of numbers. A report posted by a reconnaissance skipper in May 1537 spoke of having spotted an extraordinary number of Ottoman warships gathering in the Levant, 'so many that they could not be counted'. In June Andrea Doria arrived in Naples in command of 25 galleys. These were good warships, no doubt, but they were outnumbered by a factor of at least six-to-one.[2] When surprised by the sudden appearance of the Ottoman fleet near the island of Ponza in 1552 there was no option for Andrea Doria but to flee 'because of the disadvantage of his forces'.[3] As we have seen, in a paper of March 1562 Doria presented to the King a sober assessment of the balance of power on the seas: he expressed confidence in the seafaring capabilities of the royal forces, even though they would be outnumbered and outgunned.[4] This perspective shone through a memorandum written by the Genoese Adam Centurione in 1566, in which he began with the premise that the Turk would always have more warships. Bravura had, he continued, to be left aside, as since 1532 the Catholic Armada (the forces of the *monarquía* and its confederates), had undertaken effective and successful operations. The best means of performing the service of God and securing the good of the Christian Republic, he concluded, was to reduce the fleet into two or three bands and pursue the Islamic corsairs of North Africa, which were so numerous that they could almost form a fleet of their own. Philip II ('His Most Prudent Majesty') could surely comprehend this rationale.[5]

In the mid-1560s the Prudent King referred to the capture of Algiers as being desirable for 'the universal good of Christendom and the conservation of our estates'. But at this juncture it was something for the future, a project which might come to fruition one day. In the short term he ordered his officers to be diligent in gathering intelligence on the enemy.[6] In conversation with the Venetian ambassador, Antonio Tiepolo, in 1567 he acknowledged that he could not hope to rival 'the greatness of the Turk'.[7] As we have seen, he made a very similar observation to the Nuncio in the following year. The King was driven by a sense of realism, the recurring and unmitigated truth being that his ambitions greatly outstripped his abilities: 'I greatly regret that my forces do not match my spirit and desire.' Philip II's words on the conclusion of the Holy League resonated through the history of maritime warfare in the inland sea.[8]

Over-ambition would surely have led to hubris, and hubris would have led to disaster. On 25 November 1571 the King sought to remind the Pope of two imperatives: first, that the Christians should not allow any of the Ottoman commanders or captains captured at the battle to be ransomed; second, that to equip a big fleet in *el año que viene* was to invite problems and that the best means was to gather a large band of good warships, 'as other times I have written'.[9] In order to seize the initiative, and to make the victory at Lepanto mean something, it was necessary to renounce the approach which the Most Serene Republic had adopted to the war in the previous two summers. In 1573 Doria echoed these ideas in a paper written for Don John: a force of 20,000 men 'and a much smaller fleet' would be the best option that summer. 'There is no doubt whatsoever that taking a large fleet may cause great difficulties in the navigation, without bringing any benefit.'[10]

Having too many troops was not, however, a frequent problem. Often the number of soldiers available to the *capitanes generales* was surprisingly small, meaning that veterans had to be carefully guarded. In March 1537 the Viceroy of Naples, Don Pedro de Toledo, expressed concerns about the shortage of troops. The efforts to fortify the coastline served to increase the danger of an enemy attack. Not having men to garrison the new fortifications meant that the government had done nothing more than to prepare bastions for the enemies, '*las tierras fortificadas no teniendo gente para defenderlas es fortificarlas para los enemigos*'.[11] The viceroy was extremely concerned about his inability to defend Naples, Gaeta and Capua and that, given the shortage of infantry, he would have to depend upon the barons.[12]

There was, without doubt, a degree of exaggeration in the viceroy's tone, if not the substance of his concerns. In his *Testaments*, Charles V underlined the importance of having well-armed Spanish infantry in the Italian territories, an exigency which was born of the machinations of Pope Paul III and the many French conspiracies of the previous decades – conspiracies which, he added, had been abetted and encouraged by *el Turco* and his armada.[13] In 1560 the Viceroy of Naples expressed serious concerns about the heavy investment of men and galleys in the Djerba expedition, as did a number of officials in Spain, where the coasts were 'infested' by ships of Moors.[14] In 1562 Medinaceli offered Gian Andrea Doria 400 men for a patrol in September; typically the admiral rejected these companies and insisted upon collecting troops in La Goleta, who were (presumably) of a superior calibre.[15] In the following year Medinaceli urged Philip II to supply troops to re-inflate the *tercio* of Sicily which, as usual, was dangerously low.[16] There were only 300 veteran troops in Milan in 1565; ideally there should have been ten times that number.[17] In mid-July, as the King faced the Ottoman threat to the Hospitallers in Malta, he could not bring himself to order Alcalá, now serving as Viceroy of Naples, to remove more than three of the six companies of troops from Gaeta, Naples and Otranto.[18] Two companies, the Viceroy of Naples insisted in a letter to the King, should always be stationed in Gaeta.[19] The problem was, as ever, that he had so few troops in relation to the positions that needed defending, '*habiendo aquí tan poca gente y tantas partes donde hacer guardia'*. Spanish troops, Toledo reiterated in the following year, were the means by which the Monarchy would sustain and defend Italy, *'en la [gente] española que hay me paresce que consiste el sustentamiento y defensa de Italia'*.[20]

In July 1571 the King instructed Don John that under no circumstances was he to remove the 2,000 Spanish infantrymen from Lombardy.[21] There were no more than 6,000 Spanish troops in Naples and Sicily in the winter after Lepanto, although in total the troops, German and Italian regiments included, ran to just under 16,000. The support of this number of troops presented an enormous logistical challenge to the respective governments.[22] Certainly Habsburg diplomats felt more confident and could be more assertive when the *tercios* were at or near their full strength. Conversely when there were few Spanish soldiers in Naples, Sicily and Milan, there was a corresponding tendency to show too little respect to the interests of His Catholic Majesty, a complication which in turn affected the many ongoing negotiations in Rome.[23]

Miranda reminded the King in September 1592 that nothing was as important as having 12,000 to 14,000 Spaniards in Italy, *'que ninguna cosa es de tanta importancia como tener en Italia doce ò catorce mil españoles'*.[24] Doria, who did not always see eye-to-eye with the viceroy, certainly concurred with him on this matter.[25] For his part the King promised that he would send men in the spring; in the meantime, he instructed his Viceroy of Naples to make sure that Orbetello and Porto Ercole were provisioned.[26] Miranda repeated his warning – and plea – in December only adding, by way of parenthesis, that the galley squadron was also short of oarsmen.[27] He continued to voice these concerns throughout 1593.[28] In 1597 the governments of Naples and Sicily complained in unison that they did not have enough Spanish infantry, and that the galleys would arrive back late, if at all. In Sicily there was only enough Spanish infantry to cover 'the places that with justification we must defend', *'las plazas que justamente se han de defender'*.[29] Measures were introduced to alleviate this shortage, but in the following year the total number of infantry in Sicily came to no more than 1,500 – very few troops, warned Maqueda, in relation to the importance of the

kingdom, the 'ordinary incursions of the enemy' and the need to retain
the respect of the Sicilians.[30] He continued with warnings along these
lines in March of the following year: soldiers were needed for the galleys
'for the defence of this kingdom, upon which the most powerful of
enemies puts his eyes whenever he ventures from his house. These
troops are also needed for the quiet of this same Kingdom.'[31] In May
1602 the Viceroy of Naples warned the King that if he proceeded with
his plan to move infantry from Naples then the 100 warships that the
enemy threatened to send against the kingdom might pose a serious
threat to its coastlines.[32] Feria could spare only 800 Spanish infantrymen
for the expedition of the galleys of Sicily in 1605, even if these would be
'the best soldiers in Italy by a long way'.[33]

The oared warships were essential to the proper functioning of the
Catholic Monarchy. They were the first line of defence against an
Ottoman attack upon the crown's positions in Italy, the Balearics, North
Africa or Spain itself. One of the attractions of this system – at least, one
of the theoretical attractions – was that the relative vulnerability of the
Mediterranean regions of France and the long coastline of the Ottoman
Empire offered targets for a retaliatory attack.[34] When the Christian
garrison was besieged at Djerba in the spring of 1560, Andrea Doria
proposed a diversionary raid in the Levant, one that would pull Ottoman
forces back to defend their own seas. The King approved the idea,
mindful that his fleet was smaller than Süleyman's.[35] The idea, always
formulated in fairly vague terms, retained an inherent attraction to the
heavily outnumbered Christians in the 1560s.[36]

'Italy' was viewed as the richest region of Christendom, the key to
economic prosperity and military power, 'the true seat and sceptre to
dominate the world' as Chancellor Gattinara famously put it in the
1520s. In his *Testaments* Charles V advised his son that 'the preservation,
peace and grandeur of Spain depends on the affairs of Italy being well
ordered'.[37] The influence of trained Spanish infantry in Italy was thought
to extend far beyond the peninsula itself. For a start, companies could be
moved to the Balearic islands, which were ordinarily guarded by very
small garrisons, or to Sardinia.[38] Threats from Islam – for instance the
Ottoman siege of Oran in 1563 – were met by having the galleys bring

men, munitions and provisions over from Italy.[39] In the same year plans were made to transport 3,500 soldiers from Genoa to Valencia, where it was feared that the Moriscos were about to rebel. (Previously garrisoned in Flanders, these troops had been marched down to Milan.)[40] The 'War of Granada' (1568–70) was won – if, indeed, either side can be said to have deserved the victor's laurels – by veteran troops ferried over from Italy; as Bernard Vincent and Antonio Domínguez Ortiz noted, the authority of the Habsburgs depended upon a few thousand veteran soldiers based outside Spain.[41]

In July 1581 the King ordered that 20 reinforced galleys were to come over from Naples to try to prevent the Ottoman seizure of Morocco and Fez; his galleys in Italy were, he stated, the 'principal means' of protecting the western Mediterranean.[42] When Philip III considered intervention in Morocco in April 1608, his first step was to ask for information on the state of his forces in Italy.[43]

The role of the galleys can, therefore, be placed within a broader understanding of the military organisation of the Catholic Monarchy, that is to say its capacity to move men and materials between the major *plazas de armas*. In a letter of May 1535 Charles V set out the system and philosophy by which his states would act: *'Tous se doivent aider, les un et les autres ....'* ('They should all help each other.')[44] This was, as Federigo Chabod demonstrated in one of his pivotal studies, the essential argument advanced by the Habsburgs and their ministers to their parliaments or representative bodies: together the states were much stronger than they could have been apart. If Naples helped defend Italy and Christendom from the Turk, so Milan served to keep the French and other northern invaders out of the peninsula.[45]

In all respects, the Catholic Armada represented the unison of the politically separate and geographically dispersed parts of the Spanish Monarchy.[46] From 1532 the entire edifice of Habsburg military power depended upon making the most efficient use of its resources; markets were exploited to secure the best possible prices and quality. In 1532 money and nobles were moved from Naples to Austria in anticipation of Süleyman's prospective campaign against Vienna.[47] In 1547, 50 pieces of artillery captured from the Protestant army at Würtemberg were sent to forts in Naples. Agents of the crown continued to seek cannons in Florence, Brescia and Flanders.[48] The construction and fitting out of new hulls in the early 1560s was a collective effort: *maestranza* was brought from the 'ports of all of Spain'; masts came from Flanders, oars from Naples, firearms and yet more oars from Vizcaya.[49] Weapons, gunpowder and rope were shipped from Naples to Barcelona and elsewhere in Spain; these materials were simply unobtainable in the Principality of Catalonia.[50] From 1551 vast quantities of silver were shipped to Genoa from Spain.[51] 'No one would contest,' observed Braudel, 'the historical importance of these repeated voyages by galleys laden with chests or barrels of money.'[52] According to a contemporary diarist, 14,225,000 *scudi di oro* arrived in Genoa between 1584 and 1589; in 1616 the six galleys of Carlo Doria brought a million over from Cartagena; three oared warships carried over two million from Barcelona to Genoa in 1618.[53]

Lombardy played a key role in linking the Mediterranean with Flanders, as an excellent study by Mario Rizzo has demonstrated.[54]

> The occupation of Milan offered the Habsburgs the ability to exercise military and diplomatic control over the numerous small states of the plain of Pedana. In turn, the control of northern Italy was decisive in protecting Naples and Genoa, both of which were essential for Spain. The possession of Milan also allowed the Monarchy to threaten the south-eastern flank of the French territories, and so served as a vital point of rebuffing Bourbon interests and expansionism into Italy. Milan, therefore, was not only 'the key to Italy' but acted as the fulcrum of the entire Habsburg strategy in Europe. For Charles V Lombardy represented the only connection between his Mediterranean dominions and those of central and northern Europe, and so helped to assure the survival of his vast continental empire.'[55]

In an excellent study Davide Maffi has demonstrated that until 1640 Milan was the central strategic territory in the *monarquía's* military system. The plain of Lombardy served as a sort of trap for invading forces.[56]

The essential characteristic of Habsburg military organisation was that the Monarchy drew its strength from being more than the sum of its parts; the danger was always that its constituent elements would be isolated from one another. The very first of the major Ottoman campaigns – Barbarossa's 1534 expedition – was intended to recover Genoa for Francis I, thus denying Charles V both the link between the sea and the imperial fief of Milan and the maritime expertise of Andrea Doria.[57] The seizure of the two towns in Puglia in 1537 was, Francisco López de Gómara wrote, undertaken in the hope that it would serve as a catalyst for a general rebellion of the people of Naples against the Spanish and in favour of His Christian Majesty, who was to move against Genoa and Milan.[58] The plan in 1543 and 1544 appears to have been that Barbarossa would help to seize Genoa, although it has also been argued that the intention was merely to help defend Provence against Habsburg aggression: whatever his final objective, the Kapudan Pasha was able to exploit Toulon in order to capture ships and so underline the vulnerability of the lines of communication between Barcelona and Genoa.[59] As we have seen, in 1552 and 1554 it was rumoured that the French had formed some 'intelligence' in Naples which the Ottoman fleet would help to exploit.[60] In 1556 a similar plan was put into action: Henry II was to exploit the Pope's having declared the fief of Naples to be forfeit in order to launch a campaign against 'il Regno'. This campaign failed, but not for want of trying: later investigators uncovered incontrovertible proof that in March 1557 Cardinal Carlo Carafa, Pope Paul IV's nephew, approached Sultan Süleyman directly, asking him to concentrate his resources on an attack upon the Kingdom of the Two Sicilies. He later admitted the charge, his only justification being that the Pope himself had ordered him to undertake this embassy.[61] One of Philip II's concerns in 1558 was to reinforce the garrisons in Naples to 4,000 regular troops (half-German, half-Spanish); Piombino, Porto Ercole and Orbetello were, he ordered, to be properly garrisoned, even if this meant employing Italian infantrymen recruited in Naples or in the state of Florence.[62] One of the fears mentioned in 1572 was that His Most Christian Majesty would welcome the Ottoman fleet into Toulon in order to divide Spain from Italy, 'and so return Naples and Sicily to the French Crown'.[63] In this instance the fears were clearly far-fetched, but they nevertheless played upon an understanding of the collective nature of the Habsburg *grandeza*, the sense that this system, whatever its strengths, could be disturbed by either the 'humours' of Italy or the more direct intervention of His Most Christian Majesty and his most singular ally, the Common Enemy of Christendom.

In January 1595 Olivares, the viceroy, was fearful that Sicily might be isolated and attacked by an enemy fleet that enjoyed a clear 'superiority' on the seas,[64] while in the following year Doria warned that just a handful of galleys operating from Marseille and Toulon could cause great damage, *'por pocas que séan podrán hacer mucho daño'.*[65] There was reason to believe that the Grand Duke of Tuscany was abetting Henry IV in setting up this flotilla, and concerns increased with the appearance of a small French fleet. In September 1600 the Duke of Guise led out a flotilla of well-garrisoned *tartanas* to patrol the Provençal seas, venturing as far as Antibes. His apparent intention was to welcome the new queen of France, Marie de'Medici, who was travelling from Leghorn and to pursue three corsair ships which earlier that summer had seized a vessel carrying money being sent by the Grand Duke to Henri IV. Still, the presence of the flotilla from Toulon caused alarm in the Republic; two senators were sent along its western coastline to alert and provision the fortresses.[66] In 1604 speculation centred on the 'curiosity' of Guise, who had taken out a flotilla of five warships to reconnoitre the coastline around Monaco; further anxiety was caused by the capture of 200 slaves by the Florentine galleys, 'as if [Guise] asks for these men in order to arm [his ships], they will be given to him'.[67] Henry IV was able to dedicate considerable financial resources (specifically monies levied on the export of wheat from Languedoc and Provence) to the maintenance of the warships in Toulon and Marseille; in times of war, this flotilla would have the potential to cause enormous disruption and additional cost to the Catholic Monarchy; it would, for instance, be necessary to dispatch an entire squadron of galleys with infantry in order to send a letter from Italy to Spain.[68] In the autumn of 1605 five French galleys ventured on a patrol along the western Italian seaboard, reinforcing rumours that His Most Christian Majesty had, in conjunction with the Grand Duke, fermented a conspiracy within the Habsburg *presidios* of the Tuscan littoral or even in Gaeta. While Benavente remained very sceptical of the existence of such a plot, reports of this sort gave impetus to the fortification of the *presidio* of Porto Longone, which Don García de Toledo was overseeing.[69] A memorial submitted in 1619 by the Duke of Osuna to account for his actions as Viceroy of Sicily and Naples presents the sea as swarming with enemy vessels: on it there lurked 60 corsair ships from Tunis and Algiers, not to mention the hordes of English, French and Flemish vessels capable of throwing 10,000 men ashore.[70] At first glance the viceroy's concerns might appear a touch over the top; on the other hand, Patrick Williams has pointed out that the Councils of State and War had expressed similar concerns about the recruitment and deployment of Dutch troops and warships by the Republic of Venice in this and the previous years.[71]

The major problem for the galley squadrons of Charles V, Philip II and Philip III was their centrality, their involvement in all of the plans or strategies of His Catholic Majesty. Put another way, the fleet was of such central importance precisely because of the imbalance between the Monarchy's resources and its responsibilities. As we have seen, in 1532 and 1533 Charles V deployed his galleys on the coast of Greece with the aim of diverting Süleyman's armies from an assault on Vienna. These efforts were called into question by the Admiral of Castile, who warned that the Monarchy was caught between the might of the Ottoman Turks in the East and the growing menace of the corsairs in North Africa. His conclusion was that the greater threat from the Islamic world lay in the Mediterranean frontier, where the encroachment of *ghazi* raiders into 'Barbary' might shortly threaten the loss of Spain itself.[72]

The same essential rationale or understanding remained the prevalent strategy for later generations: as Philip II had suggested in his letters to his Italian confederates in 1561, everything depended upon galleys as they allowed the monarchy to make the most of the resources available to it. In 1566 Toledo reasoned that the best means to defend Malta, La Goleta 'and everywhere else' that summer would be to transfer the soldiers from both positions onto the royal galleys.[73] (He subsequently lamented that this policy had not been implemented.) He was aghast when a proposal was mooted during the Holy League that the armada might winter in Brindisi and Otranto. He penned a long and detailed paper on the dangers of the southern Italian coastline which, he averred, was 'the worse shoreline to sail of any that I know, even in the summer, and so much worse in winter'. To station the galleys here, on the border of Christendom, would involve an enormous risk; they needed to be in their bases, where they could be used to respond to events and to defend Naples, Sicily, Piedmont, Milan and Genoa.[74]

The role of the flotillas was often seen to extend far beyond Italy and the Mediterranean. In the summer of 1572 the King's ambassador in Rome, Zúñiga, insisted that the heretics of France and Germany were quiet precisely because of the large forces in Italy, 'a place where His Majesty can deploy them if the need should occur'.[75] This statement was the product of the extreme political and military pressures of that year, and was doubtless slightly simplistic. It did, however, draw upon an understanding of the fundamental methods by which the Catholic Monarchy organised and prepared for war.[76] In February 1583 Philip II was concerned that the Queen of England had dispatched a ship to the Sultan 'with letters in damage of my service'. With the 'shadows of the Levant and the bad offices that the French do there, asking for an armada', he expressed his concern: under no circumstances was Doria to absent himself from Italy. The King's view of his querulous Genoese admiral as a sort of coiled cobra ready to strike at the many enemies of the Catholic Monarchy reveals the really rather touching amount of faith that he had in the Prince of Melfi.[77] But it also underlines how Naples, Sicily and Milan were, like the central squares of a chess board, the positions from which Philip intended to command Europe and the Mediterranean.

The importance of the oared squadrons for the Spanish crown therefore extended beyond purely naval purposes. In order to be able to maintain this system, and to continue to operate over long distances in treacherous seas containing few safe harbours, the Habsburgs depended upon *galeras en buen orden*. The reliance upon the galley that was maintained in permanent commission meant that it would be very difficult to recover from any large-scale losses: requiring patient husbandry over many years, the oared warships were very difficult to replace. The commanders of Philip II and Philip III most often chose to use reinforced galleys for major operations; only the expedition of 1571 and the attacks on Tunis in 1573 and Algiers in 1601 saw the Habsburgs send relatively large numbers of galleys.[78] Although the reinforced vessels were faster, more seaworthy and more reliable than their 'regular' counterparts, expeditions relying upon them entailed a degree of risk that was proportionately higher. The concentration of oarsmen in a select band of vessels meant that the sinking or capture of seven reinforced galleys was the equivalent to the loss of 12 regular rowing crews (the exact proportion varied, but this was the figure – one of the many figures – given by Don García de Toledo in 1565 in relation to the reinforced Hospitaller warships), and with them a correspondingly high amount of infantry, equipment, weaponry and mariners.[79]

Any major setback – a defeat in battle; a shipwreck caused by one of the sea's sudden, violent summer storms or a dramatic change of wind direction while in an unguarded harbour – threatened to deny the Catholic Monarchy the one resource that was both vital and irreplaceable, the *galeras en buen orden*. In September 1560 the King made his concerns emphatically clear: should the remaining galleys be lost in an effort to save the garrison at Djerba then 'it would be such an irreparable damage as can be seen, not only for my kingdoms and states, but also for all of Christendom'. He instructed Andrea Doria to provide advice to the captains general, drawing upon his 'great prudence'.[80] As we have seen, in his final instructions of 1565 Philip II ordered Don García de Toledo that his priority had to be the preservation of the galleys; Malta could be retaken at some later point. Under no circumstances was the *capitán general del mar Mediterráneo* to risk an engagement on the sea, 'as the inequality is so great, the use of the 50 high-sided ships so uncertain, that to [face the enemy] would be to run a notorious risk not only our states but with all of Christendom, and if the fleet was destroyed we would be unable to rearm for a long time, as experience has taught us'.[81]

The ramifications of this strategic outlook – the very limitations inherent in it – were clear to contemporaries. The Duke of Alcalá, Viceroy of Naples, put it in August that Toledo would not try to 'relieve Malta by sea, but only by land'.[82] The phrase undoubtedly had – and has – a peculiar ring to it, but his meaning was clear: that the galleys, reduced to an elite band of reinforced vessels, would disembark the infantry and then withdraw.[83] If there was going to be a battle, it should be on land between armies, rather than at sea. Even Pope Pius IV could see the wisdom of these orders; certainly he foresaw the enormous danger to Christendom that lay in the loss of the royal fleet.[84] This same imperative shaped all subsequent campaigns. 'If any misfortune should come to my galleys,' Philip II warned Gian Andrea Doria ahead of the expedition in 1570, 'you know what damages might occur to all of Christendom. Be very careful where you place them.' The instructions contained a passage in the King's own hand in which he reminded his admiral to cast an eye on the 'state and order' of the galleys of Rome and Venice; the 'composition' of these galleys was what mattered most.[85] Needless to say, Doria entirely agreed and had anticipated the problem of what course of action to pursue if ordered by Colonna 'to do something which is not convenient'.[86] The Prince of Melfi and the King existed in a cycle of mutually reinforced conviction. Subsequent events did not demonstrate that the King or his admiral were receptive to new ideas. As we have seen, in 1574 the King forbade Don John to attempt to relieve Tunis. In 1596 Pope Clement VIII urged Philip II to undertake a campaign in Albania or the Levant, the intention being to assist the Christian war efforts in Hungary by drawing Ottoman forces to the sea; true to form, in May Doria warned the Prudent King that an operation undertaken on the coast of Albania in the proximity of the larger enemy fleet threatened 'some great disaster', *algún gran desastre*.[87]

Philip III was to prove to be more adventurous than his father, but the old principles quickly and stubbornly reasserted themselves. In 1604 the King decided to employ his armada 'in the service of God'; to this end it was to venture into the Levant to divert Ottoman forces from the war in Hungary. Benavente, Viceroy of Naples (1603–10), reported that he had heard three proposals since his arrival in Italy. The first of these, the sacking of Salonika, he took to be unfeasible as it would be very difficult for the galleys to descend upon the town without being spotted from the shoreline. The second proposal was for a raid upon Alexandria, which would be easier to achieve because the galleys could arrive without being discovered and the troops might well capture the castle of the city 'which is held with very little guard'. The best option, however, was the capture of the poorly defended *caravana*, the convoy of early spring from Alexandria to Constantinople. Benavante's thinking incorporated an intriguing caveat: 'our soldiers would not have the chance to run riot, as they would do on shore, the prize would be very good and of great reputation, and the sacking of a city would necessarily mean the galleys would be left unguarded'. The second Marquis of Santa Cruz, Captain General of the Galleys of the Kingdom of Naples, supported the viceroy's plans. He insisted that whatever the intended target of attack, the galleys should not be visible from the coast of Greece 'as it is best not to give the Greeks any encouragement to rebel against the Turk with hope of being assisted by His Majesty and subsequently to be subjected to the punishment that can readily be envisaged'. Benavente instructed Santa Cruz to achieve this – that is, to keep the fleet out of sight of the Greeks – 'in a dissimulating way', so that the other Christian commanders did not come to realise what he was doing.[88]

Given the complexity of the task facing Santa Cruz, it was perhaps not surprising that the 1604 campaign was a limited success. Undeterred, in December Benavente proposed a series of possible campaigns: he suggested that the conquest of Tripoli might be undertaken in the summer 'when the majority of the 1,000 janissaries are away [collecting] the harvest'. In order to do this, the highly reinforced fleet should carry just under 3,000 troops. Alternatively if the *caravana* was to be sought out – which 'is the expedition that would offer the most reputation and the greatest booty' – then the galleys from Genoa would be needed, along with up to 1,500 additional infantrymen from Lombardy. Failing to meet the *caramusali*, the fleet would be able to sack Alexandria ('an easy operation').[89]

Benavente's letters are worth examining in part because they demonstrate how often the ideals of holy war, *reputación* and royal service subsumed proposals which would directly enrich the viceroy and his colleagues. The recurring problem for the Christians lay in finding a meaningful offensive action. In April the Council of State met to discuss an impressive array of expert advice sent from Benavente, Santa Cruz, the Duke of Feria, Doria and the Duke of Tursi (Don Carlo Doria, son and heir of Gian Andrea Doria). Councillors were very cautious, with the Duke of Infantado capturing the general spirit when he recommended that it was necessary to rid the minds of viceroys and captains general of ideas for *empresas*. The majority opinion was that it would be best to divide the fleet into squadrons and send them to hunt the corsairs.[90] The *junta de dos*, the informal if highly influential consultative body consisting of two senior advisors to the King, recommended that the squadrons be employed chasing corsairs; if the news of civil war in Algiers proved true, the Catholic Armada might be able to head for the city.[91] Philip III delegated responsibility to Benavente and Doria. In turn Doria himself abdicated responsibility, simply stating that it was now too late to think of intercepting the *caravana* coming from Egypt or of sacking Alexandria.[92]

Finally, after much procrastination, early in June 1605 Benavente decided upon an expedition into the Levant in order to divert Ottoman land forces from the war effort in Hungary.[93] However, the Genoese pressured Benavente to limit the powers of the overall commander of the expedition, Santa Cruz. This he did. The viceroy also issued instructions that no *empresa* was to be undertaken unless it was with great certainty of success (specifically, no attempt was to be made on Alexandria unless it was with absolute confidence).[94] It was an echo of previous instructions: in 1565 Toledo had stated that he would only take risks with 'certain and well-founded hopes' of success – in which case, la Valette might well have pointed out, they were not really risks at all.[95] During the Holy League the orders issued from the humble desk in the Escorial held that any meeting with the enemy should be undertaken on the most favourable terms: there was to be no battle without having the near-total certainty of victory, '*sin tener la casi seguridad de la victoria*'.[96]

The strategy or outlook of the Catholic Monarchy was therefore shaped by a marked conservatism, one in which the preservation of the galleys was – or at least came very close to being – the overall strategic priority. There was a critical contradiction between the tactical priorities of the Habsburgs of Spain, which were based upon prudence and preservation, and their simultaneous espousal of concepts of reputation and honour. Theirs was an understated, cautious form of holy war, one that relied more upon guile than *grandeza*. Perhaps the clearest example of the dichotomy between *reputación* and prudence can be found in the exchange of September 1570: as the winter closed in, Doria clearly doubted that the Venetian fleet would be able to fight effectively with the enemy *'per non essere all'ordine'*. In complete contrast Marc'Antonio Colonna spoke in terms of glory and *grandeza*; it would be better, he solemnly informed Doria, for His Majesty to lose the entire fleet than to suffer the shame of his commanders refusing to fight and returning in safety to his kingdoms. Glorious failure was not, however, on the agenda for the Genoese admiral-prince, who replied that his (prospective) refusal to fight was based entirely upon the defects of the Venetian armada, 'for not being in order'. The tempests of autumn already loomed over all plans, as the fleet 'could not be risked in such a long navigation, and in manifest danger of misfortune'.[97]

Of course, these discussions focused on a range of issues beyond the number of ships available to the respective commanders. What is interesting, although impossible to prove, is that Charles V, Philip II and Philip III apparently formulated their strategy or instructions not only according to an understanding of the strengths and weaknesses of the military forces of the Turk, but also, implicitly, with an eye on his duties as the leader of the Muslim world and, as such, as defender of its territorial integrity. The principal consequence of this interpretation of the Ottoman Empire was that the objectives which were deemed admirable in other forms of naval warfare – the successful engagement with the enemy fleet, the capture and defence of a position of decisive strategic importance – were viewed with considerable doubt, if not overt reluctance, by the ministers of the Crown of Spain. Paradoxically, the unwillingness to be drawn into a fight betrayed a certain contempt for the forces of the enemy, an emphasis upon their reliance upon novices, *'gente nueva'*. The fundamental perspective of the Catholic Monarchy was that war, whether holy or not, was a theatre which seldom rewarded the enthusiastic 'volunteer'. For this reason Charles V, Philip II, Philip III and their ministers looked to systems, to a body of maritime knowledge and skills that could be taught and to a capacity to survive that could only be acquired *en galera*. One of the singular paradoxes in the outlook of the Habsburgs of Spain was, on the one hand, to insist that princes should be judged by their actions, not by their words, while they simultaneously expressed an insurmountable scepticism about the value of any one event or success. This paradox could only lead to a strategy which was fundamentally negative or restrictive, in that it held that a major defeat in battle might lead to the collapse of Catholic Christendom, while significant victories – even, indeed, overwhelming triumphs – were almost guaranteed to lead nowhere.

It hardly needs to be said that in adopting this stance, the Habsburgs profoundly disappointed their Christian confederates; indeed, it is clear that the actions – or inaction – of Andrea Doria provoked profound frustration among his colleagues and peers within the Monarchy.[98] Having collaborated with the Prudent King's forces in the years 1570–73 both the Papacy and Venice complained that Philip II would only be interested in a 'defensive war' against the Turks.[99] Philip III fielded similar complaints. The Emperor Rudolf II grumbled about the instructions given by Benavente to the second Marquis of Santa Cruz in the three campaigning seasons after 1604. In Vienna it had been hoped that the actions of the galleys would secure a valuable, if not decisive, advantage for the imperial forces fighting in Hungary by diverting important parts of the Sultan's army to the defence of the Mediterranean coastline.[100]

The thoughts of Charles V, Philip II or Philip III on these allegations are lost to history, but it is impossible not to speculate on how the Habsburg kings must have reacted emotionally and intellectually to them. The accusation of only being interested in a defensive form of warfare was probably fair and accurate; the problem was that no one in Venice, Vienna, the Vatican or Valetta ever set out a creditable alternative strategy for offensive war or explained how it was to be pursued or paid for: here again, the *thèse* Murphey must be applied, in that it was all but impossible to overcome the enormous Ottoman land forces in this period.

Any answer to the question of the emotional reaction of the Habsburgs to the often violent accusations levelled at them must, therefore, be speculative, but it would be logical to argue that Charles V,

Philip II and Philip III would at some point have conceded to their consciences that the complaints of the other princes of Christendom were justified; they would, on the other hand, have immediately insisted that the rationale behind them was profoundly fanciful and dubious. The one agency that guaranteed the (very different) long-term strategies of both the Republic of Venice and the Order of the Knights of the Hospital of St John of Jerusalem at Malta was the royal armada of the Catholic Monarchy; the extent of the assistance given by Philip II and Philip III to the imperial cause in the 1590s and early 1600s did rather suggest that the same argument could be effectively rehearsed for the frontier in central Europe.

If the Habsburg strategy evolved from the dictates of the *galera en buen orden* then it could also be justified by appealing to a broad set of Renaissance adages framed around the classical notion of prudence. A Florentine saying held that 'one ought not to take risks without the most urgent necessity or without being sure of victory'. Another dictum from the same tradition was to enjoy the benefit of time – '*godere el beneficio del tempo*'.[101] These ideas were the precepts upon which the Catholic Monarchy drew in formulating its strategy: they seem to have owed a great deal to history, most especially to Polybius's account of the First Punic War, which served as a direct model for sixteenth-century conflict in the *mare nostrum*. Whatever the humanist context, it was essentially true that after 1530 the avoidance of defeat was afforded greater weight and value than the quest for success. This strategy – if, indeed, it can be termed such – led the Habsburg kings to exercise a sort of caution that was extreme and not without a hint of the comical, as in 1564 when the entire fleet landed at the Peñón de Vélez, which its corsairs and inhabitants abandoned almost as soon as the large Christian armada came into view over the horizon. The campaign was celebrated as an exemplary demonstration of prudence and vigilance, not of valour and honour.[102] In 1614 the squadron of Spain took the Moroccan port of Mamora without, as Braudel says, firing a shot.[103]

The phenomenon of religious warfare inevitably raises the question of outlook, or *mentalité*, whether, or to what extent, the supernatural was seen to intervene in the physical world. Indeed, in a certain sense it goes further than this, and poses the question of consciousness, of the extent to which religious conviction was, as Lucien Febvre argued in one of the pioneering studies of early modern history, ever-present in the minds of men of the sixteenth century.[104]

The first problem in trying to address this issue lies in the obvious inconsistencies of the viceroys, captains general – and, indeed, of the King himself. The Habsburg system had a tendency towards complaint built into it; the stratagems and ambiguities of diplomatic discourse and the 'fog of war' necessarily complicate any attempt to understand *mentalité*. Marc'Antonio Colonna has on the whole been judged favourably by historians; yet it is clear that he knew how to calibrate his message to the interests of his audience. From the outset Don John treated him with considerable suspicion.[105] But everyone manipulated the news – or at least tried to do so. As Professor Fernández Álvarez notes in his invaluable biography of Charles V, the emperor certainly played down the significance of his losses at Algiers in 1541; indeed, he began to do so in letters written before he had even left the Algerian shoreline.[106]

The question of inconsistency emerges in other ways, some of them very difficult to quantify or pin down. It is noticeable, for instance, that in early July 1565 Doria made a surprisingly assertive and confident assessment of the possibility of sending relief to the besieged Hospitaller fortresses.[107] Direct comparison with expeditions that he himself led is, of course, problematic, but it is quite a challenge to reconcile the spirit of the advice that he proffered to others with the explanations of his own actions in 1570 and in other years. Before Lepanto Don John inspired his men by exhorting them to punish the arrogance of the Turk, to end the long chain of victories. Yet almost in the same breath he reminded them of the heavy losses sustained by the enemy in the previous months.[108] In a certain sense the two ideas were contradictory, in that a wretched and exhausted enemy could hardly be accused of arrogance, just as victory over such a foe could hardly be deemed to be a historical turning point.

At what point was God's providential intercession expected or required? Galley commanders were obliged to walk a fine line. The messianic objectives of Habsburg kingship were stated and formulated in numerous ways and on hundreds of occasions, but to argue that this impulse originated in religious belief invites certain difficulties. At no point did Philip II or Philip III ever plan a campaign which depended upon the intervention of divine providence; to argue that these kings believed the world might be about to end is patently absurd, as they spent so much time preparing for 'el año que viene', putting their galleys to bed early, ordering consignments of bizcocho, making plans for the improvement of their many rickety fortifications and issuing vast, lengthy and point-by-point instructions to their diplomats. It is without doubt true that the instructions issued by the kings were often so carefully balanced, so detailed and of such length that they flirted with contradiction. 'We trust in God,' wrote Philip II in his instructions of 18 June 1565, 'that not only will the Turks not succeed in what they are attempting, but that they will leave with damage and loss.' Still, the King asked his high-admiral for a paper on how to proceed should 'the opposite occur ... and if we should try to retake the island immediately, as the longer it is left the more difficult it will become'.[109] Prior to the convocation of the Holy League, the Prudent King spelt out in great detail the difficulties in waging war in the Levant: if there was one recurring assumption beneath these papers it was that God could not be relied upon to assist the forces fighting under His banner. Explanations given by the Habsburgs for the failure of major campaigns cited the scourge of el peste among the oarsmen and the terrible weather which served to delay, and sometimes derail, Christian operations.[110]

By the same standard these statesmen had a clear understanding of the likelihood of the outbreak and spread of disease among the crews. The explanations given at the time tended to focus on the 'bad airs' of a particular port or coastline, an idea that peoples from a certain region or background built up a certain type or form of immunity, and that to move peoples from one region or occupation to another was to increase the likelihood of their succumbing to disease. At Tunis the emperor ordered that the carcasses of Christians, Muslims, horses and donkeys be buried 'so that they did not infect the air'.[111] If carcasses spewed forth poisonous odours, then the airs of many regions were believed to be damaging to those unused to them. German troops found the remorseless heat of the Mediterranean summer at Tunis extremely difficult.[112] The elements had a detrimental effect upon military forces, no matter what their previous accomplishments. In February 1553 the Viceroy of Sicily wrote to commiserate with Charles V on the recent reverses in Germany. He referred to the singular triumphs of Pavia, Vienna and Tunis, before remarking that 'God had wanted to show that neither arms, nor soldiers, nor human forces were enough against the valour of Your Majesty, but only those that are superhuman, such as the cold, the airs and waters'.[113]

The Muslims were believed to think along similar lines. The principal argument advanced by Mustafa Pasha for the attack upon Cyprus rather than Granada was that of feasibility; the voyage to Spain would obviously be extremely long and dangerous. 'The arms of the Sultan are not privileged from misfortunes or storms ... knowing that Turks fall ill and are consumed when they venture away from their lands and into a different climate.' The dangers of campaigning in alien climates had been demonstrated, he observed, by the efforts of the Christian emperors and the kings of France and England to conquer Jerusalem.[114] Again, these prescriptions, while in a sense primitive and sometimes inconsistent, were at least borne out by the experience of successive generations of soldiers and sailors; indeed, they were profoundly historical in origin and nature.[115]

A good explanation of the principle that governed the deployment of the fleet after 1560 can be found in the conclusion to a detailed memorandum penned by Doria on the options for 1605: 'Your Majesty will order what you are minded to do. I would only add that the affairs of the sea are so uncertain and that they can be got right or wrong for so many different accidents that some times what is chosen for the best option ends up providing the worst result.'[116] This was the principle that had governed his career; it was the dogma that he had shared instinctively – indeed almost telepathically – with *el rey prudente*.

A fine example of the balance between God's intercession and man's actions could be found in Don Pedro de Toledo's correspondence throughout 1537. Again, the balance between heaven and earth was a fine one. Throughout the summer he repeatedly stated that the defences of Naples would be able to repel the Ottoman fleet – 'if God should allow it'.[117] It would be impossible to dismiss this belief in the possibility of providential intercession, although it should be added that from January the viceroy had meticulously prepared the coastal defences.[118] In his response to news of the brutal skirmish between Barbarossa's galleys and those of Venice in waters off Corfu in July, the viceroy observed that this event could present an opportunity to do some damage to the Turk 'sooner than he would have wanted'. But, again, this observation was framed in the light of God's providential design: the chance to do some damage would only occur 'should Our Lord want it'.[119]

In November Don Pedro de Toledo went further and penned a detailed memorandum in which he set out his belief that both Venice and Pope Paul III were planning to take advantage of Francis I's intervention in Italy in order to advance their own private interests; in the case of the Most Serene Republic these were taken to lie in Milan and in reducing the authority of Charles V in the peninsula; with regard to His Holiness, Toledo had no doubt in averring that the Pope's interests lay in Florence ('we have seen that His Beatitude has given great proof of having thirst and greed for that state').[120]

Trying to decipher what lay behind Toledo's assessment is a fiendishly difficult task; his evaluation could be read as fundamentally secular in nature, in that he was clearly aware of the importance of proper preparation and the timetable of military administration (Francis I's intervention would suffer from severe logistical shortages, he predicted, as the harvest had been gathered in and the major fortresses would be well provisioned). On the other hand, his view could be taken to be confessional, in that his perception was that both Venice and His Holiness lacked the sort of religious conviction or integrity which was emblematic of 'His Catholic Caesarean Majesty'. In either case the matter touched upon that most sacred of ambitions of the Habsburgs of Spain – to be men of their word, to abide by their solemn vows. Neither of the viceroy's assessments should be divorced from the recent history of the peninsula, or the consideration of the nature of political authority within it – namely, Clement VII's achievement in securing the imperial fief of the duchy of Florence for the Medici, or the status of Milan as a fief which had recently reverted to the imperial chamber. To this end the viceroy placed great weight on the Franco-Ottoman alliance and the presence of Neapolitan bandits or outlaws on Süleyman's galleys: again, emphasis fell on the ambiguities of Spanish rule in Italy, the paradox that the Kingdom of Naples was both the means of fighting the war and the cause of it.

The most exact demonstration of the mental outlook of the top tier of Habsburg commanders – in fact, a demonstration so surgical in nature that it may serve as almost a dissection of the different strands within it – can be found in one of the invaluable letters written in by Don García de Toledo to Don John during the Holy League. It set out the circumstances likely to be found in the summer of 1572 and compared them to those of seven years previously. His premise was a simple one: in order for the Kapudan Pasha to thwart the Christian expedition, his fleet would need to be either large enough in size to oppose that of the Holy League, or light enough to draw near and attack before withdrawing. It seemed highly unlikely that Uluç Ali Pasha would have a fleet of these dimensions or qualities ('I do not see that the enemy has the forces to fight, nor the feet to run if they should come near to Your Highness').

Toledo then moved on to consider the specifics of a prospective Christian assault on the Negroponte and the possibility of the Ottomans landing a relief expedition similar to the one that he (Toledo) had put ashore in September 1565. Toledo surmised that Don John could have four main reasons for confidence. The first was 'that God will not want to help them as He helped us' in the year of the Great Siege. The second was that, whatever design or plan he embarked upon, Don John would not be as negligent in employing a guard as Mustafa and Piyale had been at Malta. The third was that in 1565 Toledo had reinforced 60 galleys from an old fleet, *'una armada vieja'*: 'and so, strengthened and with the most skilled rowing crews, we took the flower [of our forces] to arm the said ships'. In the aftermath of *la batalla naval* the enemy, in contrast, would have to operate with a new armada, one 'little exercised at the oar';

these novice crews, Toledo reiterated, would not be able to exert the force at the oar that was necessary 'for their security'. Finally, he pointed out that in 1565 he had chosen to take only 10,000 well-armed infantry, 'judging that the smaller number would be stronger than a bigger force'. This army was to engage an Ottoman force of 20,000 ill-equipped or poorly armed troops at Malta. In contrast, in 1572 Don John would be in command of 20,000 soldiers with excellent weaponry, and the Turkish infantry would be much smaller in number.[121]

Toledo's argument, therefore, rested on four separate assessments – God's benevolent intercession; the negligent enemy; the reinforced Christian fleet; the value of veteran troops. It would be unrealistic or unfair to place emphasis on any one of these strengths. A fair summation of his advice, however, would seem to be that in 1565 God had been generous enough to give the Christians an adversary who was negligent while Toledo, in contrast, had exercised due caution in all things. This assessment referred back to the failure of the Turks to organise reconnaissance patrols around the island. Scouting missions should, Toledo added, have been relatively easy to organise.[122]

If Toledo's paper of 1572 restrospectively cast the relief of Malta as the triumph of diligence over negligence, then this line of thinking was consistent with what he had written at the time. 'We did all that we could,' he modestly concluded in September 1565, 'and our enemies have failed in everything that they should have done ... And so God has been served to have these events unfold.'[123] Toledo's expression of humility was perhaps the most revealing exposition of the ethos of the Catholic Monarchy, the idea of service to the greater cause by restraint and diligence in the exercise of arms. This is not to deny that he professed himself to be devoted to the cause of the Almighty. Fearing that his life was near its end, he hoped to spend whatever 'little remains of it' in the service of God.[124] Much as the Catholic Monarchy undertook action on His behalf, the commanders did not count on God's direct intervention. A division existed between secular realities and providential ends. In a letter to Toledo of 22 May 1565 Philip II expressed the hope that God might intervene to thwart the ambitions of the Turk, but for his part the 'principal' concern was to have skilled,

experienced men, *'gente útil y plática'*. Given the dimensions of the
enemy force, the key to success was to be alert and prepared to seize any
opportunity that the Almighty might present: 'because of the weather or
other events that tend to happen on sea and land, so that with the help
of Our Lord some good effects may be achieved, so that we can impede
and delay them'.[125] Don John of Austria's thinking and outlook followed
a similar formula. Before sailing from the Cape of San Giovanni on
16 September 1571, he expressed his belief that 'God, whose cause this
is, will have to help us …' Yet the *capitán general del mar Mediterráneo*
had previously received ample documentation on the state of the enemy
fleet and its troops – reports to which he directly referred. The enemy
fleet was superior in size but not in quality of ships or men, *'no lo es de
cualidad de navíos ní de gente'*.[126] A similar balance was struck in 1596.
Again, the messianic imperative – the drive to perform the service of
God and to secure the common good of Christendom – was set against
the probabilities of galley warfare. 'According to the reports that you will
have of the enemy, and of the quantity and quality of his fleet and our
own,' Philip II instructed Doria on 7 May 1596, '… I am very sure that
if the enemy comes with his men [and galleys] in bad order, as they say is
the case, and you have the opportunity to take advantage in some way
you will do so. Do not miss any chance. I hope in God, as this is so much
His cause, He will help you to end my concern. You are to advise me
frequently of everything you do.'[127]

The contrast with those who entered upon crusade as a demonstration of princely valour and individual derring-do was complete. As we
have seen, Colonna blamed the 'bad airs' of Corfu for his difficulties in
1572: it was a weak explanation, one which portrayed him in a bad light,
as the King and his servants had repeatedly warned him and his
colleagues that the atmosphere would disproportionately affect raw
recruits, not veterans. In his valuable studies of the Holy League,
Enrique García Hernán contrasts the messianic vision of Pius V with the
more secular and prudential outlook of the King and his ministers, a
difference of outlook that led to the complaints (mentioned above)
about His Catholic Majesty's timidity and preference for a defensive
war.[128] This is not to deny that the Habsburgs continually sought God's

intercession. In 1532 Charles V was told by his doctors that his infected leg would have to be amputated at the knee. He refused to accept this prognosis, 'preferring to die rather than lose the leg, and with his efforts, and the great remedies of the doctors and, above all, the willingness of God, who guarded him so that he could do great things in His service and to augment His faith, the illness of Caesar began to diminish'.[129] These were magnificent sentiments, but they perhaps indicated that the Habsburgs took greater risks with their physical well-being and health than they did with their royal armada.

News of the surrender of the Christian garrison at Djerba elicited laments that touched upon the mysteries of His Providential Design. The ambassador in Genoa opined that 'these are the ways of the world, and it has to be hoped that God has done it for the greater good'. [130] Yet a year previously, even before the expedition had sailed, the King had specified that with good planning and the help of God, the campaign would be undertaken 'with the security that is necessary', *'con la seguridad que conviene'*.[131] Multiple warnings were made during the expedition that God was not helping and that the right degree of care had not been taken.[132]

Man was not powerless when navigating against the forces of nature, in that experience demonstrated that His design was to allow specific winds at determined points in the calendar. In July 1554 Prince Philip issued orders to hurry preparations for the fleet that was to ferry him to England; the armada was to be *en orden* and ready to sail: 'May God be pleased to give me fair winds and a good journey.'[133] In March 1565 Toledo forbade all exports from Sicily on account of the shortage of rain. He would not be able to do anything until 'I see if God will be served to make it rain', *'hasta ver si será Dios servido que llueva'*.[134] God controlled the skies, although man could respond with intelligence and determination to His decree.

When the King wrote to his ministers to explain the successful capture of the Peñón de Vélez he explained that God had been pleased to ordain it that a number of the Turks inside had fled and those remaining had chosen to surrender the fort.[135] This was certainly true, but the enterprise had been designed to take advantage of conditions and to present the garrison with the worst possible set of circumstances – a massive and sudden descent by a Christian force towards the end of the season. In a similar vein, Santa Cruz concluded his assessment of the prospects of the Christian fleet in 1570 with the statement that the outcome of a battle with the *armada del Turco* would be a good one, 'as pleasing God I have confidence that as this is His cause He will be served to help us'.[136] But God's cause had to be assisted by man's caution and vigilance: previously the Marquis had listed the conditions which afforded the Christians a clear advantage. When these circumstances changed with the fall of Nicosia on 9 September, Santa Cruz immediately came to agree with Doria that the fleet should disband and return to its bases.

The failure of the Navarino campaign in 1572 made some statesmen wonder about the intentions of the Almighty: 'May God send us another opportunity as good as the one which has just been missed, if our sins or bad luck had not thrown us off course and along such strange roads . . .'[137] Toledo struck a similar note when he heard that the Venetians had abandoned the Holy League in 1573. 'As God has been served that the [Holy] League has not lasted,' he mused, 'this must be due to what is best for His service, and by this road He must want to give us greater victories than the past ones against His enemies.'[138] At around this point Gregory XIII cast the breakup of the League in a much more sinister light: Venice's decision to settle with the Turk was, he concluded, inspired by the Devil himself.[139] These were heady sentiments, but on the other hand, Toledo, like the King, had been painfully aware of the serious errors committed by the *Signoria* over the previous years and both men had retained profound scepticism about the long-term commitment of the Republic to the Holy League. Toledo's letter subsequently went on to set out, in regulation detail, the restrictions and limitations by which Don John would have to abide in the coming season.[140]

In 1602 the viceroy hoped to defend the coast of Naples. 'Things have been put in the best possible order,' wrote Francisco de Castro in August, 'I hope to God that the Ottoman fleet will not be able to do any damage on these coasts.'[141] God might help – if man had done everything possible as, indeed, the viceroy affirmed had been the case. In

1608 when an impressively well-armed squadron of Naples (20 reinforced galleys) sailed to Spain to undertake the capture of Larache, Benavente expressed the hope that God would give them a good journey and a good outcome, '*Dios les dé buen viaje y muy buen suceso*'.[142] It was a familiar sentiment.[143] At other times, statesmen invoked God because they were aware of the improbability of success. 'In this kingdom they are praying for the right outcome [of this campaign], asking Our Lord for the good outcome of this armada', wrote Maqueda in August 1601.[144] But he, like everyone else, surely recognised how difficult the *empresa de Argel* would be.

The loss of three galleys of the Religion of St John in 1605 was very much something to be lamented, wrote Feria in April. It must, he added, 'have been a punishment from God for His occult causes, as in the government and seamanship [of them] there was no error'.[145] Yet it was clearly recognised that to run along the coast of North Africa in April was to flirt with disaster, whatever the level of seamanship. In 1605 Carlo Doria conceded that He might be willing to assist the expedition that summer, which was to be undertaken in His cause; however, this rather devout observation immediately preceded a much more worldly discourse about the amount of noise generated by the congregation of the fleet, the large number of enemy galleys ('even if they are not of the order to come to fight with our ships, at least they will be able to put difficulties before us') and the need to refine the structure of command, allowing each commander the option to abandon the fleet at his discretion.[146] Whatever His providential design, Doria did not want to have to take direct orders from Santa Cruz.

Such statements must be understood as the point at which a basically secular outlook – that God helps those galley commanders who help themselves – merged into an understanding of divine omnipotence; in the final instance the messianic objectives may have served to inculcate a sense of humility in the Habsburgs and their ministers, for it was certainly the most glaring form of arrogance to expect or depend upon God's providential intervention. What does this tell us about the mental outlook of Doria or the King? How did they view the Ottoman Turk and his curiously ineffective fleet? Two distinct lines of thinking become tenable: first, that it was a mark of the fundamentally misguided nature of the Islamic religion to suppose that the Almighty would intervene directly to favour the Muslim peoples and forces, as theirs was manifestly a false 'sect' which He abhorred and repudiated. The second argument would be that the very thing that betrayed the falsity of the religious convictions of the Muslims was their apparent confidence that the Almighty would step in to favour their cause, as warfare functioned according to certain inexorable and incontrovertible rules which applied to all. The first interpretation was fundamentally confessional and religious in nature and origin; the second was predominantly secular in character, being essentially a rejection of the application of confessional criteria to military events (it was also, perhaps, a strain of thought derived from the Greek and Roman literature on war). Which, then, was the correct one?

The more convincing case would be the second interpretation, as the Christian approach to warfare may have drawn upon the rhetoric of the cause of God but it was not based upon the idea of entitlement born of religious certitude. The mental world-view of Philip II and Doria (as demonstrated in their correspondence in 1572) distinguished sharply between religious and military matters, between what they would, ideally, have liked to achieve and what they could realistically hope to accomplish. Fundamentally, this distinction was based upon a firm division between civilian and military personnel, between green novice and gnarled veteran. History showed that the seas and elements favoured neither Christian nor infidel. If this outlook had a theological dimension it was that it was a fundamental error to suppose that the Almighty would intervene in war in order to prove the validity of faith in Him, to use galley warfare to prove His true nature or identity. It was, moreover, a sin to put God to the test: it was one thing to pray for victory, but these entreaties could hardly compensate for any failure to make the necessary preparations. The Almighty tended to help and favour those captains who sailed aboard reinforced galleys.

The idea of military campaigns as a direct demonstration of providential blessing was an alien one. True, this line of analysis can be more easily applied to Doria, Philip II, Philip III, Toledo and Santa

Cruz than to a figure like Pope St Pius V, who saw God's design in every action; la Valette, Colonna and the Venetian commanders, moreover, tended to be so 'variable' that dissecting the precise balance between heaven and earth in their outlook might be almost impossible. As we have seen, in the summer of 1571 Pius V urged Don John of Austria to seek battle, promising him that God would certainly give victory to the Christians.[147] His Holiness clearly believed that Divine Providence would intervene to favour His cause. But all others – even, indeed, the Pope himself! – were well informed of the dramatic shortages and problems experienced by the enemy fleet during the summer, characteristics which were the consequence of the very administrative system of 'the Turk' and which had been regularly manifested since the 1530s. And in conversation with Cardinal de'Medici the Pope revealed his concerns and misgivings about both Venice and His Catholic Majesty.[148] On another occasion, a few years previously, Pius V urged the King that the best policy was to proceed under the banner of religion in the Low Countries, arguing that it was better to have His benediction and to fight against all of His enemies than to proceed with political calculation. This was not, however, quite the same as saying that God would favour those who fought under the King's banner, as the Pope's words seemed to suggest that glorious failure in His cause was more worthy than was the exercise of restraint, caution and dissimulation. His Holiness's formula was very close in tone and content to the argument put by Colonna to Doria in September 1570: it represented a world-view which was very different to that of the King and his officers.[149]

The *mentalité* of Philip II of Spain would, then, seem not only to have distinguished sharply between religious hope and military probability, but also to have rejected the very idea that divine intercession was likely to provide regular assistance to those crusading in His cause. It would clearly be mistaken to interpret this strand of thought as revealing an absence of faith, since within the providential outlook there existed the proviso that God might want to punish His people for their sins. Having said this, there must have been many who reflected that if the Almighty was not going to help His Holy Royal Catholic Majesty in the age of

Süleyman the Magnificent, Martin Luther and Jean Calvin, then when would Providential blessing be an agent in history? The kings certainly instructed their men not to blaspheme and ordered their officers to punish 'the nefarious sin' in an exemplary manner; they did not, however, operate on the basis that this provision for moral rectitude would guarantee them favourable winds or shield their forces from the scourge of disease.

It is, of course, impossible to reconstruct with absolute certainty what Andrea Doria or Philip III saw in the treacherous winds in the Channel of Málaga or the Gulf of Lion; the only historical certainty is that they envisaged that man could, through diligent husbandry over many years and decisive skill at the moment of action, make maritime disaster less likely to occur. Febvre wrote that the 'great revolution that would end by subordinating logic and mathematics to experimentation' was not yet in sight in the age of *Gargantua and Pantagruel*; a similar sort of chasm separated the seafarer from the knowledge and understanding of the pockets of high pressure above north-western Europe which provoked the sudden and fierce northerly winds of late summer and autumn, the *mistrales* or *tramontanas*.[150] Yet any sixteenth-century skipper worth his salt knew when the northerlies were likely to give way to the easterlies; since the age of Carthage and Rome mariners had warned their superiors about the sudden and fierce southerly winds which made the coastline of Sicily so treacherous in July. European sailors have perhaps always been uniquely aware of how southerly and westerly winds are warm, and easterlies and northerlies much cooler. In the year of the Great Siege the violent south-easterlies that blew Toledo and his heavily reinforced galleys from Cape Passero to Favignana were one more problem or 'inconvenience' to take into account and overcome. It was not due to divine providence that the Catholic armada was able to ride out these storms; rather the success – for it was a major, incontrovertible success – was down to that most prosaic of qualities or achievements, the fleet being *muy bien en orden*.

This is not to deny that nearly all letters contain within them a reference to the intercession of God: His intervention was sought and feared in equal quantities; so closely matched were the overall ambitions of the King of Spain with the very cause of God that His Catholic Majesty often dismissed possibilities or contingencies that would have proven unwelcome to his monarchy with the stock phrase that God would not want this to happen, *'que Dios no querrá'*.[151] It was easy to see what He would not want; conversely, few statesmen failed to express the hope that He might want to assist those fighting under the banner of the Cross in their unrelenting campaigns against heretics and infidels. But on no occasion did Charles V, Philip II or Philip III ever plan a campaign in the Mediterranean which specifically depended upon providential assistance. On the contrary, nothing was left to fate or faith: the furious allegations levelled at the Catholic Monarchy by its confederates in 1572 were not entirely unfair or ungrounded. Calculation, rather than crusade, was the byword of the Habsburgs of Spain and their officer-class.

The very point that Philip II wanted to make in moments of extreme tension was that 'a coherent rationalism', 'a well-organised rationalist system' (Febvre's terms) based upon very simple principles was inherently superior to ideas derived from a pious or confessional mentality, *'como fácilmente queriendo mirar en ello se deja entender'*. Attempting to trace the broader lineage behind this outlook is more difficult. It might be tenable to see this as a manifestation of the 'habits of mind and powers of comprehension' which had been developed in Europe during the course of the Middle Ages.[152] It seems highly possible that the influence of the Greek historian Polybius informed this line of thinking; certainly a very strong case could be made that the Prudent King, as a man of his time, held his highest ambition to be to implement the enlightening principles set down by the Greeks and Romans – at least this seems to be unequivocally and undeniably true of his aims in the *mare nostrum*. The long, dry lists of instructions issued by the King to his naval commanders may be a singularly unlikely basis from which to assess the *mentalité* of the sixteenth century; on the other hand, it could be argued with a certain degree of confidence that the most valuable insight into spirituality lies in the willingness to risk everything in this world in the hope of reward in the next. If this proviso is accepted, then the conclusion is clear: the conferment of total faith in God, the willingness to place all resources and hopes in His hands, was as difficult for the Habsburg monarchs of Spain as it has been for Christians in any period of history.

IX

The Lordship of the Sea

The concept of the command or lordship of the sea, *el señorío del mar*, was frequently employed by the captains and officers of the sixteenth and seventeenth centuries. Doria, the viceroys and senior naval officers like Diego de Brochero regularly used the idea.[1] The concept certainly had a wide currency. Francis Bacon was convinced of the historical value of the *señorío del mar*. 'But this much is certain, that he that commands the sea is at great liberty, and may take as much and as little of the war as he will. Whereas those that be strongest by land are many times nevertheless in great straits.'[2]

Implicit in Bacon's formulation were two related ideas: first, that the exercise of sea power might lead the admiral to use his guile and patience, avoiding the enemy until it served him to act; second that successful campaigns necessarily brought together resources from two or more separate and sometimes quite distant territories. Both ideas were firmly located in the record of naval warfare in the classical period;[3] both precepts were directly and immediately relevant to Habsburg operations at sea from the very beginning. In 1528 Andrea Doria switched to Charles V's side, meaning in effect that the imperialists became lords of that sea, '*señores del aquel mar*'.[4] Capelloni's biography of Doria, first published in 1569, noted that Charles V's campaigns at Tunis in 1535 and Provence in 1536 had to be supplied at every stage from the sea; the latter ran into trouble due to 'the lack of provisions, which, as they say, are the nerve of war'.[5]

The examination of the sea and the rhythm of the winds should serve to answer the question of how the Ottoman fleets, which were so often said to be poorly equipped, managed to exercise 'the lordship of the sea' and to achieve the undeniable successes that they did in the course of the sixteenth century. Christian observers identified two great advantages enjoyed by the enemy: 'not only are there many of them and few of us, but also the winds favour them and disadvantage us'.[6] There was a certain truth in this formulation, although it was drawn from a highly rhetorical piece written to celebrate chivalry in general and the Hospitaller knights in particular and cannot, therefore, be removed entirely from its political context.

If the Mediterranean is a sea of many breezes, then the prevailing summer winds run from the north-west to the north-east across the entire length and breadth of the sea.[7] As Professor John H. Pryor demonstrated in a major study, the preponderance of northerly winds throughout the summer had a dramatic effect upon seafaring for a very simple reason: this was that the North African coast was extremely dangerous, with very few safe anchorages and numerous shoals and hidden banks.[8] Skippers of ships blown towards the coast of 'Barbary' faced a very serious problem. The climate did, however, provide certain forms of assistance to seafarers. In the first place, the tides, if weak or variable, run in a counter-clockwise direction and could be exploited by skilful skippers and pilots. Moreover, the geography of the sea consists of a large number of microclimates. The exploitation of local or regional conditions allowed captains to perform a number of operations or manoeuvres, even if these (generally) light winds were necessarily of a temporary duration or of use only for short-range journeys.[9] Pryor demonstrated that trade flowed along several major sea lanes or 'trunk routes', which were the consequence of both the great weather systems that generated the prevailing northerly winds of summer and the localised microclimates formed by the interaction of chilly mountain, warm sea, dry desert and intense sunshine.[10] Thus Corsica was taken to dominate Genoa, as no ship could leave the Republic's harbour without touching on the coastline of the island (Alba put it that the Genoese saw the island as being as essential as 'the light and warmth of the sun'). It was also believed that Corsica was vital to navigation to and from Sardinia, the Mallorcas and the states of southern and central Italy.[11]

In many respects, the outlooks of both Doria and Toledo were more deterministic and more pessimistic in tone than the conclusions reached by Professor Pryor. The *capitanes generales* insisted that the 'trunk routes' which Pryor deemed to be relatively safe and well travelled were in fact capricious and unforgiving passages of sea. The diurnal land and sea breezes which he took to be an aid to navigation could also, they insisted, greatly complicate it. In their eyes the essential problem in navigation was that there were few harbours and many winds. It is true that in advancing this proposition they were not exactly making things harder for themselves, in that the picture of a cruel and tempestuous sea could only serve to underline the skills, knowledge and value of those few men who knew how to ride the waves and harness the winds.[12] The captains general perhaps knew how to play on the concerns and fears of the monarchs of Habsburg Spain, whose experiences on the seas had been far from comfortable or reassuring.[13] Finding justification or comparison for them is difficult, although it might be said that the hazardous and demanding conditions encountered in the seas of Sicily during the War of Messina (1674–78) demonstrated the dangers of sailing on that coastline. Expert seamanship and high quality ships were essential on the coastlines of the *mezzogiorno*.[14]

The case advanced by the captains general, however, went further than simply arguing that navigation was highly dangerous: they held that the use and application of the great technological innovation of the *Cinquecento* – the modern *trace italienne* fortress defended by mass-produced artillery – was in itself fundamentally limited. Above all else, this was because of the shortage of water. Larger fortresses necessarily needed larger garrisons, which in turn required greater logistical provision. The positions which Christian and Muslim fought for did not, on the whole, command major sources of water such as rivers, deep wells or streams; many did not, in fact, have a well within their walls or even boast an adequate water tank in their cellars. Very few of the major harbours commanded a productive agricultural hinterland, Messina being the chief exception. There were, consequently, relatively few harbours which offered any sort of independent strategic value; any fort depended upon continual supply and re-supply, and this could be achieved either by contact with local authorities (thus the problematic relationship with the 'King of Tunis') or from the sea, a task which the galley and the galley alone could perform with any degree of confidence.[15] This view was then set out in relation to their understanding of the reinforced galley, the obvious deduction being that the more difficult or hazardous the operation, the more high-powered the warships employed on it would have to be.

Professional seafarers constantly warned their employers about the dangers of navigation. The writer Giovanni Botero (c.1544–1617) cited Andrea Doria's assertion that there were only three safe harbours on the coast of Spain: June, July and Cartagena.[16] This seems to have been a realistic and accurate description: in 1554 the Council of State deliberated on the possibility of establishing a squadron of galleys in Catalonia, Valencia, the Balearics, Malaga or Alicante. These discussions turned on the fact that there were only four reliable harbours (Rosas, Palamós, Tortosa and Denia) in Catalonia and the Kingdom of Valencia, and that all four were hindered by major drawbacks or limitations of one sort or another.[17] In the late seventeenth century Barcelona offered nothing more than 'a cove in a poor beach'; its port was too shallow for anything but galleys to enter.[18] The coastline near to the city of Valencia remained a treacherous anchorage in the eighteenth century; only small ships would approach it, and even these could drop anchor no nearer than a half-a-mile from the city itself. Alicante, on the other hand, was a much more active sea port.[19] The Mediterranean littoral of Spain boasted few safe harbours and in one of the most reliable anchorages, La Herradura, 25 ships were lost in a few hours when the wind changed suddenly to easterly in October 1562.[20]

Few harbours were safe and secure. Even in Malta the skipper could never allow himself to fall into complacency once he had dropped anchor; the harbour of Marsascirocco was 'safe from all the winds except the *scirocco*, the southerly wind'.[21] In the winter of 1534–35 a storm wrecked as many as 30 Ottoman ships, including 12 galleys, which had been anchored in Puertofarina.[22] In March 1574 a number of ships were lost in Tripoli in a fierce storm which also caused the walls to collapse.[23] In a storm of November 1618, 25 privateering ships and 500 Turks were lost within the harbour wall of Algiers.[24] In the summer of 1567 Pope Pius V, invoking his rights as overlord of the kingdom of Naples, demanded that the Tyrrhenian be guarded by a squadron of royal galleys. This demand led to a series of concerns being voiced: that there was no port belonging to His Catholic Majesty that was appropriate for the task; Porto Ercole could not hold four galleys, let alone the 10 that were set to be sent on the expedition; Santo Stefano was large but unfortified and therefore dangerous as *fuste* (small, light ships commonly used by corsairs and skilled captains) might sneak in under dark to set fire to the galleys; His Holiness would probably not allow Civitavecchia to be used because of his natural fear of having highly armed warships belonging to a foreign prince in it for any length of time.[25] Navigation between these points could entail serious, sudden dangers: the Channel of Piombino presented a 'terribly long, uncertain and perilous undertaking'.[26] In the autumn of 1543 Barbarossa explained that his decision to winter in Toulon was largely motivated by the danger of finding a safe harbour on the voyage down to Italy.[27] This explanation bore, perhaps, a touch of exaggeration; on the other hand, it was not entirely without basis.[28] In October 1573 Doria sailed from Genoa to Portofino; using windows of good weather he then made it to Piombino (an unreliable anchorage, he complained) and then to Portoferraio, before reaching Civitavecchia. But having then sallied twice and travelled as far as 100 miles to the south, he had been forced back by unfavourable winds.[29]

Sailing the Tuscan coastline was, of course, a routine duty of the squadrons. It would have been a grave error to imagine that other stretches of sea were any less dangerous. Messina and Palermo were separated by 200 miles, 150 of which were without a port or any position in which to shelter a flotilla. These were difficult seas: 'And on account of the features of this island, these seas are infested with more winds than there are travellers who dare to cross them.' These words were penned in 1598 by the viceroy, Maqueda, who hoped that the construction of towers or small forts at Orlando and Cefalù would alleviate the danger to both the royal flotilla and to merchantmen; his proposal was dismissed out of hand by the Council of State on the grounds that these anchorages were inadequate, being neither ports nor coves, 'puertos o calas'.[30]

The southern littoral of the kingdom of Naples was at least as dangerous as the shoreline of Sicily. In August 1566, Toledo observed that there were only two ports on 'this coastline'; Messina was separated by 250 miles of hazardous, unsheltered shoreline from Taranto, and Brindisi was as far away again. 'And Your Majesty can believe that in all of the sea there is not a coast that is more dangerous, nor more full of storms [borrascas], and if the enemy wait on it, I hope that they will not leave without receiving some damage on account of the weather, because although August and September are good on other coasts, on these they are perverse.'[31] Christian statesmen were given to arguing that these geographical features favoured their cause, as they served to make the Kapudan Pasha think about how very far he was from safety as summer gave way to autumn.[32]

Toledo's correspondence contained two other points worthy of consideration. These were that at both La Goleta and Malta the diurnal breezes – the winds created by the changing temperatures of land and sea over the course of 24 hours – greatly complicated the approach to the fortresses. In a complex passage setting out various options available to sail a relief force to Malta and the dangers inherent in each one of them, he observed that only good weather would allow him to tow high-sided ships to the island. 'And this channel of Malta is so devilish that when there is neither wind nor sea elsewhere, it appears that all of the elements are found in it. And although it is a common opinion that wind is needed for the ships, the truth is what I say here.' He went on to reiterate, unambiguously, that the enemy was superior in number and to appeal to the King for precise instructions.[33] La Goleta fell into a similar category. 'The nature of the gulf is such that, even if you proceed with fresh breezes at your stern, then when you arrive at 10 or 12 miles from the shore, the winds from land get up. These breezes present a great difficulty to any ship attempting to enter the harbour, even if it is an oared vessel.' He then recounted the usual complaints about the outpost: that the anchorage at the fort offered little depth; large ships could not be accommodated there, 'and if they are light vessels then they can carry nothing but small cargoes ...' Therefore it was impossible to anchor a ship directly beneath the walls of the fort, where they would be protected by volleys of gunfire; because of this deficiency it would be possible for the enemy to approach and burn any vessel.[34]

Needless to say, Doria shared these concerns about the hazards of navigation and repeated them down the years. The coastline of southern Naples was, he warned, particularly hazardous. Between Taranto and Messina there was no harbour, and after mid-September the entire shoreline became 'very dangerous'; in a second letter he went further, stating that there was no safe harbour between Brindisi and Messina. He added that Otranto might one day accommodate a squadron but in the meantime was an inadequate anchorage for a fleet and that opening up its harbour would be a major work.[35] On the other hand, the perils of the North African coast served to offer a degree of protection to Spain. In 1565 Toledo forecast that the Turks would not dare to sail 'round ships' – high-sided freighters carrying provisions and other essential materials – as far as Oran or the Peñón de Veléz, while any vessels anchored at Algiers and Bougie could easily be attacked and put to the torch.[36] Again, this memorandum highlighted the manner in which Habsburg commanders envisaged being able to isolate the vast enemy armada by cutting its supply lines. Mers El Kebir was a uniquely safe and valuable anchorage along a desolate coastline. 'There is no other port between Larache and Portofarina.' Our source, Cabrera de Córdoba, added that only when the northern winds blew was it impossible to leave its harbour.[37] The problem, as Professor Pryor reminds us, was precisely that the prevailing wind direction was northerly. Yet it was alleged by writers such as Diego de Häedo that the sea was safer than the dry land of 'Barbary', as wild boars and lions stalked the North African coastline and fed upon Christian fugitives from Algiers.[38] Presumably the lions – or lionesses – must have been aware of the logistical constraints of hunter-predators, for in this region water was certainly a rare and valued commodity. One of the first things that the Christians did on landing at the Peñón de Vélez in 1564 was to begin digging a series of wells.[39] Nine years later, when leading statesmen came to discuss the 'Enterprise of

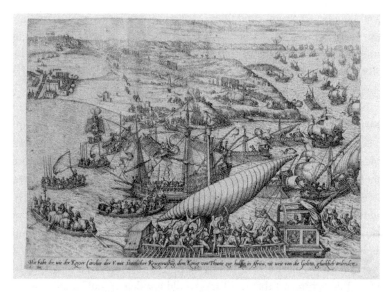

Fig. 5 The Conquest of Tunis and La Goleta by Charles V, 1535. Showing the arrival and disembarkation of the fleet near the ruins of Carthage with the north-westerly winds in their sails. Etching on paper after tapestries by Jan Cornelisz Vermeyen (dated 1546–50).

Algiers', the principle obstacle to the campaign was envisaged to be the lack of water around the city.[40]

The two great strengths of the dual *presidio* of Oran-Mers El Kebir were the harbour at the latter position and the abundant supplies of water found in the surrounding countryside. Successive governors maintained good relations with the 'Moors of Peace', local communities living within the frontiers of this 'kingdom'. Within the walls, the tradition of coexistence was continued, as Jews lived side-by-side with Christians and Muslims. This culture of tolerance was in part based upon economic necessity. This wealthy and 'abundant' region provided grain, often secured by Jewish and Muslim intermediaries, which was exported to feed parts of Spain during the agricultural crisis of the early seventeenth century.[41]

In all of these regards Oran-Mers El Kebir appears to have been exceptional. The outposts at Melilla, the Peñón de Vélez de la Gomera (lost in 1522 and regained in 1564) and the 'mole' at Algiers (lost in 1529) had to have water shipped to them.[42] Castilnuovo di Cattaro fell into the same category; the garrison stationed there by Charles V found that locating, securing and storing supplies of water was a major problem.[43] The same was true at Tripoli. In 1561 a returning captive, a man of 'credit and authority', provided a frank account of the shortcomings of the fortifications, which were numerous and would have required at least a further two years of work to address. Even then the present garrison would be unable to man more than a quarter of the walls of Tripoli. A still more serious difficulty lay in the shortage of provisions, as the 'Turks' of the garrison were at constant warfare with the indigenous 'Moors', who allowed very few foodstuffs to pass to the city. The cellars could provide for no more than eight days during a siege. But it was not at all clear that a siege of this sort would be necessary, as it seemed feasible that a sudden descent might lead to the capture of the town.[44] As Miguel Ángel de Bunes Ibarra has noted, the province of Tripoli was recognised to be a sterile sandy area, *'una esteril arenal'*.[45]

These observations were taken further in 1567 and 1568, when the government in Sicily developed a plot which might, it seemed, easily lead to the capture of the city. In July 1569 the King approved the mission to seize Tripoli with 25 or 30 well-armed galleys.[46] La Valette was convinced that, once captured, Tripoli should be dismantled. The destruction of this city would decisively restrict the scope of Ottoman operations in the western Mediterranean, while its retention would be both costly and dangerous. Tripoli was so important because it provided foods to the enemy fleet; in other words its primary value and use was as a logistical base, rather than as a fortified harbour in which a large fleet might take shelter.[47] Don Luis de Requesens, *Comendador Mayor de Castilla*, thought that the Knights of Malta might be given the city, arguing that they had sworn to hold the fort in 1530 and that they, after all, had lost it in 1551. 'But in the event of not being able to force them to take responsibility, the Grand Master's opinion appears correct, as Your Majesty cannot have so much cost in supporting so much in Barbary, as it is so far towards the Levant and it is clear that the Turk would have to try to recover it.' He concluded that the destruction of this place would serve a strategic purpose, as the demolition of Mahdia had denied a valuable base to Turgut.[48]

The incidents to which he referred – the capture (1550) and subsequent abandonment and destruction of Mahdia (1554) – were profoundly indicative of the nature of Mediterranean holy war. In the later 1540s Andrea Doria had pleaded with Charles V to do something about Turgut; these pleas led to the expedition of September 1550 and the capture, after a ferocious siege of almost three months' duration, of the fort of Africa.[49] The Ottomans insisted that this action had broken the terms of the truces signed in 1545 and 1547 and that the position had to be returned to them. Charles V refused, even when the Ottoman fleet turned up at Messina and reiterated this demand. The dilemma before him was set out by the Viceroy of Sicily in July 1551. In every respect Mahdia was superior to La Goleta: it was a relatively large harbour that might easily be fortified to a high level, 'fortísimo de sitio'. More importantly, it had abundant sources of fresh running water, 'something which is very difficult to find in Barbary and is so necessary for fleets'. The viceroy hoped that the Hospitallers might accept responsibility for it, perhaps with Malta and Tripoli being returned to the Catholic Monarchy.[50]

The other positions in North Africa were extremely limited in value. As Antonio Sánchez-Gijón points out, having surveyed the fortress at Bona in 1541 the emperor immediately decided to abandon it, his only concern being to make sure that the enemy could never again make use of the site. Perhaps this *presidio* was unfortunate, in that an explosion in 1536 and an earthquake in 1539 had rendered it, in Charles V's words, 'weak and of little importance'. Bougie (Bugía) was a rather more serious option, in that superb plans were made for the construction of an imperial fortress on a rocky promontory. It is difficult to say how realistic these designs were, but when Salah *reis* arrived at the head of an Algerian expedition in 1555 things turned sour very quickly: the 'imperial fort' was abandoned as soon as the siege began and the garrison in the town ('the great castle') held out for a mere 22 days. The commander, Luis de Peralta, was later beheaded in Valladolid for cowardice.[51]

In North Africa, therefore, the priority for the Spanish was to deny the enemy harbours or bays from which to launch raids against Christendom: fortresses were innately vulnerable and, as Antonio Sánchez-Gijón has noted, their construction was often dependent upon good relations with the indigenous Muslim populations (clauses to this effect were inserted in all capitulations with vassal rulers in North Africa). The improvement and extension of the *presidios* were badly affected by the endemic civil wars that characterised the Barbary statelets in this period.[52] Many other bastions suffered from severe logistical limitations. In 1537 the Venetian commanders of Corfu expelled from the citadels those civilians who could not take up arms. The cold and rain meant, López de Gómara tells us, that many children perished.[53] K.M. Setton notes that the 'useless mouths' were expelled from the bastions at Siena in 1554 and Famagusta in mid-April 1571.[54] In August 1551 the same decision was reached by the defenders of Tripoli.[55] In May 1595 the Governor of Menorca was planning to evacuate 'the useless people' from the island in the event of the enemy armada heading towards it.[56] How exactly he was going to do this was not made clear in his letter.

The experience of war therefore demonstrated the inadequacy of many fortresses, whose garrisons could be defeated by merely being confined to their bastions: this, in fact, was precisely the tactic adopted by Piyale Pasha at Djerba after the naval victory in May 1560. Philip II's commander, Álvaro de Sande, reported that after 34 or 35 assaults the enemy had given up trying to batter down the walls of the isolated castle. 'I understand their intention is more to defeat us by thirst than to overcome us by force.' He added that the garrison had enough food and water for six months – a considerable exaggeration.[57] As Charles Monchicourt noted in his pioneering study, the bastion at Djerba was pretty much indefensible: there were no sources of fresh water within its medieval walls; there was a cistern but, aside from being likely to crack under aerial bombardment, it was small and inadequate for the demands of modern warfare; a lagoon separated the fort or 'Castello' from the sea, meaning that no galley could be anchored within two miles of the shore and that high-sided ships, with deeper keels, had to drop anchor at a distance of eight miles or so. During the siege an enterprising soldier built and ran a distilling machine to purify seawater; unfortunately this mechanism was rendered useless by the exhaustion of the stocks of firewood.[58]

As we have seen, these logistical problems emerge even more clearly in the analysis of the fort at La Goleta. In the first place, very few Christian statesmen had any faith in the 'King of Tunis', whose assistance to the Ottomans in a prospective attack on the fort would be decisive.[59] One of Toledo's papers stated that La Goleta was a small fort with low walls. The latter problem could be remedied 'with ease'; the former could not.[60] He continued along similar lines in a memorandum sent to Don John in August 1574:

> I would not give much for the loss of La Goleta, as it is built on sand – and on flat planes of sand at that. It was clear that it would be undone with great ease, as indeed has been the case. It is a position without soil, without water, without firewood, without a port, and without a deep anchorage or harbour, meaning that, without a miracle of God a galley or ship cannot get to it.
>
> I do not know how we could receive the protection from it that that drove us to sustain it, as its role was to cover and protect the kingdoms of Sicily, Naples and Sardinia.

He added that only a limited number of soldiers could be stationed inside the bastion. Bizerta and Puerto Farina were much superior positions – Puerto Farina, in fact, was stronger in every regard.[61] After 1535 Barbarossa had used it whenever he needed an anchorage near Tunis.[62] But in comparison with the new fort that Don John had ordered to be constructed at Tunis, La Goleta was a veritable bastion! The problems of the fort at Tunis were enormous and insurmountable: among these were that it lacked a source of fresh water; it could be bombarded by two overlooking artillery positions; it was incomplete and would be quickly and easily isolated by the enemy. Toledo urged Don John to abandon it and focus all of his efforts on defending La Goleta. The *capitán general del mar Mediterráneo* thanked his predecessor and friend for his advice. But by August it was too late.[63]

By the same standard Cyprus was a very limited prize. In mid-September 1570 Santa Cruz set down his assessment of the island: this was dominated by the observation that its long coastline offered no harbour. The Ottoman fleet would be supremely vulnerable, not only to an attack launched by the Christian fleet but also to the winds.[64] Marc'Antonio Colonna agreed, pointing out to Doria and the other admirals that the enemy armada would be open to assault as its hulls had simply been dragged on the beach or shore, *la spiaggia*, of Saline to the west of Larnaca Bay.[65] Both Toledo and Colonna were writing about the specific situation of the summer and autumn of 1570, and it might be dangerous to infer from their arguments that Famagusta did not offer a safe anchorage for ten or 20 galleys. On the other hand, a strong argument could be made that the island was lost because of the severe logistical shortcomings of the forts. It seems very plausible that Famagusta was, as Philip II's spies reported, a formidable bastion: in January 1570 an Ottoman agent was captured and, having been put to torture, confessed that the Grand Signor had determined upon the conquest of the island and had dispatched him to reconnoitre the city for that purpose. 'The governor set the spy free and told him to survey the fortifications and to report back to the Sultan what was waiting for him.'[66]

It was an old story, one that had been recounted, with only small variations, since the time of the wars between Carthage and Rome. But it would seem that there was a degree of truth to it. In August 1571 the King's ambassador in Rome, Zúñiga, lamented that the Venetian land forces were in such a bad state that they were unable to resist the enemy force despite its manifest failings.[67] A few months later Alba reflected that Nicosia was lost for a shortage of men and Famagusta for a lack of provisions ('*y Famagusta se perdió por hambre*'). Had these positions been properly prepared and defended, they would have been impregnable to attack. The Venetians, he concluded, would be of little use in containing the enemy because they were concerned only with the things that brought them profit.[68]

Alba's assessment was perhaps a biased or harsh one, as it overlooked the heroism and endeavour of the defenders of these positions; whether he or his peers would have been as stringent in applying these criteria to the performance of Habsburg troops over the previous 30 or 40 years is doubtful. On the other hand, his judgement was peculiarly representative of the monarchy's approach to maritime warfare, stressing discipline, systematic preparation and the idea that warfare against the infidel Turk depended upon the capacity of a small, unflinching corps of veteran troops to defy much larger forces. In the final analysis, a considerable amount of evidence from the Venetian archives could be marshalled to support Alba's damning assessment.[69] The Venetian Gio Pietro Contarini concluded that Famagusta was lost for the shortage of charcoal and saltpetre, two of the three components of gunpowder, 'which was the salvation of the enemy and our ruination'.[70] The Republic of St Mark's other positions in the Levant were limited in a variety of ways. Corfu could accommodate 50 or so ships; Crete could offer a good anchorage at Candia; but neither island boasted the economic resources necessary to support or repair an armada.[71] Venice, remarked an official in the early seventeenth century, was not for war, 'Venezia non è da guerra'.[72]

If Alba's analysis during the Holy League of Pius V focused on the economic interests of Venice and its consequent military failings, Doria's eyes remained set on the perils on the sea. Sailing into the Greek seas represented a considerable risk. In his assessment of September 1570, Doria touched on the fact that there was not a safe anchorage from Corfu ('here') to Candia.[73] Experience had demonstrated how limited the options were. López de Gómara tells us over the winter of 1533 the troops in Koron found their circumstances insufferable: the water tanks had been cracked by the artillery bombardment; food and clothing were in very short supply, and the men became debilitated to the point that they began to fear 'illness', the outbreak of dysentery. The garrison was eating horses, donkeys or asses and the cooked soles of their shoes, 'suelas de zapatos cocidas'.[74] Preveza had such a narrow channel that in 1538 one option studied by the Christian commanders was to sink a ship in its approaches and so trap the enemy fleet inside the harbour. The belief that informed this proposal was that there were no sources of fresh water in the town. If, in other words, the Ottoman fleet could be trapped in Preveza, then it would be destroyed by thirst.[75] A very similar hope lay behind the attack upon Navarino in 1572: Don John saw that if he could seize this position, he would be able to cut the supply roads to the harbour to the south and so force the Ottoman fleet out of its anchorage at Modon. The commander who found himself trapped in harbours like Preveza or Modon would face a serious, if not insurmountable, logistical problem; it was a much better option to remain at sea, as the collection of water on the Greek coast was not deemed to present a problem. Doria's principal concern in this regard in 1572 was that the refilling of the water casks should be done in an orderly, disciplined fashion.[76] Indeed, one of the attractions – one of the few attractions – of the Greek coastline was the relative abundance of sources of water. At Igoumenitsa in July of this year the Christians had no difficulty in refilling their casks and barrels, easily rebuffing 500 cavalry who tried to prevent them from doing so. They also took water at Zante; both Christian and Ottoman galleys refilled their barrels at Cerigo.[77]

The military value of Koron, Preveza, Castilnuovo di Cattaro, Djerba, La Goleta, Oran, Mers El Kebir and Cyprus was, therefore, very limited: none of these bases could function independently, as perhaps Rhodes had done until 1522, drawing from a relatively productive economy. In a broader sense the features of geography were both a challenge and a promise to maritime forces. The microclimates that invested the seas around Sicily with its multitude of winds were, of course, a considerable danger to the warships that navigated along its shoreline; on the other hand, these *vientos* served to protect the island, in that they favoured high-grade ships over less effective ones. The treacherous coastline of the Tuscan and Roman shorelines set many challenges to the royal armada; on the other hand, it also meant that the seaboard might be effectively secured with the fortification of just a few positions (Gaeta, Piombino, Orbetello and Porto Ercole) whose retention would effectively restrict the threat from the French to the north and the Turks to the south.[78] Spain was protected by geography: the very dangers of the North African coast ensured that if the *armada del Turco* was to sail to Cartagena it would have to pass through the treacherous seas of the Balearics, where the Christian flagships did their summer hunting. Doubtless, there was a degree of exaggeration in each and every portrayal of the sea as an unforgiving mistress. But these descriptions underlined, once again, that the key to success was to sail aboard excellent ships.

In a memorable passage Braudel advanced the basic calculation that the Mediterranean was 99 days long, 'but this is surely too much'.[79] Doria and his peers very seldom discussed the time required for long-distance voyages, being preoccupied – perhaps even obsessed – with the hazards of short ones. The broader question must be whether, as has been alleged, the increased demands and scale of sixteenth-century warfare had brought about decisive changes: specifically, it has to be asked whether the distances involved in moving expeditionary forces to the point of attack and the logistical constraints inherent in these huge mobilisations meant that warfare was grinding to an end by 1580?

In the middle decades of the century Ottoman fleets were very active in the central and western Mediterranean. Yet all of these fleets were consistently reported to be of a low level of seamanship. How, then, did the fleets of Süleyman and Selim II achieve the lordship of the sea?

Again, Pryor provides a valuable framework, one which can in turn be related to patterns of trade and warfare over the previous centuries. The spring winds in the Levant run from the north-west. They had served to complicate the economic life of classical Rome, which sourced its grain from Egypt and depended upon the sailing of the fleet with provisions in April.[80] Exploiting these northerly winds was crucial to Ottoman operations. A departure after this point usually restricted the movement of the *armada del Turco*, although in 1543 or 1558, for instance, the fleet made sudden bursts of progress under sail. In 1534 Barbarossa received a gown from Süleyman, presumably in Constantinople, on 17 May 1534.[81] In 1537 Don Pedro de Toledo predicted that the enemy fleet would be ready to sail on 1 April and that it would collect the Sultan's army from La Valona before attacking Christendom – or rather, before coming to assist the ambitions of His Most Christian Majesty in Italy.[82] A captain sent to gather reconnaissance reported his astonishment that in mid-May this enormous force had yet to leave the straits of Gallipoli.[83] In 1552 the instructions passed down by the imperial council had been to sail – or to be ready to do so – by the equinox (20–21 March). The wait for oarsmen prevented this.[84] In 1565 the corsairs of North Africa were ordered on pain of death and the burning of their ships to be in Lepanto 'by the beginning of the new weather'; this timetable would allow the Kapudan Pasha to sail high-sided ships with his galleys, something which would have been much more difficult in the windless summer months.[85]

Statesmen in Italy knew that even in high summer the Sultan's fleet could make reasonable speed across the seas, although its progress was dependent upon favourable winds and was therefore irregular or unpredictable. The summer calms often stopped it in its tracks, rendering it ineffective, despite its enormous proportions. Thus in 1537 Toledo was unimpressed by the actions of the enemy armada, which he ascribed to a lack of valour; a more balanced assessment might have been that the lack of winds and the poor order of its oar stroke denied the Ottoman force the possibility of mobility and therefore the element of surprise, while the high level of defensive preparation enormously restricted its scope for action on shore.[86] As we have seen, in 1538 the fleet struggled to move under oars. Yet the Ottoman armada was able to make good progress when blessed with favourable winds; indeed it sometimes made sudden jumps over hundreds of miles. In 1543 Barbarossa's fleet left Constantinople on 17 April; in early June the people of Reggio di Calabria 'agreed to become prisoners' of the Sultan and, after much further ado, the armada arrived at Marseille on 20 July.[87] According to a reliable on-board witness, in 1552 the fleet left Constantinople on 17 May and arrived in the Negroponte on 24 May; three days later it departed for Lepanto, where it was to calk its hulls.[88] It would be June, then, before it was ready to operate against the Christians.

A valuable example of the timetable or stages of movement in high summer comes from 1558. In this year the Ottoman armada appeared on the coastline of Naples in early June; it left the coastline of Corsica on 28 June and raided Ciudadella in Minorca 12 July; yet just two days later it took on foods in Marseille, 386 km or 240 miles away. Its commander, Piyale Pasha, then declined to help the French commanders to attack Villefranche-sur-Mers, Bastia or Porto Ercole and instead began to head back to the east, stopping only to take water at Elba and momentarily to give chase to the Catholic Armada, or a part of it.[89] The best explanation for these sudden bursts of movement must be the use of the scirocco, the sometimes 'violent and dangerous' winds that burst up from the Sahara in the summer.[90] The 1589 Ottoman armada, whose 46 galleys and four galiots were consistently reported to have been in bad shape, nevertheless sailed from Modon (Methoni) to Tripoli in 11 days in August, being sighted off Sicily on or just before the 18th of the month. It was reliably reported to be carrying 8,000 troops and their provisions. Incidentally, reports of its passage were sent from Messina to Genoa in six days.[91] According to calculations made in July and August 1609, the Ottoman armada, consisting of 50 or so galleys and an unspecified number of support vessels, would have needed four days to sail from Navarino (Pylos Bay) to Sicily and another seven or eight to reach Algiers.[92]

This calculation was in part borne out by historical record, in that in 1565 the fleet had departed from Navarino under a full moon on the night of 14 May and arrived off Malta three days later.[93] Clearly, then, operations in the western Mediterranean remained a feasible option for the Sultan's fleet in the age when Cervantes was writing, just as they had been in the years in which he experienced life as a soldier and captive. In both periods there was a certain window of opportunity in early spring when the northerly or north-easterly winds were predominant; after this point things were generally harder for the Turks, as the Christians well knew.

Perhaps it would be fairer to say that it was harder for both sides to make plans after mid-May or June. 'The winds are missing in the summer,' observed Andrea Doria, 'at precisely the point when they are most needed.'[94] The observation was made in the context of the difficulty of using high-sided ships to wage war. In a long memorandum written in May 1566 Toledo echoed many of these ideas, warning that using high-sided ships for the *empresa de Argel* would entail profound difficulties, the most significant of which was that the fleet might be overcome by a calm, 'and in a month we will not be able to travel ten miles'. Having delayed too long to make plans, the winds would probably be lacking or contrary (southerly). The long navigation, and the legacy of 1541, made the campaign too much of a risk.[95]

It might be observed that Toledo's explanation of winds in 1566 was subtly different to his formulation in the previous year, in that in 1565 he and his colleagues repeatedly referred to the light northerly or north-westerly winds that ran throughout the campaigning season. It should also be said that his overall assessment of 1566 came very close to the formulation of Guilmartin, in that he held that the capture of Algiers by surprise (that is, by the sudden descent by a fleet of high-grade warships, as had occurred at the Peñón de Vélez in 1564) was unlikely and that the reduction of the North African city by siege would require a vast expeditionary force carried forth aboard a large numbers of galleons, carracks or other high-sided vessels. Yet Toledo's essential point was also that high-sided ships were, and would always be, intruders in the *mare nostrum* in June, July and August. In this he directly echoed Andrea Doria's paper of 1560: the problem, in other words, was not that gunpowder technology had rendered galleys obsolete, but rather that the peculiar geographical circumstances of the *mare nostrum* in high summer made galleons highly ineffective or unreliable as a vehicle for the transport of a large siege train. This assumption or understanding was made clear in a long discursive passage in which Toledo averred that the Ottoman fleet, consisting solely of galleys, would have the advantage over a Christian armada containing a large contingent of galleons. True, the *capitán general del mar Mediterráneo* went on to discuss the possibility of arming 150 or so galleys in Christendom, the only difficulty in doing so would be the cost; these flotillas might then be supported by squadrons of galleons or carracks from Flanders, Vizcaya and Portugal to oppose the enemy. There were, however, limits to the use of Atlantic vessels whose 'company is very bad for galleys when they have to go to look for the enemy; but when they can wait for him to come to them, their use is much more beneficial than would be the presence of a similar number of oared warships'.

Toledo clearly believed that the sailing capabilities of galleys were much greater than those of high-sided sail; the ability of sail-driven craft to tack into headwinds was not mentioned or seems to have been assumed to have been of little applicability or importance; galleons were more victims than masters of the elements. Finally the paper took into account the troubles in the Netherlands: while the conquest of Algiers would bring great reputation, 'I doubt that it would end the troubles of those states in the Low Countries, while the loss of the galleys might well destroy Your Majesty's prestige and standing'.

Galleys were assumed, therefore, to be relatively effective under sail. This insight perhaps helps to explain why Don John in 1572 urged his half-brother to build and maintain half-a-dozen galleasses, which were to be used both *en batalla* and in carrying provisions for the fleet.[96] The Ottoman high command arrived at the same conclusion.[97] It also helps to explain why the boundaries of Ottoman operations (11 May, the battle at Djerba) to 9 September (capture of Nicosia) correspond almost exactly to today's yachting season, although a few regattas are held outside this window. Races are held in exactly the seas that Gian Andrea Doria knew: Bonifaccio, for instance, hosts a series of races in autumn (the cape is described by its host club as *'cet immense stade nautique naturel'*).[98]

The summer calms, interrupted only by light northerly breezes, afforded the Christians certain advantages. Ahead of the Tunis expeditions in 1535 the Genoese Adam Centurione advised Charles V that the fleet should congregate in Sardinia in early May, with select squadrons being dispatched to Naples and Sicily to collect provisions before returning to Cagliari. 'During the summer the westerly winds reign' – Capelloni was blessed with a beautiful turn of phrase, *'regnando nella estate i venti di ponente'* – and these conditions had to be exploited; if the armada sailed from Sicily, they would hinder the operation.[99] The formulation serves to underline that the commanders of galley fleets were confident about being able to sail at an angle to the wind – in this case, using westerly or north-westerly breezes to sail to the south-east. Of course these breezes could also be expected to restrict the movement of any force coming from the Levant. The examination of the campaign does indeed show that the only serious problem came when the winds failed in the first days of June, meaning that the fleet had to proceed under oars to Mallorca.[100] Fair winds duly landed Charles V at Puerto Farina, before the ruins of Carthage, on 16 June.[101]

Of course winds could – and did – thwart even the most carefully planned campaigns. Andrea Doria's plans at Preveza in September 1538

I Capitani G.nali dell'armata Venetriana, sogliono uestire questo habite, e tale fu uisto
gia il Ser.me S. ebastiano Veniero quando frasse l'armata Turca a i Curzolari l'anno 1571
Franco forma con Priuilegio

Fig. 6 The Serene Sebastiano Veniero, 'capitano general da mar' or commander in-chief of the Venetian fleet in 1571, with Lepanto in the background. Engraving (dated c.1610).

were undone when the winds unexpectedly died down, leaving the Christian formation in disarray and the high-sided ships vulnerable to the enemy vanguard.[102] Similarly the Christian expeditions to Algiers in October 1541 and September 1601 were in a very real sense defeated by the elements.[103] Both campaigns were undertaken in the closing stages of the season, when circumstances obliged the enemy to demobilise.

By tradition the date of 15 September was the point by which the Ottoman fleet had to begin to head back to the capital to flee from the terrible storms of the Levant in autumn, '... *por huir el peligro de los horribles tempestades ordinarias en aquellos mares en el otoño*'.[104] On 13 August 1537 the Ottoman fleet set sail for the East; on 14 September it left Corfu.[105] On 23 August 1552 the fleet headed past Messina on its way back to the Levant, being spotted sailing under full sail *verso Levante*.[106] As a rule of thumb by mid-August the viceroys started to express confidence that the enemy would have to head home shortly, in part because of the poor standard of his fleet.[107] Even a foe as redoubtable as Turgut *reis* would have retired – or at least be thinking about retiring – by the last week of September.[108] In the 1590s and early seventeenth century the high admirals tended to delay their return to Constantinople; consequently, the armada was often reported to be in a desperately ragged state on its arrival back in the capital.[109]

In using autumnal winds to head towards the East, the Ottoman Kapudan Pashas were continuing patterns of action employed by Venetian traders of previous centuries.[110] After mid-October a high-pressure system forms over the Persian peninsula, generating easterly winds. The Turks took advantage of these conditions by organising a second annual convoy from Alexandria that consisted entirely of galleons or *caramusali*.[111] This was doubtless a good answer to the question of how to provision Constantinople and in this regard, as in others, the Ottomans followed the example of imperial Rome. The problem arrived when the Christian corsairs began themselves to use high-sided ships. The autumnal 'caravan' thereafter turned out to be no more secure than the one in spring.[112]

X

The Shift to the Mediterranean

The conventional approach to the history of the Mediterranean is usually set within one further argument, itself crucial to modern interpretations of sixteenth- and seventeenth-century European history. This is Braudel's celebrated argument for 'the shift to the Atlantic', that the Mediterranean was progressively abandoned by the two major powers after 1580. Philip II and Philip III were obliged to devote the bulk of their resources to wars against the rebels of the Netherlands and Elizabeth I of England; the *monarquía* came to fight in the Channel, Atlantic and Pacific, abandoning the *mare nostrum*.[1] Equally, the Ottoman sultans were drawn into a comparable series of wars against the Persian Safavid Empire and had to withdraw their forces from the Mediterranean.

The difficult in comparing Atlantic and Mediterranean warfare lies in the disparity in terms of the resources and numbers of men deployed in each theatre. The exceptional intensity of the fighting in the *mare nostrum* in the decades after 1520 complicates all assessments. In 1566 Toledo reported that the enemy fleet was 'of a small number': he meant that it was made up of just over 110 sail: Malta and La Goleta would probably be safe. At this point, the Christian fleet numbered 90 or so sail, counting both good and bad.[2]

There were, therefore, over 200 armed ships operating in the summer after the Great Siege – a figure that may serve as a starting point for comparisons. Toledo's assessment centred on the basis of the *galera en buen orden* – that the Ottoman Turk would mobilise a large armada, and the Christians an agile, frog-like one. Any assessment of the extent of imperial commitments in the *mare nostrum* must look at not only the number of active warships – itself a matter of some ambiguity, with inevitable fluctuations over the course of a single summer as hulls were laid up and their crews redirected to other ships – but also at their overall running order. This being so, the question of the commitment of the major territorial powers to the Mediterranean after 1580 becomes a more complex and challenging one, in that a judgement about the quality of the oared ships must also be incorporated into any meaningful answer. This issue is especially important when assessing the commitment of the Catholic Monarchy, which had always placed a premium on its qualitative or technical superiority over the enemy. A number of other complications – the Stradling thesis; the Thompson paradigm; the rhetorical conventions that governed the correspondence of the captains general and viceroys – further complicate any effort to measure what is, by its very nature, a complex comparison of financial investment, administrative systems and technical performance over many decades.

Two further complications should be taken into account. The first is that it is now clear that Philip II was extremely reluctant to engage in Atlantic warfare in the 1580s. In 1584, as Professor Thompson has shown, the King dismantled the force that had conquered Portugal and the Azores, disbanding the squadrons of galleons, cancelling orders of weapons and releasing the troops raised in Italy and Germany. In doing so, he rejected the proposal, made by the Marquis of Santa Cruz, that the fleet should be sent against Elizabeth.[3] The second major complication lies in the arguments developed by Spanish scholars led by José Luis Casado Soto, who have exploited the extensive documentation held in archives in Simancas, Seville and Cantabria in order to revolutionise our understanding of the events of 1588. The English fleet inflicted little damage on the Spanish armada at the Battle of the Gravelines (8 August). Even after this confrontation the Duke of Medina Sidonia, Philip II's *capitán general del mar océano*, offered battle on three successive days to Lord Admiral Howard, Elizabeth's overall commander. Each offer was declined (the English, sailing behind the Spanish, simply lowered their sails and fell back).[4] Philip II's armada failed to achieve its grand plan, but it was not defeated in battle. The principal reason for its failure lay in the ill-considered instructions which the King had given to Medina Sidonia and the Duke of Parma. These orders required them to coordinate the transport of the army of Flanders across the Channel to Kent but overlooked the fact that no deep-water harbour was available in the Spanish Netherlands.[5] As such the events of 1588 demonstrated the technological, military and administrative capabilities of the Catholic Monarchy, means of action which were the basis of its 'hegemonic position' in European history until the middle of the seventeenth century.[6]

Not all historians will be convinced of the applicability of the idea of hegemony to the study of European dynastic states. Nevertheless it is clear that the traditional interpretation of 1588 – that the Prudent King's dependence upon Mediterranean technology and a Mediterranean approach to war led to the disaster that overcame the Invincible Armada – may not be a good starting point for comparisons. But any assessment of maritime forces is problematic. How many galleys did the King have when the Mediterranean was 'in the limelight'? In 1562 the King counted 56 galleys, between those 'of his salary' and those of the Hospitallers.[7] In the following year he made a slightly different calculation, counting 70 warships with those of Malta, Florence, Savoy and the Republic of Genoa.[8] It would be possible to argue that in many years under Philip III there were around 100 or so well-equipped warships in the royal squadrons and those of his 'friends and confederates': 20 to 26 from Naples; ten to 12 from Sicily; 16 from the contractors of Genoa; 18 or so – sometimes more, sometimes fewer – from Spain; five or so from Tuscany; four from Rome; five or six in Valletta; eight from the Republic of Genoa; two or three from the Duchy of Savoy-Piedmont; four in Catalonia from 1609 and another four in Valencia from 1618.[9] In addition, another 30 ships were armed by Venice and eight or so were fitted out in Toulon under Henry IV. So might this simple comparison of figures form the basis of a new grand theory – the shift to the Mediterranean?

On its own this detail offers little grounds for comparison, although it does indicate that high-performance ships had always been at a premium. In 1535 Charles V, by his own estimate, led 74 galleys to Tunis. Six of these belonged to the Papacy and four to the Hospitallers.[10] Capelloni mentions that Paul III had ordered ten new galleys to be fitted out for the Church in Genoa for this enterprise.[11] Andrea Doria was responsible for running 20 galleys in 1538; but of these five were new, having been recently commissioned: all in all 'His Catholic Caesarean Majesty' had 54 oared battleships 'in his service'.[12] So again the great achievements of the age when the sea was 'in the limelight' were undertaken by fleets that included significant numbers of new galleys. Andrea Doria referred to the 26 reinforced galleys ('*venti sei galee rinforzate*') that he used to ferry 1,800 Italian troops to their garrisons in Sardinia in the spring and early summer of 1558.[13] As we have seen Gian Andrea Doria led 50 galleys in his much-trumpeted and long-remembered pursuit of the corsair squadron off the coast of North Africa near Gibraltar in 1567. There were 49 galleys – good galleys – belonging to His Catholic Majesty in the Christian fleet in 1570.[14] So, by any standard, the monarchy was clearly still committed to the *mare nostrum* in the immediate aftermath of the Invincible Armada, when there were 57 royal galleys in Italy and the monarchy could draw on a total of 75 with those of the 'potentates of Italy'.[15] In 1590 there were 18 galleys belonging to the businessmen-contractors of Genoa.[16] But these figures were presented as part of a long series of complaints, the point being that many of these vessels were not up to scratch, that four warships belonging to Ambrosio Spinola had been sent to patrol the English Channel and that, given the importance of the armada, the dangers in the Mediterranean and the nature of the Catholic Monarchy, to continue in this manner was to invite disaster.

In July 1565 Toledo counted 84 galleys in addition to the entirely new ones; yet he warned that among these there were many whose crews would not be able to exert a great deal of force at the oar.[17] The figure of available ships had risen to 90 in the following year and, as we have seen, he hoped (or at least thought it possible) that another 12 or 15 might be fitted out with new *chusma*.[18] Don John had 85 galleys at his disposition in June 1572, although a dozen of these had remained on the coast of Spain.[19] The fleet which made the short passage to La Goleta in 1573 consisted of 107 galleys and 31 ships.[20] On the other hand, Don John had only 54 galleys available to him in August of the following year (none of the warships based in Genoa made the sailing to Messina that summer).[21] Trying to plot the strength of individual squadrons complicates matters, in that in its peak in 1574 there were a nominal 50 galleys run in Naples *por asiento* by the Marquis of Santa Cruz, although only half of this number were sailing in September. The squadron then steadily diminished (28 galleys in 1585, 22 in 1601 and 1620, 12 in 1637).[22]

Numbers alone tell us nothing about the calibre of these warships. Santa Cruz was very proud of his 14 galleys in January 1570, which served as the core of the 20 that he fitted out for the (abortive) expedition to Cyprus in September.[23] But were these ships really any better-prepared or more seasoned than the 21 fine vessels that his son captained to Gaeta in August 1614? Certainly, this latter squadron drew the admiration of the new Captain General of the Mediterranean Sea, Prince Emanuele Filiberto of Savoy.[24] To phrase this question another way, was there really much difference between the 5,100 oarsmen available in the galleys of Naples in 1570 and the 4,600 on the oar banks of the same flotilla in 1607? The matter is immediately complicated by an inventory which tells us that in July 1571 there were in fact only 3,360 rowers available to Santa Cruz – and yet in this year he took a large number of galleys, some 38, to *'la batalla naval'*.[25]

Statistics on their own often fail to shed too much light on the subject of the commitment of the Catholic Monarchy to the Mediterranean. In other words records of the numbers of slaves, *forzati* and *buenas voyas* aboard vessels do not explain whether these were the *right sort* of captive labour force: Were they taken on land, or on sea? Were they young or old, strong or weak? And for how long had they toiled at the oar? These questions are extremely difficult to answer because the documentation does not address them in a direct and consistent manner. Captains were at once a ferociously proud and competitive group of men who, their endemic *braggadocio* notwithstanding, expressed a deep professional jealousy, if not something approaching personal insecurity, about the advantages enjoyed by their predecessors or contemporary rivals. They complained when it suited their purposes to do so, but invariably expressed confidence before a challenge.

For the Habsburgs and their *capitanes generales* the bottom line always lay in what they did rather than in what they said or complained about – actions, not words – and the 60 reinforced galleys that went to save Malta in 1565 would seem to offer a firm indication of the peak of Habsburg maritime prowess. Certainly, Philip II thought along these lines. At the end of November 1566 the King issued specific orders about the possibility of the armada having to transport him over to Italy. He sought to delay his voyage to Flanders, where he was to engineer a political settlement following the repressive measures taken by the governor, the Duke of Alba. Toledo was to wait in Genoa or Spezia with 50 well-equipped galleys; the other warships would not be needed, as they had been overworked in this and the previous years 'and even more so because the majority of them are new'.[26] So the argument could be made that 50 *galeras bien armadas* of 1566 represented something like the zenith of Habsburg naval power.

But even this assessment may have to be modified, as the testimony of one particularly valuable and forthright witness cannot be ignored. In 1565 the Duchess of Medinaceli declared that she would not travel aboard 'the galleys in Naples'. This was for two reasons: first, she had been offered only three ships which, given the importance of her person, the size of her entourage and the splendour of her wardrobe, was a woefully insufficient number; second, 'that all those who come from Naples affirm that these galleys are armed so badly with *chusma* and sailors that it is necessary for God to carry them over the seas'.[27] Now, while the duchess may not have been the best judge of the tactical strengths of a fleet, it might plausibly be argued that her status, coupled with what appears to have been a fairly frank and forthright manner, allowed her to call a spade a spade. Certainly, it would be easy to couple her dismissive assessment with similar claims made by the captains general themselves: Doria in 1566 was extremely uneasy to be sent with the fleet to Malta: the Christian armada, he averred, contained 'many ruined galleys' and would neither be large enough to fight the enemy, nor strong enough at the oar to escape in a pursuit. Just previously he had gone to the island with only his flagship; he had been much happier on this journey than on the one he was about to undertake.[28]

If these testimonies are taken at face value then it becomes extremely difficult to explain or understand the relief of Malta in the previous year when, without doubt, very significant feats of seamanship were achieved by the armada. The only real answer that can be given is that judgements were always defined in relation to the strength of the enemy, the demands of the operation that was about to be undertaken and the interests and concerns of the commander who made them.

If the Habsburgs of Spain never really abandoned the inland sea, then what about the Ottoman Empire? Michel Fontenay, Idris Bostan, Pál Fodor and Emilie Themopoulou have demonstrated that from 1603 the Ottoman fleet was equipped with larger rowing crews (184 men per galley), and that criminal and slave oarsmen constituted more than 50 per cent. In other words, fleets in the early seventeenth century were manned to a higher level than previously had been the case. Indeed, the conquest of Venetian fortresses in Crete in the first years of the war begun in 1645 allowed the Kapudan Pasha to fit out galleys to an even higher specification by using large numbers of captives as oarsmen.[29]

Long after the sultanate of Selim II (1566–74), the Ottomans were capable of sending out fleets that were at least as large as their counterparts from Amsterdam, London or Plymouth. In the summer of 1589 the reports consistently state that the Ottoman fleet carried 8,000 troops – almost as many as the English navy had in the Channel in the previous summer.[30] In 1594 a fleet of 100 or so sail gathered to run along the coastline of Naples and Sicily. Reggio di Calabria was sacked and burnt, but the topography of this town appears to have made it particularly vulnerable to assault from the sea. An armada of 100 sail carrying only 8,000 soldiers (some reports said 11,000) was clearly incapable of mounting a serious attack upon 'the Kingdom'.[31] Fleets of similar proportions gathered in Greece over the next years. Reports arriving in Naples in late summer of 1596 stated that the Turkish fleet numbered some 90 galleys: it had arrived in Navarino by mid- or late August, 'mal armadas de remo, y bien de gente de guerra' – 'badly armed by oar but well for men of war'. The Kapudan Pasha showed no intention of planning to leave 'his seas'.[32] As happened so often, the two armadas and their respective strengths and weaknesses nullified each other: 'The reports state that in the Levant they are as afraid of our fleet as we are of theirs,' concluded the Viceroy of Naples, the Count of Olivares.[33]

Two years later the enemy did at least venture from his bases. The Ottoman Kapudan Pasha, again Cigala-zade Yusuf Sinan Pasha, arrived with a fleet of 55 galleys and anchored four off Messina. Braudel observes that the high admiral arranged to receive his mother and extended family aboard the flagship and that 'such official indulgence would have been unheard of twenty years earlier'. A slightly different perspective was offered by the Viceroy of Sicily, Maqueda, who confessed that he was surprised to see an enemy fleet of these proportions on the coastline, especially since it ran the risk of being confronted by the superior Christian force which would destroy it 'without any doubt'. Among the weaknesses of the Sultan's armada, the viceroy picked out the fact that it could only disembark 3,000 soldiers.[34] His meaning was that it carried a total of twice that number of troops: the usual calculation was that the Turks had to retain a fighting force equal to the number of troops aboard the Christian fleet, which might attack it while the raiding party was ashore.

The same pattern of events was to dominate the campaigns of the following years. Statesmen called the galleys to Messina to confront the enemy fleet, but this gathering was clearly meant to be a deterrent, a means of avoiding an engagement and so saving the cost of the full-scale mobilisation of the militias. The viceroys remained relatively serene about their chances of defending the coastlines. True, in 1597 the President of the Kingdom of Sicily, Giovanni III Ventimiglia, Marquis of Geraci, did express concern about what might happen if 100 enemy ships arrived in Apulia and Calabria, but this fed back into the concerns (mentioned above) about the exhaustion and isolation of Sicily.[35] In 1603 the most reliable reports held that the Ottoman fleet, gathered in the Negroponte, numbered over 50 galleys and was manned by well-equipped janissaries, *sepahis* and 'other men' of the region. Still Feria was very confident of being able to defend the coastlines; Benavente thought it unlikely that the enemy would venture from his seas, and that he 'certainly will not try to land in Calabria, because he must know that Your Majesty has gathered a quantity of galleys together in these seas'.[36] In fact the Kapudan Pasha soon headed home. In 1606 Feria refused to believe that the Kapudan Pasha would dare to leave the Archipelago, while Benavente took the reports of 8,000 janissaries aboard 70 galleys to be an inflated figure bandied about by the Republic of St Mark.[37] Still, other intelligence sources held that the armada was carrying more than 7,000 'marksmen', *tiradores*; on receipt of these dispatches the viceroys immediately put the coastal defences of Naples and Sicily on alert. With this measure they expected the end of the campaigning season to pass without incident; as, indeed, it did.[38]

The reaction to these events conveyed a sense of their futility. 'In Italy everybody believes that the small and ruined Turkish armada has advanced so far in response to the call of the Venetians, and has been provided with the assistance of their ports and galleys', reported Philip III's ambassador in Genoa.[39] In August 1607 it was known that some 60 Ottoman galleys had arrived in waters near Zante. The new viceroy in Messina, the Duke of Escalona, saw no cause for panic, in part because the report was unconfirmed but also because it seemed unlikely that the enemy would leave the safety of his own seas. He would, in the meantime, take the usual precautions.[40] In these cases the assumption underpinning the responses of the viceroys was that a force of around 60 galleys carrying 6,000 or so soldiers would not be enough to launch an attack – much less a meaningful attack – upon the coastlines of Naples and Sicily.

Futile though they may have been, these expeditions saw the mobilisation of large numbers of warships. Cigala-*zade* Yusuf Sinan Pasha led out 100 galleys in 1596, not counting the corsairs. Doria set out with 44 reinforced galleys; when he heard that the enemy fleet had remained in Modon, without showing any intention of moving ahead, he headed back to Messina.[41] In December 1605 Santa Cruz calculated that the Catholic armada would number 71 galleys in the following summer, a figure which did not include the squadron of Spain.[42] In fact the 1606 fleet, numbering 45 'very reinforced' warships, gathered in Messina in late summer in order to face the Ottoman armada. The Christian vessels were technically far superior to those of their adversary, although both sides were handicapped by the very poor weather.[43]

So in 1596 and 1606 the combined fleets of the Catholic King and the Ottoman Sultan numbered a total of at least 140 specialised warships; these were hugely expensive vessels with large crews which devoured provisions. If we assume that 160 oarsmen were serving aboard each ship – another conservative estimate – then the total number of rowers reached just over 22,000. If 60 *gente de cabo* and troops – again, another conservative estimation of the soldiers, sailors and officials – were aboard each ship then another 10,000 or so were engaged in war. The militia in Naples included 23,000 men, and in Sicily it mustered just under 10,000 volunteers. And many other years saw large numbers of warships on patrol. In September 1610 the Ottoman fleet consisted of 60 galleys (it had been reinforced in order to concentrate the best oarsmen in these hulls).[44] Philip III's galleys, around 50 well-drilled ships, were employed in the removal of the Moriscos from Spain. So 110 good warships were in operation, not counting the 20 or galiots belonging to the various corsairs or the squadrons of the Republics of Genoa and Venice, the Holy See, the small squadron based in Nice or the dozen or galleys fitted out in Toulon. In 1614 a fleet of some 80 Ottoman galleys landed briefly at Malta before being driven back.[45] The greatest concern of the Count of Lemos, Viceroy of Naples, in this year was that the young *capitán general del mar Mediterráneo*, Prince Emanuele Filiberto of Savoy, would feel himself compelled to go in search of the enemy and glory.[46]

Relatively large Ottoman fleets continued to threaten the shores of Christendom until the last years of Philip III's reign. In the spring of 1618 a spy reported the Sultan's fleet would consist of 60 vessels; as ever they were 'badly reinforced for the lack of officers (*gente de cabo*), oarsmen and captains of valour and experience to govern galleys. And they will not be able to leave port until between the end of April or the middle of May.'[47] In July the *armada del Turco* gave little cause for concern: its galleys were 'in poor order' and would not be capable of making long voyages.[48] Unsurprisingly, in this year the Kapudan Pasha achieved very little. There was, however, one exception to this rule. In 1620 the sacking of Manfredonia was accomplished by an armada carrying 7,000 troops, although it is revealing that the capture of the town was seen as a singular disaster by the government of Naples. Had the garrison put up any resistance – even the governor fled – then its chances of success would have been good. It was certainly well equipped with munitions – part of the booty presented to the Sultan by the Kapudan Pasha included 400 powder-barrels.[49]

The application of Doria's criteria to Atlantic warfare in the sixteenth, seventeenth and eighteenth centuries casts it into three periods: the first of these ran from around 1570 to 1640 and was highlighted by the amphibian operations at which the Elizabethans excelled and which the early Stuarts found so difficult to imitate; the second phase began in 1650 and was characterised by the emergence of the battle fleet, the specialised warship and line-ahead formation; the third dated from the time of the War of Spanish Succession (1701–13) onwards, when the Catholic Monarchy was dismembered following the death of the last Habsburg, Charles II (1665–1700), and the British acquired the strategically decisive positions of Gibraltar and Minorca.

Only this first phase concerns us here. In this period English fleets were constrained by problems which were almost identical to those found in the history of Mediterranean galley warfare: if in theory high-sided vessels were able to remain at sea for relatively long periods of time, it was also true that every day that they spent away from bases reduced their operational capacity due to the outbreak and spread of illness among the crew; the key reason for this ill-health lay in the reliance upon inexperienced and inadequate crews, who were prone to fall quickly and irredeemably sick.

In 1572–73, Sir Francis Drake led a raid on the Caribbean and Indies which would culminate with his successful assault upon mule trains carrying the silver from Peru; this attack took place near to Nombre de Dios and led to a life-and-death chase through the forest and back to the small ships or pinnaces. He himself captained one ship, the *Pascha*, with a crew of 47 men; his brother skippered the *Swan*, with 26. By January 1573, 28 crewmen had died, including two of his brothers, John (from infected wound) and Joseph (from yellow fever, the surgeon finding 'his liver swolne, his heart as it were sodden, and his guts all fair').[50] Did Drake encounter any serious, organised opposition in his circumnavigation of the globe in 1577–80? By the standards of Mediterranean warfare, he certainly did not. The merchant vessels in Callao harbour were unguarded; treasure ships like the *Cacafuego* carried no armament at all – not even small arms.[51] His other expeditions met with little resistance. 'Francisco Draque,' writes Cabrera de Córdoba of the 1585–86 campaign, 'left Plymouth to go to the Indies with 11 large ships, 8 small ones and some *pataches*, and provisions for a year and three thousand soldiers ...'[52] (The figure of 3,000 troops appears to have been a considerable exaggeration, as mariners and soldiers numbered no more than 2,300, the soldiers being raw recruits who had been pressganged or 'volunteered'.) Again, he launched a series of amphibian raids against unfortified and poorly defended positions. Santo Domingo was won within 24 hours by an expeditionary force consisting of only 800 men (some sources reported 1,000 troops); Cartagena de Indias was taken by Drake at the head of 1,000 men, there being no 'artillery, nor powder, neither harquebuses nor men experienced in war' in the town.[53] Another account, based on slightly different sources, has it that the arch-privateer had under him no more than 1,900 men, of whom over a third were sailors; of these 750 men lost their lives, almost always as a result of disease.[54] By 27 February 1586, he had only 700 fit men under his command, 'very many of the better minds and men being either consumed by death, or weakend by sickness and hurts'. By April, his crews were throwing a corpse overboard every day.[55]

Not surprisingly, in his account of the expedition Drake spoke of the 'slenderness of our strength' due to the 'inconvenience of continual mortality'.[56] The logistical restraints on Elizabethan galleons were considerable, as Dr Cheryl A. Fury has demonstrated in her excellent recent study. The storage of foods and water was extremely inadequate. The successes of the Elizabethan navy were, therefore, possible only in a relatively short window of opportunity. This was true in two senses: first, when sailing to the Indies, captains operated on a timetable determined by the winds and the deteriorating health of the crews (an unknown hand set down where Drake's squadron would be on a specific date in its 1585 campaign, estimating the booty to be had at Dominica, Margarita island, Río de la Hacha, Santo Domingo, Santa Marta, Cartagena, Nombre de Dios, Panama and Havana);[57] second, the achievements of the Elizabethans were possible only in the years before the fortification of important seaside positions in the Indies, a process which Philip II began in the last decade or so of his life. Drake's final campaign saw him unable to overcome a succession of relatively small fortifications at Las Palmas in the Canaries, San Juan at Puerto Rico (where hastily erected earthworks and the scuttling of large ships in the harbour mouth served to close off the approaches), and at Nombre de Dios. He died, as John Cummins noted, within a few miles of the scenes of his greatest successes.[58] But the standards and size of the Spanish forts and defensive battlements in the Indies were still, by Mediterranean measurements, extremely low: the final defeat of the 1595–96 expedition was achieved by 80 or 90 Spanish troops at La Capirilla, a hastily improvised position on the road between Nombre de Dios and Panama.[59]

The other great actions of the Elizabethan age fell within these boundaries. In August 1585 the Queen agreed to send 6,350 troops and 1,000 cavalry to try to save Antwerp; this force failed to rescue the city, which was seized by the army led by Alessandro Farnese, Duke of Parma and Piacenza. This was her decisive commitment, the point of no return. In 1588 there were around 10,000 soldiers aboard the English fleet; Drake's squadron in 1595 sailed from England with just under 2,500 men, of whom less than 1,000 were soldiers.[60] The Anglo-Dutch expedition that stormed Cadiz in 1596 carried around 10,000 troops; before setting sail the English overall commander, the Earl of Essex, lamented the quality and discipline of his men, who were not experienced in war and only partly trained and so manifestly unfit 'to make any great progress in Spain itself'. His strategy was largely shaped by an understanding of the quality of Philip II's forces in Flanders and

France, where the King maintained the 'most disciplined army in Christendom'. Essex's plan was to bring 'insolent' Spain very low by attacking the most vulnerable part of the Habsburg domains, the exposed ports and harbours of the Iberian peninsula. 'It is better to make war offensive than defensive,' he concluded.[61] Having seized Cadiz, his (tentative) plan was to hold it and to use it as a base from which to attack the fleets coming from the West and East Indies, 'whereby we shall cut his sinews and make war upon him with his own money'.[62] The campaign was initially successful because it faced no concerted opposition at Cadiz: cannon lay without carriages on the ground; towers were bereft of artillery; at one point the city's medieval walls could be easily scaled by the attackers, being 'no higher than in many places a man might reach with his hand'.[63]

The details of the 1596 expedition, like those of Drake's earlier raids, underlined the extent to which the policy of seaborne attack was predicated upon amphibian operations conducted with the advantage of surprise on undefended or (very) poorly fortified positions. In a memorandum written in the immediate aftermath of the Anglo-Dutch assault on Cadiz, Doria lamented that the necessary preparations had not been made in good time. Properly fortified by the English, the city would offer excellent shelter to their fleet. Yet he downplayed the likelihood of any long-term outcome beyond the loss of property and reputation: if the enemy sailed from the city and the fleet from New Spain arrived safely in Seville, then Essex's expedition would have achieved nothing more than a bonfire of straw, *'un fuego de pajas'*.[64] This observation may have served to remind the King that his doughty old Genoese admiral was more concerned with military contingencies than financial calculation; by the same standard Elizabeth was furious that her men, having secured the city, did not capture the Indies galleons which, laden with produce, were anchored in the inner harbour and were burnt by the Spanish. Yet this sort of failure, born of a lack of discipline, was exactly what could be expected of an expeditionary force of volunteers and 'adventurers'.

The case advanced by figures such as Essex for conducting offensive warfare was that haughty, arrogant Spain, while appearing to be supremely powerful, was in fact highly vulnerable in Iberia and the Indies.[65] By the same standard he argued that a narrow defensive strategy was destined to fail, largely because the coastlines of England and Ireland were so vulnerable to amphibious attack: in his paper of August 1596 Doria had urged the King to undertake the enterprise of England, reasoning that it was better to fight abroad than at home. The English 'blue water' strategy might, therefore, be summarised as a plan to exploit the vulnerability of Spain in order to mask England's military failings in Kent and Cornwall.

The outstanding features of the campaigns launched by Elizabeth I and Charles I was their amphibian nature and dependence upon *gente nueva*; the inevitable consequence of this was that they suffered very high levels of mortality and had to sail directly to their objective, bring the attack to a successful conclusion and return within a short space of time. The recourse to impressment meant that royal ships were inadequately manned by 'tailors, potters, and the like', 'landlubbers', 'idlers and boys' and 'rouges taken up in the street', 'the scum and dregs of the country'. Raleigh acknowledged that seamen worked for their sovereign 'with great grudging' and viewed such duty as equivalent to being galley slaves. Royal ships in 1588 were manned by 'poor Fishermen and Idlers ... insufficient for such labour', men who were 'poor, unserviceable and of weak spirit'.[66] As was the case in the Mediterranean, health – or the lack of it – was the vital consideration in any operation. 'God of his mercy keep us from the sickness,' wrote the Lord Admiral in a famous passage, 'for we fear that more than any hurt that the Spanish will do.' Unfortunately He was not listening. 'The fleet had been ravaged by infection before it had even left port, and this same infection plagued the English navy throughout the summer.' Hawkins declared that the fleet had been decimated by disease and was 'utterly unfitted and unmeet to follow any enterprise'.[67]

These words perhaps underline the value of health and, in historiographical terms, of Manuel Gracia's valuable studies of Spanish medical provision in 1588 and 1591, when galleys were deployed in Brittany.[68] Similar constraints affected English naval operations until at least 1630. In 1625 just 10,448 men, nearly all of them green recruits, were dispatched by Charles I to attack Cadiz. Inevitably, the expedition suffered from terrible ill-health and mortality, not to mention an almost total lack of discipline when ashore.[69] The first attempted intervention by the English at the Île de Ré, near La Rochelle, in 1627 carried only 6,000 troops and 1,000 cavalry, and the second (in 1628) only 4,000 in total.[70] The calibre of the men recruited for this expedition was lamentable: 'Such a rotten, miserable fleet, set out to sea, no man ever saw. Our enemies seeing it may scoff at our nation.' It was almost inevitable that this expedition should end in disaster with extremely heavy mortality rates.[71] The reverses of the early years of Charles I's reign therefore served to cast the Elizabeth's reign as a golden age of naval action. 'There were now no more Drakes in England,' lamented one observer, 'all were hens.'[72] In a similar vein Raleigh once compared the performance of English soldiers in the New World and in Ireland, ascribing the poor performance in the latter theatre to the lack of an incentive. 'No man makes haste to the market where there is nothing to be bought but blows.'[73] Doria would have argued that this description entirely missed the point: every sailor, tinker, idler and hen who ventured to sea made haste to a market where blows would rain down upon him, as these knocks were part of taking to the seas on insalubrious and cramped wooden hulls which were almost invariably stocked with deteriorating biscuit and algae-filled water.

The remarkable successes of the Elizabethans, and the extraordinary failures under Charles I, led many contemporaries to conclude that there had been a precipitous decline in the standards of English seafaring in the early seventeenth century. It is not clear that this perception was justified. Approached from the level of professionalism and the number and calibre of available crews – that is to say with the criteria which Doria and Philip II applied with such rigour to Mediterranean warfare – it is clear that the English campaigns in years as different in outcome as 1588 and 1628 were largely consistent in scale and calibre. To be precise, at the height of its Elizabethan pomp the English navy was capable of transporting around 6,000 to 8,000 soldiers to attack positions on the Iberian peninsula; something between a quarter and a third of this number could be ferried to the Indies; whatever the intended target, there was a direct inverse correlation between the amount of time spent at sea and the operational capacity of the fleet or squadron. The one expedition which exceeded the boundaries of this equation, the 1589 campaign against Corunna and Lisbon, was marked by an outbreak of disease which was remarkable and devastating even by the standards of the day. Between 8,000–10,000 men died.[74]

It is obviously true that the distinction must be made between naval activity and war on the one hand, and trade and commerce on the other. Few would doubt that the Dutch and, to a lesser extent, the English and French clearly came to dominate in trade after 1580 and throughout the seventeenth century. Technology was also rapidly progressing, in that in 1650 the fleets of men-o'-war under admirals such as Robert Blake and Michiel de Ruyter were clearly distinct from those of converted merchantmen of the sort which had dominated in the later 1500s. From 1650 or so squadrons of ships of the line could remain at sea for longer periods, although English operations in the 1650s were dependent upon the use of Portuguese and Tuscan harbours. Fleets of this kind were almost indestructible in battle – or could only be destroyed in specific circumstances such as those of 1639. Their indestructibility was, in fact, the problem: henceforth war at sea became a long-term commitment requiring vast funds. The English state was singularly unable to meet this commitment until the foundation of the Bank of England (1694), itself a consequence of the profound revolutionary changes brought about by 'the first modern revolution' in 1688.[75]

The conclusion is, therefore, clear: the traditional historiographical image of an abandoned Mediterranean and an Atlantic bustling with combatants fitted out with the latest technology presents an exact inversion of the actual state of affairs. Major campaigns in the inland sea came to a halt after 1574 precisely because the Habsburgs of Spain and the Ottoman Turks were able to mobilise such impressive naval forces, different though they were in size and nature. Armed deterrence, not abandonment, was the salient characteristic of the Mediterranean in the later sixteenth and early seventeenth centuries. The unheralded and unhappy armadas that, year after year, sailed from the Golden Horn and, having battled the elements and terrible health problems, limped back to port in November or December hardly seem to deserve a place within Braudel's grand narrative of civilisations and empires. But simply more men, and perhaps even tougher, more resolute and more dedicated men, sailed aboard the fleets of Murad III and Mehmed III (1595–1603) than took to the seas on Tudor galleons. Guilmartin writes of the symbiotic relationship between the fortified port and the war galley, arguing that technology had tipped the balance in favour of the former in the course of the sixteenth century.[76] The problem with this formulation is twofold: first, that practically no fortress stood on its own as a major harbour base boasting access to abundant water supplies, the support of a prosperous hinterland, and a chain of watchtowers or smaller fortresses guarding the watering points. More fundamentally, the idea of command of the sea was a distant improbability in 1580 or 1600 – or, indeed, in 1620. Guilmartin's comparison implicitly compared the fleet under Don John with the performance of British squadrons under Lord Admiral Nelson, which was able to shadow the Franco-Spanish fleet for over two years before eventually bringing it to battle in October 1805. If sixteenth- and seventeenth-century galleons were theoretically capable of remaining at sea for long periods, then they were constrained by precisely the same problems of health which so dominated warfare in the *mare nostrum*.

There were no major battles in the Mediterranean between 1580 and 1620 precisely because such large fleets and well-drilled, disciplined garrisons continued to guard the shores and patrol the seas. The relative calm of the sea in these decades was a tribute to the extreme strategic importance of the Mediterranean sea, upon which the two most advanced territorial states of their day depended. The difficulty in pursuing this line of argument lies in the limitations that so characterised all forms of sea power. Toledo would have been surprised to be told in late July 1565 that he presided over the zenith of a military system. The one recurring assumption found in his correspondence from that year was that the war in the Mediterranean was one that the Christians might lose but could never win. On the same note the King's apparent conviction that the Ottoman fleet had sustained such heavy losses in the summer of 1571 that it could already be considered defeated casts Lepanto as a triumph of endurance rather than as a pivotal clash of religiously certified empires.

Until 1590 or so the Atlantic and Indies were *'lugares abiertos'*, undefended territories that were open to attack. The one real window of opportunity for European powers intent upon raiding the territories of the Catholic Monarchy in the New World lay in the time between the dramatic expansion of the output of the silver mines of Potosí in the middle decades of the *Cinquecento* and the fortification of the key strategic harbour positions of *'las Indias'* towards the end of it. This window of opportunity was, of course, precisely the one that Drake and Elizabeth exploited with such ruthlessness and guile. The Queen and her pirate have sometimes been admired for their defence of a certain set of principles; the admiration for them has hardly been diminished by the incontrovertible observation that they, like any good corsairs, developed a sense of principled action which was never entirely divorced from a consideration of how and where they might come across some of the King of Spain's silver. In many respects their defiance of the Catholic Monarchy was all the more remarkable than the traditional narrative allows, in that the Prudent King not only commanded vastly superior forces, but also viewed war as a sort of trial of endurance in which the enemy would be invited to exhaust his – or her – strengths before the decisive blow fell. The odds were never in favour of the Queen of England: on the other hand, the decision to go to war with 'insolent Spain' was not hers. Philip II demanded restraint and discipline from his commanders precisely because he was aware of how the search for lucre tended to dissolve military order and operational coherence; this was especially true during amphibian operations. And His Catholic Majesty certainly had a good idea of where Drake might next strike and what he might be looking for.

The Virgin Queen and her rosy-cheeked privateer occupy a unique position within English history, but their prominence is primarily because they offered a conclusion to an older theme of amphibian raiding rather than because they pointed the way forward to a new form of oceanic warfare. They were closer in spirit to the Vikings than to Nelson. The simple truth of the matter is that their chosen method of fighting was, at the end of their lives, already obsolete: Drake's death on 27 January 1596 off Porto Belo, Panama, was the changing of the guard, the point at which an instinctive and opportunistic series of amphibian raids encountered a constrictive system designed to confront the enemy with the terrible dilemma of being in command of the seas as the seasons changed and the crew became 'consumed' by disease. The application in the Caribbean of a system based upon the exploitation of gunpowder technology, the Italian design of geometric fortification and an understanding of how the changing of the seasons directed and constrained man's ability to make war on the seas – that is to say, a strategy of calculated prudence – brought about a sudden and irreversible change. In the next century Atlantic warfare would follow the advanced lines set down in the *mare nostrum* in the age of Barbarossa and Andrea Doria: maritime conflict became a test of guile and endurance; the crucial factor in it was administrative provision rather than inspired improvisation. The employment of oared warships and the construction and manning of modern forts in the Indies meant that a page had been turned. The days of magic mirrors and games of bowls on Plymouth Hard belonged to the past: the Elizabethan system of warfare at sea had reached an evolutionary dead end. True to Darwin's prescription, it had been superseded by an invasive species, one based upon the crocodilian precept that an effective predator sometimes simply conserves his energies, waiting for his prey to make the fatal mistake.

XI

The Problem of Holy War in the Sixteenth Century

'Privateering is a weapon of the weak and, in the final analysis, one without a future.' Professor Enrique Otero Lana's assessment is an extremely useful and suggestive one.[1] It has been confirmed by many recent studies. It could probably be applied to the Uskoks of Senj, who turned to raiding to make up for the wretched terrain around their base and their inadequate wages. These were desperate men, willing, as one Habsburg official put it, to fight for many days for a single loaf of bread.[2] From the very beginning, governments were conscious of the dangers of piracy. In 1489 Ferdinand the Catholic prohibited the practice of *el corso*. The history of the outpost of Oran was characterised by a constant struggle between the desire for trade (with 'the Moors of peace') and for violence (against 'the Moors of war'). It would be too simplistic to describe this dialectic as the inevitable consequence of poverty as there was considerable variation, but it again underlined how difficult it was for Mediterranean society to support professional military forces.[3] The activities of the corsairs of Algiers might be profitably interpreted in these terms: *el corso* was often the activity of the desperate and is perhaps best understood as a consequence of overpopulation and poverty than as the manifestation of any religious sentiment.[4] This perspective perhaps explains why the *ghazi* raiders were so active in despoiling the very subjects of the Sultan in Greece and the Levant, intidimidating local officials and bribing admirals (the phenomenon represents 'a paradox of Ottoman institutions').[5] A slightly different – and more sympathetic – interpretation is that Algerian piracy can in part be viewed as a reaction to the unfair trading conditions imposed upon the 'regency' by the Christian powers in general, and by the consuls of Marseille in particular. 'When commerce dies, *la course* flourishes.'[6]

Professor Faroqhi has demonstrated that complicated trading relationships existed in the Levant, ones that transcended the religious divide.[7] Her conclusions have been echoed by a number of recent studies, which have focused on the complexity of the Mediterranean and the trading networks within it. Even in Malta there was a constant impulse towards commerce: put another way, there was always a chance that peace would break out.[8] The rhetoric of holy war tended to serve the interests of those who espoused it. K.R. Andrews observed apropos of the genteel Elizabethan raiders that 'those most deeply influenced by the knightly ideal were nearly always the most in need of money'. Again, it is a conclusion which has been echoed in recent studies.[9] These lines of thinking can be traced back to Michel Fontenay's pivotal essay describing the Knights of Malta as *rentiers* who lived on the profits of their vast estates, and Bartolomé and Lucile Bennassar's examination of the sad realities of the corsairs of North Africa and their forced conversion of Christian children.[10]

If the social history of privateering underlined that the rhetoric of raiding and violence was often a direct reflection of the interests of those who espoused it, then the history of Mediterranean naval campaigns is similarly filled with paradoxes and ambiguities. In 1538 and 1565, in 1571 and 1596 the crusading expeditions collapsed beneath the contradiction between man's ambitions and God's will. The paradox in the history of holy war is that, having been legitimised and convened in the service of the Almighty, the combatants immediately discovered that providence seemed determined to offer the infidel or misbeliever exactly the same rights and opportunities as those given to the forces fighting in His cause. Disease wreaked havoc among the Ottoman fleet in 1537; it was no kinder to the Christian expeditionary force in the winter of 1559–60 or to the Venetian squadrons in Crete and Corfu in June and

July 1570. Winds wrecked the Christian fleet formation on 25 September 1538, but then dashed the Ottoman armada against the shores of Greece a few weeks later. Charles V's ships fared no better at Algiers in 1541. Mustafa Pasha faced a terrible problem at the walls of St Elmo in June 1565; the realisation of the traps, both political and military in nature, that awaited him became very clear to Don John of Austria on 29 August 1571. Both sides could claim that the weather patterns offered the enemy certain advantages in the early part of the season: Doria and Toledo argued forcefully that that the *vientos* seemed to set a trap for the Christians in September and October, almost daring them to venture too far to the East.

Engagement in crusade and *jihad* therefore reminded the *capitanes generales*, viziers and Kapudan Pashas of the profoundly secular and mechanical nature of warfare: any mobilisation began with inventories of biscuit and *chusma*, sails and cisterns, water and shot, before turning to considerations of the capricious sea, the corrosive elements and the ubiquitous 'bad airs'. If anything the absolute terms by which these conflicts were understood – those of Islam and Christendom, the righteous and the damned – served to underline the fundamental impossibility of victory in that only a succession of major victories could bring about a triumphant resolution of the war and it seemed very unlikely that the enemy would fight on terms manifestly disadvantageous to his cause in successive campaigns. Not only did the nature of the two fleets seem to make any sort of conclusion to the war unlikely, but the very limitations of any one harbour or port as a strategic base served to underline the reality that no one blow could be decisive. Having said this it should be added that there was one eventuality which might have proven to be decisive – the destruction or capture of the fleet of His Catholic Majesty.

At every moment Mediterranean holy war pitted two competing interpretations against each other: on the one side was the ideal of secular prudence based upon the legacy of the Greeks, Romans and Carthaginians; on the other stood the 'messianic imperialism', the appeal to the service of God and the programme to defeat and conquer all infidels. It is true that the kings of Spain repeatedly tried to convince their confederates that, if the latter strategy was to be applied or accepted as the final objective, then it should be pursued using tactics derived and designed from the pages of Thucydides and Polybius: it would be difficult to claim that their efforts at persuasion were successful. The dialectic between these two interpretations was present in both the planning of expeditions and the subsequent assessment of them: Lepanto was celebrated as the greatest victory for a thousand years and the manifestation of celestial blessing; yet the idea of providential preference was precisely the pitfall against which the King had warned his confederates so assiduously in the 16 or so months leading up to it: his warnings and prognosis, moreover, were unequivocally justified and confirmed by the unfolding of events in the 12 months after it.

Braudel says that the statesmen of the sixteenth century were more acted upon than actors, meaning that vast historical forces carried them forward; it might be added that in a very real sense they were all literally actors, aware of the imperative never to betray their true thoughts or feelings.[11] In a different context Robin Briggs notes the 'operatic' terms used by contemporary historians to describe the motivations of rebels in seventeenth-century France.[12] Throughout his long career Gian Andrea Doria found the operatic or theatrical demands of his profession particularly difficult to perform: his refusal to dissimulate or deny what he held to be self-evident truths set him apart from his contemporaries. It is easy to dismiss his spectacularly forthright manner as a stratagem employed by a *munitionnaire* intent on preserving his galleys at all costs; a more generous assessment, however, would be that as a man of honour and integrity he found it impossible to suppress things that he considered to be self-evident truths, to say one thing in dispatches to the King and another in councils of war held *en galera*. Doria has often been dismissed as a man of dissimulation and calculation whose only purpose was to confound the efforts of men of far greater endeavour and spirit. He, like Toledo in 1565, struggled to make the King's confederates recognise the dichotomy between the ideal of holy war and the reality of fighting the Ottoman Turk with galleys. In 1571 Don John confronted this same problem; a year later, at Navarino, he was overwhelmed by it.

In 1573 he succumbed to the temptation of empty glory, much as Toledo, Doria and his half-brother warned him about the inevitable outcome of trying to defend the isolated and waterless bastions at Tunis against an enemy that could easily build or adopt positions allowing it to fire down on the walls from a superior position; in 1574 he was surely forced to conclude that they had been right to do so.

The problems involved in waging 'offensive war' were perhaps especially acute for the Christians, as the attempt to gain territories ran up against a number of serious limitations: that reinforced galleys were irreplaceable; that there were few positions of decisive strategic value in the Levant; that 'the Turk' stood as the leader of the Muslim community, and therefore could not allow any lands to be alienated from the domains of Islam. This study has touched upon the fort only as a sort of hindrance, a diversion of energies and resources that would have been better invested in sustaining galleys. It was very difficult to identify deep-water, fortified anchorages offering access to abundant supplies of water and a rich agricultural hinterland. Harbours were not only comparatively unsafe, but even the most advanced fortresses required constant replenishment and re-supply. The conditions of Mediterranean warfare and geography dictated that this logistical operation could only really be achieved by oared vessels.

Yet if the Christians saw little purpose in the war, then those Ottoman statesmen and chroniclers who addressed the problem of maritime conflict found it difficult to believe that 'the Muslims' could triumph. Writing in 1655, Katip Çelebi drew a stark conclusion about Lepanto: 'For future campaigns, the commanders must consider the possibility of peace first even if it is thought that the power of the enemy can be overcome.' Peçevi concluded that the seas of the Islamic states – if not those of the whole world – had not seen such an unblessed war since the invention of the ship by the Prophet Noah.[13]

Of all the coastal positions that the Christians fought for, Castilnuovo di Cattaro clearly provoked the most attention and, indeed, controversy; the very nature of the interest in this small fort lay in the difficulty of the landward approach to it through the mountains of the Balkans. It was, moreover, located in the Adriatic, 'the Gulf of Venice'. Its isolation and seclusion beg the question of the motivations of Charles V in 1538 and 1539: having professed his desire to serve God and re-conquer Constantinople in order to resurrect the old title of 'Emperor of the East', it was curious that he should have chosen to invest his resources in defending this remote and mountainous, if picturesque, Adriatic town.[14] It seems entirely plausible that his true intention was to avoid a war, rather than start one.

The criteria which western statesmen rigorously applied to their own fleets – that is, an awareness of the vast human and financial expense involved in maintaining an armada at sea over a campaigning season – served, when applied to the forces of the enemy, to highlight its recurring qualities and inevitable failures. A very strong element within the western mindset was the perception that the Turk had been provoked into a fight; this was specifically true after 1560, when the Franco-Ottoman collaboration gave way during the French *guerres de religion*. In 1562 Süleyman had reportedly issued 'express orders' to Turgut *reis* that he was to take the galleys of Malta 'if he can'.[15] In November 1563 the Ottoman preparations were directed at the Knights: 'the Turk is in a great fury for the damages that the galleys of the Religion and of the Duke of Florence have done in the Levant and the fleet will come upon Malta and then Apulia'.[16] A year later the spies had no doubt about the intentions of the Sultan and his men. 'They have a desire to go to the island of Malta, which they very much hate, but it being so strong and well provisioned, it appears that they have little hope of being able to destroy it' (*'de poder la expugnar'*).[17] Francesco Balbi di Correggio's account of the origins of the Great Siege set it in the light of the constant attacks by the Christian corsairs upon the Sultan's trade and peoples; Antonio Fajardo y Azevedo gave a similar explanation in his general history of the Ottoman Empire.[18] The Hospitaller Giacomo Bosio's account of deliberations in Constantinople from October 1564 dwelt on the many outrages perpetrated by the Knights over the previous decades and the Sultan's twin duties to protect the pilgrimage routes ('to allow us to visit the Holy House of Mecca in peace') and to come to the rescue of the Muslims who languished in the dungeons of *il Burgo*. More remarkably, Bosio also mentioned that the Hospitallers had broken the vow made by the-then Grand Master, Philippe de Villiers de l'Isle-Adam, to Süleyman in return for free passage from Rhodes in January 1523.[19] Süleyman himself gave an explanation along similar lines.[20] His instructions to Hasan Pasha, governor general of Algiers, were specific:

> The island of Malta is a headquarters for infidels. The Maltese have already blocked the route utilised by Muslim pilgrims and merchants to the Eastern Mediterranean, on their way to Egypt. I have ordered Piyale Pasha to take part in the campaign with the Imperial Navy, and you must bring all of the volunteer captains in the area who will participate in the Malta campaign.

A parallel interpretation was set out in the Ottoman histories dealing with Süleyman's motivation in moving against Rhodes in 1522.[21]

At this point the problem lies in describing the basic character of the Ottoman Empire. One jurist, Taliki-*zade* Mehmed el-Fenari, proudly boasted it was more thoroughly dedicated to the implementation of the precepts of the *şeriat* (holy law) than any previous regime in history.[22] Modern scholarship has tended to argue that the rationale informing the writings of jurists such as Taliki-*zade* ('as long as the holy law is observed, the realm will flourish, the treasury will be full, and the army will be victorious') was somehow simplistic and outdated. But his writings served to underline, once again, how much attacks on the pilgrimage routes offended the basic rationale and duties of the Islamic state. When Taliki-*zade* came to list the qualities necessary for the government of the state, he listed as his priority 'adherence to Islam'. The second duty was guardianship of the holy cities, Mecca and Medina; the fourth was to maintain authority over both land and sea.

A great deal of evidence might be found in both the Ottoman sources and the Christian archives to suggest that the Sultan's principal concern in 1565 was to deal with the Hospitaller corsairs, rather than to prepare the ground for the conquest of Italy. If the latter had been the case, Süleyman could certainly have chosen positions (Siracusa and Augusta and the adjacent city-fort of Carlentini in Sicily; Alghero in Sardinia; the Balearics) whose conquest would have been far easier to achieve, as the King, Toledo and many others well knew.[23] Foremost among the list of vulnerable positions was La Goleta, limited though this *presidio* was in value.

The one act guaranteed to transform the complex web of diplomatic and economic ties into a simple, stark confessional contest between Islam and Christendom, the *Dar al-Harb* and the *Dar al-Islam*, was to attack Muslim pilgrims in the seas ruled by the Ottomans. This was, precisely, the activity at which the Christian corsairs excelled. Spy reports seemed to confirm this thesis: in the lead up to the Great Siege an intelligence report stated that the Chief Mufti, 'who is like the Pope of the Turks', had issued a ruling that all those who died on the campaign or within ten years of returning from it would be martyrs.[24] Again, the detail may well be accurate as the Ottoman campaign register refers to those who were killed as being 'fallen martyrs'.[25]

If the Mediterranean campaigns after 1530 were far from straightforward or heroic, then, as Setton, Braudel and Thompson noted, the majority of the galleys available to His Catholic Majesty were based in Italy.[26] The very elements that triumphed at Lepanto – the disciplined professionalism found in Philip II's infantry and reinforced fleet – were the consequence of long years of diligent improvement. The very tactical strengths that gave the Christians victory at *la batalla naval* enforced the strategic decisions that determined that it would lead nowhere; the *política de prudencía* that so limited the Christian offensive potential in the months after *la batalla naval* was based upon the centrality of the oared fleet to the survival of Catholic Christendom. In the simplest terms, the Catholic Monarchy operated within very fine margins. When, in December 1614, the Duke of Osuna set out his plans for the defence of Sicily against 150 Ottoman galleys he asked for 4,000 Spaniards to be sent to the island, arguing that without a core of Spanish infantry the Italian militia, being '*gente inesperta y de poco servicio*', would flee to the mountains and the island, so exposed, might be lost to the Turk.[27]

Osuna's concerns were, of course, exaggerated in order to serve his immediate cause and interests. Yet his case contained an essential truth, and this was that the military system depended upon the presence of professional infantry in Naples, Sicily and Milan. Clearly, there were very marked limits to the operation of this system; it could not fight in more than one theatre at any one time, or at least found it very difficult to do so. This observation immediately refers back to the question of the outlook or strategic priorities of *el rey prudente*, to the dialectical rivalry between messianic objectives and the limitations of galley warfare. While the King pledged himself to the service of God, he believed that the only genuine and beneficial option was to improve his fleet in patrols around the islands of the western Mediterranean. The commitment of the Order of the Knights of the Hospital of St John of Jerusalem went far beyond the merely rhetorical. Its very *raison d'être* was 'to sack, ravage, seize and despoil persons and property belonging to pagans and to retrieve the loss, in whole or in part, both from the guilty as from the innocent followers of that sect'.[28] In a brilliant paper based upon the records of the later seventeenth century, Professor Fontenay argued that the Hospitallers exploited their acts of *corso* as a means of justifying the many estates held by the Order across Catholic Europe.[29]

Did the violent *corso* of the Hospitaller Knights in the Levant serve any military purpose other than to irritate the Turk and stir him to send his fleet against Christendom? A moment's thought reveals how much the squadrons of Philip II and Philip III would have benefited from the presence of four or five highly reinforced Hospitaller galleys on their summer patrols around the islands. This was, in fact, exactly the perspective set out by the King in a letter to the Grand Master of March 1563, in which he linked the 'service of God' to the protection of Christendom and 'security and conservation of my states and your land', '*la seguridad y conservación de mis estados y de vuestra tierra*'. This objective was to be achieved by employing the fleet in two bands to chase the Islamic corsairs.[30] The Hospitallers could never entirely ignore the requests made by His Catholic Majesty; on the other hand, they very rarely overlooked their own interests: in 1563 la Valette sent four Hospitaller galleys to help the armada; concurrently he dispatched his two private ships into the Levant, where they took 400 slaves.[31] In the following year a similar pattern of events unfolded: having pledged the squadron to the King, la Valette sent all seven warships on a raid into the eastern seas. Again, he provided an explanation of his decision: he had received reports of Turgut's squadron being in La Valona; when the Hospitaller squadron investigated it found this information to be false, but happily it did manage to intercept and overcome a large merchant-man near Modon. The viceroy was disappointed that the squadron from Malta would arrive late to the campaign against the Peñón de Vélez. The King was more forthright in his response. Having stated that the captured ship was a good prize, he again reiterated that the service of God and 'the benefit or profit of Christendom' lay in the prosecution and eradication of corsairs, 'our common enemies, who seeing that there are no galleys in these seas will believe that they can proceed more freely and insolently than they have done up to now'. It had appeared to him, he added, that the Hospitaller galleys should return to Malta in order to achieve this aim.[32]

Instead, therefore, of acting in a defensive and constructive role, the galleys from Valetta and Leghorn raided the eastern Mediterranean, constantly provoking the Turk.[33] The consequent Ottoman offensives in 1565 and 1570 entailed precipitous risks for the Catholic Monarchy based in Naples, Milan, Genoa, Sicily and Spain, as the loss of the royal galleys would have led to disaster in Milan, Piedmont, Flanders, Artois – perhaps even in Spain itself. If the Ottoman campaigns after 1580 (in 1594, 1599, 1602 and 1614) were undertaken on a lower level of intensity and smaller scale, then they clearly entailed great expense to the exchequers in Naples and Messina.

The relationship between the Catholic Monarchy and the Christian privateers was certainly an ambiguous one. In part this was because of the Hospitaller dedication to *el corso* and in part because their contribution to major campaigns tended to be relatively half-hearted – this was true even when, as in 1559–60, the expedition was undertaken to recover the fief of Tripoli for the Order of the Hospital.[34] As we have seen, in 1551 and 1552 there were considerable doubts about the willingness and the capacity of this organisation, dominated by Frenchmen, to defend its territories. Aside from the military protection extended to the Knights, the Catholic Monarchy also allowed the Order to export large quantities of provisions from Sicily on very favourable terms.[35]

The reaction to the siege of Malta again made manifest the profound suspicions which had been voiced by Charles V and his ministers in the wake of the conquest of Mahdia in 1550. In February 1566 Toledo wrote that la Valette was attempting to transfer his institution of crusading monks to a coastal position in Sicily, having set his eyes on Augusta. 'But I feel that I should advise your Majesty,' Toledo wrote on 26 November, 'that Augusta not a place for one Frenchman to live in, let alone many.' This matter was one of absolute importance, as this transfer could not be allowed in any way.[36] He was preaching to the converted; the King was pleased with Toledo's efforts to prevent the Grand Master from moving to Sicily, 'as with this and the other accommodations you have made him and will make him, he cannot excuse, nor deal nor think of moving to Augusta, as this, as you say, is something that would not be appropriate in any way, and nor could I permit'.[37]

The war in the Mediterranean, therefore, can in part be understood within the context of the uniquely unfavourable conditions that bound princes to privateers, the Habsburgs of Spain to the Hospitallers of Malta. It seems logical to enquire, from this perspective, what common ground they shared? The answer to this question lies in two overlapping areas: the first of these was, as Philip II's correspondence of the first half of the 1560s suggested, that the crown and the corsairs of Malta were driven by a common dedication to 'the public cause of our holy faith', 'the service of God';[38] the second was that both the Hospitallers and the Grand Duke of Tuscany were subjects or vassals of the Catholic Monarchy by virtue of the multiple investitures agreed by the Habsburg emperor and the Medici Pope at Bologna in the four months from November 1529.[39]

In this light the determination of the Habsburgs of Spain to defend Latin Christendom can be seen as the consequence of what they swore to do in order to inaugurate their kingship; it can be directly tied to their unique historical predicament as an example of kingship-by-investiture. If the territorial extent of Habsburg possessions ('an empire on which the sun never set') was enormous, then their military power in the *mare nostrum* largely depended upon a few thousand troops billeted in Milan and garrisoned in bastions dotted around the coastlines of Naples and

Sicily. In 1510 and then again in 1521, 1529, 1554, 1555 and 1599, the Crown of Spain confirmed its possession of the Norman crusader fief by acknowledging its status as a feudatory of the Holy and Apostolic See of Rome: in doing so, it undoubtedly assumed the role of a 'great power', but it also committed itself to the Constantinian ethos of the Church, to the 'cause of God', the unrelenting campaign for the propagation of the faith and the struggle against heretics and Saracens. It can be postulated that the liege bond between Habsburgs and popes was cemented not only by the perception that the barons and princes of *il Regno* looked to the Papacy as their overlord and thus as the guardian of their sweeping prerogatives and rights, but also by the realisation that His Most Christian Majesty would do anything – including allying himself with the Turk – in order to recover his patrimony in Italy. Venice and Florence were almost as untrustworthy: to put it another way, they had almost as much to gain from the confiscation of the fiefs of the Spanish Habsburgs as did His Most Christian Majesty.

In this panorama, Mediterranean holy war was not the product of a 'messianic imperialism'; nor was it the consequence (*pace* Braudel) of the determining cycles of economic development; it was the result of royal feudalism, of the very resonances of political authority within the various crowns worn by the Habsburgs of the House of Spain. The division of sovereignty was not a by-product of the jagged dynastic rivalries and confessional disputes of the early modern period: it was the cause of them. If, in other words, the messianic objectives of the Habsburgs of Spain are seen to originate in their feudal obligations in Italy, then the problem of the motivations of Charles V, Philip III and Philip III becomes a more complex one. On one level it would be impossible to deny a degree of military rationale to the campaigns in the Mediterranean: Philip II could not, for instance, have been anything other than concerned – and perhaps even fearful – about the prospect of an Ottoman conquest and occupation of Malta. Similarly the loss of Tripoli, La Goleta and perhaps even of Cyprus must, on some level, have increased concerns about the capacity of the Catholic Monarchy to defend its own territories or, crucially, to communicate with them across the seas. Yet in all cases the discussions were set in the context of a

Franco-Ottoman, rather than purely Ottoman, advance: the response to the loss of Tripoli in 1551 centred around the 'national' allegiance of the French knights, who at the very least had been too willing and eager to exchange their freedom for their honour; Philip II's instructions in 1565 alluded to the hidden enmities which would recur in the event of the loss of the island. Similar concerns underlay all assessments in 1572, when the basic dilemma facing the King lay in the question of what His Most Christian Majesty and the Queen of England might try to do while Don John led his quixotic crusade in the Levant on behalf of the Republic of St Mark. It is not unduly cynical to postulate that the concerns about the Moriscos were tied up with ideas about how 'some evil spirit' might use the New Christians of Granada and Valencia in order to advance their interests elsewhere. This was certainly true in 1596, when the Queen of England, His Most Christian Majesty and the Dutch rebels seemed to be coordinating their actions with those of the Ottoman Turk – or, at least, so the Marquis of Denia clearly believed.

The difficulty with this line of interpretation lies in determining the limits of Habsburg obligations. Thus in 1566 the King famously vowed in a letter to Pius V that he would rather lose all of his states and kingdoms than fail in the service of God and tolerate a heretic as a subject.[40] The context for this declaration was his decision to impose a repressive religious settlement in the Netherlands, a resolution which in turn seemed to abrogate the complex political and legal framework of these 17 separate fiefs of the Low Countries. Philip II's words have been seen as the manifestation of extreme religious devotion; alternatively they have been taken as representative of the conviction that political allegiance was somehow dependent upon confessional uniformity. It seems remiss, however, to fail to point out that the King had already pledged himself to the Holy See, and that in doing so he – or, strictly speaking, his proxy – had solemnly vowed in the Vatican chamber decorated by Raphael that the King of Naples, as an obedient son of the Church, would never tolerate a heretic as a subject, but that he would instead persecute them all with great rigour, *sed illos efficaciter persequentur*.

In other words, if the proposition is accepted that the Habsburgs of Spain were compelled to a war of certain characteristics – many of them unfavourable to the interests of the *monarquía* – in the Mediterranean by the terms of investiture in Italy, then it seems inevitable that the question be posed about the scope of Habsburg 'obligations' in northern Europe and the Atlantic. One incident unites both theatres of action. As Professor Parker notes, in the summer of 1569 both Alba and the King sought to improve relations with the Queen of England.[41] On 2 November 1569 Philip II's ambassador in Rome, Zúñiga, reported news of the revolt of English Catholics against Elizabeth I ('the Northern Rebellion'), and the possibility that the Pope would move on this matter too soon. The Pontiff was already toying with the idea that His Catholic Majesty should be the one to punish the Queen; Zúñiga was particularly aware of danger that Pius V might leave himself open to French manipulation on this matter.[42] On 4 November the Pope informed Zúñiga that he would write to Alba to instruct him to see what he could do to depose the Queen and to place the kingdom, a papal fief, in the hands of a Catholic Englishman who might then marry the Queen of Scotland. In response Zúñinga underlined the need to concede the *cruzada* and other monies to the King if he were to undertake 'the Enterprise of England' ('it being impossible for His Majesty to deal with so many problems as are daily put in his hands'). He added that the Pope recognised that His Catholic Majesty would never allow a Frenchman to set foot in England, and vice versa. The letter of 4 November was received in Madrid on 11 December; on 16 Philip II wrote to Alba to confirm the Pope's instructions.[43]

In February 1570 Pius V declared Elizabeth to be a heretic and deposed. Experienced statesmen in Italy reacted to this news in a very specific way, in part because it was increasingly evident that an Ottoman attack upon Cyprus was being prepared. In a letter dated 7 March 1570 Zúñiga reported his ongoing efforts to persuade Pius V that the existing funds generated by the Three Graces did not cover the cost necessary for the defence of the King's realms 'and still less [enable him to] undertake at the same time two such difficult wars as this one [in the Mediterranean] and the [proposed] war against England. The Pope replied that he would do as much as his conscience would allow.'[44]

An extraordinary ambassador, Luis de Torres, was dispatched by Pius V to convince Philip II that the Holy League was a necessity. The instructions, dated 6 March 1570, read:

> Another matter of business that we want to be dealt with His Majesty on this occasion is to exhort His Majesty to embrace the affairs of England by helping the rebels, from whom we have letters that beg for our assistance and ask that we recommend them to His Catholic Majesty. The Nuncio has already touched on this matter and has reported that the King has sent 200,000 ducats to the Duke of Alba for this effect. We want you to encourage His Majesty to proceed with this [operation against] that wretched Queen, [who is] so perverse and who robs everyone on the seas. These are the two things that we want to deal with His Majesty ...

The mission undertaken by Torres has always been seen in the context of the Holy League, but he was in fact sent to ask for the prosecution of two separate wars in the Mediterranean and Atlantic.[45] Of course in his audiences and speeches Torres first dealt with the need to conclude the capitulations of the Holy League. But the affairs of England were not forgotten. Having thanked the King for the 200,000 *scudi* sent via Alba to the rebels in the previous year, he beseeched him not to forget the affairs of England. 'And once again His Holiness implores His Majesty that he should wish to continue an enterprise which is as holy as all of his others. In this passage he listened to me with enthusiasm [*con gusto*], and he said that he would never fail to give to His Holiness complete contentment with all his power, as was his duty and desire.'[46]

On 12 May 1570 Philip II replied to Torres that he had decided to do what the Pope asked of him with regard to the Holy League with Venice. However, the King insisted that Pius V should feel no gratitude for this, '[as I am] obliged, as his most obedient son, to give the Pope satisfaction in all affairs, as would always be seen by events', '*come si vedrebbe per gli effetti sempre*'. The King then touched upon one of his favourite themes – the difference between words and deeds, rhetoric and action – before asserting that the only thing that could challenge the integrity of the

League would be 'some evil spirit' who might seek to disturb the good understanding upon which it was based.[47]

There was not much doubt about where this evil spirit might have lived – very possibly, somewhere near Paris – but at this juncture (mid-May) Philip II again instructed his diplomats in Rome to impress upon Pius V that his responsibilities far outstripped his incomes: under no circumstances was talk of the League to be allowed to proceed unless it was done with the explicit understanding that the Three Graces would be granted.[48] In mid-May the King again reaffirmed to the nuncio that he would never fail to obey His Holiness with regards to England, '*che non mancherebbe in questa parte d'ubbidir S.Santità*'.[49] But, finally, the Prudent King had to accept in an audience with Torres on 3 August that his sacred obligation to the service and honour of God and of His Holy See compelled him to help to return England to obedience to the Church – an achievement which, he pointed out, he had already brought about once (by his marriage to Mary I). He did, however, stress the need not to do something simply for the sake of appearance or vanity: when the moment came for action, the campaign should be carried out with determination, resolve and genuine prospects of success. Philip II lamented that the Northern Rebellion had been undertaken without foresight or preparation; it had unnecessarily revealed the intentions of the rebels and had thus inevitably ended in defeat. Success depended upon seizing opportunities when they presented themselves. Finally the King explained that he would give instructions to Alba to intervene in the event of this being possible.[50]

Before, then, he had begun to fight the war in the Mediterranean, Philip II had pledged himself to the war in the Atlantic. It is true that he did so in a strange way: one of Zúñiga's complaints in an audience (11 August) was that the Bull of deprivation did not bestow the investiture of England upon Philip II; it might, he had initially suspected, have been the work of Frenchmen, 'and [His Catholic Majesty] can never accept that a Frenchman should put his foot in that kingdom' of England.[51] The very logic employed by Philip II in his audiences with Torres underlined that the Bull of 1570 was self-defeating, in that the progress of the Holy League could only invite Elizabeth to consider what His Catholic

Majesty might do in the event of a successful resolution to the Mediterranean campaigns. It was said that Pius V himself came to regret the decision to move against the Queen of England and Ireland. Francis Borja, for one, did all he could to smooth troubled waters, realising that the declaration of forfeiture could only complicate the plans for the defence and extension of Catholic Christendom.[52] But his efforts were in vain.

Conclusion

The study of imperial organisation and holy war in the Mediterranean therefore leads from the consideration of *chusma* to the tactical features of oared warships, the strategic timetable and the mental outlook of the protagonists. It ends with the thesis that the dictates of political sovereignty, rather than considerations of military purpose, were the determining features of war between Christian and Islamic states in the Mediterranean in the sixteenth and early seventeenth centuries.

This conclusion is not entirely novel. In his time as ambassador in Rome Cardinal Ferdinando de'Medici wrote a series of letters to his brother, the Grand Duke Francesco, whose basic assumption was the centrality of Rome to European affairs. 'In Ferdinando's eyes, the pontiff was the potential arbiter of international questions and equilibria far more than the spiritual head of the church.' For this reason ecclesiastical affairs were often governed by secular considerations: this was especially true of the creation of cardinals.[1] Cardinal Richelieu expressed a similar idea in his *Testament Politique*: the negotiations in Rome were pivotal to the humours of Christendom. A crucial plank of his plan to strengthen the crown of France was to arm galleys in Marseille with the aim of severing communications between Spain and Italy.

It has generally been assumed that the Habsburgs of Spain had to choose between the *mare nostrum* and northern Europe. This was true, but in a very limited sense: it was applicable, or partially applicable, to finances, resources and to the deployment of trained, veteran troops, who were always in short supply. In relation to the galley, almost the precise opposite was the case. Rather than being conceived of as a choice between the Mediterranean and the North, success in the two theatres of arms was in fact dependent upon one and the same resource, the royal armada, upon which everything depended in 1528, 1535, 1563, 1588, 1596, 1609 and 1614. The Catholic Monarchy increased its capacity to fight in both theatres by strengthening its *chusma* in summer patrols and by resting the rowing crews through the dark winter months. Sending its flotillas to hunt in the coves and capes around Sardinia and Minorca in April and May improved the Catholic Monarchy's ability to respond not only to the threat posed by Islam in the southern sea but also to emergencies in central Europe or on Spain's Atlantic seaboard.

Far, then, from being an anachronistic relic of a previous age, the Mediterranean war galley was the vehicle upon which the most advanced and successful states of their day based their fighting systems. No fortress could operate without receiving an array of supplies from across the seas – many, in fact, depended upon the galleys to ferry that most basic of supplies, water, to them – and very few military campaigns on land could be sustained without the continual assistance of the elegant, sleek warships that were capable of both navigating into and across winds and rowing through the summer calms. For the Ottomans, the oared flotillas served to bring the wealth of the Orient and the fertility of the Nile delta to its capital. This basic economic imperative blurred into the fundamental obligation of 'the Turk' as the Servant of the Two Holy Cities to protect pilgrimage routes to Mecca and Medina, a duty which in turn allowed the dynasty to locate itself within the history and traditions of Islam stretching back to Four Rightly Guided Caliphs and to the Prophet himself.

All of the campaigns seen in the century after 1530 could be interpreted as a struggle between the rival dictates of valour and prudence. For the Habsburgs of Spain there was a direct and recurring conflict between the final ambition – the service of God, with the attendant notion that He might come to the assistance of His people – and the refusal to take any risk with the oared squadrons or to place any faith in fate or providence. It is more difficult to be precise about the

Ottoman intentions, but the recurring problem for the sultans would seem to have lain in the tension between the defence of the lands, seas and peoples of Islam and the existence of the Order of the Knights of the Hospital of St John of Jerusalem at Malta, a wealthy and privileged institution whose very purpose was to inflict as much damage upon the infidel as was possible.

This dialectic clash of valour and vigilance dominated the sea in the lifetimes of princes like Andrea Doria and privateers like Barbarossa; Don García de Toledo and Turgut *reis* were trapped by it, as were Don John of Austria and Uluç Ali Pasha, Gian Andrea Doria and Murad *reis el grande*, the most formidable corsair of his day. Trying to understand this dynamic, to see why intelligent and superbly well-informed individuals took the risks that they did is, of course, the central problem in the history of the sixteenth and seventeenth centuries. One interpretation would be that they were driven by faith in God or Allah; the problem with this line of interpretation is that only the naive or uninformed placed much faith in the galleys of Venice, the integrity of the Hafsid 'King of Tunis', the sailing conditions along the coasts of Greece in September or the utility of the small and isolated fortress on the sandy isthmus guarding the lagoon of Tunis. Above all else, every judgement turned on the capacity of oarsmen to withstand the ferocious assault upon their health and well-being that life *en galera* unleashed upon them.

If holy war was not driven by religious faith, then an alternative explanation is required: that Philip II and Süleyman were prisoners of history, rather than its agents. It would be difficult to claim originality for this interpretation, although in this case it would be argued that the actors were fully conscious of the role that the fates had asked them to play, and that their awareness of their obligations was derived from the ceremonies in which sovereignty was conferred upon them. The duties to which His Catholic Majesty and the Shadow of God on Earth committed themselves at the moment of their investiture or coronation were decisive in forging their subsequent policies.

The Habsburgs of Spain and the Ottomans of Turkey have nearly always been studied as independent rulers located within narratives of national grandeur and decline; this classification overlooks the vast international panorama in which they placed themselves. The Ottomans cast themselves as heirs of the Umayyad and Abbasid Caliphs; their motivation for doing so was the need to legitimise their government over vast parts of the Arab lands as a result of the conquest of 1516/17; the Habsburg devotion to the cause of God was explicable by the 'obligations' which they accepted in return for the conferral of the decisive fiefs in Italy. This line of analysis would seem to offer by far the most convincing interpretation of the Prudent King, as in other respects it is difficult to reconcile the paradox that the figure who so often and so emphatically found himself in agreement with Gian Andrea Doria about the benefits of his galley squadrons patrolling the capes of Bonifaccio, Passero and Denia, was also the ruler who sent three major fleets against England and pledged himself to burn the stain of Protestantism from Christendom. Peace in Italy came at a high price: the achievement of 'la tranquilidad de Italia' committed the King of Spain to war everywhere else.

To view the fighting in the inland sea as being waged by Spain and the Turk is one tradition; to view it as a contest between His Catholic Majesty and the Caliph of the Muslims offers new perspectives on Mediterranean and, indeed, world history. Rather than view Charles V, Philip II and Philip III in terms of the future development of imperial powers – 'the rise and decline of Spain' – it might be profitable to view them in terms of the legacies of the medieval period: they were heirs not only to the legacy of coexistence in Spain, but also to the black-and-white crusading ethos of the Church militant and to the bewildering array of jurisdictions within the Holy Roman Empire. In 1530 they accepted as their vassals the Hospitaller Knights, a crusader body whose origins and entire *raison d'être* lay in the legacy of the First Crusade ('*su profesión es guerrear a los infieles*', as Juan de Vega put it in 1551). A consideration of the vast scale of Habsburg obligations may have served to deepen concerns about the Moriscos: much as '*la empresa de España*' seemed inherently unlikely for both geographical and military reasons, the Habsburgs could extrapolate from their own quixotic and herculean campaigns in the service of God and easily understand how 'the Turk' might be compelled or convinced to come to the rescue of the minorities in Granada, Aragon and Valencia. In any case, the Morisco dilemma once again returned discussions to the relationship between Spain and the Italian fiefs of the crown, in that in the final instance the defence of the coastlines of Iberia would surely have depended upon the regular forces stationed in the Republic of Genoa, the Duchy of Milan and the Kingdom of the Two Sicilies.

While the Ottomans insisted that they sought peace, the Habsburgs were convinced that they could not afford war. The fighting at La Goleta in June 1535 or August 1574, at St Elmo in June 1565 or at Lepanto in October 1571 offered unequivocal proof of the limits of what either side could achieve or realistically hope to achieve. Attempting to understand the intensity of the fighting reveals the paradoxes and contradictions of early modern holy war: that the decisively new forms of political and military organisation that emerged in the *Cinquecento* served to reinvigorate older institutions and patterns of action and thought; that the emergence of powerful centralised bureaucracies serving the crowns of France and Spain reinvigorated the medieval mechanisms of international feudalism just as the ranks of *kapikulus* or slaves of the imperial household in Constantinople served to create a state which based its claim to legitimacy on the pristine model of early Islam; that the discovery and exploration of vast new worlds in the Indian and Atlantic Oceans served to underline the centrality of the Mediterranean and its ancient war galley, whose characteristics had hardly changed from the times of Thucydides and Polybius; that the modern technology of Italian-design fortress and gunpowder weaponry offered extraordinary new opportunities to those relics of the medieval past, the Hospitaller warrior monk and *ghazi* raider; that the ferocious siege of the bastions at Malta underlined the unique value of fleets, and that the Christian victory at Lepanto demonstrated that the Ottoman Turk could not be definitively defeated at sea. Finally, it might be suggested that the catalyst to the emergence of forms of national consciousness was found in the great overarching programmes of Church and Empire and that the phenomenon of holy war ultimately underlined the value of the dispassionate assessment of Islamic civilisation and must therefore have contributed at some level towards the secularisation of the European world-view or *mentalité*.

No sooner have these arguments been advanced than they immediately lead to a series of new problems: the Treaty of Tordesillas (1494), which divided the New Worlds between Portugal and Spain, was also promulgated under Papal jurisdiction; in turn, this accord must be interpreted in the light of two Bulls of May 1493, profoundly contradictory and ambiguous in nature, by which Pope Alexander VI conferred upon Isabella *la Católica* the recently discovered territories in the Indies; it is perhaps worth noting that Neapolitan jurists insisted upon the Holy See's claims to the vast territories in the Atlantic and Pacific. By definition dynastic states functioned through the ceremony of marriage and the papacy controlled the crucial prerogatives to dispense from the diriment impediments of consanguinity – in other words, it could allow cousins or other close-relatives to marry. It might also be wondered why the investiture of Ireland should have been so important to Philip II and Philip III.[2] These themes and questions lead back to the finest of historiographical traditions, the study of the Mediterranean and the Mediterranean world in the age of Philip II of Spain, King of Jerusalem, King of the Two Sicilies, Duke of Milan, *Su Sacra Real Católica Majestad*. It is obviously true that this study has provided only tentative or partial answers to them. But it is hoped that it has at least demonstrated that, like Süleyman the Lawgiver, the Habsburgs of Spain were men of their word.

Notes

Introduction

1. AGS, Sec.Prov.leg.987 sf CCI Madrid, 17 December 1598.
2. Fernand Braudel, *The Mediterranean and the Mediterranean World in the Age of Philip II*, translated by Siân Reynolds, 2 volumes, Collins: London 1973, ii, pp.1139–42, 1184–85.
3. José Luis Casado Soto, *Los Barcos Españoles del siglo XVI y la Gran Armada de 1588*, Editorial San Martin: Madrid-Spain 1988, *passim*.
4. Geoffrey Parker, *The Grand Strategy of Philip II*, Yale University Press: New Haven and London 1998, p.176.
5. Braudel, *Mediterranean*, ii, pp.1088–1185; Andrew C. Hess, 'The Battle of Lepanto and Its Place in Mediterranean History', in *Past & Present*, No.57 (Nov. 1972), pp.53–73; I.A.A. Thompson, *War and Government in Habsburg Spain 1560–1620*, UCL: London 1976, pp.13–14; C.H. Imber, 'The Navy of Süleyman the Magnificent', in *Archivum Ottomanicum*, vol. VI (1980), p.220.
6. A.T. Mahan, *The Influence of Sea Power upon History, 1660–1783*, reprinted London 1965, *passim*. Mahan's arguments are examined and set in context by Paul Kennedy, *The Rise and Fall of British Naval Mastery*, Penguin edition: London 2001, pp.1–9.
7. John Francis Guilmartin, Jr., *Gunpowder and Galleys. Changing Technology and Mediterranean Warfare at Sea in the 16th Century*, 2nd edition, Conway Maritime Press: London 2003.
8. Carlo M. Cipolla, *Guns, Sails and Empires. Technological Innovation and the Early Phases of European Expansion, 1400–1700*, Sunflower University Press: Manhattan, Kansas 1985, see especially pp.100–01.

9. For a valuable recent overview, Jan Glete, *Warfare at Sea, 1500–1650, Maritime Conflicts and the Transformation of Europe*, Routledge: London and New York 2000, see especially p.5.

10. Braudel, *Mediterranean*, ii, p.994. The numerous problems encountered in the constuction of La Goleta are examined by Antonio Sánchez-Gijón, 'La Goleta, Bona, Bugía y los presidios del reino de Túnez en la política mediterránea del Emperador', in C.J. Hernando Sánchez ed., *Las fortificaciones de Carlos V*, Ministerio de Defensa, AEAC, CECCFC: Madrid 2000, pp.625–51.

11. Philip II himself referred to '*las ruines intenciones del dicho rey de Túnez, y cuan de mala gana provee las cosas que está obligado a dar para aquella fuerza*', CODOIN, xxix, pp.78–79.

12. AGS, Est.leg.1126, fol.39 Medinaceli to King, Palermo 26 April 1561.

13. AGS, Est.leg.1127 fol.14 Grand Master of Hospitallers to Viceroy of Sicily, Malta 25 February 1562.

14. Manuel Fernández Álvarez, *Carlos V, el César y el Hombre*, Fundación Academia Europea de Yuste: Madrid 1999, pp.504, 509.

15. Francisco López de Gómara, *Guerras de mar del Emperador Carlos V*, SECCFC: Madrid 2000, edited by Miguel Ángel de Bunes Ibarra and N.E. Jiménez, pp.171, 175.

16. Anne Brogini and María Ghazali, 'Un enjeu espagnol en Méditerranée: les présides de Tripoli et de La Goulette au XVIᵉ siècle', *Cahiers de la Méditerranée*, 70 (2005), para 97,'mis en ligne le 12 mai 2006'.

17. CODOIN, xxix, pp.177–79, 181–83.

18. Enrique García Hernán, 'La conquista y pérdida de Túnez por don Juan de Austria', in G. Candiani and L. Lo Basso eds, *Mutazioni e permanenze nella storia navale del Mediterraneo secc. XVI–XIX* in *Guerra e pace in età moderna. Annali di storia militare europea*, II (2010), Franco Angeli: Milan pp.39–95, pp.44–48, 89–95.

19. Between 1571 and 1577 the government of Sicily spent 1,600,000 *scudi* on defence and supplies for the fleet. Rossella Cancila, *Fisco Ricchezza Comunità nella Sicilia del Cinquecento*, ISI: Rome 2001, p.62; the cost of foods to the Kingdom of Sicily in 1571, 1572 and 1572 ran to 1,250,000 ducats, García Hernán and García Hernán, *Lepanto*, p.86 ; on the reduced, but still significant, contribution made by Sicily in the 1640s and 1650s, Davide Maffi, *Il baluardo della corona. Guerra, esercito, finanze e società nella Lombardia seicentesca (1630–1660)*, Le Monnier Università: Florence 2007, pp.328–31, 344.

20. I.A.A. Thompson, *War and Government in Habsburg Spain, 1560–1620*, UCL: London 1976, *passim* and see especially pp.163–84, 230–31; David Parrott, *The Business of War. Military Enterprise and Military Revolution in Early Modern Europe*, CUP: Cambridge 2012.

21. David Parrott, 'France's Wars against the Habsburgs, 1624–1659: the Politics of Military Failure', in García Hernán and Maffi eds, *Guerra y sociedad*, i, pp.31–48, p.34; Thompson, *War and Government*, p.256.

22. Thompson, *War and Government*, *passim* and especially his 'Conclusion', pp.274–87; Parrott, *Business of War*, Chapter VI.

23. Parrott, 'France's Wars', p.47.

24. David Parrott, 'A *"prince souverain"* and the French crown: Charles de Nevers, 1580–1637' in Robert Oresko, G.C. Gibbs and H.M. Scott eds, *Royal and Republican Sovereignty in Early Modern Europe. Essays in memory of Ragnhild Hatton*, CUP: Cambridge, New York and Melbourne 1997, pp.149–87, especially pp.176–83.

25. Robert Oresko, 'The House of Savoy in search for a royal crown in the seventeenth century' in Oresko, Gibbs and Scott eds, *Royal and Republican Sovereignty*, pp.272–350.

26. Oresko, 'House of Savoy', p.273.

27. Palmira Brummett, *Ottoman Seapower and Levantine Diplomacy in the Age of Discovery*, State University of New York Press: New York 1994, pp.102–03, 108–09, 116–17, 121; Pál Fodor, 'Ottoman Policy Towards Hungary, 1520–1541' reproduced in *In Quest of the Golden Apple. Imperial Ideology, Politics and Military Administration in the Ottoman Empire*, Isis Press: Istanbul 2000, pp.105–69; M.J. Rodríguez-Salgado, '¿Carolus Africanus?: el Emperador y el turco', in José Martínez Millán ed., *Carlos V y la quiebra del humanismo politico en Europa (1530–1558)*, 4 volumes, SECCFC: Madrid 2001, i, pp.487–531, p.490; Colin Imber, *The Ottoman Empire, 1300–1650. The Structure of Power*, Palgrave Macmillan: Basingstoke and New York 2002, p.125; Daniel Goffman, *The Ottoman Empire and Early Modern Europe*, CUP: Cambridge 2002, p.103.

28. C.R. Boxer, *The Dutch Seaborne Empire 1600–1800*, Hutchinson: London 1965, pp.25–28; Glete, *Warfare at Sea*, pp.85–89; Philip J. Stern, *The Company-State. Corporate Sovereignty & the Early Modern Foundations of the British Empire in India*, OUP: Oxford 2011.

29. Hugh Brogan, *The Penguin History of the United States*, Penguin: London 1986, pp.18–50.

30. Brogan, *Penguin History of the United States*, p.85.

31. The bibliography on piracy is enormous. For valuable recent overviews, Gonçal López Nadal, 'El Corsarismo Mediterraneo', in Luis Ribot García and Ernest Belenguer Cebriá eds, *Las sociedades ibéricas y el mar a finales del siglo XVI*, 6 volumes, Sociedad Estatal Lisboa '98: Clarendon: Madrid 1998, iii, pp.233–60; G. Fisher, *Barbary Legend. War, Trade and Piracy in North Africa (1415–1830)*, Oxford 1957; S. Bono, *I corsari barbareschi*, ERI: Turin 1964; P. Earle, *Corsairs of Malta and Barbary*, Sidgewick and Jackson: London 1970; Alberto Tenenti, *Piracy and the Decline of Venice 1580–1615*, translated by Janet and Brian Pullan, Longmans: London 1967; S. Bono, *Corsari nel Mediterraneo. Cristiani e musulmani fra guerra, schiavitù e commercio*, A Mondadori: Milan 1993; E. Sola Castaño, *Un Mediterráneo de piratas: corsarios, renegados y cautivos*, Tecnos: Madrid 1988; Mirella Mafrici, *Mezzogiorno e pirateria nell'età moderna*, Edizioni Scientifiche Italiane: Naples etc. 1995; Peter Earle, *The Pirate Wars*, Methuen: London 2004; Catherine Wendy Bracewell, *The Uskoks of Senj. Piracy, Banditry and Holy War in the Sixteenth Century Adriatic*, Cornell: Ithaca and London 1992; Moulay Belhamissi, *Marine et marins d'Alger (1518–1830)*, 3 volumes, BNA: Algiers 1996; M.A. de Bunes Ibarra, 'Bases y logística del corso berberisco', in *La expulsión de los moriscos y la actividad de los corsarios norteafricanos*, in Instituto de Historia y Cultura Naval: *Jornadas de Historia Marítima*, No.61 (October 2010), pp.83–102.

32. A recurring theme of Géraud Poumarède, *Pour en finir avec la Croisade. Mythes et réalités de la lutte contre les Turcs aux XVIᵉ et XVIIᵉ siècles*, Quadrige/PUF: Paris 2004, part III.

33. Mario Rizzo, 'Centro spagnolo e periferia lombarda nell'impero asburgico tra Cinque e Seicento', in *Rivista Storica Italiana*, CIV (1992), pp.315–48; Mario Rizzo, 'Non solo guerra. Risorse e organizzazione della strategia asburgica in Lombardia durante la seconda metà del Cinquecento' in Enrique García Hernán and Davide Maffi eds, *Guerra y sociedad en la Monarquía Hispánica. Política, estrategia y cultura en la Europa moderna (1500–1700)*, 2 volumes, Laberinto, CSIC and Fundación Mapfre: Madrid 2006, i, pp.217–52; on Milan's contribution in the crucial period of 1647 to 1653, Maffi, *Il baluardo della corona*, p.395; on Naples, Antonio Calabria, *The Cost of Empire. The Finances of the Kingdom of Naples in the Time of Spanish Rule*, CUP: Cambridge 1991, pp.1–6, 76–103; Giulio Fenicia, *Il Regno di Napoli e la difesa del Mediterraneo nell'età di Filippo II (1556–1598)*, Cacucci Editore: Bari 2003; Mafrici, *Mezzogiorno e pirateria*, pp.181–245; for a recent overview, Giovanni Muto, 'Strategie e Strutture

del Controllo Militare del Territorio nel Regno di Napoli nel Cinquecento', in García Hernán and Maffi eds, *Guerra y sociedad*, i, pp.153–70.

34. Thompson, *War and Government*, pp.21–23, 32, 34–35, 119–20, 127–28, 180, 182–84.

35. Thompson, *War and Government*, pp.179–82.

36. Enrique Solano Camón, *Poder monárquico y estado pactista (1626–1652). Los Aragoneses ante la Unión de Armas*, Institución Fernando el Católico: Zaragoza 1987, p.218.

37. Solano Camón, *Poder monárquico y estado pactista*, pp.60–61.

38. Juan Francisco Pardo Molero, *La defensa del imperio. Carlos V, Valencia y el Mediterráneo*, with a prologue by Bernard Vincent, SECCFC: Madrid 2001; Jordi Buyreu Juan, *Institucions i conflictes a la Catalunya moderna*, Rafael Dalmau: Barcelona 2005.

39. Thompson, *War and Government*, pp.19, 127–28, 137–39, 143; on the Guards of Castile, see also Enrique Martínez Ruiz, 'La difícil supervivencia del "ejército interior": las Guardas, los aposentamientos y la escasez de dinero a fines del siglo XVI', in P. Sánz Camañez ed., *La Monarquía Hispánica en tiempos del Quijote*, Sílex: Madrid 2005, p.433–61.

40. Antonio Jiménez Estrella, 'Ejército permanente y política defensiva en el Reino de Granada durante el siglo XVI', in García Hernán and Maffi eds, *Guerra y sociedad*, i, pp.579–610.

41. Rizzo, 'Alloggiare in casa d'altri', especially pp.86–88, 92.

42. J.H. Elliott, *The Revolt of the Catalans. A Study in the Decline of Spain*, CUP: Cambridge 1963, pp.237, 244–45, 391, 414–15; Thompson, *War and Government*, p.129; K.M. Setton, *The Papacy and the Levant (1204–1571)*, 4 volumes, American Philosophical Society: Philadelphia 1976, 1978, 1984, iv, p.891.

43. 'In 1604 there were only seven galleys under oars' in Spain, Thompson, *War and Government*, p.180; 26 galleys in Naples, Calabria, *Cost of Empire*, p.88 n16; Phillip Williams, 'Past and Present. The forms and limits of Spanish naval power in the Mediterranean, 1590–1620' in Mario Rizzo, José Javier Ruiz Ibáñez and Gaetano Sabatini eds, *Le forze del principe. Recursos, instrumentos y límites en la práctica del poder soberano en los territorios de la Monarquía Hispánica* (Acts of a Conference held in Pavia, 22 to 24 September 2000), 2 volumes, Universidad de Murcia: Murcia 2003, i, pp.237–78, p.271, 959–60.

44. Hernando Sánchez, *Castilla y Nápoles en el siglo XVI*, pp.160, 334.

45. For monies sent to Milan in the 1500s, Mario Rizzo, 'Porte, chiavi e bastioni. Milano, la geopolitica italiana e la strategia asburgica nella seconda

metà del XVI secolo', in Rossella Cancila ed., *Mediterraneo in armi (sec. XV–XVIII), Quaderni di Mediterraneo,* n° 4, 2 volumes, Palermo 2007, ii, pp.467–511, pp.496–507, 510–11.

46. Mafrici, *Mezzogiorno e pirateria,* pp.193–94.

47. Calabria, *Cost of Empire,* pp.89–90.

48. E. Otte and F. Trasselli cited by Arturo Pacini, *La Genova di Andrea Doria nell'Impero di Carlo V,* Olschki: Florence 1999, especially chapters II and IV; Friedrich Edelmayer, 'Génova en la encrucijada entre el Sacro Imperio y la Monarquía Católica', in Manuel Herrero Sánchez, Yasmina Rocío Ben Yessef Garfia, Carlo Bitossi and Dino Puncuh eds, *Génova y la Monarquía Hispánica,* 2 volumes, Società Ligure di Storia Patria: Genoa 2011, ii, pp.617–26.

49. Mario Rizzo, 'Gli *Austrias* e l'Italia centrosettentrionale nella prima età moderna. Una rapsodia geopolitica', in E. Fasano Guarini and F. Bonatti eds, *Atti del Convegno di Studi: Feudi di Lunigiana tra Impero, Spagna e Stati Italiani (XV–XVIII secolo)* ('Memorie della Accademia Lunigianese di Scienze "Giovanni Capellini"') pp.67–113, p.67; Arturo Pacini, ' "Poiché gli stati non sono portatili…": geopolitica e strategia nei rapporti tra Genova e Spagna nel Cinquecento', in Herrero Sánchez *et al* eds, *Génova…,* ii, p.413–57.

50. Henry Kamen, *Spain's Road to Empire. The Making of a World Power, 1492–1763,* Allen Lane: London etc. 2002; Óscar Recio Morales, 'La gente de naciones en los ejércitos de los Austrias hispanos: servicio, confianza y correspondencia', in García Hernán and Maffi eds, *Guerra y sociedad,* i, pp.651–79.

51. For example, Muto, 'Strategie e strutture', pp.159–60; Carlos Belloso Martín, *La antemuralla de la monarquía. Los tercios españoles en el Reino de Sicilia en el siglo XVI,* Adalid-Ministerio de Defensa: Madrid 2010; on militias see José Javier Ruiz Ibáñez ed., *Las milicias del rey de España. Sociedad, política e identidad en las Monarquías Ibéricas,* Fondo de Cultura Económica: Madrid 2009. For plans for reform, Enrique García Hernán, *Milicia general en la edad moderna. El batallón de don Rafael de la Barreda y Figueroa,* Ministerio de Defensa: Madrid 2003.

52. Karen Barkey, *Empire of Difference. The Ottomans in Comparative Perspective,* CUP: Cambridge 2008, p.294.

53. Pál Fodor, 'The organization of defence in the Eastern Mediterranean (end of the 16th century)', in Elizabeth Zachariadou ed., *The Kapudan Pasha, His Office and His Domain,* Crete University Press, Rethymnon 2002, pp.87–94; Phillip Williams, 'The Sound and the Fury: Christian Perspectives on

Ottoman naval organisation, 1590–1620', in Cancila ed., *Mediterraneo in armi*, ii, pp.557–92, pp.566–71, 582–84.

54. Gerald MacLean, *The Rise of Oriental Travel. English Visitors to the Ottoman Empire, 1580–1720*, Palgrave: London and New York 2004, p.126.

55. Bernard Lewis, *Istanbul and the Civilization of the Ottoman Empire*, Oklahoma University Press: Oklahoma 1963, pp.26–27.

56. For a masterly study of coastal towers, earthquakes, privateering and economic change, César Olivera Serrano, *La actividad sísmica en el Reino de Granada (1487–1531). Estudio histórico y documentos*, Stock Cero: Madrid 1994.

57. A point explored for the 1550s in Gilles Veinstein, 'Les préparatifs de la campagne navale franco-turque en 1552 à travers les ordres du divan ottoman' in *Revue de l'Occident musulman et de la Méditerranée*, No.39 (1985) pp.35–67; G. Veinstein, 'Les campagnes navales franco-ottomanes au XVIe siècle', in I. Malkin ed., *La France et la Méditerranée. Vingt-sept siècles d'interdépendance*, Leyde 1990, pp.311–34, 329. Note the delays caused by the wait for oarsmen and sailors in 1574, AGS, Est.leg.1141 fol.67 Reports from Constantinople, April 1574.

58. AGS, Est.leg.1120 fol.133 Juan de Vega to Prince, Messina 10 October 1551 (marked as both 1551 and 1552).

59. The Duke of Osuna, Viceroy of Sicily, predicted that 82 galleys would be available to Philip III in Italy in this summer, AGS, Est.leg.1888, fol.26 CCE Madrid 2 December 1614. These were: the Royal flagship and six galleys from Osuna's own squadron; 24 from Naples; 12 from Sicily; 16 from the contractors of Genoa; eight from the Republic of Genoa; six from the Papacy; five from Hospitaller Malta; the 20 or so galleys belonging to the squadrons of Catalonia, Portugal and Spain would remain on their own coasts. (The viceroy's mathematical skills were not the best, although he may have been following standard practice in counting the flagships and vice-flagships as three rather than two ships.) In a *consulta* (discussion), the Marquis of Villafranca pointed out that Osuna had overlooked the six highly reinforced galleys of Florence, which had enough oarsmen to arm ten regular warships, '*pues tiene buques y chusma de sobra*'. Incidentally Osuna predicted at this point that the Turk would arm 157 warships; in fact (at least) 60 Ottoman galleys were reported to be in operation, AGS, Est. leg.1359 fol.193 Marquis of Bedmar to Philip III, Venice 20 June 1615. Venice would have armed around 30, Tenenti, *Piracy and the Decline of Venice*, pp.113, 120–21; Luca Lo Basso, *Uomini da remo. Galee e galeotti del Mediterraneo in età moderna*, Selene Edizioni: Milan 2003, p.41.

60. For efforts to provision Oran in the early 1600s, Manuel Lomas Cortés, 'Las galeras en el aprovisionamiento marítimo de Orán-Mazalquivir' in Miguel Ángel de Bunes Ibarra and Beatriz Alonso Acero eds, *Orán. Historia de la Corte Chica*, Ediciones Polifemo: Madrid 2011, pp.195–221. See also Esteban Mira Caballos's excellent overview, 'Defensa terrestre de los reinos de Indias', in Hugo O'Donnell y Duque de Estrada ed., *Historia Militar de España. Vol. III. Edad Moderna. I. Ultramar y la Marina*, Laberinto and Ministerio de Defensa: Spain 2012, pp.143–93.

61. John Cummins, *Francis Drake*, Weidenfeld & Nicolson: London 1995, pp.251, 253.

62. Beatriz Alonso Acero, *Orán-Mazalquivir, 1589–1639: Una sociedad española en la frontera de Berbería*, CSIC: Madrid 2000, p.82.

63. On Mediterranean fortifications, a great deal of information can be found in Hernando Sánchez ed., *Las fortificaciones de Carlos V*; on raids, Mafrici, *Mezzogiorno*, pp.57–67.

64. Parker, *Grand Strategy*, p.286.

65. Lo Basso, *Uomini da remo*, *passim*.

66. García Hernán, 'Túnez', pp.88–89.

Chapter I

1. M. Mallett and C. Shaw, *The Italian Wars, 1494–1559*, Pearson: Harlow, London etc. 2012, pp.238, 243, 264.

2. There are many general narratives of these conflicts, and several valuable shorter accounts: Setton, *Papacy*, iii and iv, *passim*; Braudel, *Mediterranean*, ii, pp.904–1237; R.C. Anderson, *Naval Wars in the Levant 1559–1853*, LUP: Liverpool 1952, pp.1–120; Goffman, *Ottoman Empire and Early Modern Europe*, pp.137–64; Ann Williams, 'Mediterranean conflict' in Metin Kunt and Christine Woodhead eds, *Süleyman the Magnificent and His Age*, Longman: London and New York 1995, pp.39–54; Rodríguez-Salgado, '¿Carolus Africanus?'; Beatriz Alonso Acero, 'El norte de África en el ocaso del emperador (1549–1558)', in Martínez Millán ed., *Carlos V y la quiebra*, i, pp.387–414; Malta is presented as a crucial geostrategic position in Anne Brogini, *Malte, frontière de Chrétienté (1530–1670)*, EFR: Rome 2006, part one; Lemnour Merouche, *Recherches sur l'Algérie à l'époque Ottomane. II. La course mythes et réalité*, Editions Bouchene: Paris 2007, part one; N. Housley, *Crusading and the Ottoman Threat, 1453–1505*, OUP: Oxford 2012.

3. Kenneth Gouwens, 'Clement and Calamity: The Case for Re-evaluation' in Kenneth Gouwens and Sheryl E. Reiss eds, *The Pontificate of Clement VII. History, Politics, Culture*, MPG Books: Bodmin 2005, pp.3–14; Barbara McClung Hallman, 'The "Disastrous" Pontificate of Clement VII: Disastrous for Giulio de'Medici?' in ibid., pp.29–40; Charles L. Stinger, 'The Place of Clement VII and Clementine Rome in Renaissance History' in ibid., pp.165–84; G. Signorotto, 'Papato e principi italiani nell'ultima fase del conflitto tra Asburgo e Valois', in Martínez Millán ed., *Carlos V y la quiebra*, i, pp.259–80.

4. On the historical development of the investiture from the papal perspective, Cardinal S. Borgia, *Breve storia del dominio temporale della Sede Apostolica nelle Due Sicilie*, Rome 1788, especially pp.223–31; see also S. Reynolds, *Fiefs and Vassals. The Medieval Evidence Reinterpreted*, OUP: Oxford 1994, pp.210–13; Aurelio Musi, 'Carlo V nella *Historia della Città e Regno di Napoli* di G.A. Summonte', in B. Anatra and F. Manconi eds, *Sardegna, Spagna e Stati italiani nell'età di Carlo V*, Carocci: Rome 2001, pp.51–61.

5. David Abulafia, 'Introduction' in David Abulafia ed., *The French Descent into Renaissance Italy. Antecedents and Effects*. Variorum: Aldershot and Brookfield 1995 p.1–25; Cecil H. Clough, 'The Romagna campaign of 1494: a significant military encounter', in ibid., pp.192–215; Mallett and Shaw, *Italian Wars*, p.28.

6. For the following passage, L. Suárez, *Los Reyes Católicos*, Ariel: Barcelona 2004, pp.833–35, 848–49, 854–56, 862–63, 869–73.

7. Ferdinand to ambassador in Rome, 12 September 1503: '*cuanto a lo de la guerra de Nápoles creemos que gran parte del bien de aquel negocio o del contrario está en quien será papa.*' Cited by A. Serio, 'Una representación de la crisis de la unión dinástica: los cargos diplomáticos en Roma de Francisco de Rojas y Antonio de Acuña (1501–1507)', in L. Ribot, J. Valdeón and E. Maza eds, *Isabel la Católica y su época. Actas del congreso internacional 2004*, 2 volumes, Instituto Universitario de Historia Simancas, Universidad de Valladolid: Valladolid 2007, ii, pp.849–62, 853–54.

8. Borgia, *Breve storia*, p.227.

9. Ferrara was claimed as an apostolic fief, Suárez, *Reyes Católicos*, pp.882–83, 905, 910–13, 938–39; Setton, *Papacy*, iii, p.72–73, 75, 87; Mallett and Shaw, *Italian Wars*, p.99.

10. Luis Cabrera de Córdoba, *Historia de Felipe II, Rey de España*, 3 volumes, edited and with a preliminary study by José Martínez Millán and Carlos J. de Carlos Morales, *Felipe II (1527–1598). La configuración de la Monarquía Hispana*, Junta de Castilla y León: Salamanca 1998, i, p.61.

11. Also involved were Venice, the Republic of Florence and Francesco Sforza, Duke of Milan. Setton, *Papacy*, iii, pp.241–43.

12. McClung Hallman, 'The "Disastrous" Pontificate of Clement VII', p.38; Setton, *Papacy*, iii, pp.303–10; Pacini, *La Genova...*, chapters I and II.

13. Fernández Álvarez, *Carlos V*, pp.225–33.

14. Borgia, *Breve storia*, *passim*; see also S. Reynolds, *Fiefs and Vassals. The Medieval Evidence Reinterpreted*, OUP: Oxford 1994, pp.210–13. A copy of the investiture document can be found in AGS, Est.leg.971 sf 'Sumario de lo que contienen las bullas de Clemente Sexto, Julio 2°, Leon X^{mo}, Julio 3° sobre las Investiduras...' with letter of Duke of Sessa to King, Rome 4 June 1599.

15. McClung Hallman, 'The "Disastrous Pontificate" of Clement VII', pp.38–39.

16. Clough, 'Clement VII and Francesco Maria Della Rovere', pp.77–78, 105–06.

17. Victor Mallia-Milanes, 'Introduction to Hospitaller Malta', in Victor Mallia-Milanes ed., *Hospitaller Malta. Studies on Early Modern Malta and the Order of St John of Jerusalem*, Mireva: Msida 1993, pp.2–3.

18. Setton, *Papacy*, iii, p.351–52; Rubén Mayoral López, 'Los halcones de la Orden de San Juan y la caza real durante el reinado de Felipe III' in F. Ruiz Gómez and J. Molero García eds, *La Orden de San Juan en tiempos de Quijote*, EUCLM: Cuenca 2010, pp.182–90.

19. McClung Hallman, 'The "Disastrous" Pontificate', pp.38–39.

20. CSPV, vol 4. (1527–33), no.524; Mallett and Shaw, *Italian Wars*, p.219.

21. Venice held them from 1495 to 1509 and from 1528 to 1529, Carol Kidwell, 'Venice, the French invasion and the Apulian ports', in Abulafia ed., *French Descent*, pp.295–309.

22. Kidwell, 'Venice, the French...', pp.298–300.

23. Setton, *Papacy*, iii, p.332 and iv, p.879.

24. Franco Angiolini, 'I Presidios di Toscana: cadena de oro e llave y freno de Italia', in García Hernán and Maffi eds, *Guerra y sociedad*, i, pp.171–88.

25. Mario Rizzo, 'Alloggiare in casa d'altri. Le implicazioni economiche, politiche e fiscali della presenza militare asburgica nel territorio finalese fra cinque e seicento' in Paolo Calcagno ed., *Finale tra le potenze di antico regime. Il ruolo del Marchesato sulla scena internazionale (secoli XVI–XVIII)*, Società Savonese di Storia Patria: Savona 2009, pp.77–91; Friedrich Edelmayer, 'La Lucha por el camino español. Felipe II y el marquesado de Finale Ligure', in Alberto Marcos Martín ed., *Hacer historia desde Simancas*.

Homenaje a José Luis Rodríguez de Diego, JCL: Valladolid 2011, pp.293–304.

26. Rizzo, 'Non solo guerra', pp.251–52.

27. Giorgio Spini, 'Italy after the Thirty Years War' in F.L. Carsten ed., *The New Cambridge Modern History. Volume V: the Ascendancy of France 1648–88*, Cambridge 1969, pp.458–60; Michael Levin, *Agents of Empire: Spanish Ambassadors in Sixteenth-Century Italy*, Cornell University Press: Ithaca and London 2005, pp.38–42.

28. Mario Rizzo, 'Sticks, Carrots and all the Rest: Lombardy and the Spanish strategy in northern Italy between Europe and the Mediterranean', *Cahiers de la Méditerranée*, vol.71 (2005) December 2005, pp.145–84; Levin, *Agents of Empire, passim*; B.J. García García, *La Pax Hispanica. Política exterior del Duque de Lerma*, LUP: Leuven 1996, pp.83–88; Edelmayer, 'La Lucha por el camino español', *passim*.

29. Mario Rizzo, 'Gli Austrias e l'Italia centrosettentrionale nella prima età moderna. Una rapsodia geopolitica', in Elena Fasano Guarini and Franco Bonatti eds, *Feudi di Lunigiana tra Impero, Spagna e Stati Italiani (XVI–XVIII secolo)*, Accademia Lunigianese di Scienze 'Giovanni Capellini': La Spezia 2008, pp.67–113; Rizzo, 'Alloggiare in casa d'altri', p.77; Oresko, 'House of Savoy', p.285.

30. For an exploration of loyalty, nationalism and the tensions generated by Spanish rule over a Neapolitan aristocracy and nobility in which an important element were of Norman or Angevin origin, C.J. Hernando Sánchez, 'Españoles e Italianos. Nación y lealtad en el Reino de Nápoles durante las Guerras de Italia', in A.A. Álvarez-Ossorio Alvariño and B.J. García García eds, *La Monarquía de las Naciones. Patria, nación y naturaleza en la Monarquía de España*, FCA: Madrid 2004, pp.423–81; for the quotation from Julius II, pp.450–51; see also A. Spagnoletti, 'El concepto de naturaleza, nación y patria en Italia y el reino de Nápoles con respecto a la Monarquía de los Austrias', in ibid., pp.483–503; C.J. Hernando Sánchez, *Castilla y Nápoles en el siglo XVI. El virrey don Pedro de Toledo. Linaje, estado y cultura (1532–1553)*, Junta de Castilla y León: Salamanca 1994, chapter IV; C.J. Hernando Sánchez, *El reino de Nápoles en el Imperio de Carlos V: la consolidación de la conquista*, CECCFC: Madrid 2001; M.A. Visceglia, 'Un groupe social ambigu. Organisation, stratégies et représentations de la noblesse napolitaine, XVIe-XVIIe siècles' in *Annales. Économies, Sociétés, Civilisations*, 48th year, No.4 (1993), pp.819–51, translated by Judith Revel.

31. Tommaso Astarita, *The Continuity of Feudal Power. The Caracciolo di Brienza in Spanish Naples*, CUP: Cambridge 1992, p.235.
32. Aurelio Musi, *Mezzogiorno Spagnolo: la via napoletana allo stato moderno*, Guida: Naples 1991.
33. Sean T. Perrone, *Charles V and the Castilian Assembly of the Clergy. Negotiations for the Ecclesiastical Subsidy*, Brill: Leiden Boston 2008; Aurelio Espinosa, *The Empire of the Cities. Charles V, the Comunero Revolt, and the Transformation of the Spanish System*, Brill Leiden Boston 2008; Ruth MacKay, *The Limits of Royal Authority. Resistance and Obedience in Seventeenth-Century Castile*, CUP: Cambridge, 2007
34. Maria Antonietta Visceglia, *Guerra, diplomacia y etiqueta en la Corte de los Papas (siglos XVI y XVII)*, Ediciones Polifemo: Madrid 2010, p.68.
35. Angelantonio Spagnoletti, *Prìncipi italiani e Spagna nell'età barocca*, ESBM: Milan 1996, pp.129–45.
36. Levin, *Agents of Empire*, p.47.
37. AGS, Est.leg.1026 fol.48 Toledo to King, Naples 10 and 11 July 1537.
38. On Antonello di Sanseverino's intrigues with Charles VIII in 1494, Michael Mallett, 'Personalities and pressures: Italian involvement in the French invasion of 1494', in Abulafia ed., *French Descent*, pp.151–63.
39. Hernando Sánchez, *Castilla y Nápoles en el siglo XVI*, pp.332–33.
40. The reference was to Pietrantonio Sanseverino, fourth prince of Bisignano (1490–1599), AGS, Est.leg.1120 fol.69 de Vega to Charles V, Messina 7 July 1552.
41. AGS, Est.leg.1120 fols.73–74 Résumé of letters of viceroy of Sicily, 3, 4, 6, 7 and 8 of July 1552.
42. Setton, *Papacy*, iv, pp.582–84.
43. 'Henri II returned almost immediately to his obsession with Italy.' Braudel, *Mediterranean*, ii, pp.925–26.
44. Levin, *Agents of Empire*, p.56–57; see also Maria Antonietta Visceglia, 'Factions in the Sacred College in the Sixteenth and Seventeenth Centuries' in Gianvittorio Signorotto and Maria Antonietta Visceglia eds, *Court and Politics in Papal Rome, 1492–1700*, CUP: Cambridge 2002, pp.99–131.
45. Levin, *Agents of Empire*, pp.60–63.
46. Levin, *Agents of Empire*, pp.90–91. The study of diplomacy in Italy has undergone a transformation in recent years, Daniela Frigo, 'Introduction' to Daniela Frigo ed., *Politics and Diplomacy in Early Modern Italy. The Structure of Diplomatic Practice, 1450–1800*, translated by Adrian Belton, CUP: Cambridge 2000; for an excellent case study, see Frigo, '"Small states" and diplomacy: Mantua and Modena', in ibid., pp.147–75.

47. Frigo, '"Small States"', p.174.
48. Frigo, '"Small States"', p.155.
49. See the numerous references to the investiture of Ferrara and other fiefs in E. García Hernán, *La acción diplomática de Francisco de Borja al servicio del Pontificado, 1571–1572*, Generalitat Valenciana: Valencia 2000, pp.335–82, especially 336–37.
50. J. Ignacio Tellechea Idígoras, 'Lo que el Emperador no supo. Proceso de Paulo IV a Carlos V y Felipe II', in Martínez Millan ed., *Carlos V y la quiebra*, iv, pp.181–95.
51. Setton, *Papacy and the Levant*, iv, p.750.
52. M.J. Rodríguez-Salgado, *The Changing Face of Empire. Charles V, Philip II and Habsburg Authority, 1551–1559*, CUP: Cambridge 1988, p.148.
53. On the Pope's ambitions for Siena, Braudel, *Mediterranean*, ii, pp.938–39; Parker, *Grand Strategy*, pp.80–81.
54. Patrick Williams, *Philip II*, Palgrave: Basingstoke and New York 2000, p.28.
55. Visceglia, 'Factions in the Sacred College', p.104.
56. Friedrich Edelmayer, 'Carlos V y Fernando I. La quiebra de la monarquía universal', in Martínez Millan ed., *Carlos V y la quiebra*, i, pp.151–61.
57. F. de Laiglesia, *Estudios históricos (1515–1555)*, 3 volumes, Imprenta Clásica Española: Madrid 1918, i, p.101.
58. '...y si saliesse un Papa atravesado o mal christiano tengo por cierto que yria por tierra lo que queda de la christiandad.' Lucian Serrano, *Correspondencia Diplomática entre España y la Santa Sede durante el pontificado de S. Pio V*, 4 volumes, Instituto Pio IX: Madrid 1914, i, p.54.
59. Serrano, *Correspondencia*, i, pp.88–89.
60. Luciano Serrano, *La Liga de Lepanto entre España, Venecia y la Santa Sede (1570–1572). Ensayo historico a base de documentos diplomaticos*, 2 volumes, Escuela Española de Historia y Arqueología en Roma: Madrid 1918, i, p.190 n.1.
61. He also specified the improvement of the galleys, infantry and fort of Porto Longone, and weapons for 20,000 men, AGS, Est.leg.1102, fol.85 Benavente to Philip III, Naples 26 April 1605; in both Naples and Sicily the fortifications were built with an eye on domestic control, Carlos José Hernando Sánchez, 'El reino de Nápoles. La fortificación de la ciudad y el territorio bajo Carlos V', in Hernando Sánchez ed., *Las fortificaciones de Carlos V*, pp.514–53; Nicola Soldini, 'El Gobernante Ingeniero: Ferrante Gonzaga y las estrategias del dominion en Italia', in ibid., pp.354–87; this may help to explain why the castles in Sicily were often judged to be inadequate for defence against attack from the sea, V. Favarò, *La*

modernizzazione militare nella Sicilia di Filippo II, Quaderni Mediterranea: Palermo 2009, chapter II.

62. Rodriguez Salgado, '¿Carolus Africanus?', pp.495–99.

63. Gülru Necipoğlu, 'Süleyman the Magnificent and the Representation of Power in the Context of Ottoman-Habsburg-Papal Rivalry', in H. İnalcık and C. Kafadar eds, *Süleyman the Second and His Time*, Isis Press: Istanbul 1993, pp.163–91.

64. Idris Bostan, 'The Establishment of the Province of *Cezayir-i Bahr-i Sefid*', in Zachariadou ed., *Kapudan Pasha*, pp.241–51; Miguel Ángel de Bunes Ibarra, *Los Barbarroja. Corsarios del Mediterráneo*, Alderabán: Madrid 2004.

65. On Tunis 1535, see the collection of essays, A.A. Ezquerra and J.I. Ruiz Rodríguez eds, *Túnez, 1535. Halcones y halconeros en la diplomacia de la monarquía española*, CSIC etc.: Spain 2012.

66. Veinstein, 'Les campagnes...', *passim*; M.Á. de Bunes Ibarra, 'Carlos V, Venecia y la Sublime Puerta: la embajada de Diego Hurtado de Mendoza en Venecia', in Martínez Millán ed., *Carlos V y la quiebra*, i, pp.591–617.

67. Hernando Sánchez, *Castilla y Nápoles en el siglo XVI*, pp.353–54.

68. Setton, *Papacy*, iii, p.397 n.10.

69. Fernández Álvarez, *Carlos V*, pp.613–17.

70. Christine Isom-Verhaaren, *Allies with the Infidel. The Ottoman and French Alliance in the Sixteenth Century*, I.B.Tauris: London, New York 2011.

71. Karl Brandi, *The Emperor Charles V: The Growth and Destiny of a Man and of a World Empire*, translated by C.V. Wedgwood, Jonathan Cape: London 1965, pp.512–13, 566, 557–58, 575, 577–80, 58; Hubert Jedin, *A History of the Council of Trent*, 3 volumes, translated by Dom Ernest Graf, Nelson & Sons: London, Edinburgh etc. 1957–61, i, pp.220–409 (especially 224, 227–8), 496–504.

72. Charles V had previously complained to Constantinople that Turgut reis had effectively broken the truce, Mafrici, *Mezzogiorno e pirateria*, p.52.

73. Braudel, *Mediterranean*, ii, pp.908–11, 918–21, 924.

74. Brogini and Ghazali, 'Un enjeu espagnol en Méditerranée...', paragraph 47.

75. AGS, Est.leg.1119 fol.240 'Lo que respondió Juan de Vega al comendador que envio el papa', September 1551.

76. AGS. Est.leg.1119 fol.228 'Copia de carta de...virrey de Sicilia ...a Su Md al último de noviembre de 1551'.

77. Alonso Acero, 'El norte de África', pp.397–98.

78. Braudel, *Mediterranean*, ii, pp.932–33, 940; Setton, *Papacy*, iv, p.833.

79. Josep Juan Vidal, 'La defensa del reino de Mallorca en la época de Carlos V (1535–1558)' in Martínez Millán ed., *Carlos V y la quiebra*, pp.541–89, especially 548.

80. Veinstein, 'Les préparatifs', p.56.

81. AGS Est.leg.1120 fol.160 Prince to Viceroy of Sicily, Zaragoza 6 October 1552; fol.164 to Viceroy of Naples.

82. CODOIN, xxx, pp.266–67.

83. Braudel, *Mediterranean*, ii, pp.944–45, 973–87.

84. Exactly how many ships were lost at Djerba remains a difficult question, with contemporaries alternatively stating that 12, 19 or 28 galleys had been taken, Braudel, *Mediterranean*, ii, p.980; Setton, *Papacy*, iv, p.762.

85. Braudel, *Mediterranean*, ii, pp.990–91; M.J. Rodríguez-Salgado, '"El león animoso entre las balas": los dos cercos de Orán a mediados del siglo XVI', in Bunes Ibarra and Alonso Acero eds, *Orán. Historia de la Corte Chica*, pp.13–54.

86. Braudel, *Mediterranean*, ii, pp.1081–87; Setton, *Papacy*, iv, pp.984–85, 993–94 n.73, 996.

87. García Hernán, *La acción diplomática, passim*; David García Hernán and Enrique García Hernán, *Lepanto: el día después*, Actas editorial: Madrid 1999, pp.70, 79.

88. Anderson, *Naval Wars in the Levant*, pp.56–57.

89. Braudel, *Mediterranean*, ii, p.1139.

90. Braudel, *Mediterranean*, ii, pp.1139–42, 1165–66, 1176–85.

91. Cited by Julio Caro Baroja, *Los moriscos del reino de Granada*, 2nd edition, Ediciones ISTMO: Madrid 1976, p.236; Pierre Chaunu, 'Minorités et conjoncture. L'expulsion des Morisques en 1609', in *Revue Historique*, ccxxv (1961), pp.81–98; R. Benítez Sánchez-Blanco, *Heroicas decisiones. La Monarquía Católica y los moriscos valencianos*, Institució Alfons el Magnànim: Valencia 2002, chapter IV especially pp.374–78, 418–19.

92. Antonio Domínguez Ortiz and Bernard Vincent, *Historia de los moriscos. Vida y tragedia de una minoría*, Alianza: Madrid 1978, p.179; 'la inminencia de la pérdida de la república', M. Lomas Cortés, *El proceso de expulsión de los moriscos de España (1609–1614)*, University of Valencia: Valencia 2011 pp.44–46, 544.

93. Patrick Williams, *The Great Favourite. The Duke of Lerma and the Court and Government of Philip III of Spain, 1598–1621*, MUP: Manchester and New York 2006, p.157.

94. AGS, Est.leg.1435 fol.17 Don Juan Vivas to King, Genoa 29 December 1610.

95. Parker, *Grand Strategy*, pp.5–7, 80, 85–86, 93–95, 98–99, 104–09, 155, 159–60, 162, 179–80, 190, 268, 281, 286, 292; Cabrera de Córdoba, *Felipe II*, i, p.375; see the numerous references in Levin, *Agents of Empire*.

Chapter II

1. On the orders in 1565, Setton, *Papacy*, iv, pp.857, 862, 868–69; for the royal instructions in 1570, which merged into the controversy over Doria's action or inaction, ibid., pp.965–67, 972–73, 977–79, 983; the king forbade Don John from trying to save Tunis in 1574, ibid., p.1095.
2. AGS, Est.leg.1126 fol.156 and 157 King to Viceroy of Sicilia and Grand Master, Toledo 27 January 1561.
3. AGS, Est.leg.1126 fol.164 'Instrucción a Fernando de Silva Marqués de la Favara...primero de abril de 1561'.
4. AGS Est.leg.1126 fol.165 King to Medinaceli, Guisado [?] 1 April 1561; fol.166 to Grand Master.
5. CODOIN, xxix, pp.59–60.
6. CODOIN, xxix, pp.121–85.
7. See his letter of 5 July, CODOIN, xxix, pp.247–55 especially p.250.
8. CODOIN, xxix, pp.310–13.
9. Serrano, *Liga de Lepanto*, i, pp.276–78; Vargas-Hidalgo, *Correspondencia*, pp.806–08 and especially p.806.
10. See Perrone, *Charles V and the Castilian Assembly of the Clergy*; Thompson, *War and Government*, p.16.
11. M.J. Rodríguez-Salgado, *Felipe II, el «Paladín de la Cristiandad» y la paz con el Turco*, Colección Síntesis XI, Universidad de Valladolid, Valladolid 2004; pp.30–35, 66–67, 103–08, 118–19, 174–75.
12. Serrano, *Correspondencia*, ii, pp.294–95, 297.
13. Perrone, *Charles V*, p.224; on the Emperor's claims to be performing the 'service of God', see p.175.
14. Of the 1.1 million *escudos* brought in by the Three Graces in 1574, 800,000 was sent to Flanders, García Hernán, *Armada española*, p.94.
15. Braudel, *Mediterranean*, ii, p.1056 n.172.
16. Serrano, *Correspondencia*, iv, p.441.
17. AGS, Est.leg.1127 fol.173 Medinaceli to King, Messina 29 July 1563; note also concerns about the 'bad intentions' in Italy, Rodríguez-Salgado, '"El león animoso"', p.44.
18. Rodríguez-Salgado, *Paladín de la Cristiandad*, especially pp.116–19, 120, 129, 174–75.

19. For a similar perspective, Thompson, *War and Government*, p.16.

20. Cited by J.R. Hale, 'Sixteenth century explanations of War and Violence', in *Past & Present*, No. 51 (May 1971), p.22; see also Poumarède, *Pour en finir*, chapter IV.

21. García Hernán and García Hernán, *Lepanto*, p.113.

22. For left-field proposals on how to cut costs, Fenicia, *Regno di Napoli*, pp.8–9; cost is a crucial consideration in Miguel Ángel de Bunes Ibarra, 'La defensa de la cristiandad; las armadas en el mediterráneo en la edad moderna', in *Cuadernos de Historia Moderna*, V (2006), pp.77–99.

23. AGS, Est.leg.1428 fol.158 King to Prince Doria, Madrid 29 February 1596.

24. AGS, Est.leg.1127 fol.64 Medinaceli to King, Palermo 19 July 1562.

25. M. Fontenay, 'Les galères de Malte 1530–1798', in *Quand voguaient les galères*, Catalogue of an exhibition held in 1990 at the Musée de la Marine, Paris, Rennes, 1991; Lo Basso, *Uomini da remo*, chapter VI; Brogini, *Malte*, pp.259–62.

26. Given the dimensions of the Ottoman mobilisations, it would have been impractical to use experienced oarsmen, Imber, *Ottoman Empire*, p.305.

27. Michel Fontenay, 'Chiourmes turques au XVIIe siècle', in Rosalba Ragosta ed., *Le genti del mare mediterraneo*, 2 volumes, Lucio Pironti: Naples 1981, ii, pp.877–903, pp.901–02.

28. Lucile and Bartolomé Bennassar, *Les chrétiens d'Allah. Histoire extraordinaire des rénegats XVIe–XVIIe siècles*, Perrin: Paris 1989, pp.318, 321, 358–62.

29. Imber, *Ottoman Empire*, pp.307–08; see also Veinstein, 'Les préparatifs', pp.44–45.

30. Imber, *Ottoman Empire*, pp.221–25, 249–50; Emilie Themopoulou, 'Les Kürekçi de la flotte ottomane au XVIIe siècle', in Zacharoadou ed., *Kapudan Pasha*, pp.165–79, especially 167–71.

31. Robert Bartlett, *The Making of Europe. Conquest, Colonialization and Cultural Change, 950–1350*, Penguin: London 1993, p.190; Susan Rose, 'Islam Versus Christendom: The Naval Dimension, 1000–1600', *The Journal of Military History*, Vol.63, No.3 (July 1999), pp.561–78; Arnold Cassola, *The 1565 Ottoman Malta Campaign Register*, PEG: Malta 1998, p.62.

32. Girón, *Crónica del Emperador Carlos V*, p.118.

33. Isom-Verhaaren, *Allies with the Infidel*, pp.129, 157, 189.

34. Setton, *Papacy*, iv, p.1085.

35. CODOIN, xxix, p.558.

36. Words attributed to Hassan Pasha, Anonymous, *La batalla naval del señor Don Juan de Austria según un manuscrito anomino contemporáneo'*, with a prologue by Admiral Julio Guillen Tato, Homenaje del Instituto Histórico de Marina IV Centenario de Lepanto: Madrid 1971, pp.155–56.

37. CODOIN, iii, p.8.

38. Halil İnalcık, *The Ottoman Empire. The Classical Age 1300–1600*, London 1973, p.41.

39. W. Montgomery Watt, 'Islamic Conceptions of Holy War', in T.P. Murphy ed., *The Holy War*, Ohio State University Press: Columbus 1974, pp.141–56; Lewis, *Istanbul and the Civilization of the Ottoman Empire*, pp.36–64; Imber, *Ottoman Empire*, pp.115–27; Colin Imber, 'The Ottoman Dynastic Myth', *Turcica* 19 (1987), pp.7–27; Suraiya Faroqhi, *The Ottoman Empire and the World Around It*, I.B.Tauris: London and New York 2004, pp.114–18; see also the essays by Daniel Goffman, Gábor Ágoston, Douglas A. Howard and Baki Tezcan in Virginia H. Aksan and Daniel Goffman eds, *The Early Modern Ottomans. Remapping the Empire*, CUP: Cambridge 2007.

40. Faroqhi, *Ottoman Empire and the World Around It*, p.80.

41. Suraiya Faroqhi, *Pilgrims and Sultans*, I.B.Tauris: London 1994, p.184.

42. Isom-Verhaaren, *Allies with the Infidel*, p.189.

43. Lewis, *Istanbul and the Civilization of the Ottoman Empire*, pp.45–46.

44. Giancarlo Casale, *The Ottoman Age of Exploration*, OUP: Oxford etc. 2010, pp 44, 82–83, 147–51.

45. AGS, Est.leg.1121 fol.234 de Vega to Emperor, Messina 4 October 1553.

46. Fenicia, *Regno di Napoli*, p.9.

47. AGS Est.leg.1394 f.388 Reports from Constantinople, 8 to 12 of March 1565.

48. CODOIN, iii, pp.270–72; views of the Ottoman Empire are explored in M. Rivero Rodríguez, *La batalla de Lepanto. Cruzada, guerra santa e identidad confesional*, Sílex: Madrid 2008, pp.39–60 and Alain Servantie ed., *L'Empire ottoman dans l'Europe de la Renaissance*, LUP: Leuven 2005; Nancy Bisaha, *Creating East and West: Renaissance Humanists and the Ottoman Turks*, UPP: Philadelphia 2006; and M. Meserve, *Empires of Islam in Renaissance Historical Thought*, HUP: Cambridge Massachusetts 2008; Christian writers were aware of both the universalist pretensions ('King of Kings') and that at times the Moors rejected Ottoman claims to leadership, M.A. de Bunes Ibarra, *La imagen de los musulmanes y del norte de África en la España de los siglos XVI y XVII: Los caracteres de una hostilidad*, CSIC: Madrid 1989, chapter V.

49. Fodor, 'Ottoman Policy Towards Hungary', pp.113–18.

50. Brummett, *Ottoman Seapower, passim*; Faroqhi, *Ottoman Empire and the World Around It*, pp.100–01, 137–60.

51. Most recently by Rhoads Murphey, *Ottoman Warfare, 1500–1700*, UCL: London 1999, *passim*.

52. Setton, *Papacy*, iv, p.855.

53. Imber, *Ottoman Empire*, p.126; for the rhetoric of later wars, see Svat Soucek's paper in Zachariadou ed., *Kapudan Pasha*.

54. Lewis, *Istanbul and the Civilization of the Ottoman Empire*, p.59; on the corsairs Bennassar and Bennassar, *Les chrétiens d'Allah*, *passim*.

55. Faroqhi, *The Ottoman Empire and the World Around It*, pp.98–100, 114, 117.

56. Setton, *Papacy*, iii, pp.364–65, 382.

57. Setton, *Papacy*, iii, pp.370–73.

58. James Gairdner ed., *Letters and Papers, Foreign and Domestic. Henry VIII*, vol.8 (January to July 1535), London 1885, No.826.

59. García Hernán and García Hernán, *Lepanto*, pp.75–76.

60. For this and similar statements, Setton, *Papacy*, iii, pp.364–65, 376, 378, 382.

61. AGS, Est.leg.1547 fol.201 'Lo que dijo el hebreo que vino por el Turco a Venecia', no date (1540?)

62. De Laiglesia, *Estudios históricos*, i, p.98.

63. Braudel, *Mediterranean*, ii, p.1047.

64. Stéphane Yérasimos, 'Les relations franco-ottomanes et la prise de Tripoli en 1551' in Gilles Veinstein ed., *Soliman le magnifique et son temps. Actes du colloque de Paris, Galeries Nationales du Gran Palais, 7–10 mars 1990*, Louvre: Paris 1992, pp.529–47.

65. Victor Mallia-Milanes, *Venice and Hospitaller Malta 1530–1798. Aspects of a Relationship*, PEG: Malta 1992, p.72.

66. The season was well advanced, AGS, Est.leg.1121 fols.249–50 Prince Philip to de Vega, 6 August 1553.

67. AGS, Est.leg.1498 fols.44–46 King to Francisco de Vargas, London(?) 6 de January 1555.

68. Diarmaid MacCulloch, *Reformation. Europe's House Divided, 1490–1700*, Penguin: London 2003, pp.331–32.

69. Francis Bacon, *The Essays*, Macmillan: London and New York 1900, p.78.

70. Serrano, *Correspondencia*, iv, pp.534–35.

71. Parker, *Grand Strategy*, pp.157–60, 162.

72. Parker, *Grand Strategy*, pp.100–01.

73. See his letter to Zúñiga of 14 February 1571, Serrano, *Correspondencia*, iv, pp.185–87. It proved very difficult to convince the Venetians to undertake a localised campaign with realistic goals, *'una empresa particular'*; their intention was, reportedly, to inspire a rebellion among the Ottoman subjects, ibid., pp.211–12.

74. See his letter of 12 April 1571, Serrano, *Correspondencia*, iv, p.247.

75. Serrano, *Correspondencia*, iii, p.427.

76. See the letter of the negotiators to the king, Rome 9 June 1570, Serrano, *Correspondencia*, iii, p.391.

77. For a scathing assessment of the Venetian forces at Souda in Crete, Cabrera de Córdoba, *Felipe II*, ii, pp.564–65.

78. For Venetian sources and testimony that confirm the bleak picture of their fleet, Setton, *Papacy*, iv, pp.967, 974–76, 980, 982–83, 986, 990, 1001, 1002, 1010–11, 1026, 1072.

79. AGS, Est.leg.1134 fol.61 Don Juan to King, Messina 29 August 1571; Est. leg.1501 fol.2, 30 August 1571; almost identical letters addressed to Don García de Toledo are reprinted in CODOIN, iii, pp.17–18; the 60 Venetian galleys that came from 'Cyprus' (surely 'Crete') were also found to be *'muy mal en orden'*, ibid., p.260.

80. On 28 September Philip II expressed the same concerns, Serrano, *Correspondencia*, iv, p.444.

81. Serrano, *Liga Lepanto*, i, p.159; CODOIN, iii, pp.20–21; Cabrera de Córdoba, *Felipe II*, ii, p.588.

82. Anonymous, *La batalla naval del Señor Don Juan de Austria*, p.121; the governor of Otranto blamed this misfortune on their being in poor order for *chusma* and lacking in expertise among their captains, AGS, Est.leg.1134 fol.38 'Por carta de Bautista de Frías ...' Otranto 30 July 1571.

83. See his letter of 28 September, Serrano, *Correspondencia*, iv, p.444.

84. AGS, Est.leg.1401, fol.242 Reports from Constantinople 19 March 1571; for very similar reports Vargas-Hidalgo, *Correspondencia*, pp.721–22.

85. Intelligence from Dimitri Risicari, *'hombre muy esperto'*, AGS, Est.leg.1401 fol.141 Reports from Corfu, 30 May 1571; Vargas-Hidalgo, *Correspondencia*, pp.733–34.

86. AGS, Est.leg.1401 fol.149 Reports from Otranto, 13 June 1571; fol.159 Reports from Corfu,24 June 1571.

87. AGS, Est.leg.1134 fol.8 Reports from Zante 5 July.

88. AGS, Est.leg.1134 fol.21 'Avvisi di 21 di luglio 1571 venuti da Corfù.' For similar reports from the Venetian archives, Setton, *Papacy*, iv, p.1022.

89. AGS, Est.leg.1134, fol.62 'En Messina a 31 de Agosto 1571'. For additional reports from Est.leg.1060 on the shortages and deficiencies of the Ottoman fleet, Braudel, *Mediterranean*, ii, p.1099.

90. Serrano, *Correspondencia*, iii, p.447, iv, pp.405–06, 414–15; for papal efforts to speed up Don John, Vargas-Hidalgo, *Correspondencia*, p.747.

91. Onur Yildirim, 'The Battle of Lepanto and its impact on Ottoman History and Historiography', in Cancila ed., *Mediterraneo in armi*, ii, pp.533–66, especially 541–42, 547–52.

92. AGS, Est.leg.1401 fol.95 'Relatione de N[ove] arrivato a Lecce alli xii di luglio 1571'.

93. Yildirim, 'Battle of Lepanto', p.541.

94. CODOIN, iii, pp.250, 259–60.

95. His assessment of the intentions of the Pope and of Venice was restated, Serrano, *Correspondencia*, iv, pp.483–84; see also García Hernán and García Hernán, *Lepanto*, p.67.

96. See his letter of 1 August 1571, CODOIN, iii, pp.8–10.

97. CODOIN, iii, p.220.

98. 'Y después hicimos embestir en tierra tantas que es vergüenza decirlo…' CODOIN, iii, p.225. The 'great ease and speed' with which Ottoman ships were overcome was mentioned by Fray Juan de San Gerónimo, ibid., p.245.

99. D. Panzac, *La marine ottomane. De l'apogée à la chute de l'Empire (1572–1923)*, CNRS: Paris 2009, p.32.

100. CODOIN, iii, pp.216–17.

101. Yildirim, 'Battle of Lepanto', p.549.

102. Rivero Rodríguez, *Lepanto*, chapter VI.

103. Braudel, *Mediterranean*, ii, pp.843, 1100–06; Rafael Vargas-Hidalgo, *La Batalla de Lepanto*, ChileAmérica: Santiago 1998; Roger Crowley, *Empires of the Sea. The Final Battle for the Mediterranean 1521–1580*, Faber and Faber: London 2008; Hugh Bicheno, *Crescent and Cross. The Battle of Lepanto 1571*, Phoenix: London, 2003; Andrew Wheatcroft, *Infidels. A History of the Conflict between Christendom and Islam*, 2nd edition, Penguin: London 2004, pp.3–38; Ricardo Cerezo Martínez, *Años cruciales en la historia del Mediterráneo (1570–1574)*, Junta Ejecutiva del IV Centenario de la Batalla de Lepanto: Madrid 1971; Andrew C. Hess, 'The Battle of Lepanto and Its Place in Mediterranean History', *Past & Present*, No. 57 (Nov.1972), pp.53–73; Serrano, *Liga de Lepanto*, passim; Alberto Guglielmotti, *Marcantonio Colonna alla Battaglia di Lepanto*, Felice le Monnier: Florence 1862, passim; Setton, *Papacy*, iv, pp.1045–1100; A. Dragonetti de Torres, *La Lega di Lepanto nel carteggio diplomatico inedito di*

don Luys de Torres nunzio straordinario di S. Pio V a Filippo II, Fratelli Bocca Editori: Turin 1931, *passim*; Williams, 'Mediterranean conflict', *passim*; Manuel Rivero Rodríguez, '¿Monarquía Católica o Hispánica? África o Levante: la encrucijada de la política mediterránea entre Lepanto (1571) y el proyecto de la jornada real de Argel (1618)', in Porfirio Sanz Camañes ed., *La Monarquía Hispánica en tiempos del Quijote*, UCLM Sílez: Madrid 2005, pp.593–613; Poumarède, *Pour en finir*, pp.233–45; N. Housley, *The Later Crusades, 1274–1580: From Lyon to Alcazar*, OUP: Oxford 1992; Niccolò Capponi, *Victory of the West. The Story of the Battle of Lepanto*, Pan Books: London, Basingstoke and Oxford 2006; Alessandro Barbero, *Lepanto. La batalla de los tres imperios*, Pasado & Presente: Barcelona 2011

104. See his letter to Zúñiga of 14 February 1571 cited above; see also his reaction to the peace accord made between the Most Serene Republic and Selim II in April 1573, Serrano, *Liga de Lepanto*, ii, p.301.

105. García Hernán and García Hernán, *Lepanto*, *passim*.

Chapter III

1. For quotations in this paragraph, National Maritime Museum, *The Maritime Siege of Malta 1565*, London, no date, p.7.

2. Ernle Bradford, *Shield and Sword. The Knights of Malta*, Hodder and Stoughton, London and Glasgow 1972, p.80. See also Jean Claude Hocquet, 'Gens de mer à Venise', in Ragosta ed., *Le genti del mare Mediterraneo*, i, pp.103–68, pp.166–67.

3. J.S. Morrison and J.F. Coates, *The Athenian Trireme. The History and Reconstruction of an Ancient Greek Warship*, CUP: Cambridge 1986, pp.115–16.

4. Morrison and Coates, *Athenian Trireme*, pp.61, 120.

5. Morrison and Coates, *Athenian Trireme*, pp.115–16, 117–18; Polybius, *The Rise of the Roman Empire*, translated by Ian Scott-Kilvert, edited by F.W. Walbank, Penguin: London 1979, pp.345–46; see Jane Gardner's edition of Caesar, *The Civil War*, Penguin: London, New York etc. 1967, pp.172–73.

6. Frederic C. Lane, 'Merchant Galleys, 1300–34: Private and Communal Operation', reprinted in *Venice and History. The Collected Papers of Frederic C. Lane*, John Hopkins Press: Baltimore 1966, pp.193–226, 219–20; Antony Luttrell, 'Late-Medieval Galley Oarsmen' in Ragosta ed., *Le genti...*, i, pp.87–101; Hocquet, 'Gens de mer à Venise', pp.144–50.

7. AGS, Est.leg.1026 fol.63 'Por letras de Príncipe Andrea Doria de 22 de julio 4 milas de Corfu se entiende lo siguiente'.

8. Braudel, *Mediterranean*, i, p.457.

9. CODOIN, iii, pp.313–15.

10. Lo Basso, *Uomini da remo*, p.66.

11. AGS, Est.leg.1423 fol.76 Doria to Philip II, Loano 1 March 1591.

12. CODOIN, xxix, pp.149, 207, 249–51; Braudel, *Mediterranean*, ii, pp.1018–19.

13. AGS, Est.leg.1422 fol.110 Doria to Philip II, Genoa 25 June 1590; Est. leg.1092 fol.34 Miranda to Philip II, Naples 19 June 1590.

14. On health – or the lack of it – aboard Elizabethan ships, Cheryl A. Fury, *Tides in the Affairs of Men. The Social History of Elizabethan Seamen, 1580–1603*, Greenwood Press: Westport, Connecticut and London 2002, pp.137–95.

15. CODOIN, xxix, p.14.

16. I.A.A. Thompson, 'A Map of Crime in Sixteenth-Century Spain', in *War and Society in Habsburg Spain*, Variorum: Aldershot 1992, p.261; Tenenti, *Piracy and the Decline of Venice*, pp.113, 116.

17. Zysberg, *Les galériens*, pp.381, 383.

18. AGS, Est.leg.1098 fol.46 'Relación de los forzados que han venido de las carceles de Viqueria y de otras partes desde los diez de octubre 1601 hasta marzo siguiente 1602'.

19. AGS, GA leg.680 sf 'Relación de los esclavos ....último de diciembre 1607'.

20. CODOIN, xxviii, p.400.

21. Richard Overy, *The Dictators. Hitler's Germany, Stalin's Russia*, Penguin edition: London, New York, etc. 2005, pp.613–15.

22. On health and medical provision on the galleys, Manuel Gracia Rivas, *La sanidad en la jornada de Inglaterra (1587–1588)*, Editorial Naval: Madrid 1988, pp.36–41

23. AGS, Est.leg.1134 fol.43 'Lo que le señor Marqués de Sancta Cruz ha de hacer por servicio del Rey mi señor es lo siguiente'.

24. Zysberg, *Les galériens*, pp.248–49

25. Those oarsmen who were unable to serve should be placed aboard a galley 'that serves as a hospital'. AGS, Est.leg.1156 fol.57 Doria to King, Messina 16 July 1588.

26. Zysberg, *Les galériens*, p.220.

27. Cited by Enrique García Hernán, *La Armada española en la monarquía de Felipe II y la defensa del Mediterráneo*, Tempo: Madrid 1995, p.158.

28. He was fitting out four galleys for the Papacy in Venice. Serrano, *Correspondencia*, iii, pp.446–47.

29. He suggested that the convalescents be left in Genoa to recuperate, even though they had been paid for the full summer, Vargas-Hidalgo, *Correspondencia*, p.910.

30. AGS, Est.leg.1128 fol.149 King to Toledo, Madrid 2 September 1564.

31. AGS, Est.leg.1100 fol.57 Benavente to Philip II, Naples 31 May 1604.

32. AGS, Est.leg.1424 fol.167 Don Juan Portocarrero to Philip II, Barcelona 4 June 1592.

33. For technical detail on how to mix new and experienced oarsmen on one bank so that the oar stroke remained steady, Zysberg, *Les galériens*, pp.246–48.

34. AGS, Est.leg.1058 fol.51 Santa Cruz to King, Corfu 13 October 1570.

35. Setton, *Papacy*, iv, pp.997–98.

36. Vargas-Hidalgo, *Correspondencia*, p.856.

37. '... *que bastaría que fuesen armadas de tres en tres pues las del enemigo no deben de armar à mas, y algunas no à tanto, como se entiende por avisos*', AGS, Est.leg.1136 fol.166 King to Don John of Austria, Madrid 28 September 1571.

38. AGS, Est.leg.1433 fol.160, Vives to King, Genoa 7 March 1606.

39. CODOIN, xxviii, p.399; CODOIN, iii, p.316.

40. AGS, Est.leg.1428 fol.160 King to Doria, Madrid 20 April 1598.

41. AGS, Est.leg.1420 fol.161 Doria to King, Genoa 27 April 1588.

42. Vargas-Hidalgo, *Correspondencia*, p.1222.

43. See his letter of 20 August 1566, CODOIN, xxx, pp.384–85.

44. AGS, Est.leg.1130 fol.22 'Copia de carta que don Garcia de Toledo escribió al duque de Alcalá a los 13 de febrero de 1566'; fol.24 Toledo to King, Catania 16 February 1566; CODOIN, xxx, p.140.

45. AGS, Est.leg.1431 fol.70 Doria to Philip III, Loano 13 January 1601. Doria was able to compel the contractors to run galleys in the order stipulated in the contracts, but not to replace experienced oarsmen with similarly skilled and strong rowers. Again, this point underlined the damage done by winter navigation.

46. García Hernán, *Armada española*, pp.158–59.

47. CODOIN, xxx, p.236.

48. AGS 1130, fol.142 Juan de Villaroel to King, Messina 7 December 1566.

49. Lo Basso, *Uomini da remo*, p.289.

50. AGS, Est.leg.1422 fol.138 Doria to Philip II, Genoa 26 September 1590.

51. AGS, GA leg.430 fol.103 Doria to King, Pegli 12 August 1595; CODOIN, xxviii, pp.398–99; Francesco Caracciolo, *Uffici, difesa e corpi rappresentativi*

nel Mezzogiorno in età spagnola, Editori meridionali riuniti: Reggio Calabria 1974, pp.149–51.

52. CODOIN, xxviii, p.193.

53. Those whose crimes had been atrocious were to be excluded from the scheme, CODOIN, xxviii, pp.264–65.

54. '*Pues por mozo y gallardos que sean el primer año son inútiles y el segundo empiezan a ser de algún servicio y así importaría mucho ordenar no se condenasen por menos de tres y que sean hábiles al remo*', AGS, Est.leg.1422 fol.175 Recommendations made by Doria for the improvement of the galley squadrons, 1590.

55. Note that the context of this letter was the complaint of a contractor that he had not been allocated the *forzados* stipulated in his contract. AGS, Est. leg.1058 fol.54 Santa Cruz to King, Naples 2 June 1570.

56. AGS, GA leg.422 fol.196 CCG 20 June 1594.

57. The Council of War reminded all concerned that the exchange of slaves in this manner was forbidden AGS, GA leg.741 sf Don Luis Bravo de Acuña to 'A J C', Lisbon 9 November 1610; sf King to Villafranca, no date (July?) 1610.

58. Anita Gonzalez-Raymond, *La croix et le croissant. Les inquisiteurs des îles face à l'Islam 1550–1700*, Edition du Centre Nationale de la Recherche Scientifique: Paris 1992, pp.223–24.

59. Bennassar and Bennassar, *Les chrétiens d'Allah*, p.49.

60. Miguel de Cervantes Saavedra, *The Ingenious Hidalgo Don Quixote de la Mancha*, translated with an Introduction and Notes by John Rutherford, Penguin: London 2000, p.181.

61. This document also refers to the high mortality rate among an unspecified number of English captive oarsmen, of whom only 55 were now alive, AGS, GA leg.489 fol.86 Doria to King, Cadiz 7 September 1597.

62. CODOIN, xxix, p.122.

63. Note also the problem of slaves bought in Sardinia, CODOIN, xxx, pp.362, 382.

64. AGS, Est.leg.1058 fol.51 Santa Cruz to King, Naples 14 May 1570.

65. AGS, GA leg.741 sf Elda to A J C, Gibraltar 9 October 1610. He hoped that half of the new galley convicts would be sent to his squadron.

66. AGS, Est.leg.3479 fol.3 CCE 22 January 1632.

67. '*Qu'ils rament ou pas, d'une période à l'autre, leur chance de survie reste la même.*' Zysberg, *Les galériens*, p.381. In 1572 Toledo advised Don John that to station the fleet in Corfu for any length of time while waiting for Colonna

to arrive would be to run a serious risk, *'la gente podría enfermar padesciendo incomodidades en la mar y venir á se deshacer'*, CODOIN, iii, p.86.

68. Cabrera de Córdoba, *Felipe II*, i, p.151.

69. Lo Basso, *Uomini da remo*, pp.281–82.

70. AGS, Est.leg.1432 fol.188 Doria to Philip III, Pegli 4 August 1604 '... *y así como el hacerlas navegar de invierno las destruye, así no las hace ningún provecho el estar de verano en los puertos* ...'; Est.leg.1433 fol.59 Doria to Philip III, Loano 11 February 1605.

71. AGS, Est.leg.1428, fol.101 Doria to King, Messina 21 September 1596.

72. AGS, Est.leg.1105 fol.100 Santa Cruz to Philip III, Naples 10 December 1608.

73. AGS, GA leg.492 fol.67 Duke of Feria to King, Barcelona 18 December 1597.

74. AGS, Est.lib.'K'1678 fol.4 Avisos 21 November 1607.

75. They were also, of course, *'muy bien armadas de chusma'*, AGS, Est.leg.1428 fol.107 Doria to Philip II, 'Golfo de la Espezia' 11 October 1596.

76. Braudel, *Mediterranean*, ii, p.977; Setton, *Papacy*, iv, pp.758, 761.

77. AGS, Est.leg.1127 fol.26 Medinaceli to King, Palermo 4 April 1562.

78. Jurien de la Gravière, *Les Chevaliers de Malta et la marine de Philipppe II*, 2 volumes, Librairie Plon: Paris 1887, i, pp.69–71.

79. AGS, Est.leg.1435 fol.108 Tursi to Philip III, Genoa 14 February 1611.

80. CODOIN, xxx, pp.315–16, 335–36.

81. AGS, Est.leg.1105 fol.90 Benavente to Philip III, Naples 7 November 1608.

82. AGS, Est.leg.1105 fol.97 Benavente to Philip III, Naples 5 December 1608.

Chapter IV

1. R.B. Wernham, *The Return of the Armadas. The Last Years of the Elizabethan War against Spain 1595–1603*, Clarendon: Oxford 1994, p.100.

2. Thompson, *War and Government*, p.30; N.A.M. Rodger, *The Safeguard of the Sea. A Naval History of Great Britain. Volume 1 660–1649*, Harper Collins: London 1997, p.246.

3. Cabrera de Córdoba, *Felipe II*, iii, p.1137.

4. AGS, GA leg.567, sf *Adelantado Mayor de Castilla'* to Philip III, Puerto de Santa María 25 April 1600

5. '... *no está armada una galera con el buque y con la jarcia ni con otros aparejos muertos, que después la falta de gente de cabo y remo que es tan difícil*

de haber de cualquiera cualidad que sea cuanto más ejercitada y hábil para el servicio', AGS, Est.leg.1094 fol.15 Count of Miranda to Philip II, Naples 13 February 1594.

6. In 1564 Don García de Toledo envisaged using 184 oarsmen aboard each vessel, Guilmartin, *Gunpowder and Galleys*, p.212. Yet in the following year he demobilised one of every three galleys – using 60 of the 90 or so available to him, Braudel, *Mediterranean*, ii, p.1018. For detailed technical discussions by Toledo and his colleagues on these matters (whether to sail with '*cincuenta galeras ... muy reforzadas y muy buenas*'), see CODOIN, xxix, pp.250–51, 492. In 1571 the 10 galleys of Sicily were armed with between 190 and 225 oarsmen; the *capitana* required 314 rowers, Maurice Aymard, 'Chiourmes et galères dans la seconde moitié du XVIe siècle', in G. Benzoni ed., *Il Mediterraneo nella seconda metà del Cinquecento alla luce di Lepanto*, Olschki: Florence 1974, p.75.

7. On the growth of the size of the galley see Anderson's tables, *Oared Fighting Ships*, p.68. Philip III's royal flagship, the *Real*, required 388 oarsmen in 1602; at this time the *capitana* of Sicily was equipped with 300, although the *Adelantado Mayor de Castilla'* wanted to recruit another 80 rowers, AGS, Est.leg.1431 fol.257 '*Relación de la chusma que hay en la galera real.*' December 1602

8. '*pues para pelear poco importa tengan ruines pies, consistiendo el negocio en tener buenas manos ...*', AGS, Est.leg.457 sf, 'Discurso de lo que se podría hacer para ofender a la armada enemiga'.

9. Vargas-Hidalgo, *Correspondencia*, p.17, 1063, 1090–91, 1188–89.

10. AGS, Est.leg.1126 fol.127 Medinaceli to King, Palermo 21 November 1561.

11. AGS, Est.leg.1432 fol.68, Doria to Philip III, Loano 20 January 1603.

12. AGS, Est.leg.1095 fol.243, Olivares to Maqueda, Naples 13 August 1598; Est. leg.1164 fol.83 Cardinal Doria to Philip III, Palermo 13 November 1610.

13. Tenenti, *Piracy and the Decline of Venice*, pp.27, 34; Setton, *Papacy*, iv, p.861; for a valuable comparative study, Candiani, 'Galee forzate o di libertà'.

14. F.F. Olesa Muñido, *La Galera en la navegación y combate*, 2 volumes, Museo Naval: Madrid 1971, i, pp.35–51.

15. The current generation of galleys was also reckoned to carry more provisions in proportion to the number of men serving aboard it, AGS, GA leg.662 sf Ramon Doms to Philip III, Barcelona 9 August 1606.

16. Guilmartin, *Gunpowder and Galleys*, pp.209–20; John H. Pryor, *Geography, Technology and War. Studies in the Maritime History of the Mediterranean, 649–1571*, CUP: Cambridge 1988, *passim* and especially pp.35–36.

17. Guilmartin, *Gunpowder and Galleys*, p.211; thus on leaving port in calm conditions the French fleet might row for 2 hours, Zysberg, *Les galériens*, pp.267–68.

18. AGS, Est.leg.1026 fol.27 'Lo que se entiende de Levante por diversas vias.' May–June 1537.

19. '*Que las mas de las galeras van muy mal al remo y de manera que no pueden hacer fuerza ninguna*', AGS, Est.leg.1119 fol.247 'Relación de Juan Biscaíno español renegado'.

20. CODOIN, xxix, p.364.

21. AGS, Est.leg.1057 fol.17 Reports from Constantinople, 8 January 1569.

22. Serrano, *Liga de Lepanto*, i, p.78 ; Setton, *Papacy*, iv, p.974.

23. Vargas-Hidalgo, *Correspondencia*, p.694.

24. AGS, Est.leg.1545 fol.93 Reports from Constantinople, 10 and 11 July 1595.

25. Girón, *Crónica del Emperador Carlos V*, p.265.

26. See Álvaro de Bazán's letter to García de Toledo, CODOIN, xxx, p.269.

27. He found Cadiz and Malaga very difficult, even in early July, Vargas-Hidalgo, *Correspondencia*, pp.509–10, 513–15.

28. See Toledo's letter of 25 May, CODOIN, xxix, pp.372–73.

29. Zysberg, *Les galériens*, p.269; Olesa Muñido, *La Galera*, i, pp.193–99.

30. CODOIN, xxx, p.308.

31. CODOIN, xxix, pp.21–22.

32. AGS, Est.leg.1136 fol.148 King to Don Juan, no place or date 1571.

33. Steve Redgrave, *Steve Redgrave's Complete Book of Rowing*, Partridge Press: London, New York, Toronto, Sydney and Auckland 1992, p.100.

34. Christopher Chant, *Rowing for Everyone*, David & Charles: London and Vancouver 1977, p.8.

35. Zysberg, *Les galériens*, pp.247–48; also Lo Basso, *Uomini da remo*, pp.352–53.

36. Lionel Casson, *Ships and Seamanship in the Ancient World*, John Hopkins: Baltimore and London 1995, p.104 n.34.

37. D. Panzac, 'Affrontement maritime et mutations technologiques en mer Egee: l'Empire ottoman et la République de Venise (1645–1740)', in Zachariadou ed., *Kapudan Pasha*, pp.119–39, especially 127–28.

38. Redgrave, *Book of Rowing*, p.101; Chant, *Rowing for Everyone*, pp.18–20.

39. 'And once things start to improve it is like a vicious circle in reverse: the eradication of one fault will soon make you able to get rid of another two and so on.' Chant, *Rowing for Everyone*, pp.16, 41, 57.

40. Chant, *Rowing for Everyone*, pp.60–64.

41. Turgut noticed that the stroke of the majority of the Sicilian galleys in 1561 was '*mal ordonnée et confuse*' on account of their being '*galères nouvellement armées*'. Jurien de la Gravière, *Les Chevaliers de Malta et la marine de Philipppe II*, i, pp.60–62.

42. Setton, *Papacy*, iv, pp.993–94 n.73, 996.

43. For other examples of chases, AGS, Est.leg.1429 fol.33, Binasco to Philip II, Genoa 16 August 1597; Est.leg.1096 fol.87, no title – account of a pursuit, Messina 22 July 1599; Est.leg.1433 fol.27, Don Diego Ferrer to Philip III, Genoa 29 June 1605.

44. Girón, *Crónica del Emperador Carlos V*, p.265.

45. López de Gómara, *Guerras de mar*, p.206.

46. For a chase from the Gulf of Cagliari to just off the coast of North Africa, Jurien de la Gravière, *Chevaliers de Malte et la Marine de Philippe II*, pp.100–01.

47. For efforts to find artillery and 'wheels and carriages' for the majority of galleys, Vargas-Hidalgo, *La Batalla de Lepanto*, p.120.

48. AGS, Est.leg.1103 fol.109 Santa Cruz to Philip II, Crotone 9 June 1606.

49. For a very similar chase, AGS, Est.leg.1433 fol.216, Carlo Doria to Philip II, Genoa 23 November 1606.

50. On sailing techniques and their impact on the hull, its buoyancy and structural integrity, Olesa Muñido, *La Galera*, i, pp.188–207.

51. The appointment of Prince Emanuele Filiberto led to an investigation into the prizes awarded to previous high admirals, AGS, Est.leg.1945 sf 'Papeles sobre las decimas de las presas que se han hecho en Italia que dicen toca al Sr Príncipe Filiberto por razón de su cargo, mayo 1614'.

52. AGS, Est.leg.1161 fol.46 Santa Gadea to King, Messina 4 August 1604.

53. AGS, Est.leg.1394 fol.206 Doria to King, Genoa 8 December 1565. For similar incidents, Est. leg.1426 fol.12 Don Pedro de Mendoza to King, Genoa 4 February 1594; Est.leg.1945 sf CCE on three letters from Don Juan de Cardona to King, 17 January 1603.

54. AGS, GA leg.588 sf Feria to King, Barcelona 5 December 1601.

55. AGS, Est.leg.1161 fol.39 Feria to King, Palermo 9 June 1604.

56. See the 'Relación verdadera …' 15 November 1612, reproduced in Henry Ettinghausen, *Notícies del segle XVII. La Premsa a Barcelona entre 1612 i 1628*, Ajuntament de Barcelona: Barcelona 2000 number 4.

57. AGS, Est.leg.1162 fol.209 Escalona to King, Palermo 20 August 1607.

58. AGS, Est.leg.8796 fol.28 Marquis of Aytona to Duke of Escalona, Rome 12 July 1607.

59. CODOIN, iii, p.120; CODOIN, xxix, pp.458–59, 469; (Doria's advice in 1572),Vargas-Hidalgo, *Correspondencia*, p.826.

60. Note the many difficulties experienced by Juan Zanoguera in his reconnaissance of 1566, Setton, *Papacy*, iv, p.902.

61. López de Gómara, *Guerras de mar*, p.159.

62. CODOIN, iii, p.88.

63. Orhan Koloğlu, 'Renegades and the case of Uluç / kiliç Ali', in Cancila ed., *Mediterraneo in armi*, ii, pp. 528–29, 531.

64. The two galleys commanded by Andrea Doria belonged to his father, Gian Andrea, AGS, GA leg.289 fol.232 Andrea Doria to Philip II, Palamós 28 October 1590.

65. AGS, Est.leg.1104 fol.80 Benavente to Philip III, Naples 20 July 1607.

66. Setton, *Papacy*, iii, pp.534–35.

67. AGS, Est.leg.1090 fol.80 Oratio Lercaro to Antonio de Barrientos, 'en galera' 4 July 1589.

68. AGS, GA leg.288 fols.223–24, Don Pedro de Acuña to Philip II, Los Alfaques 19 and 26 September 1590.

69. For Doria's luckless patrol in 1569 (the enemy corsairs were active on the coast of Sicily), Vargas-Hidalgo, *Correspondencia*, p.578.

70. For a good example, Cabrera de Córdoba, *Felipe II*, ii, p.783.

71. Pardo Molero, *La defensa del imperio*, p.161.

72. Lorenzo Capelloni, *Vita del principe Andrea Doria...*, Gabriel Giolito: Ferrara 1569, pp.157–58; for additional details Anderson, *Naval Wars in the Levant*, pp.27–28; Braudel, *Mediterranean*, ii, p.924; López de Gómara, *Guerras de mar del emperador Carlos V*, pp.254–55.

Chapter V

1. Braudel, *Mediterranean*, i, p.16.

2. In November 1572, Vargas-Hidalgo, *Correspondencia*, pp.844–45.

3. AGS, Est.leg.1093 fol.96 Miranda to Philip II, Naples 3 December 1596.

4. Fernández Álvarez, *Carlos V*, p.495.

5. Braudel, *Mediterranean*, ii, p.1008.

6. Vargas-Hidalgo, *Correspondencia*, pp.371–72.

7. AGS, Est.leg.1127 fol.70 Medinaceli to King, Monreale 18 August 1562.

8. AGS, Est.leg.1127 fol.99 Medinaceli to King, Palermo 31 December 1562.

9. CODOIN, xxix, pp.63–64, 111, 336. Of course, the question of cost was also important, in that the arming of new ships was financially demanding, ibid., pp.150–01.

10. CODOIN, xxix, pp.144–5, 251.

11. CODOIN, xxx, pp.64, 70–71.

12. CODOIN, xxx, p.175.

13. Thompson, *War and Government in Habsburg Spain*, pp.167–68, 170–71; Caracciolo, *Uffici, difesa e corpi rappresentativi*, pp.146–48.

14. AGS, Est.leg.1058 fol.58 Santa Cruz to King, Naples 8 June 1570.

15. The Republic was selling pardons to exiles if they would serve in Candia or pay for the recruitment of oarsmen, Setton, *Papacy*, iv, p.1002.

16. AGS, Est.leg.1136 fol.142 don Juan de Cardona to King, Palermo 14 December 1571.

17. Caracciolo, *Uffici, difesa e corpi rappresentativi*, p.157; Mafrici, *Mezzogiorno e pirateria*, pp.201; Vargas-Hidalgo, *Correspondencia*, pp.923–25.

18. Vargas-Hidalgo, *Correspondencia*, p.930.

19. Vargas-Hidalgo, *Correspondencia*, p.1202.

20. Lo Basso, *Uomini da remo*, pp.296, 328–29; see also Mafrici, *Mezzogiorno e pirateria*, pp.190–208.

21. Salvatore Bono, 'Schiavi Musulmani sulle Galere e nei Bagni d'Italia', in Ragosta ed., *Genti del mare mediterraneo*, pp.837–75; note (pp.847–48) the high proportion of slaves on the galleys of Sicily; Fontenay, 'Chiourmes turques …', *passim*.

22. Imber, 'Navy…', pp.265–69; Murat Çizakça, 'Ottomans and the Mediterranean: an Analyis of the Ottoman Shipbuilding Industry as reflected by the Arsenal Registers of Istanbul 1520–1650', in Ragosta ed., *Genti*, ii, pp.773–87; AGS, Est.leg.971 sf Reports from Constantinople, 13 January 1599.

23. Setton, *Papacy*, iv, pp.861–62.

24. Lo Basso, *Uomini da remo*, part II.

25. AGS, Est.leg.1945 sf CCE 9 March 1619.

26. For examples Setton, *Papacy*, iv, p.583; Panzac, *La marine ottomane*, p.117.

27. On diplomatic complaints made to La Valette, see Mallia-Milanes, *Venice and Hospitaller Malta; passim*; Molly Greene, *Catholic Pirates and Greek Merchants. A Maritime History of the Mediterranean*, PUP: Princeton and Oxford 2010; on mortality on those unaccustomed to the oar, Lo Basso, *Uomini da remo*, pp.344–45; northern seafarers found conditions in the Mediterranean to be extremely difficult, Guido Candiani, 'Stratégie et diplomatie Vénitiennes: navires anglo-hollandais et blocus des Dardanelles,

1646–1659', *Revue d'histoire maritime. Histoire maritime. Outre-mer. Relations internationals*, IX (2008), pp.251–82, p.257; Professor Panzac has argued persuasively that, the Alexandria convoy aside, there was relatively little Ottoman commerce (ships owned, captained and crewed by Muslims) to rob, *La marine ottomane*, p.121.

28. AGS, Est.leg.1432 fol.146 Don Juan Vivas to King, Genoa 4 April 1604.
29. AGS, Est.leg.1433 fol.160 Vivas to King, Genoa 7 March 1606.
30. AGS, Est.leg.457 sf CCE 'Sobre lo que propone fray Roberto Datti...' Valladolid August 1605.
31. AGS, GA leg.618 sf Feria to King, Palermo 7 June 1603.
32. AGS, Est.leg.1430 fol.267 Doria to King, Genoa 28 September 1600.
33. AGS, Est.leg.457 sf '*Relación del estado de las galeras que Su Majestad tiene en Italia.*' 1595.
34. AGS, Est.leg.1435 fol.277, 'La junta de galeras ...' 18 July 1612.
35. Pardo Molero, *La defensa del imperio*, p.161.
36. Francesca Ortalli ed., *Lettere di Vicenzo Priuli Capitano delle Galee di Fiandra al Doge di Venezia, 1521–1523*, with appendices and index by Bianca Lanfranchi Strina, CPFRSV: Venice 2005, p.55.
37. Rodríguez-Salgado, '¿Carolus Africanus?', p.491; López de Gómara, *Guerras de mar*, pp.132–33, 135–36.
38. López de Gómara, *Guerras de mar*, p.206.
39. Caracciolo, *Uffici, difesa e corpi rappresentativi*, pp.153–55.
40. Vargas-Hidalgo, *Correspondencia*, p.17.
41. Vargas-Hidalgo, *Correspondencia*, p.242.
42. Vargas-Hidalgo, *Correspondencia*, p.351.
43. Vargas-Hidalgo, *Correspondencia*, pp.397–98.
44. AGS, Est.leg.1127 fol.115 King to Viceroy of Sicily, Madrid 14 June 1562; Vargas-Hidalgo, *Correspondencia*, pp.408–10; Braudel, *Mediterranean*, ii, p.991; note Sancho de Levia's view in September 1565, CODOIN, xxix, pp.492–93.
45. AGS, Est.leg.1127 fol.65 La Valette to King, Malta 21 July 1562.
46. AGS, Est.leg.1127 fol.72 La Valette to King, Malta 7 September 1562.
47. CODOIN, xxx, p.382.
48. AGS, Est.leg.1132 f.38 Copy of Royal Instructions to Don Garcia de Toledo, 18 March 1567.
49. AGS, Est.leg.1431 fol.138 Doria to Philip III, Genoa 7 November 1601.
50. It seems that the enemy craft ran aground on the North African coastline, their crews escaping. Vargas-Hidalgo, *Correspondencia*, pp.507–08.

51. Two of these galiots had been operating in May from the very mouth of the Tiber, Serrano, *Correspondencia*, ii, p.192.

52. Vargas-Hidalgo, *Correspondencia*, p.575.

53. See the successful expedition of Marcelo Doria in 1581, Vargas-Hidalgo, *Correspondencia*, p.1078.

54. Serrano, *Correspondencia*, iii, pp.505–06.

55. AGS, Est.leg.1136 fols.202 and 203 King to Santa Cruz, Madrid 20 February 1571; fol.225 to Juan de Cardona, Aranjuez 7 May.

56. Vargas-Hidalgo, *Correspondencia*, pp.816–19, 835.

57. For this paragraph, CODOIN, xxviii, pp.205–15.

58. Vargas-Hidalgo, *Correspondencia*, pp.1161–62, 1171–72; AGS, Est.leg.456 sf, King to Doria, 7 January 1589.

59. AGS, Est.leg.1424 fol.138 Doria to King, Genoa 2 September 1592.

60. AGS, Est.leg.1424 fol.141 Doria to King, Genoa 13 October 1592.

61. Nicolas Vatin, 'L'Empire ottoman et la piraterie en 1559–1560', in Zachariadou ed., *Kapudan Pasha*, pp.371–408, especially p.405; Vargas-Hidalgo, *Correspondencia*, p.434.

62. AGS, Est.leg.1102 fol.275 Benavente to King, Naples 1 December 1605.

63. For examples from the later 1570s, Rodríguez-Salgado, *Paladín de la Cristiandad*, pp.55, 104, 117–18.

64. Mayoral López, 'Los halcones', pp.182–90.

Chapter VI

1. See also his highly favourable assessment of Doria's service at the Peñón in 1564, CODOIN, xxix, pp.34, 248, 484–85.

2. Vargas-Hidalgo, *Correspondencia*, p.982.

3. AGS Est.leg.1130 fol.95 Doria to King, 1 July 1566; Vargas-Hidalgo, *Correspondencia*, p.1078.

4. Having lost a number of galleys in the previous winters, he had again been commanded to take to the seas, 'so I must believe that this order can be motivated by no other reason than to desire to see me lose one galley after another, as happened last year. Your Majesty must forgive me for complaining, as someone who is at a point such as I am, cannot leave to complain to his friends.' AGS, Est.leg.1394 fol.207, Doria to King, 8 December 1565; see also his letters of the same date, Vargas-Hidalgo, *Correspondencia*, p.466–70.

5. AGS, Est leg.1394 fol.204 Doria to Francisco Erasso, Leghorn 19 November 1564.

6. For example, Vargas-Hidalgo, *Correspondencia*, p.239.

7. As in July 1569, '. . . I ask that Your Majesty must forgive me for the effrontery I use in reminding you of things that, with your great prudence, you must know better than anybody.' Vargas-Hidalgo, *Correspondencia*, p.579.

8. Vargas-Hidalgo, *Correspondencia*, pp.227, 259.

9. Vargas-Hidalgo, *Correspondencia*, p.286.

10. He claimed to be losing 26,830 ducats annually, Vargas-Hidalgo, *Correspondencia*, pp.160–62.

11. Vargas-Hidalgo, *Correspondencia*, pp.252–53.

12. Vargas-Hidalgo, *Correspondencia*, p.287 n.624.

13. Vargas-Hidalgo, *Correspondencia*, p.307.

14. Braudel, *Mediterranean*, i, p.251; on the 'usury of merchants' and the galleys not having enjoyed one hour's rest in the last six years, Vargas-Hidalgo, *Correspondencia*, pp.271–72.

15. Vargas-Hidalgo, *Correspondencia*, pp.440–41.

16. Thompson, *War and Government*, p.78.

17. Caracciolo, *Uffici, difesa e corpi rappresentativi*, pp.140–41.

18. In August 1596, the Count of Olivares pointedly observed that there could be no doubt that with a younger and healthier *capitán-general* a core of good galleys could enter into the Archipelago, throwing the Turks in confusion and forcing them to flee, AGS, Est.leg.1094 fol.247 Olivares to Philip II, Naples 6 August 1596.

19. In the wake of the burning of Reggio Calabria, Miranda, Viceroy of Sicily, argued that the destruction 'could have been excused if the enemy had faced any opposition on the seas'. In fairness, he was willing to accept that the roots of this setback lay in a number of problems, the longer-term decay of the squadrons being one of them, AGS, Est.leg.1094 fol.114 Miranda to Philip II, Naples 13 September 1594.

20. William Robertson, *The History of the Reign of Emperor Charles V*, J.&J. Harper edition: New York 1830, p.227

21. CODOIN, xxix, p.445.

22. CODOIN, xxix, p.461.

23. García Hernán and García Hernán, *Lepanto*, p.85.

24. Toledo's request for greater authority to run the galleys was motivated by the intrusions and interventions of the viceroy and the Council of the Sommaria. He also made the following complaints: his galleys did not possess winter awnings; the *chusma* was weak and sick; and the mariners *ruines*, poorly paid and fewer than they should be. Moreover he had just

been forced to hand over 300 of the best oarsmen to Doria, AGS, Est. leg.170 fol.128 Don Pedro de Toledo to King, Colibre (? – Collioure) 14 October 1593.

25. 'Quisiera yo acrecentar esta escuadra de galeras aunque fuera dando para ello la sangre de mis brazos,' AGS, Est.leg.1161 fol.72 Feria to King, Messina 13 November 1604.

26. AGS, Est.leg.1168 fol.81 Osuna to King, 23 December 1614.

27. R.A. Stradling, *Europe and the Decline of Spain. A Study of the Spanish System, 1580–1720*, George Allen & Unwin: London 1981, pp.115–16. For a different interpretation, David Goodman, *Spanish Naval Power, 1589–1665. Reconstruction and Defeat*, CUP: Cambridge 1997, pp.39–67.

28. Caracciolo, *Uffici, difesa e corpi rappresentativi*, pp.215, 224; Hernando Sánchez, *Castilla y Nápoles en el siglo XVI*, p.348; James D. Tracy, *Emperor Charles V, Impresario of War. Campaign Strategy, International Finance, and Domestic Politics*, CUP: Cambridge 2002, *passim*; Rodríguez-Salgado, *Changing Face of Empire*, pp.35, 50–54, 341; CODOIN, xxix, pp.320–21; Calabria, *Cost of Empire*, pp.99–101; Fenicia, *Regno di Napoli*, 'Conclusion'; in Sicily annual expenditure was outstripping income by 500,000 *escudos*, AGS, Est.leg.1163 fol.121 CCE 29 October 1608.

29. CODOIN, xxviii, pp.181–84; on his financial difficulties, Serrano, *Liga de Lepanto*, ii, pp.91–93.

30. García Hernán, 'La conquista y la pérdida', pp.44, 45, 63, 69–70, 73, 86.

31. AGS, Est.leg.1420 fol.137, Doria to King, Loano 1 March 1588.

32. Vargas-Hidalgo, *Correspondencia*, p.1225.

33. This letter also contains one of the relatively few references to the use of 'hospital ships', AGS, Est.leg.1156 fol.67, Doria to Philip II, Messina 16 July 1588.

34. The sailing of galleys in December and January 1566 was essential for the monarchy but would pose grave risks to the galleys and would lead to the 'loss' of many of the rowers, '*con mucho riesgo de las galeras y con mucha perdición de chusma*', Vargas-Hidalgo, *Correspondencia*, p.480.

35. Girón, *Crónica del Emperador Carlos V*, p.192.

36. Braudel, *Mediterranean*, ii, pp.909–10.

37. Hernando Sánchez, *Castilla y Nápoles en el siglo XVI*, pp.399–400, 402.

38. The squadron of contractors was the one 'that works most, serves best and [even though it is based] in a place where everything is more costly, it also costs the least', AGS, Est.leg.1423 fol.67 Doria to Philip II, Loano 12 February 1591.

39. The *asiento* for the two galleys provided by the Duke of Tursi took in 1608 stipulated that 15 new *forzados* would be provided each year from the kingdom of Naples to the Genoese, AGS, Est.leg.1105 fol.2 Benavente to Philip III, Naples 31 January 1608.

40. See Andrea Doria's lament about Don Juan de Mendoza enjoying a '*ventaja sobre mí*' in the matter of payments, 'I appear to be treated worse than all the others', Vargas-Hidalgo, *Correspondencia*, pp.253–54.

41. Braudel, *Mediterranean*, ii, p.1013; Thompson, *War and Government*, p.167.

42. Don García de Toledo to King, 22 February 1565, CODOIN, xxix, p.33.

43. CODOIN, xxix, pp.351–52.

44. For complaints about the employment of slaves in the houses and gardens of captains and other abuses, Caracciolo, *Uffici, difesa e corpi rappresentativi*, p.160.

45. AGS, Est.leg.456 sf Doria to Philip II, Puçol (?) 16 October 1588; Est. leg.1427 fol.65 Doria to Philip II, Pegli 2 August 1595; Est.leg.457, sf 'Relación del estado de las galeras que Su Majestad tiene en Italia.'; Est. leg.1422 fol.128 Doria to Philip II, Turrilla (?) 10 August 1590.

46. For examples of his limited authority, CODOIN, xxx, pp.262–63, 269.

47. 'I know for certain,' he added a little later, 'that others are trying to occupy the place that should be mine.' CODOIN, xxviii, pp.98–99, 104–05.

48. See his long letter of 6 September 1575 in relation to the dispute over his plans for three expeditions, CODOIN, xxviii, pp.205–15 and especially pp.213–14.

49. García Hernán and García Hernán, *Lepanto*, p.159.

50. Toledo's recall in 1566 was the direct result of the king's eventually deciding to take the side of the Viceroy of Naples, the Duke of Alcalá, H.G. Koenigsberger, *The Practice of Empire,* Cornell University Press: Ithaca 1969, p.181.

51. Serrano, *Correspondencia*, iii, pp.399–400.

52. Rivero Rodríguez, *Lepanto*, pp.228–29.

53. AGS, Est.leg.1129, fol.102 Doria to King, Messina 5 July 1565; Toledo, incidentally, agreed that in the summer the wheat and wine had been more expensive than usual, fol.104 Toledo to King, Messina 5 July 1565. The king tried to ensure that Doria received the *tratas de Sicilia* in 1565 and that 'some reasonable' sum of money be sent to him, Vargas-Hidalgo, *Correspondencia*, pp.455, 457–58, CODOIN, xxix, p.224.

54. Rafael Vargas-Hidalgo, *Batalla de Lepanto*, pp.265–66; Setton, *Papacy*, iv, p.1048.

55. Serrano, *Correspondencia*, ii, pp.426–27.

56. CODOIN, xxix, pp.495–96.

57. AGS, Est.leg.1394 fol.204 Doria to King, Leghorn 19 November 1564 (cited above also).

58. In fairness, he went on to say that his intuition was driven by his desire to serve, Vargas-Hidalgo, *Correspondencia*, p.817.

59. He was asking for some of Salerno's estate, AGS, Est.leg.1120 fol.145 de Vega to King, 1552.

60. CODOIN, xxix, pp.491–92.

61. Vargas-Hidalgo, *Correspondencia*, p.691 n.1281.

62. 'dejando estas otras que se han armado de nuevo, podríamos encontrándonos con las galeras que el bajá saca rompelles muy fácilmente la cabeza', CODOIN, xxix, pp.301–02.

63. King to Toledo, 9 March 1565, CODOIN, xxix, pp.59–60.

64. CODOIN, xxix, pp.174, 365–66.

65. Vargas-Hidalgo, *Correspondencia*, pp.546–47, 578.

66. Vargas-Hidalgo, *Correspondencia*, p.458; AGS, Est.leg.1394 fol.206 Doria to King, Genoa 9 December 1565.

67. Andrea Doria was perhaps more conscious of the problems encountered by his officials and sailors. Vargas-Hidalgo, *Correspondencia*, pp.19–20, 26.

68. Letter of 4 February 1571 to Zúñiga, Serrano, *Correspondencia*, iv, p.188.

69. See his letter of July 1570, Serrano, *Correspondencia*, iii, p.481.

Chapter VII

1. Fodor, 'Ottoman Policy Towards Hungary', p.143 n.5.

2. Panzac, *La marine ottomane*, pp.78–80.

3. Girón, *Cronica del Emperador Carlos V*, pp.221, 223.

4. Luis Ribot, 'Las Provincias Italianas y la defensa de la Monarquía', reproduced in *El arte de gobernar. Estudios sobre la España de los Austrias*, Alianza: Madrid 2006, pp.92–118; Valentina Favarò, 'La Sicilia fortezza del Mediterraneo', in *Mediterranea: ricerche storiche*, I (June 2004) pp.31–48.

5. Liliane Dufour, 'El reino de Sicilia. Las fortificaciones en tiempos de Carlos V'. in Hernando Sánchez ed., *Las fortificaciones de Carlos V*, pp.492–513; Antonino Giuffrida, 'La fortezza indifesa e il progetto del Vega per una ristrutturazione del sistema difensivo siciliano', in Cancila ed., *Mediterraneo in armi*, i, pp.227–88; Favarò, 'La Sicilia fortezza', p.35 ff.

6. Hernando Sánchez, 'El reino de Nápoles', *passim*; on the militias and troops in Naples, Mafrici, *Mezzogiorno e pirateria*, pp.208–28.

7. Alonso Acero, 'El norte de África', p.401.

8. Rhoads Murphey, 'A Comparative Look at Ottoman and Habsburg Resources and Readiness for War circa 1520 to circa 1570', in García Hernán and Maffi eds, *Guerra y sociedad*, i, pp.75–102.

9. From: *Letters and Papers, Foreign and Domestic, Henry VIII*, Volume 8: January–July 1535 (1885), pp.305–25; available at: www.british-history.ac.uk/report.aspx?compid=75537 (accessed 18 September 2013).

10. From: *Letters and Papers, Foreign and Domestic, Henry VIII*, Volume 15: 1540 (1896), pp.364–76; available at: www.british-history.ac.uk/report.aspx?compid=76173 (accessed 18 September 2013).

11. Braudel, *Mediterranean*, ii, p.1140.

12. Vargas-Hidalgo, *Correspondencia*, pp.693–98 especially p.696.

13. Imber, 'Navy of Süleyman the Magnificent', p.227.

14. Christine Woodhead, 'The Present Terrour of the World? – Contemporary Views of the Ottoman Empire c1600', in *History*, Vol 72 No.234 (February 1987), p.31.

15. Veinstein, 'Les préparatifs', pp.55, 60.

16. Imber, *Ottoman Empire*, p.315.

17. Aurelio Espinosa, 'The Grand Strategy of Charles V (1500–1558): Castile, War, and Dynastic Priority in the Mediterranean', *Journal of Early Modern History*, volume 9.3 (2005), pp.239–83.

18. Braudel, *Mediterranean*, ii, p.927; see also Mafrici, *Mezzogiorno*, pp.50–51.

19. Vargas-Hidalgo, *Correspondencia*, pp.425, 428–29.

20. AGS, Est.leg.1127 fol.156 'Instrucción y orden de lo que ...' Messina 18 May 1563.

21. Vargas-Hidalgo, *Correspondencia*, pp.434, 578–79; Braudel, *Mediterranean*, ii 881; CODOIN, xxx, pp.269–70.

22. Guilmartin, *Gunpowder and Galleys*, p.198; CODOIN, xxix, pp.293–94.

23. Cassola, *1565 Ottoman Malta Campaign Register*, p.437.

24. Caracciolo, *Uffici, difesa e corpi rappresentativi*, p.156.

25. AGS, Est.leg.1422 fol.177 'Tercero parecer [de Doria]'.

26. Imber, 'Navy of Süleyman the Magnificent', pp.265–69; Imber, *Ottoman Empire*, pp.305–06.

27. Murphey, 'Comparative Look', pp.82, 88.

28. Murphey, 'Comparative Look' p.97; Murphey, *Ottoman Warfare*, pp.25–34.

29. AGS, Est.leg.900 sf Reports from Messina 2 June 1565; *'gente desarmada y sin orden no puede competir con la ordinaria de VM'*, CODOIN, xxix, pp.167–70 (especially p.168), 364–68.

30. R. Murphey, 'Introduction', in Colin Imber, Keiko Kiyotaki and Rhoads Murphey eds, *Frontiers of Ottoman Studies*, 2 volumes, I.B.Tauris: London 2005, ii, p.16; Imber, *Ottoman Empire*, pp.309–10.

31. See Williams, 'Sound and the Fury', pp.557–63.

32. Setton, *Papacy*, iii, p.84.

33. Girón, *Crónica del Emperador Carlos V*, p.217.

34. AGS, Est.leg.1498 fol.167 Reports from Constantinople, June 1559.

35. AGS, Est.leg.1161 fol.38 Feria to King, Messina 6 June 1604.

36. For reports of 1531 and 1532, Setton, *Papacy*, iii, p.356; López de Gómara, *Guerras de mar*, p.138.

37. Girón, *Crónica del Emperador Carlos V*, pp.199, 201–02, 204–05, 208.

38. Bostan, 'The Province of *Cezayir-i Bahr-i Sefid*', p.246.

39. Note also that the fleet required 2,305 tonnes of biscuit, Imber, *Ottoman Empire*, pp.305, 312.

40. Giles Veinstein, 'La dernière flotte de Barberousse', in Zachariadou ed., *Kapudan Pasha*, pp.181–97.

41. Vargas-Hidalgo, *Correspondencia*, pp.20, 22.

42. Vargas-Hidalgo, *Correspondencia*, pp.56–59, 64, 66–67.

43. Vargas-Hidalgo, *Correspondencia*, pp.260, 264.

44. AGS, Est.leg.1498 fol.178 Reports from Constantinople, 19 July 1559.

45. Vargas-Hidalgo, *Correspondencia*, pp.392–93.

46. AGS, Est.leg.1324 fol.118 Reports from Constantinople, 20 January 1563.

47. The Pashas would have been bribed by the Signoria, AGS, Est.leg, 1324 fol.119 García Hernández to King, Venice 10 March 1563.

48. AGS, Est.leg.1127 fol.126 Viceroy of Sicily to King, Palermo 11 February 1563.

49. AGS, Est.leg.1325, fol.44, Hernández to King, Venice 8 October 1564.

50. CODOIN, xxix, p.366.

51. Imber, 'Navy of Süleyman', pp.246–47, 263–64, 265–66, 268; Setton, *Papacy*, iv, p.856 n.99; similar assessments were made of the fleet in 1572, Panzac, *La marine ottomane*, chapter I.

52. Among the casualties were 4,000 janissaries, AGS, Est.leg.1325 fol.129 Garcí Hernandez to King, Venice 22 December 1565; Est.leg.1324 fol.209 Reports from Constantinople, 22 October 1565; Est.leg.900 sf Reports from Constantinople, 22 October 1565.

53. Vargas-Hidalgo, *Correspondencia*, p.476.

54. Setton, *Papacy*, iv, pp.894–99, 903–06.

55. See Zúñiga's letter from Rome, 9 July 1568, Serrano, *Correspondencia*, ii, p.405.

56. AGS, Est.leg.1326 fol.135 Julian López to King, Venice 25 September 1568; note also García Hernán, *La acción diplomática*, p.109.

57. Vargas-Hidalgo, *Correspondencia*, pp.676–77; Vargas-Hidalgo, *Batalla de Lepanto*, pp.125–26.

58. AGS, Est.leg.1058 fol.11 Reports from Constantinople 13 January 1570.

59. AGS, Est.leg.1327 fol.149 Reports from Constantinople 4 June 1570.

60. Setton, *Papacy*, iv, p.988 n.55.

61. This report included the detail on the Christians being dismissed as chickens; by his own account, he had reneged 12 years previously, AGS, Est.leg.1134 fol.55 'Relación del renegado que se dice Martín de Morales...' 30 August 1571.

62. Vargas-Hidalgo, *La Batalla de Lepanto*, pp.105–06, 125–26.

63. Vargas-Hidalgo, *Correspondencia*, p.823.

64. See his letters of 26 May and 12 August 1572, CODOIN, iii, pp.86–89, 94–95.

65. AGS, Est.leg.1157 fol.67 Reports from Constantinople 8 December 1590; additional details, Imber, *Ottoman Empire*, p.310.

66. AGS, Est.leg.1159 fol.97 Reports from Corfu 14 June 1600.

67. Alexander H. de Groot, 'The Ottoman Threat to Europe, 1571–1830: Historical Fact or Fancy?' in Mallia-Milanes ed., *Hospitaller Malta 1530–1798*, pp.199–254, p.219.

68. Imber, *Ottoman Empire*, pp.306–07.

69. Vargas-Hidalgo, *Correspondencia*, p.540; AGS, Est.leg.1098 fol.19 Reports from Istanbul 10 December 1601.

70. Braudel, *Mediterranean*, ii 944–95, 971, 979; Vargas-Hidalgo, *Correspondencia*, pp.278–79; Cabrera de Córdoba, *Felipe II*, i, p.167.

71. Vatin, 'L'Empire ottoman...' p.376.

72. CODOIN, xxix, pp.273, 282, 293–94, 509–10.

73. López de Gómara, *Guerras de mar*, pp.137–41.

74. Girón, *Crónica del Emperador Carlos V*, p.217.

75. López de Gómara, *Guerras de mar*, pp.198, 202; Braudel, *Mediterranean*, i, p.249.

76. Mafrici, *Mezzogiorno*, p.50.

77. Yildirim, 'Battle of Lepanto', p.550.

78. Braudel, *Mediterranean*, ii, pp.1139–40; for other reports, Setton, *Papacy*, iv, p.1095.

79. AGS, Est.leg.1134, fol.55 'Relación del renegado... Martin de Morales... 25 de agosto 1571', cited above in n.61.

80. Yildirim, 'Battle of Lepanto', pp.541–42.

81. Serrano, *Liga de Lepanto*, ii, p.91.

82. One hundred and fifty new hulls were to be built in Istanbul and elsewhere over the winter of 1537–38, Girón, *Crónica del Emperador Carlos V*, pp.214–15; Imber, 'The Reconstruction of the Ottoman Fleet after Lepanto', *passim*.

83. Braudel, *Mediterranean*, ii, pp.1046–47, 1058–60, 1073.

84. Serrano, *Liga de Lepanto*, ii, pp.21–22; Vargas-Hidalgo, *Correspondencia*, p.831.

85. '*150 galeras para estorbar con ellas los designios del enemigo*', see Toledo's letter of 8 July 1573, CODOIN, xxviii, pp.196–98.

86. AGS, Est.leg.1327 fol.138 Reports from Pera [Constantinople], 22 December 1569.

87. AGS, Est.leg.1326 fol.205 Thomas de Zornoza to King, Venice 24 January 1569.

88. Phillip Williams, *Piracy and Naval Conflict in the Mediterranean, 1590–1610/20*, unpublished D.PHIL thesis Oxford University 2001, p.126.

89. AGS, Est.lib.'K'1675 fol.24, 'Lo que avisa el embajador que el emperador tiene...' 2 February 1591.

90. AGS, Est.leg.1094 fol.114 Miranda to Philip II, Naples 13 September 1594.

91. CSPV 1613–15 no.179 Morosini, Madrid 30 January 1614.

92. AGS, Est.leg.1888 fol.26 CCE Madrid 2 December 1614. The Marquis of Villafranca also thought that the fleet might be of these proportions; Williams, *Piracy*, pp.34–35.

93. John Keegan, *Battle at Sea from Man-of-War to Submarine*, Pimlico: London 1993, p.154.

94. Yildirim, 'Battle of Lepanto', p.543.

95. Note the deep divisions on strategy in 1570–72, Serrano, *Liga de Lepanto*, i, pp.60–61.

96. Serrano, *Liga de Lepanto*, ii, p.323.

97. His meaning was that similar battle-gambles might easily have taken place in 1570 and 1572, 23 December 1572, CODOIN, iii, pp.101–02.

98. Toledo's assessment in May 1565: with the loss of the king's galleys and regular infantry in a battle at sea '*quedarían sus reinos desnudos de dos remedios tan grandes para su defensa*', CODOIN, xxix, p.167.

99. Salvatore Bono, 'Naval Exploits and Privateering', in Mallia-Milanes ed., *Hospitaller Malta*, pp.351–98, especially 356–57, 360, 363–64, 367; Brogini, *Malte*, chapter VI especially pp.291–303; Williams, 'Sound and the Fury', pp.582–84.

100. Serrano, *Liga de Lepanto*, ii, p.46 n.1.

101. Cabrera de Córdoba, *Felipe II*, ii, p.684; CODOIN, xxviii, pp.188–89.

102. AGS, Est.leg.1103, fol.146 Benavente to King, Naples 30 July 1606.

103. García Hernán, *Armada española*, pp.101–02.

104. AGS, Est.leg.1105 fol.114 Proposal for an attack in the Levant, with letter of 25 December 1608.

105. AGS, Est.leg.1108 fol.47 Santa Cruz to King, Messina 23 April 1614.

106. AGS, Est.leg.1102 fol.80 Benavente to King, Naples 25 April 1605; again, similar proposals had been discussed during the early 1570s, García Hernán and García Hernán, *Lepanto*, p.62.

107. AGS, Est.leg.457 sf Philip II to Count of Olivares, Madrid 27 May 1594. In March 1563 the king dangled before his Italian confederates the possibility of a hunt for corsairs in the waters of the 'Levant' – if the enemy fleet failed to appear, Vargas-Hidalgo, *Correspondencia*, pp.409–10.

108. AGS, Est.leg.457 sf Doria to Philip II, Genoa 7 December 1594.

109. AGS, Est.leg.1127 fols.32, 46 Grand Master of Malta to viceroy of Sicily, Malta 24 April and 4 May 1562.

110. AGS, Est.leg.456 sf Doria to Philip II, Genoa 18 June 1589.

111. By the time, for instance, that the Council of State met to discuss the Duke of Osuna's crusading schemes in March 1614 the moment had passed, for that summer at least. AGS, Est.leg.1888 fol.3 CCE 'sobre las cartas del duque de Osuna' Madrid (?) 21 March 1614.

112. Setton, *Papacy*, iii, p.446.

113. Guilmartin, *Gunpowder and Galleys*, pp.120–22.

114. Works on the Moriscos include Tulio Halperin Donghi, *Un conflicto nacional. Moriscos y cristianos viejos en Valencia*, Institució 'Alfons el Magnànim': Valencia 1980; L. Cardaillac, *Moriscos y cristianos. Un enfrentamiento polémico (1492–1640)*, with a preface by Fernand Braudel, Fondo de Cultura Economico: Madrid, Mexico, Buenos Aires 1979; Miguel Ángel de Bunes Ibarra, *Los moriscos en el pensamiento histórico. Historiografía de un grupo marginado*, Catedra: Madrid 1983; Rafael Benítez Sánchez-Blanco, 'La política de Carlos V hacia los moriscos granadinos' in Martínez Millán ed., *Carlos y la quiebra*, i, pp.415–46; Míkel Epalza, 'Moriscos contra Carlos V: Argel y el nuevo modelo de inserción de los musulmanes hispanos en el Magreb (1516–1541)', in ibid., pp.447–67.

115. Joan Reglà, 'La cuestión morisca y la coyuntura internacional en tiempos de Felipe II' (revised version of original) in *Estudios sobre los moriscos*, Anales de la Universidad de Valencia: Valencia 1964, pp.137–57; Pascual Boronat y Barrachina, *Los moriscos españoles y su expulsión*, 2 volumes, first printed

Valencia 1901 reprinted with a preliminary study by Ricardo García Cárcel, Universidad de Granada: Granada 1992; Andrew Hess, 'The Moriscos. An Ottoman Fifth Column in Sixteenth-Century Spain', *American Historical Review*, LXXIV, Number 1 (October 1968), pp.1–25.

116. Braudel, *Mediterranean*, ii, pp.921–22; Juan Francisco Pardo Molero, 'El reino de Valencia y la defensa de la Monarquía en el siglo XVI', in Maffi and García Hernán eds, *Guerra y sociedad*, ii, pp.611–50, pp.640–41, 644; Rodríguez-Salgado, '"El león animoso"', p.29.

117. Thompson, *War and Government*, pp.22–23; on plots and collaboration, Pardo Molero, *La defensa del imperio*, pp.269, 275–76, 337–41, 421; Jiménez Estrella, 'Ejército permanente', pp.588, 591–93.

118. In addition to the pages above, see Braudel, *Mediterranean*, ii, pp.944–45, 1064–66, 1140; Hess, 'The Moriscos', p.21 n.81.

119. Vargas-Hidalgo, *Correspondencia*, pp.246–47.

120. Vargas-Hidalgo, *Correspondencia*, p.324.

121. Vargas-Hidalgo, *Correspondencia*, p.349.

122. See the royal instruction of 22 May, CODOIN, xxix, pp.158–63, especially p.159.

123. Vargas-Hidalgo, *Correspondencia*, pp.544–46.

124. AGS, Est.leg.456 sf Philip II to Doria, Madrid 22 March 1591.

125. AGS, Est.leg.456 sf Philip II to Duke of Sesa, Grand Master, Grand Duke and Republic of Genoa Nuestra Señora de la Estrella 20 October 1592.

126. AGS, Est.leg.1428, fols.168 King to Prince Doria, Toledo 12 July 1596.

127. See AGS, Est.leg.1888 fol.26 CCE, Madrid 2 December 1614 (cited above).

128. AGS, Est.leg.1326 fol.314 Reports from Constantinople, 26 December 1569.

129. See Toledo's letter of 8 July 1574 (incorrectly dated) cited above, CODOIN, xxviii, pp.198.

130. AGS, Est.leg.456 sf 'Discurso del Príncipe Doria sobre prevenciónes' 16 October 1588.

131. For similar contemporary assessments, Ricardo García Cárcel, *Herejía y sociedad en el siglo XVI. La inquisición en Valencia 1530–1609*, Ediciones Península: Barcelona 1980, p.102; Boronat y Barrachina, *Los moriscos españoles y su expulsión*, ii, p.469.

132. AGS, GA leg.455 fol.55 Denia to King, Valencia 20 May 1596; ibid., fol.56 'Relación de la visita...'; GA leg.457 fol.204 and 205, 13 July 1596; ibid. fol.276, 17 July; GA leg.458 fol.256, 20 August; Est. leg.343 fol.21 Denia to King, Valencia 14 August 1596; ibid. fol.42 'Puntos de carta de marqués de

Denia ...Valencia 3 agosto 1596'; ibid. fol.46 Denia to King, Valencia 3 August 1596; ibid. fol.52, 24 July. 'It does not appear that the Turkish armada is coming here this summer,' he concluded in his letter of 20 August, 'and so there will be quiet among the new Christians of this kingdom.' The attachment of the Moriscos to their land was a powerful deterrent to any sort of rebellion that was not assisted by a *gruessa armada del Turco*', as he explained in his letter of 17 July.

133. Braudel, *Mediterranean*, ii 794; T. Halperin Donghi, 'Recouvrements de civilisation: les Morisques au Royaume de Valence au XVI siècle', *Annales. Economies. Sociétés. Civilisations*, xi (1956), pp.154–82, p.178; Halperin Donghi, *Un conflicto nacional*, pp.126–27.

134. The viceroy recorded this confession in person, see his letter of 20 August cited above.

135. Espinosa, 'Grand Strategy', pp.267–68.

136. De Groot, 'Ottoman Threat', p.216. On 1596 see pp.233–34.

137. AGS, GA leg.518, fol.82 Benavente to King, Valencia 15 August 1598.

138. Domínguez Ortiz and Vincent, *Historia de los moriscos*, p.167; Boronat, *Los moriscos españoles y su expulsión*, ii, p.38.

139. Domínguez Ortiz and Vincent, *Historia de los moriscos*, pp.167–68.

140. Boronat, *Los moriscos españoles y su expulsión*, ii, pp.466–67.

141. Sam White, *The Climate of Rebellion in the Early Modern Ottoman Empire*, CUP: Cambridge 2011, pp.180–85. AGS, Est.leg.1105 fol.63 Benavente to King, Naples 15 August 1608; Williams, *Piracy*, pp.69, 73, 83–85, 88–89.

142. AGS, Est.leg.988 sf Aytona to King, Roma 11 November 1608.

143. AGS, Est.leg.'K'1679 fol.16 Reports from Constantinople, 24 January 1609; fol.17 don Alonso de la Cueba to King, Venice 31 January 1609 (received 10 March); fol.26 Reports from Constantinople 'de 22 de hebrero 1609'; fol.28 de la Cueva to King, Venice 28 February 1609 (received 4 April) 'con avisos de Constantinopla de 24 de enero'.

144. AGS, Est.leg.1326 fol.92 Reports from Constantinople, 12 July 1567; Braudel, *Mediterranean*, ii, pp.1198, 1224–25; Williams, 'Sound and the Fury', pp.570–72.

145. AGS, GA leg.457 fol.439 count of Alcaudete to King, Oran 26 July 1596.

146. García García, *Pax Hispanica*, pp.86–88 n.14; Parrott, 'A "prince souverain"', pp.164–65.

147. AGS, Est.leg.1105 fol.211 Wignacourt to Benavente, Malta 4 July 1609; see also the documents sent by Lerma to the king with his note of 14 October 1609 in Est.leg.214 sin folio and also ibid. sf 'Relación suscinta de

todas las diligencias...del reyno de Mallorca', August 1609 and ibid. sf 'Copia de los avisos...'.

148. 'Some say it will be 60 or 70 galleys, others say 90, 120 or 130 and some go as far as 200' with 20,000 janissaries, AGS, Est.leg.493 sf CCE, 3 June 1609 'Sobre los avisos ... de armada del turco ...'; Williams, *Piracy*, pp.69, 86–87.

149. Boronat, *Los moriscos españoles y su expulsión*, ii, pp.116–19, 150–51; M. Lomas Cortés, *La expulsión de los moriscos del reino de Aragón. Política y administración de una deportación (1609–1611)*, CEM: Teruel 2008; Lomas Cortés, *El proceso de expulsión*, passim.

Chapter VIII

1. Braudel, *Mediterranean*, ii, p.1236.
2. AGS, Est.leg.1026 fol.27 'Lo que se entiende de Levante por diversas vias', May–June 1537; fol.35 Pedro de Toledo to King, Naples 23 June 1537.
3. Capelloni, *Vita del principe Andrea Doria*, pp.157–58; Anderson, *Naval Wars in the Levant*, pp.27–28. See also Braudel, *Mediterranean*, ii, p.924.
4. Vargas-Hidalgo, *Correspondencia*, pp.397–98.
5. Vargas-Hidalgo, *Correspondencia*, pp.450–51.
6. See his letter of 4 June 1566, CODOIN, xxx, pp.278–79.
7. Setton, *Papacy*, iv, pp.890–91.
8. Serrano, *Liga de Lepanto*, ii, p.334.
9. CODOIN, iii, pp.234–36.
10. Vargas-Hidaldo, *Correspondencia*, pp.935–36.
11. AGS, Est.leg.1026 fol.3 and 4 Toledo and Collatoral Council to King, Naples 21 March 1537.
12. AGS, Est.leg.1026 fol.13 Toledo to King, Naples 25 March 1537.
13. Laiglesia, *Estudios históricos*, pp.104–07.
14. Braudel, 'Los españoles y África del norte de 1492 a 1577', reproduced in *En torno del Mediterráneo*, p.90. See also, *Mediterranean*, ii, pp.970, 979.
15. AGS, Est.leg.1127 fol.100 'Lo que contiene cinco cartas del visorey de Sicilia a Su Md de xviii de agosto xii y xiii de setiembre y 22[?] de enero 1563...'
16. AGS, Est.leg.1127 fol.126 Viceroy of Sicily to King, Palermo 11 February 1563.
17. CODOIN, xxix, p.568.
18. CODOIN, xxix, pp.145–46, 152–53, 161, 223–24, 318–20, 326 especially 290–91.

19. CODOIN, xxix, pp.449–50.

20. CODOIN, xxx, p.300.

21. AGS, Est.leg.1136 fol.145 King to Don John of Austria, San Lorenzo 16 July 1571.

22. CODOIN, iii, p.44; García Hernán and García Hernán, *Lepanto*, pp.89, 98, 94–110.

23. See Zúñiga's letter of 14 October 1569, Serrano, *Correspondencia*, iii, pp.165–66.

24. AGS Est.leg.1093 fol.83 Miranda to King, Naples 21 September 1592; see also his letter of 12 August, fol.62.

25. AGS, Est.leg.1424 fol.141 Doria to King, Genoa 13 October 1592.

26. AGS, Est.leg.1093 fol.99 King to Miranda, 30 March 1592.

27. AGS, Est.leg.1093 fol.96 Miranda to King, Naples 3 December 1592; see also his letters of 15 and 22 November, fols.92, 95.

28. AGS, Est.leg.1093 fol.123 Miranda to King, Naples 25 March 1593.

29. AGS, Est.leg.1158 fol.130 Marquis of Hierace to King, Palermo 18 April 1597.

30. AGS, Est.leg.1158 fol.148 Duke of Maqueda to King, Palermo 15 May 1598.

31. AGS, Est.leg.1159 fol.21 Maqueda to King, Palermo 21 March 1599.

32. AGS, Est.leg.1098 fol.38 Don Francisco de Castro to King, Naples 11 May 1602.

33. AGS, Est.leg.1161 fol.184 Feria to King, Palermo 2 May 1605.

34. Fernand Braudel, 'A modo de introducción: Primeras investigaciones' reprinted in Roselyne de Ayala and Paule Braudel eds, *En torno al Mediterráneo*, with prologue by Maurice Aymard, Barcelona 1997, p.37.

35. Braudel, *Mediterranean* ii, p.981; note Andrea Doria's misgivings about the delay in bringing the galleys over from Spain, Vargas-Hidalgo, *Correspondencia*, pp.334–35, 350–52.

36. For Doria's proposal for 1563, Vargas-Hidalgo, *Correspondencia*, pp.405–06.

37. Rodríguez-Salgado, *Changing Face*, pp.31–32; Parker, *Grand Strategy*, p.82.

38. As in 1558 and 1560, Vargas-Hidalgo, *Correspondencia*, pp.201, 326.

39. Braudel, *Mediterranean*, ii, pp.927, 998, 1002; Rodríguez-Salgado, '"El león animoso"', pp.35–41.

40. Cabrera de Córdoba, *Felipe II*, i, p.261.

41. Vincent and Domínguez Ortiz, *Historia de los moriscos*, pp.39–40; Thompson, *War and Government*, pp.21, 25–26, 147, 237.

42. Vargas-Hidalgo, *Correspondencia*, pp.1072–73, 1076–77.

43. See his annotation to the *Consulta* AGS, Est.leg.2025, fol.97 CCE '*sobre Cartas del duque de Medina Sidonia y del Rey de Fez Muley Xeque*' San Lorenzo 8 April 1608.

44. Fernández Álvarez, *Carlos V*, pp.494–95.

45. Giuffrida, 'La fortezza indifesa e il progetto', pp.229–30; A. Musi, 'L'Italia nel sistema imperiale spagnolo' in A. Musi ed., *Nel sistema imperiale. L'Italia spagnola*, Edizioni Scientifiche Italiane: Naples 1994, p.60; Rizzo, 'Centro spagnolo', pp.324–25; Cancila, *Fisco Ricchezza Comunità*, pp.60–66; Favarò, *La modernizzazione, passim*; Belloso Martín, *La antemuralla*, pp.17–25; Ribot, 'La Provincias Italianas', pp.115–16 makes some valuable observations about links between the monarchy, the Church and the ruling elites. For the success of the system after 1640, Stradling, *Europe and the Decline of Spain*, pp.116–22; Maffi, *Il baluardo della corona*, pp.64–66.

46. See the insightful comments by Thompson, 'Spanish Armada', p.72 and Braudel, *Mediterranean*, ii, pp.997–98.

47. Hernando Sánchez, *Castilla y Nápoles en el siglo XVI*, pp.384–85.

48. Hernando Sánchez, *Castilla y Nápoles en el siglo XVI*, pp.392–93; CODOIN, xxix, pp.208–09.

49. Cabrera de Córdoba, *Felipe II*, i, p.261.

50. AGS, GA leg.492 fol.67 Duke of Feria to King, Barcelona 18 December 1597; Est. leg.1098 fol.4 Francisco de Castro to Philip III, Naples 14 January 1602.

51. Setton, *Papacy*, iii, pp.554–55.

52. Braudel, *Mediterranean*, i, pp.488–93.

53. For details, Lo Basso, *Uomini da remo*, pp.222–27.

54. Mario Rizzo, 'Milano e le forze del principe. Agenti, relazioni e risorse per la difesa dell'impero di Filippo II', in J. Martínez Millán ed., *Felipe II (1527–1598). Europa y Monarquía Católica*, Parteluz: Madrid 1998, i, pp.731–66.

55. Rizzo, 'Centro spagnolo e periferia lombarda', pp.324–25.

56. Maffi, *Baluardo della corona*, pp.18–19.

57. Tied into this was the idea that the Habsburg positions would starve without the corn of Sicily, López de Gómara, *Guerras de mar*, pp.154–56; Pacini, *La Genova*, pp.304–07, 588.

58. López de Gómara, *Guerras de mar*, pp.184–86.

59. Isom-Verhaaren, *Allies with the Infidel*, pp.116–19, 136–38, 158–64.

60. AGS, Est.leg.1120 fol.200 'Relación que se tomó de Agustín de la Seta escribano de las galeras de Sicilia de la armada del Turco.' 1552; Caracciolo, *Uffici, difesa e corpi rappresentativi*, pp.128–29, 131–32.

61. Setton, *Papacy*, iv, p.678–80.

62. Vargas-Hidalgo, *Correspondencia*, pp.180–81, 186.

63. Serrano, *Liga de Lepanto*, ii, p.292.

64. AGS, Est.leg.1158 fol.44 Olivares to King, Palermo 27 January 1595.

65. AGS, Est.leg.1428 fols. 133 and 134 Doria to King, Loano 23 December 1596.

66. AGS, Est.leg.1430 fol.207 Count of Biñasco to King, Genoa 25 August 1600; fol.218, 1 October 1600; fol.263, Doria to King, 13 September 1600.

67. AGS, Est.leg.1432 fol.160 Vivas to King, Genoa 11 August 1604.

68. AGS, Est.leg.1432 fol.19 and 20 Vivas to duke of Lerma, Genoa 9 May 1603; fol.25, 12 May.

69. There were also concerns about Gaeta, AGS, Est.leg.1102 fols.118, 119 Benavente to Philip III, Naples 3 June 1605 and ibid. fol.248, 22 December 1605.

70. Avelino Sotelo Álvarez ed., *Diarios de Francesco Zazzera (1616–1620) sobre el megalómano, arbitrario, populista y voyeur virrey de Nápoles, duque de Osuna*, Àristos: Torrevieja 2002, pp.194–96.

71. Williams, *Great Favourite*, pp.218–21, 227.

72. Espinosa, 'Grand Strategy', pp.267–68; for the very limited resources available to the crown in Valencia and Catalonia to combat the threat, Pardo Molero, *La defensa del imperio*, pp.251–58.

73. CODOIN, xxx, pp.310–11.

74. CODOIN, iii, pp.111–13.

75. Serrano, *Liga de Lepanto*, i, p.347.

76. For Doria's understanding of the system in 1570, Vargas-Hidalgo, *Correspondencia*, pp.630–31.

77. Doria was to receive certification of his new title of 'Captain General of the Mediterranean Sea', Vargas-Hidalgo, *Correspondencia*, pp.1112–13.

78. One hundred and seven galleys sailed under Don John of Austria in 1573, Braudel, *Mediterranean*, ii, p.1132.

79. Three galleys of Malta, armed four-by-four, had the crews of five regular ships, CODOIN, xxix, pp.207, 251.

80. Vargas-Hidalgo, *Correspondencia*, p.364.

81. See his letter of 27 July, CODOIN, xxix, pp.311–12.

82. CODOIN, xxix, p.450.

83. The king's words on 18 June, CODOIN, xxix, p.228.

84. CODOIN, xxix, p.471.

85. Vargas-Hidalgo, *Correspondencia*, p.684.

86. Vargas-Hidalgo, *Correspondencia*, pp.700–01.

87. AGS, Est.leg.1428 fol.82 Doria to King, Genoa 25 May 1596.

88. AGS, Est.leg.1100 fol.42 Instruction given to Marquis of Santa Cruz by Benavente, 1 May 1604.

89. AGS, Est.leg.1100 fol.180 Benavente to King, Naples 18 December 1604.

90. AGS, Est.leg.457 sf CCE Valladolid April 1605.

91. AGS, Est.leg.457 sf Villalonga to Lerma, Valladolid 14 April 1605.

92. AGS, Est.leg.1433 fol.84 Doria to King, Genoa 27 May 1605.

93. AGS, Est.leg.1433 fol.87 Doria to King, Genoa 6 June 1605.

94. AGS, Est.leg.457 sf CCE 'sobre lo que el conde de Benavente escrive en carta de 7 de julio [1605] ...' Valladolid, August 1605.

95. See his letter of 2 June, CODOIN, xxix, p.174.

96. Serrano, Liga de Lepanto, i, p.107 n.4.

97. Vargas-Hidalgo, Correspondencia, pp.693–98 especially 697.

98. Espinosa, 'Grand Strategy', p.268; Hernando Sánchez, Castilla y Nápoles en el siglo XVI, pp.276–77.

99. García Hernán, Armada española, p.73.

100. AGS, Est.leg.1105 fol 28 Benavente to King, Naples 30 April 1608; fol.29 'Copia de Carta del Archiduque Maximiliano escrita al Conde de Benavente', Graz 17 April 1608; fol.30 original in Italian; fol.31 Philip III to Benavente, Madrid 14 April 1606.

101. Cited by Felix Gilbert, Machiavelli and Guicciardini. Politics and History in Sixteenth Century Florence, Princeton University Press: Princeton 1965, p.33.

102. CODOIN, xxviii, pp.569–71; Braudel, Mediterranean, ii, p.1000; Thompson, War and Government, p.13.

103. Braudel, Mediterranean, ii, p.885.

104. Lucien Febvre, The Problem of Unbelief in the Sixteenth Century. The Religion of Rabelais, translated by Beatrice Gottlieb, HUP: Cambridge Massachusetts and London 1982.

105. For Don John's suspicions in August 1571, Serrano, Correspondencia, iv, p.422. For Colonna's stringent criticism of Doria, Poumarède, Pour en finir, pp.241–42; however, in 1573 he blamed the Venetians for the failure of the Holy League, Setton, Papacy, iv, p.1084.

106. Fernández Álvarez, Carlos V, p.616.

107. CODOIN, xxix, p.246.

108. Cabera de Córdoba, Felipe II, ii, p.588.

109. As was the case with his instructions of 18 June 1565, CODOIN, xxix, pp.220–25.

110. Toledo in 1565, CODOIN, xxix, pp.26, 39; Doria on the unfavourable winds of 1573, Vargas-Hidalgo, Correspondencia, pp.956–57; for the

difficult conditions in 1596, AGS, Est.leg.1428 fol.84 Doria to Philip II, Genoa 8 June 1596; Est.leg.1428 fol.99 Doria to Philip II, Rizol (?) 14 July 1596.

111. López de Gómara, *Guerras de mar*, p.171.

112. Capelloni, *Vita del principe Andrea Doria*, pp.67–68.

113. AGS, Est.leg.1121 fol.99 de Vega to Emperor, Palermo 12 February 1553.

114. Cabrera de Córdoba, *Felipe II*, i, p.508.

115. On the unhealthy autumn weather in Apulia and Brundisium, Caesar, *Civil War*, pp.106–07.

116. AGS, Est.leg.1433 fol.59 (60 duplicated) Doria to King 11 February 1605; Philip II used almost identical terms when giving orders to Santa Cruz in 1587, Parker, *Grand Strategy*, p.263.

117. AGS, Est.leg.1026 fol.69 Toledo to King, Naples/Melfi 4 August 1537.

118. See the numerous letters to this effect in AGS, Est.leg.1026 fols.4, 13, 34 etc.

119. AGS, Est.leg.1026 fol.65 Toledo to King, La Cidonia 1 August 1537.

120. AGS, Est.leg.1026 fol.116 'Copia de la carta que el virrey de Nápoles escribió al marqués de Aguilar a 15 de noviembre de 1537'.

121. See his letter of 12 August 1572, CODOIN, iii, pp.93–97, especially 95–96.

122. Cassola, *1565 Ottoman Malta Campaign Register*, pp.347–49.

123. CODOIN, xxix, p.483.

124. CODOIN, xxx, p.261.

125. CODOIN, xxix, pp.159–61, especially 160.

126. CODOIN, iii, pp.26–27.

127. Vargas-Hidalgo, *Correspondencia*, p.1458.

128. García Hernán, *Armada española*, pp.72–73.

129. This was a hereditary illness, Girón, *Crónica del Emperador Carlos V*, pp.12–13.

130. Vargas-Hidalgo, *Correspondencia*, p.363.

131. Vargas-Hidalgo, *Correspondencia*, p.250.

132. Vargas-Hidalgo, *Correspondencia*, pp.262–63; Braudel, *Mediterranean*, ii, pp.975–79.

133. AGS, Est.leg.1498 fol.10 Prince Philip to Francisco de Vargas, Corunna 6 July 1554.

134. CODOIN, xxix, p.332.

135. AGS, Est.leg.1128 fol.135 King to Viceroy of Sicily, 20 September 1564.

136. Vargas-Hidalgo, *Correspondencia*, p.692.

137. '… *si pecados nuestros o mala fortuna no nos la hubieran desviado por tan extraños caminos.*' Serrano, *Liga de Lepanto*, ii, p.381.

138. CODOIN, xxviii, pp.196–98.

139. Serrano, *Liga de Lepanto*, ii, p.290.

140. Serrano, *Correspondencia*, iv, pp.9–10; see also Setton, *Papacy*, iv, pp.963–64.

141. AGS, Est.leg.1098 fol.117 Francisco de Castro to Philip III, Naples 20 August 1602.

142. AGS, Est.leg.1105 fol.41 Benavente to Philip III, Naples 3 July 1608.

143. Galleys carrying money to Italy in the early summer of 1592 would have a clear voyage 'with the help of God', as Philip II put it. AGS, Est.leg.456 sf Philip II to Don Juan Puerto Carrero, Segovia 8 June 1592.

144. AGS, Est.leg.1159 fol.246 Maqueda to Philip III, Palermo 6 August 1601.

145. AGS, Est.leg.1162 fol.43 Duke of Feria to Philip III, Palermo 13 April 1606.

146. AGS, Est.leg.1102 fol.130 Carlo Doria to Philip III, Naples 28 June 1605.

147. See above, chapter II.

148. Elena Fasano Guarini, ' "Rome, workshop of all the practices of the world": from the letters of Cardinal Ferdinando de'Medici to Cosimo I and Francesco I', in Signorotto and Visceglia eds, *Court and Politics*, pp.53–77, p.69.

149. Serrano, *Correspondencia*, ii, p.52 *ff.*

150. Febvre, *Problem of Unbelief*, p.151.

151. For examples regarding the possible loss of Malta, CODOIN, xxix, pp.309–13.

152. R.W. Southern, *Western Views of Islam in the Middle Ages*, HUP: Cambridge Massachusetts 1962, *passim* and especially p.109; for a specific example, Housley, *Crusading and the Ottoman Threat*, pp.20–22.

Chapter IX

1. '*Correr el campo como a señores del mar*', AGS, Est.leg.456 sf Doria to Philip II, Genoa 18 June 1589; '*podrán correr el mar a su salvo*', Est.leg.1428 fol.54 Doria to King, Loano 9 March 1596; GA leg.492 fol.49 Feria to King, Barcelona 6 December 1597.

2. Bacon, *Essays*, pp.77–78.

3. Caesar, *Civil War*, pp.125–35, 163.

4. Laiglesia, *Estudios históricos*, i, p.136.

5. The shortages were exacerbated by the remorseless heat and terrible conditions, which killed many of the Emperor's German troops, Capelloni, *Vita del principe Andrea Doria*, pp.67–68.

6. CODOIN, xxix, p.402.

7. Pryor, *Geography, Technology and War*, pp.6–7, 16–20.

8. Pryor, *Geography, Technology and War*, pp.20–24, 38–39, 92.

9. Pryor, *Geography, Technology and War*, especially pp.14–15, 95.

10. Pryor, *Geography, Technology and War*, chapters I and III.

11. Pacini, '"Poiché gli stati non..."', pp.447–53.

12. '...*y digo en este arte que tracto de la mar hay muy pocos que lo sepan hacer* ...' AGS, Est.leg.1130, fol.24 Toledo to King, Catania 16 February 1566.

13. Braudel, *Mediterranean*, ii, pp.952–53 and especially n.260; Vargas-Hidalgo, *Correspondencia*, pp.268–69; for Toledo's comments, CODOIN, xxx, p.403.

14. Luis Ribot, *La Monarquía de España y la Guerra de Mesina (1674–1678)*, Actas: Madrid 2002 pp.51–115, 209–16, 417–21.

15. On collaboration between the *presidio* troops and the 'Moors of Peace', Alonso Acero, 'El norte de África', pp.405–06; Alonso Acero, *Orán-Mazalquivir*, chpt.III; Alonso Acero, 'Trenes de avituallamiento'.

16. Cited by Braudel, *Mediterranean*, i, p.257.

17. Note that the governments of both Aragon and Catalonia proposed to arm separate squadrons, Pardo Molero, *La defensa del imperio*, pp.408–09.

18. G. Rowlands, 'The King's Two Arms: French Amphibious Warfare in the Mediterranean under Louis XIV, 1664–1697', in D.J.B. Trim and M.C. Fissel eds, *Amphibious Warfare 1000–1700. Commerce, State Formation and European Expansion*. Brill: Leidon & Boston 2006, pp.263–314, pp.272–73, 287.

19. Ricardo Franch, *Crecimiento comercial y enriquecimiento burgués en la Valencia del siglo XVIII*, Institució Alfons el Magnànim: Valencia 1986, pp.14–17.

20. Braudel, *Mediterranean*, i, p.253, ii, p.995.

21. Setton, *Papacy*, iv, p.855.

22. AGS, Est.leg.1111, f.100 'Nuevas de Barbarossa que embia Andrea Doria 12 de enero 1535'.

23. AGS, Est.leg.1141 fol.42 Reports from Tripoli provided by don Sciptio Ansalone, 26 March 1574.

24. AGS, Est.leg.1945 sf 'Relación de lo que contienen las cartas...' 18 November to 12 March 1618–19 (?).

25. Serrano, *Correspondencia*, ii, pp.185–86.

26. Braudel, *Mediterranean*, i, p.251.

27. Isom-Verhaaren, *Allies with the Infidel*, p.133.
28. See the numerous references to the dangers of navigation along the coastline of Italy in Abulafia, 'Introduction', Clough, 'Romagna Campaign' and Pacini, ' "Poiché . . ." '
29. See his letter of 22 October 1573, Vargas-Hidalgo, *Correspondencia*, p.956.
30. With response on reverse, AGS, Est.leg.1158 fol.7 Maqueda to King, Messina 7 December 1598.
31. CODOIN, xxx, pp.271–72, 383.
32. 'No teniendo por acá donde poder abrigarse en caso de un temporal', AGS, Est.leg.1158 fol.180 Maqueda to King, Messina 19 September 1598.
33. CODOIN, xxix, pp.249–50.
34. See his paper of 25 March 1566, CODOIN, xxx, p.199.
35. AGS, Est.leg.1428 fol.101 Doria to King, Messina 21 September; fol.113 Doria to King, Genoa 20 October 1596 with fol.114 copy of letter from Olivares to Doria, 29 September 1596.
36. CODOIN, xxix, pp.25–26.
37. Cabrera de Córdoba, *Felipe II*, i, pp.265, 267.
38. Braudel, *Mediterranean*, ii, p.400.
39. CODOIN, xxviii, pp.569–70.
40. García Hernán, 'La conquista y la pérdida', p.50.
41. Alonso Acero, *Orán-Mazalquivir*, pp.14–15.
42. Braudel, 'Los Españoles y África del norte', pp.79–80; Alonso Acero, 'Trenes de avituallamiento', pp.746–47.
43. Fernández Álvarez, *Carlos V*, p.580.
44. AGS Est.leg.1126 fol.5 'Relación de Cintio Calvo Milanés, uno de los criados del duque de Medinaceli que se perdio en los Gelves' 27 February 1561.
45. Bunes Ibarra, *La Imagen*, pp.25–26.
46. AGS Est.leg.1132 f.186 King to Marquis of Pescara, Madrid 12 July 1569.
47. A plot had been prepared for the seizure of the city, AGS, Est.leg.1132 fol.48 'Relacion de lo que don Pedro Velázquez dijo al gran maestre sobre el particular de Tripoli . . . Palermo a x de enero de 1568'.
48. AGS, Est.leg.1132 fol.72 Comendador Mayor de Castilla to King, Puerto de Santa María 24 June 1568.
49. On the impressive fortifications at Mahdia or África, 'the most formidable of the kingdom of Tunis', Sánchez-Gijón, 'Presidios del reino de Túnez', pp.631, 648; on the occupation of Africa during 1550–54, Alonso Acero, 'El norte de África', pp.394–99; Setton, *Papacy*, iii, pp.533–34; Braudel, *Mediterranean*, ii, pp.909–11.

50. AGS, Est.leg.1120 fol.59 Juan de Vega to King, Messina 18 June 1551.
51. Sánchez-Gijón, 'Presidios del reino de Túnez', pp.642–45; Braudel, *Mediterranean*, ii, pp.933–34.
52. Sánchez-Gijón, 'Presidios del reino de Túnez', p.626, 635–36, 648.
53. López de Gómara, *Guerras de mar*, p.190.
54. Setton, *Papacy*, iv, p.1028.
55. Yérasimos, 'Les relations franco-ottomanes', p.539 .
56. AGS, GA leg.425 fol.25 Diego de Heredia to King, Cuitadela 3 May 1595.
57. See Álvaro de Sande's letter to the Duke of Medinaceli, 11 July 1560, Vargas-Hidalgo, *Correspondencia*, pp.348–49.
58. Charles Monchicourt, 'L'Expédition espagnole de 1560 contre l'île de Djerba' in *Revue Tunisienne*, XX (Tunis, 1913) (also printed Ernest Leroux: Paris 1913), chpt. IV; Setton, *Papacy*, iv, pp.759–65 especially 761.
59. See Doria's assessment in 1563, Vargas-Hidalgo, *Correspondencia*, p.405.
60. CODOIN, xxix, p.490.
61. CODOIN, iii, pp.160–67.
62. Sánchez-Gijón, 'Presidios del reino de Túnez', p.628.
63. CODOIN, iii, pp.138–39, 157–58; on water shortages in the forts, García Hernán, 'La conquista y la pérdida', pp.64, 68, 70, 79, 81.
64. AGS, Est.leg.1058 fol.109 'El parecer que dio el Marqués de Santa Cruz sobre la ida de las armadas a Chipre', 16 September 1570.
65. Guglielmotti, *Marcantonio Colonna alla Battaglia di Lepanto*, pp.77–78; Setton, *Papacy*, iv, p.972.
66. AGS, Est.leg.1327 fol.143 Reports from Cyprus 24 February 1570. Efforts to fortify Famagusta can be traced back to at least the beginning of the century, Setton, *Papacy*, iii, p.45.
67. Serrano, *Correspondencia*, iv, pp.410–11.
68. CODOIN, iii, p.303.
69. Setton, *Papacy*, iv, pp.848, 939–40, 941–43, 1028–37, 1070.
70. Setton, *Papacy*, iv, p.908.
71. Setton, *Papacy*, iv, p.986.
72. Luciano Pezzolo, 'Stato, guerra e finanza nella Repubblica di Venezia fra medioevo e prima età moderna', in Cancila ed., *Mediterraneo in armi*, i, pp.67–112, p.110.
73. Guglielmotti, *Marcantonio Colonna alla Battaglia di Lepanto*, pp.58–59.
74. López de Gómara, *Guerras de mar*, p.143.
75. López de Gómara, *Guerras de mar*, pp.193–97.
76. Braudel, *Mediterranean*, ii, pp.1122–23; Vargas-Hidalgo, *Correspondencia*, p.827.

77. Setton, *Papacy*, iv, pp.1081–82.

78. Angiolini, '*I Presidios di Toscana*: cadena de oror e llave freno de Italia', *passim*.

79. Braudel, *Mediterranean*, i, pp.358–79; see also Pryor, *Geography, technology and war*, pp.71–75.

80. Casson, *Ships and Seamanship in the Ancient World*, p.297–99; Pryor, *Geography, Technology and War*, p.19–20.

81. He headed back to the capital in November, Bostan, 'The Province of *Cezayir-i Bahr-i Sefid*', p.246; another source speaks of his having departed by 28 March, Setton, *Papacy*, iii, p.395 n.4.

82. AGS, Est.leg.1026 fol.13 Toledo to King, Naples 25 March 1537.

83. AGS, Est.leg.1026 fol.27 'Lo que se entiende de Levante por diversas vias.' May–June 1537.

84. Veinstein, 'Les préparatifs', pp.38–39, 53.

85. CODOIN, xxix, pp.6, 8–9, 363; for similar instructions in 1566, Setton, *Papacy*, iv, pp.879–80.

86. AGS, Est.leg.1026 fol.65 Viceroy of Naples to King, 'de la Cidonia' 1 August 1537; see also fols.61 (last day of July), 69 (4 August), 76 (1, 4 and 9 August).

87. Isom-Verhaaren, *Allies with the Infidel*, pp.124–26, 186.

88. AGS, Est.leg.1120 fol.251 'Lo que refiere Antonio Serrano ... a xi de junio [1552] es lo siguiente'.

89. Vargas-Hidalgo, *Correspondencia*, pp.193, 201–02; Braudel, *Mediterranean*, ii, pp.944–45; Pierre Antonetti, *Sampiero. Soldat du Roi et rebelle corse 1498–1567*, France Empire: Paris 1987, pp.110–13.

90. Pryor, *Geography, Technology and War*, pp.20, 93.

91. AGS, Est.leg.1421 fol.88 'Relación de cuatro cartas...' August and September 1589; on Hasan Pasha's purpose in 1589 see Hess, *Forgotten Frontier*, p.113.

92. AGS, Est.leg.214 sf 'Copia de los avisos ... de Mallorca desde Menorca'.

93. Cassola, *1565 Ottoman Malta Campaign Register*, p.114.

94. See his letter of 19 June 1560, Vargas-Hidalgo, *Correspondencia*, p.340.

95. CODOIN, xxx, pp.246–50.

96. García Hernán and García Hernán, *Lepanto*, pp.121–22.

97. Imber, *Ottoman Empire*, p.290.

98. The Real Club Náutico de Palma organises a competition in mid-April; see www.palmavela.es.

99. Capelloni, *Vita del principe Andrea Doria*, pp.57–59.

100. Fernández Álvarez, *Carlos V*, p.502; López de Gómara, *Guerras de mar*, p.162.

101. The emperor sailed from Barcelona on 30 May and reached Cagliari on 12 June, Setton, *Papacy*, iii, pp.395–96; on the expedition, Alfredo Alvar Ezquerra, 'Los mediterráneos de Carlos V y la empresa de Túnez' in Ezquerra and Ruiz Rodríguez eds, *Túnez, 1535*, pp.185–235.

102. Guilmartin, *Gunpowder and Galleys*, p.66.

103. Fernández Álvarez, *Carlos V*, p.614–16; García García, *Pax Hispanica*, pp.77–78.

104. Cabrera de Córdoba, *Felipe II*, ii, p.587.

105. Girón, *Crónica del Emperador Carlos V*, pp.120–21.

106. Capelloni, *Vita del principe Andrea Doria*, p.158; Setton, *Papacy*, iv, pp.583–84.

107. AGS, Est.leg.1095 fol.243, Olivares to Maqueda, Naples 13 August 1598.

108. AGS, Est.leg.1127 fol.180 Viceroy of Sicily to King, Messina 25 September 1563.

109. Williams, 'Sound and the Fury', pp.585–87.

110. Frederic C. Lane, 'Rhythm and Rapidity of Turnover in Venetian Trade of the Fifteenth Century', in *Collected Papers of Frederic C. Lane*, p.110.

111. Pryor, *Geography, Technology and War*, pp.318; Brummett, *Ottoman Seapower*, p.129.

112. Braudel, *Mediterranean*, ii, p.878; Poumarède, *Pour en finir*, chapter VII; Mallia-Milanes, *Venice and Hospitaller Malta*, chapter VI; on convoys after 1645, Panzac, 'Affrontement maritime et mutations technologiques', pp.126–27.

Chapter X

1. The argument is set out throughout the second volume of his work, but see especially, *Mediterranean*, ii, pp.1139–42, 1184–85.

2. CODOIN, xxx, pp.310–11.

3. I.A.A. Thompson, 'The Invincible Armada', reprinted in *War and Society*, pp.1–2.

4. Casado Soto, *Los barcos españoles del siglo XVI*, *passim*. The details of Medina Sidonia's offers on 9, 10 and 11 August are found on p.240.

5. On the Gravelines, Casado Soto, *Barcos*, pp.237–40, 256.

6. Casado Soto, *Barcos*, pp.253–57. See also José Luis Casado Soto, 'Flota Atlántica y tecnología naval hispana en tiempos de Felipe II', in Ribot García and Belenguer Cebriá eds, *Las sociedades ibéricas y el mar*, ii (*La*

monarquía. Recursos, organización y estrategias), pp.339–63; José Luis Casado Soto, 'Entre el Mediterráneo y el Atlántico: los barcos de los Austrias', in García Hernán and Maffi eds, *Guerra y sociedad*, i, pp.861–89.

7. AGS, Est.leg.1127 fol.115 King to Medinaceli, Madrid 14 June 1562.

8. AGS, Est.leg.1127 fol.208 King to Medinaceli, Escorial 8 March 1563.

9. Valentina Favarò, 'La escuadra de galeras del Regno di Sicilia: costruzione, armamento, amministrazione', in Cancila ed., *Mediterraneo in armi*, pp.289–313, pp.312–13; for Naples Caracciolo, *Uffici, difesa e corpi rappresentativi*, pp.141–46, Calabria, *Cost of Empire*, p.88 n.16; there were 20 galleys in Spain in 1598, 7 in 1604 and 12 in 1621, Thompson, *War and Government*, pp.179–84; Philip III had six well equipped galleys in Genoa in 1610, with the Republic manning eight, the Hospitallers five and Order of St Stephen five and France ten or 11, although these were inferior to the warships of His Catholic Majesty, AGS, Est.leg.1435 fol.21 Rodrigo de Mendoza to King, Genoa 18 June 1610, see also n.59 on p.277.

10. Fernández Álvarez, *Carlos V*, pp.501–02; Guilmartin, *Gunpowder and Galleys*, p.114; Setton, *Papacy*, iii, pp.396–97.

11. Capelloni, *Vita del principe Andrea Doria*, p.57.

12. Capelloni, *Vita del principe Andrea Doria*, pp.84, 86.

13. Also cited in Chapter II above, Vargas-Hidalgo, *Correspondencia*, p.193.

14. Vargas-Hidalgo, *Correspondencia*, p.692.

15. With three galleys in Savoy. AGS, Est.leg.456 sf 'Relación de las galeras de la armada de su majestad en Italia y de los potentados'. Undated, around 1589.

16. Although only a dozen were serving, AGS Est.leg.1422 fol.133 'Relación del numero de las galeras de la escuadra de Genoa y del estado dellas'.

17. CODOIN, xxix, p.301.

18. CODOIN, xxx, pp.310–11.

19. Naples 32; Sicily 14; Spain 12; Doria 12; Order of St John three; contractors 12; García Hernán and García Hernán, *Lepanto. El día después*, pp.120–21.

20. Braudel, *Mediterranean*, ii, p.1132.

21. These were: Naples 25, Sicily 15; the Pope three; the Religion four; Spain seven without the flagship or *patrona*; Vargas-Hidalgo, *Correspondencia*, p.986.

22. Ribot, 'Provincias Italianas', pp.80–81.

23. AGS, Est.leg.1058 fol.13 Santa Cruz to King, Naples 14 January 1570; there had been 13 galleys in Naples in 1568, with just over 2,130 slaves and *forzati* (163 per galley); in 1575, when 50 galleys were being paid for, only

40 were available; that there were 4,252 slaves and criminal oarsmen (106 for each of the 40 galleys), Mafrici, *Mezzogiorno e pirateria*, p.197.

24. AGS, Est.leg.1108 fol.75 Prince Filiberto to Philip III, Naples 21 August 1614; note also Osuna's claim to have equipped 20 *galeras reforzadas*, Sotelo Álvarez, *'Diarios' de Francesco Zazzera*, p.196.

25. AGS, Est.leg.1134 fol.16 'Relación de los officiales, gentilshombres, marineros...' 16 July 1571.

26. CODOIN, xxx, pp.424–25.

27. AGS, Est.leg.900 fol.147 'Por cartas de Don Luys de Torres al Com [endador] Mayor de Castilla de Roma' 2 November 1565.

28. AGS, Est.leg.1130 fol.84 Doria to Francisco de Eraso (the king's secretary), Messina 14 July 1566.

29. Panzac, *La marine ottomane*, pp.69–73; Fodor, 'Organisation of Defence ...', pp.87–94, especially 93; Themopoulou, 'Les kürekçi...', pp.174–75.

30. Braudel, *Mediterranean*, ii, pp.1189–90.

31. AGS, Est.leg.1094 fol.108 Miranda to King, Naples 18 September 1594; Est.leg.1158 fol.23 'Relación que embia el Marques de Hierache ...' 21 September 1594.

32. AGS, Est.leg.1094 fol.251 Count of Olivares to Francisco de Idiáquez, Naples 3 September 1596; '...mal armadas de gente de remo y medianamente de gente de pelea...', Est.leg.1158 fol.99 'Relación que hace una persona ...'.

33. AGS, Est.leg.1094 fol.247 Olivares to King, Naples 6 August 1596.

34. Braudel, *Mediterranean*, ii, pp.1187–88, 1231–32; AGS, Est.leg.1158 fol.182, Maqueda to King, Messina 28 September 1598.

35. AGS, Est.leg.1158 fol.130 Prince of Hierace to Philip II, Messina 18 April.

36. AGS, Est. leg.1099 fol.98 Benavente to King, Naples 9 September 1603.

37. AGS, Est.leg.1162 fol.53 Feria to King, Palermo 26 April 1606; Est. leg.1162 fol.87, Feria to Philip III, Palermo 17 August 1606; Est.leg.1103 fol.175 Benavente to Philip III, Naples 15 September 1606.

38. AGS, Est.leg.1103 fol.190 Benavente to King, Naples 5 October 1606.

39. AGS, Est.leg.1433 fol.194, Don Juan Vivas to King, Genoa 13 October 1606.

40. AGS, Est.leg.1162 fol.209 Escalona to King, Messina 20 August 1607.

41. AGS, Est.leg.1428 fol.71 Doria to King, Loano 19 April 1596; fol.97 Pegli 1 July; fol.101 Messina 21 September 1596.

42. AGS, Est.leg.1102 fol.260 Santa Cruz to Philip II, Naples 22 December 1605.

43. AGS, Est.leg.1103 fol.194 Benavente to Philip III, Naples 5 October 1606; Anderson, *Naval Wars in the Levant*, pp.70–71.
44. AGS, Est.leg.1106 fol.64 Lemos to Philip III, Naples 4 September 1610.
45. De Groot, 'Ottoman Threat to Europe', pp.220–21.
46. AGS, Est.leg.1108 fol.77 Lemos to King, Naples 26 August 1614.
47. AGS, Est.leg.1930 fol.119 Reports 25 May 1618.
48. AGS, Est.leg.1930 fol.202 Reports 6 July 1618.
49. Mafrici, *Mezzogiorno e pirateria*, p.65; de Groot, 'Ottoman Threat to Europe', p.224.
50. Cummins, *Francis Drake*, pp.45, 55, 60.
51. Cummins, *Francis Drake*, pp.96–67, 101.
52. Cabrera de Córdoba, *Felipe II*, iv, p.1134.
53. On his entrance at Santo Domingo, Cabrera de Córdoba, *Felipe II*, iv, p.1136; for additional details Cummins, *Francis Drake*, pp.148–49, 154–56; R.B. Wernham, 'Amphibious Operations and the Elizabethan Assault on Spain's Atlantic Economy 1585–1598', in Trim and Fissel eds, *Amphibious Warfare*, pp.181–215, pp.183–87.
54. Parker, *Grand Strategy*, pp.175–76.
55. At this point *el corsario* was also experiencing serious problems with contrary winds and a shortage of water, Cummins, *Francis Drake*, pp.156–57; on Indies forts, Mira Caballos, 'Defensa', pp.159–81.
56. Fury, *Tides in the Affairs of Men*, p.161.
57. Cummins, *Francis Drake*, pp.135–36.
58. Cummins, *Francis Drake*, pp.242.
59. Cummins, *Francis Drake*, pp.251, 253.
60. Williams, *Philip II*, p.187–89; Wernham, 'Assault on Spain's Atlantic Economy', pp.200–01.
61. Wernham, 'Assault on Spain's Atlantic Economy', p.203; Wernham, *Return of the Armadas*, pp.126–28.
62. Rodger, *Safeguard of the Sea*, pp.282–86.
63. When the English commanders assessed the possibility of holding Cadiz they envisaged that they would have to send munitions and artillery ashore, Wernham, *Return of the Armadas*, pp.102–04, 107–08.
64. AGS, Est.leg.1428 fol.100 Doria to Philip II, Messina 13 August 1596.
65. J.H. Elliott, *The Old World and the New*, CUP: Cambridge 1972, pp.90–91.
66. Fury, *Tides in the Affairs of Men*, pp.27–32.
67. Fury, *Tides in the Affairs of Men*, pp.158–85 especially 176–77, 182.
68. Manuel Gracia Rivas, 'La Jornada de Don Juan de Águila de 1591 y sus aspectos sanitarios', in Enrique García Hernán, Miguel Ángel de Bunes,

Óscar Recio Morales and Bernardo J. García García eds, *Irlanda y la Monarquía Hispánica: Kinsale 1601. Guerra, política, exilio y religión*, CSIC and University of Alcalá: Madrid 2002, pp.153–72, 159, 170–72.

69. Charles Carlton, *Charles I. The Personal Monarch*, second edition, Routledge: London and New York 1995, pp.72–76. On the expeditions of the 1620s, Rodger, *Safeguard of the Sea*, pp.357–63, 399–403.

70. Carlton, *Charles I*, pp.91–92, 95, 103.

71. Of the 8,000 men Buckingham had taken to the Île de Ré of La Rochelle only 3,000 returned, and of these 1,600 were too sick or wounded to walk and had to be carried from their ships, Carlton, *Charles I*, pp.90–95; Rodger, *Safeguard of the Sea*, p.363.

72. Rodger, *Safeguard of the Sea*, pp.362–63, 376, 384.

73. G.M. Thompson, *Sir Francis Drake*, Seeker and Warburg: London 1972 pp.188–89.

74. MacCaffrey, *Elizabeth I*, p.247; Fury, *Tides in the Affairs of Men*, p.171.

75. Steve Pincus, *1688. The First Modern Revolution*, Yale University Press: New Haven and London 2009; Wernham, 'Assault on Spain's Atlantic Economy', pp.181–82, 212–13.

76. Guilmartin, *Gunpowder and Galleys*, pp.111–36.

Chapter XI

1. Enrique Otero Lana, *Los corsarios españoles durante la decadencia de los Austrias. El corso español del Atlántico peninsular en el siglo XVII (1621–1697)*, Ministerio de Defensa: Madrid 1992, especially pp.333–40, 343–54.

2. Bracewell, *Uskoks*, chapter IV.

3. M. García Arenal and M.A. de Bunes Ibarra, *Los españoles y el norte de África, siglos XV–XVIII*, Mapfre: Madrid 1992, p.28; Alonso Acero, *Orán*, chapter IV especially pp.388–98.

4. The decline of Algerian privateering is analysed with reference to improvements in economic and agricultural conditions in Merouche, *Recherches sur l'Algérie*, ii, part III ('Une course déclinante (1700–1830)').

5. Vatin, 'L'Empire ottoman . . .', pp.372–73.

6. Belhamissi, *Marine et marins d'Alger*, i, p.57–61.

7. Faroqhi, *Ottoman Empire and World Around It*, p.3.

8. R. Cancila, 'Il Mediterraneo, storia di una complessità', in *Mediterranea: ricerche storiche*, XIII (August 2008), pp.243–54; Gigliola Pagano di Divitiis, *English Merchants in Seventeenth-Century Italy*, CUP: Cambridge 1998; Francesca Trivellato, *The Familiarity of Strangers. The Sephardic Diaspora,*

Livorno, and Cross-Cultural Trade in the Early Modern Period, Yale: New Haven and London 2009; Brogini, *Malte, passim*; Mallia-Milanes, *Venice and Hospitaller Malta, passim*; see also the essays by Antony Luttrell and de Groot in Mallia-Milanes ed., *Hospitaller Malta*.

9. Quoted by Keith Thomas, *The Ends of Life. Roads to Fulfilment in Early Modern England*, OUP: Oxford and New York 2009, p.58; Poumarède, *Pour en finir*, part 3; on the manipulation of crusade for political purposes, Housley, *Crusading and the Ottoman Threat*, pp.212, 215.

10. Fontenay, 'Chevaliers...'; Bennassar and Bennassar, *Les chrétiens...*, *passim*.

11. Braudel, *Mediterranean*, i, p.19.

12. Robin Briggs, 'Noble conspiracy and revolt in France, 1610–60', *Seventeenth Century French Studies*, 1990, 12 (1), pp.158–76, p.159.

13. Yildirim, 'Battle of Lepanto', pp.548, 550.

14. Doria observed in 1573 that one of the attractions of Castilnuovo was that cavalry could not be employed in the surrounding countryside, Vargas-Hidalgo, *Correspondencia*, p.832.

15. AGS, Est.leg.1127 fol.37 'Avisos de Tripoli' April 1562.

16. AGS, Est.leg.1324 fol.186 Secretary García Hernández to King, Venice 13 November 1563.

17. AGS, Est.leg.1325 fol.59 Reports from Constantinople, 11 November 1564.

18. Cassola, *1565 Ottoman Malta Campaign Register*, p.86.

19. Jurien de la Gravière, *Chevaliers de Malte dans la marine de Philippe II*, ii, pp.145–55 and especially pp.147–49; for details on Hospitaller raids in the 1560s, Anderson, *Naval Wars in the Levant*, pp.17–18; Setton, *Papacy*, iv, p.843.

20. Cassola, *1565 Ottoman Malta Campaign Register*, pp.96–98, 102–04.

21. On the motivation for the attack upon Rhodes in 1522, A.C. Hess, 'The Evolution of the Ottoman Seaborne Empire in the Age of the Oceanic Discoveries', *1453–1525, American Historical Review*, LXXIV, No.7 (December 1970), pp.1892–1919, especially pp.1902, 1906, 1907–08, 1911–12, 1919; for a broader context, Goffman, *Ottoman Empire and Early Modern Europe*, pp.99–101.

22. For this and the following paragraph, Woodhead, 'Present Terrour of the World', pp.24, 27–28, 33; Kochu Bey advanced a similar case about the Ottoman caliphate in 1630, Lewis, *Istanbul*, p.42.

23. CODOIN, xxix, pp.25, 26, 38, 184–85; Setton, *Papacy*, iv, pp.890–91; on efforts to fortify the eastern seaboard, Soldini, 'Gobernante ingeniero',

pp.359–71; the medieval castle of Marchetti at Siracusa had been badly affected by an earthquake in 1542 and had to be completely destroyed and rebuilt again from 1578, Dufour, 'Reino de Sicilia', p.505, 511–12.

24. Reports from Constantinople, 10 February 1565, CODOIN, xxix, p.346.

25. See the numerous references in Cassola, *1565 Ottoman Malta Campaign Register*, pp.177, 179, 247, 249, 297 etc. On Islamic law and seaborne robbery, see Suraiya Faroqhi's paper in Zachariadou ed., *Kapudan Pasha*, and Maria Pia Pedani, 'Some Remarks on the Ottoman Geo-Political Vision of the Mediterranean in the Period of the Cyprus War (1570–1573)' in Imber, Kiyotaki and Murphey, *Frontiers of Ottoman Studies*, ii, pp.23–35; for a comparable attack upon Muslim pilgrims, Stern, *Company-State*, pp.134–35.

26. Setton, *Papacy*, iv, p.759; Braudel, *Mediterranean*, ii, pp.1008–12; Thompson, *War and Government*, p.17.

27. AGS, Est.leg.1168 fol.81 Osuna to King, Palermo 23 December 1614.

28. Mallia-Milanes, *Venice and Hospitaller Malta*, p.93.

29. M. Fontenay, 'Corsaires de la foi ou rentiers du sol? Les chevaliers de Malte dans le *corso* Méditerranéen au XVIIe siècle', in *Revue d'Histoire moderne et contemporaine*, XXXV (July–September, 1988), pp.361-84.

30. These patrols were contingent on there being no danger from the enemy fleet, AGS, Est.leg.1127 fol.207 King to Grand Master, no place (Madrid?) 8 March 1563.

31. AGS, Est.leg.1127 fol.164 Grand Master to King, Malta 6 June 1563.

32. AGS, Est.leg.1128 fols.127 and 128 King to Grand Master, Madrid 29 August 1564.

33. On Hospitaller actions see Bono, 'Naval Exploits and Privateering', pp.356–57, 360, 363–64, 367.

34. The Grand Master recalled the galleys in April 1560, Setton, *Papacy*, iv, p.761.

35. Mallia-Milanes, *Venice and Hospitaller Malta*, pp.105–07, 250.

36. CODOIN, xxx, pp.11–13.

37. 18 January, CODOIN, xxx, p.82.

38. For other examples, AGS, Est.leg.1159 fol.167 Philip III to Alof de Wignacourt, San Lorenzo 1 November 1600; CODOIN, xxix, pp.243–44; Poumarède, *Pour en finir*, pp.446–47, 455, 519.

39. Fernández Álvarez, *Carlos V*, p.496; Setton, *Papacy*, iv, p.859; CODOIN, xxx, p.288.

40. Setton, *Papacy*, iv, p.910.

41. Parker, *Grand Strategy*, pp.157–58

42. Serrano, *Correspondencia*, iii, pp.183–84.
43. Serrano, *Correspondencia*, iii, pp.188–89.
44. Serrano, *Liga de Lepanto*, i, p.58 n.2.
45. Dragonetti de Torres, *Lega di Lepanto*, p.46.
46. See his Memorial of 4 May 1570, Serrano, *Correspondencia*, iii, pp.324–25; letter of 24 April 1570 (Cordoba) detailing audience of 21 April, Dragonetti de Torres, *Lega di Lepanto*, pp.97–115 especially 103–04.
47. Dragonetti de Torres, *Lega di Lepanto*, pp.133–38.
48. Serrano, *Liga de Lepanto*, i, p.59 n.2; Serrano, *Correspondencia*, iii, pp.330–34.
49. Dragonetti de Torres, *Lega di Lepanto*, p.157.
50. Serrano, *Correspondencia*, iii, p.493–94.
51. Serrano, *Correspondencia*, iii, p.499.
52. García Hernán, *La acción diplomática*, pp.66–75, 182–89, 382–86; on fears in England in 1570, Rivero Rodríguez, *Lepanto*, pp.106–13.

Conclusion

1. Fasano Guarini, "'Rome, workshop of all the practices of the world...'", p.60.
2. García Hernán, *La acción diplomática*, pp.310–11, 401, 434, 438; Óscar Recio Morales, *España y la pérdida del Ulster. Irlanda en la estrategia política de la Monarquía Hispánica (1602–1649)*, Laberinto: Madrid 2003.

Select Bibliography

Printed Primary Sources

BON, Ottaviano, *The Sultan's Seraglio. An Intimate Portrait of Life at the Ottoman Court*, edited and with an introduction by Geoffrey Goodwin, Saqi Books: London 2000

CABRERA DE CÓRDOBA, Luis, *Historia de Felipe II, Rey de España*, 4 volumes, edited and with a preliminary study by José Martínez Millán and Carlos J. de Carlos Morales, *Felipe II (1527–1598). La configuración de la Monarquía Hispana*, JCL: Salamanca 1998

CAPELLONI, Lorenzo, *Vita del principe Andrea Doria...*, Gabriel Giolito: Ferrara 1569

CASSOLA, Arnold, *The 1565 Ottoman Malta Campaign Register*, PEG: Malta 1998

CODOIN, Colección de Documentos inéditos para la historia de España, 112 volumes, Madrid 1842–95

    Volume III, 'Correspondencia entre don García de Toledo y don Juan de Austria', compiled by don Martín Fernández Navarrete, don Miguel Salvá and don Pedro Sainz de Baranda, Imprenta de la Viuda de Calero: Madrid 1843

    Volume XXVIII, 'Correspondencia de Felipe II y de otras personas con don Juan de Austria desde 1568 y 1570', compiled by Marquis of Pidal and don Miguel Salvá, Imprenta de la Viuda de Calero: Madrid 1856

    Volume XXIX, 'Correspondencia de Felipe II con don García de Toledo y otros', compliled by Marquis of Pidal and don Miguel Salvá, Imprenta de la Viuda de Calero: Madrid 1856

Volume XXX, 'Continuación de la correspondencia de Felipe II con don García de Toledo y otros', compiled by Marquis of Pidal and don Miguel Salvá, Imprenta de la Viuda de Calero: Madrid 1857

CONTRERAS, Alonso de, *The Adventures of Captain Alonso de Contreras, a Seventeenth Century Diary*, translated by Philip Dallas, Paragon House: New York 1989

DAN, Pierre, *Histoire de Barbarie et de ses corsaires...*, second edition, Pierre Rocolet: Paris 1649

DIGBY, Sir Kenelm, *Journal of a Voyage into the Mediterranean 1628*, Publications of the Camden Society Vol.96, Westminster 1868

GIRÓN, Pedro, *Crónica del Emperador Carlos V*, CSIC: Madrid 1964

HÄEDO, Diego de, *Topografía e historia general de Argel* and *Epitome de los Reyes de Argel*, Valladolid 1612 (published in one volume, reprinted by Sociedad de bibliófilos españoles, Imprenta de Ramona Velasco: Madrid 1927)

LAIGLESIA, F. de, *Estudios históricos (1515–1555)*, 3 volumes, Imprenta Clásica Española: Madrid 1918

LÓPEZ DE GÓMARA, Francisco, *Guerras de mar del Emperador Carlos V*, edited by Miguel Ángel de Bunes Ibarra and N.E. Jiménez SECCFC: Madrid 2000

ORTALLI, Francesca Ortalli ed., *Lettere di Vicenzo Priuli Capitano delle Galee di Fiandra al Doge di Venezia, 1521–1523*, with appendices and index by Bianca Lanfranchi Strina, CPFRSV: Venice 2005

SERRANO, Luciano, *Correspondencia diplomática entre España y la Santa Sede durante el pontificado de S. Pío V*, 4 volumes, Instituto Pío IX: Madrid 1914

SOTELO ÁLVAREZ, Avelino, ed., *Diarios de Francesco Zazzera (1616–1620) sobre el megalómano, arbitrario, populista y voyeur virrey de Nápoles, duque de Osuna*, Àristos: Torrevieja 2002

VARGAS-HIDALGO, Rafael, *Guerra y Diplomacia en el Mediterráneo: Correspondencia inédita de Felipe II con Andrea Doria y Juan Andrea Doria*, Ediciones Polifemo: Madrid 2002

Studies

ABULAFIA, David, ed., *The French Descent into Renaissance Italy. Antecedents and Effects*. Variorum: Aldershot and Brookfield 1995

AKSAN, Virginia H. and GOFFMAN, Daniel, *The Early Modern Ottomans. Remapping the Empire*, CUP: Cambridge 2007

ALONSO ACERO, Beatriz, *Orán-Mazalquivir, 1589–1639. Una sociedad española en la frontera de Berbería*, CSIC: Madrid 2000

ALONSO ACERO, Beatriz, 'El norte de África en el ocaso del emperador (1549–1558)', in José Martínez Millán ed., *Carlos V y la quiebra del humanismo político en Europa (1530–1558)*, 4 vols, SECCFC: Madrid 2001, i, pp.387–414

ALONSO ACERO, Beatriz, *Cisneros y la conquista española del norte de África*, Ministerio de Defensa: Madrid 2006

ALONSO ACERO, Beatriz, 'Trenes de avituallamiento en las plazas españoles de Berbería', in García Hernán and Maffi eds, *Guerra y sociedad en la Monarquía Hispánica. Política, estrategia y cultura en la Europa moderna (1500–1700)*, 2 volumes, Laberinto, CSIC and Fundación Mapfre: Madrid 2006, i, pp.739–66

ÁLVAREZ-OSSORIO ALVARIÑO, A., and GARCÍA GARCÍA, Bernardo J., eds, *La Monarquía de las Naciones. Patria, nación y naturaleza en la Monarquía de España*, Fundación Carlos de Amberes: Madrid 2004

ANATRA, Bruno, and MANCONI, Francesco, eds, *Sardegna, Spagna e Stati italiani nell'età di Carlo V*, Carocci editore: Rome 2001

ANGIOLINI, Franco, *I cavalieri e il principe. L'Ordine di Santo Stefano e la società toscana in età moderna*, EDIFIR: Florence 1996

ANGIOLINI, Franco, 'I Presidios di Toscana: cadena de oro e llave freno de Italia', in García Hernán and Maffi eds, *Guerra y sociedad*, i, pp.171–88

ARDIT, Manuel ed., *Els moriscos i la seua expulsió*, in *Afers. Fulls de recerca i pensament*, vol.XXIV (62/63), Editorial Afers: Catarroja 2009

ASTARITA, Tommaso, *The Continuity of Feudal Power. The Caracciolo di Brienza in Spanish Naples*, CUP: Cambridge 1992

BACCAR-BOURNAZ, Alia and HADDAD-CHAMAKH, Fatma eds, *L'écho de la prise de Grenade dans la culture européenne aux XVIe et XVIIe siècles. Actes du Colloque de Tunis (18–21 novembre 1992)*, Cérès: Tunis 1994

BARKEY, Karen, *Empire of Difference. The Ottomans in Comparative Perspective*, CUP: Cambridge 2008

BELLOSO MARTÍN, Carlos, *La antemuralla de la monarquía. Los Tercios españoles en el reino de Sicilia en el siglo XVI*, Adalid-Ministerio de Defensa: Madrid 2010

BENNASSAR, Bartolomé and BENNASSAR, Lucile, *Les chrétiens d'Allah. L'histoire extraordinaire des renégats XVIe–XVIIIe siècles*, Perrin: Paris 1989

BONO, Salvatore, *I corsari barbareschi*, ERI: Turin 1964

BONO, Salvatore, *Corsari nel Mediterraneo. Cristiani e musulmani fra guerra, schiavitù e commercio*, A. Mondadori: Milan 1993

BONO, Salvatore, 'Schiavi Musulmani sulle Galere e nei Bagni d'Italia', in Rosalba Ragosta ed., *Le genti del mare mediterraneo*, 2 volumes, Lucio Pironti: Naples 1981, ii, pp.837–75

BORONAT Y BARRACHINA, Pascual, *Los moriscos españoles y su expulsión*, 2 volumes, reprinted with a preliminary study by Ricardo García Cárcel, Universidad de Granada: Granada 1992

BOSTAN, Idris, 'The Establishment of the Province of *Cezayir-i Bahr-i Sefid*', in Elizabeth Zachariadou ed., *The Kapudan Pasha, His Office and His Domain*, Crete University Press: Rethymnon 2002, pp.241–51

BRACEWELL, Catherine Wendy, *The Uskocks of Senj. Piracy, Banditry and the Holy War in the Sixteenth-Century Adriatic*, Cornell: Ithaca and London 1992

BRAUDEL, Fernand, *The Mediterranean and the Mediterranean World in the Age of Philip II*, 2 volumes, translated by Siân Reynolds, Collins: London 1973

BROGINI, Anne, *Malta, frontière de chrétienté*, École française de Rome: Rome 2006

BROGINI, Anne, and GHAZALI, María, 'Un enjeu espagnol en Méditerranée: les présides de Tripoli et de La Goulette au XVIᵉ siècle', *Cahiers de la Méditerranée*, 70 (2005) (available online: http://cdlm.revues.org/840? lang=en; accessed March 2010)

BRUMMETT, Palmira, *Ottoman Seapower and Levantine Diplomacy in the Age of Discovery*, State University of New York Press: New York 1994

BUNES IBARRA, Miguel Ángel de, *La imagen de los musulmanes y del norte de África en la España de los siglos XVI y XVII. Los caracteres de una hostilidad*, CSIC: Madrid 1989

BUNES IBARRA, Miguel Ángel de, *Los Barbarroja. Corsarios del Mediterráneo*, Alderabán: Madrid 2004

BUNES IBARRA, Miguel Ángel de, *Los moriscos en el pensamiento histórico. Historiografía de un grupo marginado*, Catedra: Madrid 1983

CALABRIA, Antonio, *The Cost of Empire. The Finances of the Kingdom of Naples in the Time of Spanish Rule*, CUP: Cambridge 1991

CANCILA, Rossella, 'Corsa e pirateria nella Sicilia della prima età moderna', in *Quaderni storici*, 'La schiavitù nel Mediterraneo', 107 XXXVI (August 2001), pp.363–78

CANCILA, Rossella, *Fisco Ricchezza Comunità nella Sicilia del Cinquecento*, ISI: Rome 2001

CANCILA, Rossella ed., *Mediterraneo in armi (secc.XV-XVIII)*, 2 volumes, Quaderni Mediterranea: Palermo 2007

CANCILA, Rossella, 'Il Mediterraneo, storia di una complessità', in *Mediterranea. Ricerche storiche*, No.13 (August 2008), pp.243–54

CANDIANI, Guido, 'Stratégie et diplomatie Vénitiennes: navires anglo-hollandais et blocus des Dardanelles, 1646–1659', *Revue d'histoire maritime. Histoire maritime. Outre-mer. Relations internationals*, IX (2008), pp.251–82

CANDIANI, Guido, 'Galee forzate o di libertà: una comparazione tra la marina veneziana e quella spagnola all'indomani della contesa dell'interdetto (1607)', in García Hernán and Maffi eds, *Guerra y sociedad*, i, pp.947–65

CARACCIOLO, Francesco, *Uffici, difesa e corpi rappresentativi nel Mezzogiorno in età spagnola*, Editori meridionali riuniti: Reggio Calabria 1974

CASADO SOTO, José Luis, *Los Barcos Españoles del siglo XVI y la Gran Armada de 1588*, Editorial San Martin: Madrid 1988

CASADO SOTO, José Luis, 'Flota Atlántica y tecnología naval hispana en tiempos de Felipe II', in Luis Ribot and Ernest Belenguer eds, *Las sociedades ibéricas y el mar a finales del siglo XVI*, 6 volumes, Sociedad Estatal Lisboa '98: Madrid 1998, ii (*La Monarquía. Recursos, organización y estrategias*) pp.339–63

CASADO SOTO, José Luis, 'Entre el Mediterráneo y el Atlántico: los barcos de los Austrias', in García Hernán and Maffi eds, *Guerra y sociedad*, i, pp.861–89

CASALE, Giancarlo, *The Ottoman Age of Exploration*, OUP: Oxford 2010

ÇIZAKÇA, Murat, 'Ottomans and the Mediterranean: an Analysis of the Ottoman Shipbuilding Industry as reflected by the Arsenal Registers of Istanbul 1520–1650', in Rosalba Ragosta ed., *Le genti del mare mediterraneo*, 2 volumes, Lucio Pironti: Naples 1981, ii, pp.773–87

CUMMINS, John, *Francis Drake*, Weidenfeld and Nicolson: London 1995

DE LA PEÑA, José F. and SOLA CASTAÑO, Emilio, *Cervantes y la Berbería. Cervantes, mundo turco-berberisco y servicios secretos en la época de Felipe II*, FCE: Madrid 1995

DRAGONETTI DE TORRES, A., *La Lega di Lepanto nel carteggio diplomatico inedito di don Luys de Torres nunzio straordinario di S. Pio V a Filippo II*, Fratelli Bocca Editori: Turin 1931

EARLE, Peter, *Corsairs of Malta and Barbary*, Sidgewick and Jackson: London 1970

EDELMAYER, Friedrich, 'La Lucha por el camino español. Felipe II y el marquesado de Finale Ligure', in Alberto Marcos Martín ed., *Hacer historia desde Simancas. Homenaje a José Luis Rodríguez de Diego*, JCL: Valladolid 2011, pp.293–304

EDELMAYER, Friedrich, 'Carlos V y Fernando I. La quiebra de la monarquía universal', in Martínez Millán ed., *Carlos V y la quiebra...*, i, pp.151–61

EDELMAYER, Friedrich, 'Génova en la encrucijada entre el Sacro Imperio y la Monarquía Católica', in Manuel Herrero Sánchez, Yasmina Rocío Ben Yessef Garfia, Carlo Bitossi and Dino Puncuh eds, *Génova y la Monarquía Hispánica*, 2 volumes, Società Ligure di Storia Patria: Genoa 2011, ii, pp.617–26

ESPINOSA, Aurelio, 'The Grand Strategy of Charles V (1500–1558): Castile, War, and Dynastic Priority in the Mediterranean', *Journal of Early Modern History*, volume 9.3 (2005), pp.239–83

ESPINOSA, Aurelio, *The Empire of the Cities. Charles V, the Comunero Revolt, and the Transformation of the Spanish System*, Brill Leiden: Boston 2008

ESTEBAN ESTRÍNGANA, Alicia, *Guerra y finanzas en los Países Bajos católicos. De Farnesio a Spínola (1592–1625)*, Laberinto: Madrid 2002

EZQUERRA, A.A. and RUIZ RODRÍGUEZ, J.I. eds, *Túnez, 1535. Halcones y halconeros en la diplomacia de la monarquía española*, CSIC etc: Spain 2012

FAROQHI, S., *The Ottoman Empire and the World Around It*, I.B.Tauris: London 2004

FASANO GUARINI, Elena, '"Rome, workshop of all the practices of the world": from the letters of Cardinal Ferdinando de'Medici to Cosimo I and Francesco I', in Gianvittorio Signorotto and Maria Antonietta Visceglia eds, *Court and Politics in Papal Rome, 1492–1700*, CUP: Cambridge 2002, pp.53–77

FAVARÒ, Valentina, 'La escuadra de galeras del Regno di Sicilia: costruzione, armamento, amministrazione', in Cancila ed., *Mediterraneo in armi*, i, pp.289–313

FAVARÒ, Valentina, *La modernizzazione militare nella Sicilia di Filippo II*, Quaderni Mediterranea: Palermo 2009

FERNÁNDEZ ÁLVAREZ, Manuel, *Carlos V, el César y el Hombre*, Fundación Academia Europea de Yuste: Madrid 1999

FONDEVILA SILVA, Pedro and SÁNCHEZ BAENA, Juan José, 'Las galeras de la monarquía hispánica', in A.A. Ezquerra and J.I. Ruiz Rodríguez eds, *Túnez, 1535. Halcones y halconeros en la diplomacia de la monarquía española*, CSIC etc: Spain 2012, pp.89–119

FENICIA, Giulio, *Il Regno di Napoli e la difesa del Mediterraneo nell'età di Filippo II (1556–1598)*, Cacucci Editore: Bari 2003

FERNÁNDEZ ÁLVAREZ, Manuel, *Carlos V, el césar y el hombre*, Fundación Academia Europea de Yuste: Madrid 1999

FODOR, Pál, *In Quest of the Golden Apple. Imperial Ideology, Politics and Military Administration in the Ottoman Empire*, Isis Press: Istanbul 2000

FODOR, Pál, 'The organization of defence in the Eastern Mediterranean (end of the 16th century)', in Zachariadou ed., *The Kapudan Pasha*, pp.87–94

FONTENAY, Michel, 'L'empire ottoman et le risque corsaire au XVIIe siècle', *Revue d'histoire moderne et contemporaine*, XXXII (April–June 1985), pp.185–208

FONTENAY, Michel, 'La place de la course dans l'économie portuaire: l'exemple de Malte et des ports barbaresques', *Annales. Économies, Sociétés, Civilisations*, n.43 (1988), pp.1321–47

FONTENAY, Michel, 'Corsaires de la foi ou rentiers du sol? Les chevaliers de Malte dans le *corso* Méditerranéen au XVIIe siècle', in *Revue d'Histoire moderne et contemporaine*, XXXV (July–September, 1988), pp.361–84

FONTENAY, Michel, 'L'esclavage en Méditerranée occidentale au XVIIe siècle', in *Bulletin de l'Association des Historiens Modernistes*, 14 (1990), pp.11–50

FONTENAY, Michel, 'Les missions des galères de Malta 1530–1798', in M. Vergé-Franceschi ed., *Guerre et commerce en Méditerranée, IXe–IXXe siècles*, Henri Veyrier: Paris 1991, pp.103–22

FONTENAY, Michel, 'Le Maghreb barbaresque et l'esclavage méditerranéen aux XVIe–XVIIe siècles.' Communication au Ve congrès d'Histoire de Civilisation du Maghreb, *Le Maghreb et les pays de la Méditerranée. Échanges et contacts* (Tunis, October 1989), published in *Les Cahiers de Tunisie*, volume XLV (1991), special number 157–58, Tunis 1993, p.7–43

FONTENAY, Michel, 'Le développement urbain du port de Malte du XVIe au XVIIe siècle', in *Revue de l'Occident Musulman et de la Méditerranée*, 71 (1994/1) pp.91–108

FONTENAY, Michel, 'Malte au temps de Charles Quint et Philippe II: un enjeu de la politique Espagnole en Méditerranée', in Ernest Belenguer Cebrià ed., *Felipe II y el Mediterráneo. vol.4 La monarquía y los reinos (II)*, 4 volumes, CECCFC: Madrid 1999, pp.277–291

FONTENAY, Michel, 'Chiourmes turques au XVIIe siècle', in Rosalba Ragosta ed., *Le genti del mare mediterraneo*, ii, pp.877–903

FRIEDMAN, Ellen G., *Spanish Captives in North Africa in the Early Modern Age*, University of Wisconsin Press: Wisconsin 1984

FRIGO, Daniela, ed., *Politics and Diplomacy in Early Modern Italy. The Structure of Diplomatic Practice, 1450–1800*, translated by Adrian Belton, CUP: Cambridge 2000

FURY, Cheryl A., *Tides in the Affairs of Men. The Social History of Elizabethan Seamen, 1580–1630*, Greenwood Press: Westport, Connecticut and London 2002

FUSARO, Maria, 'Cooperating mercantile networks in the early modern Mediterranean', *Economic History Review*, No.65 (2012/2), pp.701–18

GALASSO, Giuseppe, *Dalla 'libertà d'Italia' alle 'preponderanze straniere'*, Editoriale scientifica: Naples 1997

GALASSO, Giuseppe, *En la periferia del imperio. La Monarquía Hispánica y el reino de Nápoles*, Península: Madrid 2000

GARCÍA ARENAL, Mercedes, and BUNES IBARRA, Miguel Ángel de, *Los españoles y el norte de África, siglos XV–XVIII*, Editorial Mapfre: Madrid 1992

GARCÍA CÁRCEL, Ricardo, *Herejía y sociedad en el siglo XVI. La Inquisición en Valencia 1530–1609*, Ediciones Península: Barcelona 1980

GARCÍA GARCÍA, Bernardo José, *La Pax Hispanica. Política exterior del Duque de Lerma*, LUP: Leuven 1996

GARCÍA HERNÁN David and GARCÍA HERNÁN, Enrique, *Lepanto. El día después*, Actas editorial: Madrid 1999

GARCÍA HERNÁN, Enrique, *La armada española en la monarquía de Felipe II y la defensa del Mediterráneo*, Tempo: Madrid 1995

GARCÍA HERNÁN, Enrique, *La acción diplomática de Francisco de Borja al servicio del Pontificado, 1571–1572*, Generalitat Valenciana: Valencia 2000

GARCÍA HERNÁN, Enrique, 'La conquista y pérdida de Túnez por don Juan de Austria', in G. Candiani and L. Lo Basso eds, *Mutazioni e permanenze nella storia navale del Mediterraneo secc. XVI–XIX* in *Guerra e pace in età moderna. Annali di storia militare europea*, II (2010), Franco Angeli: Milan pp.39–95

GARCÍA HERNÁN, Enrique and MAFFI, Davide, eds, *Guerra y sociedad en la Monarquía Hispánica. Política, estrategia y cultura en la Europa moderna (1500–1700)*, 2 volumes, Laberinto, CSIC and Fundación Mapfre: Madrid 2006

GARCÍA MARTÍNEZ, Sebastián, *Bandolerismo, piratería y control de moriscos en Valencia durante et reinado de Felipe II*, University of Valencia: Valencia 1977

GILBERT, Felix, *Machiavelli and Guicciardini. Politics and History in Sixteenth Century Florence*, PUP: Princeton 1965

GIUFFRIDA, Antonino, 'La fortezza indifesa e il progetto del Vega per una ristrutturazione del sistema difensivo siciliano', in Cancila ed., *Mediterraneo in armi*, i, pp.227–88

GLETE, Jan, *Warfare at Sea, 1500–1650, Maritime Conflicts and the Transformation of Europe*, Routledge: London and New York 2000

GOFFMAN, Daniel, *The Ottoman Empire and Early Modern Europe*, CUP: Cambridge 2002

GOODMAN, David, *Spanish Naval Power, 1589–1665. Reconstruction and Defeat*, CUP: Cambridge 1997

GORROCHATEGUI SANTOS, Luis, *Contra Armada. La mayor catástrofe naval de la historia de Inglaterra*, Ministerio de Defensa: Madrid 2011

GRACIA RIVAS, Manuel, *La sanidad en la jornada de Inglaterra (1587–1588)*, Instituto de Historia y Cultura Naval: Madrid 1988

GREENE, Molly, *A Shared World. Christians and Muslims in the early Modern Mediterranean*, PUP: Princeton and Chichester 2000

GREENE, Molly, 'Beyond the Northern Invasion', *Past and Present*, No.174 (1) (2002), pp.41–70

GREENE, Molly, *Catholic Pirates and Greek Merchants. A Maritime History of the Early Modern Mediterranean*, PUP: Princeton and Oxford 2010

GROOT, Alexander H. de, 'The Ottoman Threat to Europe, 1571–1830: Historical Fact or Fancy?', in Victor Mallia-Milanes ed., *Hospitaller Malta 1530–1798. Studies on Early Modern Malta and the Order of St John of Jerusalem*, Mireva: Msida 1993, pp.199–254

GUARNIERI, G., *I Cavalieri di Santo Stefano: contributo alla storia della marina militare italiana 1562–1859*, Nistri-Lischi: Pisa 1928

GUILMARTIN, John Francis, Jr., *Gunpowder and Galleys. Changing Technology and Mediterranean Warfare at Sea in the 16th Century*, 2nd Edition Conway Maritime Press: London 2003

GUILMARTIN, John Francis, Jr., 'The Siege of Malta, 1565', in D.J.B. Trim, and M.C. Fissel eds, *Amphibious Warfare 1000–1700. Commerce, State Formation and European Expansion*, Brill: Leiden and Boston 2006, pp.148–79

HALPERIN DONGHI, Tulio, *Un conflicto nacional. Moriscos y cristianos viejos en Valencia*, Institució Alfons el Magnànim: Valencia 1980

HERNANDO SÁNCHEZ, Carlos José, *Castilla y Nápoles en el siglo XVI. El Virrey don Pedro de Toledo. Linaje, estado y cultura (1532–1553)*, JCL: Salamanca 1994

HERNANDO SÁNCHEZ, Carlos José, *El reino de Nápoles en el Imperio de Carlos V. La consolidación de la conquista*, CECCFC: Madrid 2001

HERNANDO SÁNCHEZ, Carlos José ed., *Las fortificaciones de Carlos V*, Ministerio de Defensa, AEAC and CECCFC: Madrid 2000

HESS, Andrew C., 'The Moriscos. An Ottoman Fifth Column in Sixteenth-Century Spain', *American Historical Review*, LXXIV, No. 1 (October 1968), pp.1–25

HESS, Andrew C., 'The Evolution of the Ottoman Seaborne Empire in the Age of the Oceanic Discoveries', *1453–1525, American Historical Review*, LXXV, No. 7 (December 1970), pp.1892–1919

HESS, Andrew C., 'The Battle of Lepanto and Its Place in Mediterranean History', in *Past and Present*, No.57 (November 1972), pp.53–73

HESS, Andrew C., *The Forgotten Frontier. A History of the Sixteenth-Century Ibero-African Frontier*, University of Chicago Press: Chicago 1978

İNALCIK, Halil, 'State Sovereignty and Law during the Reign of Süleyman', in İnalcık and Kafadar eds, *Süleyman the Second and His Time*, Isis Press: Istanbul 1993, pp.59–92

İNALCIK, Halil, and KAFADAR, Cemal eds, *Süleyman the Second and His Time*, Isis Press: Istanbul 1993

IMBER, Colin, 'The Navy of Süleyman the Magnificent', *Archivum Ottomanium*, VI (1980), pp.211–82

IMBER, Colin, 'Süleymân as Caliph of the Muslims: Ebû's-Su'ûd's Formulation of Ottoman Dynastic Ideology', in Gilles Veinstein ed., *Soliman le Magnifique et son temps. Actes du colloque de Paris, Galeries Nationales du Grand Palais, 7–10 mars 1990*, Louvre: Paris 1992, pp.179–84

IMBER, Colin, *The Ottoman Empire, 1300–1650. The Structure of Power*, Palgrave Macmillan: Basingstoke and New York 2002

JIMÉNEZ ESTRELLA, Antonio, 'Ejército permanente y política defensiva en el Reino de Granada durante el siglo XVI', in García Hernán and Maffi eds, *Guerra y sociedad*, i, pp.579–610

KAMEN, Henry, *Spain's Road to Empire. The Making of a World Power, 1492–1763*, Allen Lane: London etc 2002

KIDWELL, Carol, 'Venice, the French invasion and the Apulian ports', in David Abulafia ed., *The French Descent into Renaissance Italy. Antecedents and Effects*. Variorum: Aldershot and Brookfield1995, pp.295–309

KIRK, Thomas Allison, *Genoa and the Sea. Policy and Power in an Early Modern Maritime Republic, 1559–1684*, John Hopkins University Press: Baltimore 2005

LEPEYRE, Henri, *Geografía de la España morisca*, translated by Luis C. Rodríguez García, University of Valencia, etc.: Valencia, 2009

LO BASSO, Luca, *Uomini da remo. Galee e galeotti nel Mediterraneo in età moderna*, Selene Edizioni: Milan 2003

LÓPEZ NADAL, Gonçal, 'El Corsarismo Mediterraneo', in Ribot García and Belenguer Cebriá eds, *Las sociedades ibéricas y el mar a finales del siglo XVI*, iii (*El área del Mediterráneo*), pp.233–60

MAFFI, Davide, *Il baluardo della corona. Guerra, esercito, finanze e società nella Lombardia seicentesca (1630–1660)*, Le Monnier Università: Florence 2007

MAFRICI, Mirella, *Mezzogiorno e pirateria nell'età moderna*, Edizioni Scientifiche Italiane: Naples etc 1995

MALLETT, Michael and SHAW, Christine, *The Italian Wars, 1494–1559*, Pearson: Harlow, London etc. 2012

MALLIA-MILANES, Victor, *Venice and Hospitaller Malta, 1530–1798. Aspects of a Relationship*, PEG: Malta 1992

MALLIA-MILANES, Victor, ed., *Hospitaller Malta. Studies on Early Modern Malta and the Order of St John of Jerusalem*, Mireva: Msida 1993

MARCOS MARTÍN, Alberto ed., *Hacer historia desde Simancas. Homenaje a José Luis Rodríguez de Diego*, JCL: Valladolid 2011

MARTÍNEZ-HIDALGO Y TERNÁN, José, *Lepanto, la batalla, la galera 'Real'*, Museo Marítimo: Barcelona 1971

MARTÍNEZ RUIZ, Enrique, 'La difícil supervivencia del "ejército interior": las Guardas, los aposentamientos y la escasez de dinero a fines del siglo XVI, in Porfirio Sánz Camañes ed., *Monarquía Hispánica en tiempos del Quijote*, Sílex: Madrid 2005, pp.433–61

MIGLIO, Massimo, 'Continuità e fratture nei rapporti tra Papato e Spagna nel Quattrocento', in *En los umbrales de España. La incorporación del reino de Navarra a la Monarquía Hispana*, Gobierno de Navarra: Pamplona 2012, pp.279–95

MOLINER PRADA, Antonio ed., *La expulsión de los moriscos*, Nabla: Barcelona 2009

MONCHICOURT, Charles, *L'Expédition espagnole de 1560 contre l'île de Djerba. Essai bibliographique, récit de l'expédition, document originaux*, Ernest Leroux: Paris 1913

MURPHEY, Rhoads, *Ottoman Warfare, 1500–1700*, UCL: London 1999

MURPHEY, Rhoads, 'A Comparative Look at Ottoman and Habsburg Resources and Readiness for War circa 1520 to circa 1570', in García Hernán and Maffi eds, *Guerra y sociedad*, i, pp.75–102

MUSI, Aurelio, *Mezzogiorno spagnolo. La via napoletana allo stato moderno*, Guida: Naples 1991

MUSI, Aurelio, 'L'Italia nel sistema imperiale spagnolo', in A. Musi ed., *Nel sistema imperiale: L'Italia spagnola*, Edizioni Scientifiche Italiane: Naples 1994

MUSI, Aurelio, 'Carlo V nella *Historia della città e Regno di Napoli* di G.A. Summonte', in B. Anatra and F. Manconi eds, *Sardegna, Spagna e Stati italiani nell'età di Carlo V,* Carocci: Rome 2001, pp.51–61

MUTO, Giovanni, *Le finanze pubbliche napoletane tra riforme e restaurazione (1520–1634),* Edizioni scientifiche italiane: Naples 1980

MUTO, Giovanni, 'Strategie e Strutture del Controllo Militare del Territorio nel Regno di Napoli nel Cinquecento', in García Hernán and Maffi eds, *Guerra y sociedad,* i, pp.153–70

NECIPOĞLU, Gülru, 'Süleyman the Magnificent and the Representation of Power in the Context of Ottoman-Habsburg-Papal Rivalry', in H. İnalcık and C. Kafadar eds, *Süleyman the Second and His Time,* Isis Press: Istanbul 1993, pp.163–91

NICHOLSON, Helen, *The Knights Hospitaller,* Boydell and Brewer: Woodbridge 2001

O'DONNELL Y DUQUE DE ESTRADA, Hugo, 'Lepanto. Creación, triunfo y consecuencias de la Santa Liga', in *La Monarquía Hispánica Felipe II, un monarca y su época,* SECCFC: Madrid 1998, pp.275–84

OLIVERA SERRANO, César, *La actividad sísmica en el Reino de Granada (1487–1531). Estudio histórico y documentos,* Stock Cero: Madrid 1994

ORESKO, Robert, 'The House of Savoy in search for a royal crown in the seventeenth century', in Oresko, Gibbs and Scott eds, *Royal and Republican Sovereignty in Early Modern Europe. Essays in memory of Ragnhild Hatton,* CUP: Cambridge, New York and Melbourne 1997, pp.272–350

OTERO LANA, Enrique, *Los corsarios españoles durante la decadencia de los Austrias. El corso español del Atlántico peninsular en el siglo XVII (1621–1697),* Ministerio de Defensa: Madrid 1992

PACINI, Arturo, *La Genova di Andrea Doria nell'Impero di Carlo V,* Olschki: Florence 1999

PACINI, Arturo, ' "Poiché gli stati non sono portatili…": geopolitica e strategia nei rapporti tra Genova e Spagna nel Cinquecento', in Herrero Sánchez *et al.* eds, *Génova…,* ii, pp.413–57

PAGANO DE DIVITIIS, Gigliola, *English Merchants in Seventeenth-Century Italy,* CUP: Cambridge 1997

PANZAC, Daniel, *La marine ottomane. De l'apogée à la chute d'Empire, 1572–1923,* CNRS: Paris 2009

PARDO MOLERO, Juan Francisco, *La defensa del imperio. Carlos V, Valencia y el Mediterráneo,* prologue by Bernard Vincent, SECCFC: Madrid 2001

PARKER, Geoffrey, *The Grand Strategy of Philip II,* Yale University Press: New Haven and London 1998

PARROTT, David, *The Business of War. Military Enterprise and Military Revolution in Early Modern Europe*, CUP: Cambridge 2012

PEDANI, M.P., 'Some Remarks upon the Ottoman Geo-Political Vision of the Mediterranean in the Period of the Cyprus War (1570–1573)', in Colin Imber, Keiko Kiyotaki and Rhoads Murphey eds, *Frontiers of Ottoman Studies*, 2 volumes, I.B.Tauris: London 2005, ii, pp.23–35

PERRONE, Sean T., *Charles V and the Castilian Assembly of the Clergy. Negotiations for the Ecclesiastical Subsidy*, Brill: Leiden and Boston 2008

PRYOR, John H., *Geography, Technology and War. Studies in the Maritime History of the Mediterranean, 649–1571*, CUP: Cambridge 1988

RECIO MORALES, Óscar, 'La gente de naciones en los ejércitos de los Austrias hispanos: servicio, confianza y correspondencia', in García Hernán and Maffi eds, *Guerra y sociedad*, i, pp.651–79

REGLÀ, Joan, *Estudios sobre los moriscos*, Anales de la Universidad de Valencia: Valencia 1964

RIBOT GARCÍA, Luis Antonio, *La Monarquía de España y la guerra de Mesina*, Actas: Madrid 2002

RIBOT GARCÍA, Luis Antonio, *El arte de gobernar. Estudios sobre la España de los Austrias*, Alianza: Madrid 2006

RIZZO, Mario, 'Centro spagnolo e periferia lombarda nell'impero asburgico tra Cinque e Seicento', in *Rivista Storica Italiana*, CIV (1992), pp.315–48

RIZZO, Mario, 'Milano e le forze del principe. Agenti, relazioni e risorse per la difesa dell'impero di Filippo II', in José Martínez Millán ed., *Felipe II (1527–1598). Europa y Monarquía Católica*, 4 volumes, Parteluz: Madrid 1998, i, pp.731–66

RIZZO, Mario, 'Sticks, Carrots and all the Rest: Lombardy and the Spanish strategy in northern Italy between Europe and the Mediterranean', *Cahiers de la Méditerranée*, vol.71 (2005) December, 2005, pp.145–84

RIZZO, Mario, 'Alloggiare in casa d'altri. Le implicazioni economiche, politiche e fiscali della presenza militare asburgica nel territorio finalese fra cinque e seicento', in Paolo Calcagno ed., *Finale tra le potenze di antico regime. Il ruolo del Marchesato sulla scena internazionale (secoli XVI–XVIII)*, Società Savonese di Storia Patria: Savona 2009, pp.77–97

RIZZO, Mario, 'Gli *Austrias* e l'Italia centrosettentrionale nella prima età moderna. Una rapsodia geopolitica', in E. Fasano Guarini and F. Bonatti eds, *Atti del Convegno di Studi: Feudi di Lunigiana tra Impero, Spagna e Stati Italiani (XV–XVIII secolo)* ('Memorie della Accademia Lunigianese di Scienze "Giovanni Capellini" ') pp.67–113

RIZZO, Mario, 'Non solo guerra. Risorse e organizzazione della strategia asburgica in Lombardia durante la seconda metà del Cinquecento', in García Hernán and Maffi eds, *Guerra y sociedad*, i, pp.217–52

RIZZO, Mario, 'Porte, chiavi e bastioni. Milano, la geopolitica italiana e la strategia asburgica', in Cancila ed., *Mediterraneo in armi*, ii, pp.467–511

RODGER, N.A.M., *The Safeguard of the Sea. A Naval History of Great Britain. Volume 1 660–1649*, Harper Collins: London 1997

RODRÍGUEZ-SALGADO, M.J., *The Changing Face of Empire. Charles V, Philip II and Habsburg Authority, 1551–1559*, CUP: Cambridge 1988

RODRÍGUEZ-SALGADO, M.J., *Felipe II, el «Paladín de la Cristiandad» y la paz con el Turco*, Colección Síntesis XI, Universidad de Valladolid: Valladolid 2004

RODRÍGUEZ-SALGADO, M.J., '¿Carolus Africanus?: el Emperador y el turco', in José Martínez Millán ed., *Carlos V y la quiebra...*, i, pp.487–531

RUIZ GÓMEZ, Francisco, and MOLERO GARCÍA, Jesús, *La Orden de San Juan en tiempos del Quijote*, Ediciones de la Universidad Castilla-La Mancha: Spain 2010

RUIZ IBÁÑEZ, José Javier ed., *Las milicias del rey de España. Sociedad, política e identidad en las Monarquías Ibéricas*, Fondo de Cultura Económica: Madrid 2009

SÁNCHEZ-GIJÓN, Antonio, 'La Goleta, Bona, Bugía y los presidios del Reino de Túnez en la política mediterránea del Emperador', in Carlos José Hernando Sánchez ed., *Las fortificaciones de Carlos V*, Ministerio de Defensa, AEAC and CECCFC: Madrid 2000, pp.625–51

SERIO, A., 'Una representación de la crisis de la unión dinástica: los cargos diplomáticos en Roma de Francisco de Rojas y Antonio de Acuña (1501–1507)', in L. Ribot, J. Valdeón and E. Maza eds, *Isabel la Católica y su época. Actas del congreso internacional*, 2 volumes, Instituto Universitario de Historia Simancas, Universidad de Valladolid: Valladolid 2007, ii, pp.849–62

SERRANO, Luciano, *La Liga de Lepanto entre España, Venecia y la Santa Sede (1570–1573). Ensayo histórico a base de documentos diplomáticos*, 2 volumes, Escuela Española de Historia y Arqueología en Roma: Madrid 1918–19

SETTON, Kenneth M., *The Papacy and the Levant (1204–1571)*, 4 volumes, American Philosophical Society: Philadelphia 1976, 1978, 1984

SETTON, Kenneth M., *Venice, Austria and the Turks in the Seventeenth Century*, American Philosophical Society: Philadelphia 1991

SIGNOROTTO, Gianvittorio, and VISCEGLIA, Maria Antonietta eds, *Court and Politics in Papal Rome, 1492–1700*, CUP: Cambridge 2002

SIGNOROTTO, Gianvittorio, 'Papato e principi italiani nell'ultima fase del conflitto tra Asburgo e Valois', in Martínez Millán ed., *Carlos V y la quiebra...*, i, pp.259–80

SOLA CASTAÑO, Emilio, *Un Mediterráneo de piratas. Corsarios, renegados y cautivos*, Tecnos: Madrid 1988

SOLANO CAMÓN, Enrique, *Poder monárquico y estado pactista (1626–1652). Los Aragoneses antes la Unión de Armas*, Institución Fernando el Católico: Zaragoza 1987

SPAGNOLETTI, Angelantonio, *Principi italiani e Spagna nell'età barocca*, ESBM: Milan 1996

STERN, Philip J., *The Company-State. Corporate Sovereignty and the Early Modern Foundations of the British Empire in India*, OUP: Oxford 2011

STRADLING, R.A., *Europe and the Decline of Spain. A Study of the Spanish System, 1580–1720*, George Allen and Unwin: London, Boston and Sydney 1981

STRADLING, R.A, *The Armada of Flanders. Spanish Maritime Policy and European War, 1568–1668*, CUP: Cambridge 1992

SUÁREZ, Luis, *Los Reyes Católicos*, Ariel: Barcelona 2004

TAMBORRA, Angelo, *Gli stati italiani, l'Europa e il problema turco dopo Lepanto*, Olschki: Florence 1961

TELLECHEA IDÍGORAS, J. Ignacio, 'Lo que el Emperador no supo. Proceso de Paulo IV a Carlos V y Felipe II', in Martínez Millan ed., *Carlos V y la quiebra...*, iv pp.181–95

TENENTI, Alberto, *Piracy and the Decline of Venice 1580–1615*, English translation by Janet and Brian Pullan, Longmans: London 1967

THOMPSON, I.A.A., *War and Government in Habsburg Spain, 1560–1620*, UCL: London 1976

THOMPSON, I.A.A., 'Las galeras en la política militar española en el Mediterráneo durante el siglo XVI', *Manuscrits*, 24 (2006), pp.95–124

TRACY, James D., *Emperor Charles V, Impresario of War. Campaign Strategy, International Finance, and Domestic Politics*, CUP: Cambridge 2002

TRIM, D.J.B. and FISSEL, M.C., eds, *Amphibious Warfare 1000–1700. Commerce, State Formation and European Expansion*, Brill: Leiden and Boston 2006

VARRIALE, Gennaro, 'Nápoles y el azar de Corón (1532–1534)', in *Tiempos Modernos*, vol.7, No.22 (2011/1), 30 pages (available online: www.

tiemposmodernos.org/tm3/index.php/tm/article/viewArticle/222; accessed March 2012)

VEINSTEIN, Gilles, 'Les préparatifs de la campagne navale franco-turque en 1552 à travers les ordres du divan ottoman', in *Revue de l'Occident musulman et de la Méditerranée*, No.39 (1985), pp.35–67

VEINSTEIN, Gilles, 'Les campagnes navales franco-ottomanes au XVIe siècle', in I. Malkin ed., *La France et la Méditerranée. Vingt-sept siècles d'interdépendance*, Brill: Leiden 1990, pp.311–34

VEINSTEIN, Gilles ed., *Soliman le magnifique et son temps. Actes du colloque de Paris, Galeries Nationales du Gran Palais, 7–10 mars 1990*, Louvre: Paris 1992

VILAR, Pierre, *Catalunya dins l'Espanya moderna*, 4 volumes, Catalan translation by Eulàlia Duran, Edicions 62: Barcelona 1966

VILLARI, Rosario, *La rivolta antispagnola a Napoli. Le origini (1585–1647)*, Editori Laterza: Bari 1967

VISCEGLIA, Maria Antonietta, 'Un groupe social ambigu. Organisation, stratégies et représentations de la noblesse napolitaine, XVIe–XVIIe siècles', in *Annales. Économies, Sociétés, Civilisations*, 48th year, No.4 (1993), pp.819–51, translated by Judith Revel

VISCEGLIA, Maria Antonietta, *Guerra, diplomacia y etiqueta en la Corte de los Papas (Siglos XVI y XVII)*, Ediciones Polifemo: Madrid 2010

WERNHAM, R.B., *The Return of the Armadas. The Last Years of the Elizabethan War against Spain 1595–1603*, Clarendon Press: Oxford 1994

WILLIAMS, Patrick, *Philip II*, Palgrave: Basingstoke and New York 2000

WILLIAMS, Patrick, *The Great Favourite. The Duke of Lerma and the Court and Government of Philip III of Spain, 1598–1621*, MUP: Manchester and New York 2006

WOODHEAD, Christine, 'The Present Terrour of the World? – Contemporary Views of the Ottoman Empire c1600', in *History*, Vol 72 No.234 (February 1987), pp.20–37

ZACHARAIADOU, Elizabeth ed., *The Kapudan Pasha, His Office and His Domain*, Crete University Press: Rethymnon 2002

ZYSBERG, André, *Les galériens. Vies et destins de 60,000 forçats sur les galères de France 1680–1748*, Éditions du Seuil: Paris 1987

Index